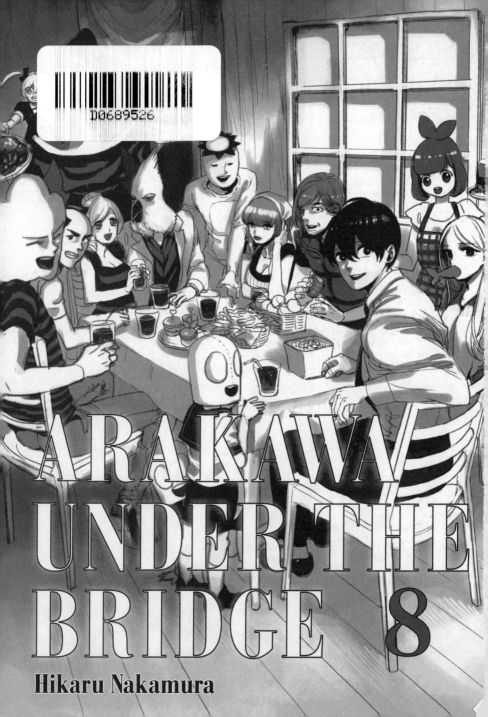

ARAKAWA UNDER THE BRIDGE

8

Hikaru Nakamura

CONTENTS

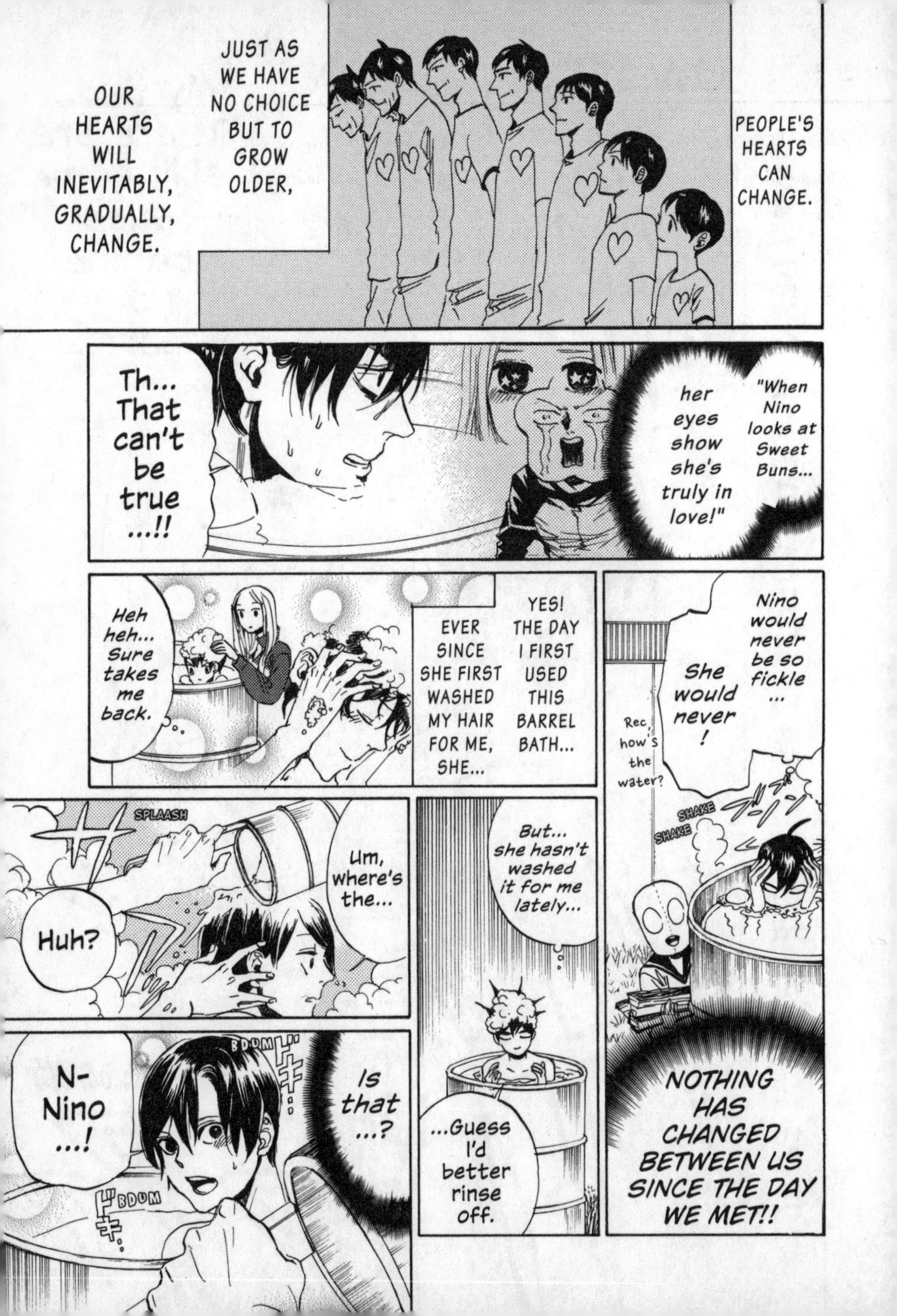
PEOPLE'S HEARTS CAN CHANGE.
JUST AS WE HAVE NO CHOICE BUT TO GROW OLDER,
OUR HEARTS WILL INEVITABLY, GRADUALLY, CHANGE.
"When Nino looks at Sweet Buns...
her eyes show she's truly in love!"
Th... That can't be true ...!!
Nino would never be so fickle...
She would never!
Rec, how's the water?
SHAKE
SHAKE
NOTHING HAS CHANGED BETWEEN US SINCE THE DAY WE MET!!
YES! THE DAY I FIRST USED THIS BARREL BATH...
EVER SINCE SHE FIRST WASHED MY HAIR FOR ME, SHE...
Heh heh... Sure takes me back.
But... she hasn't washed it for me lately...
...Guess I'd better rinse off.
Um, where's the...
SPLAASH
Huh?
BDOM
Is that...?
N-Nino...!
BDUM

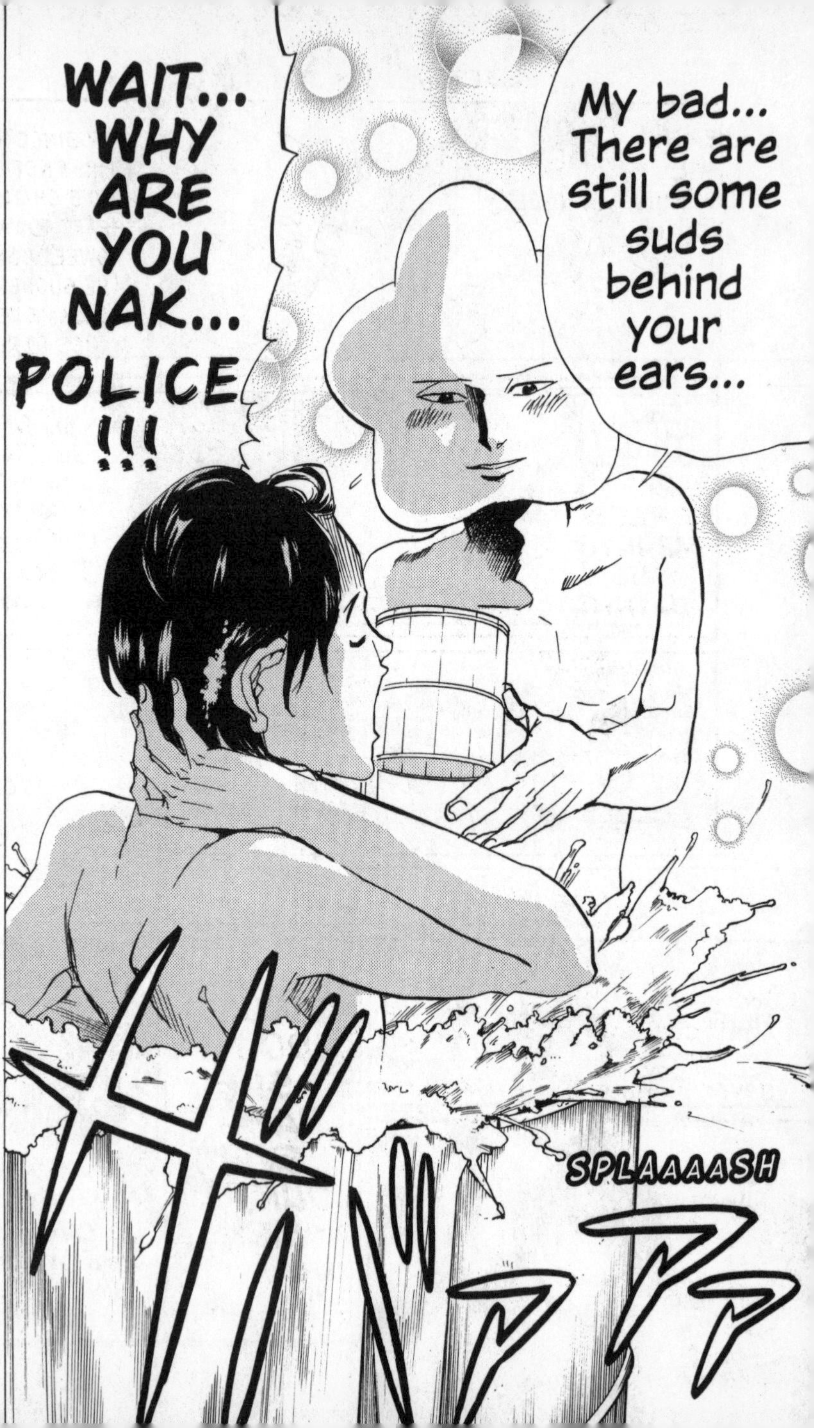
My bad... There are still some suds behind your ears...
WAIT... WHY ARE YOU NAK... POLICE!!!
SPLAAAASH

THE HUMAN HEART MAY EXCITEDLY LEAD US TO WHERE WE LEAST EXPECT.

Chapter 378: War Buddies

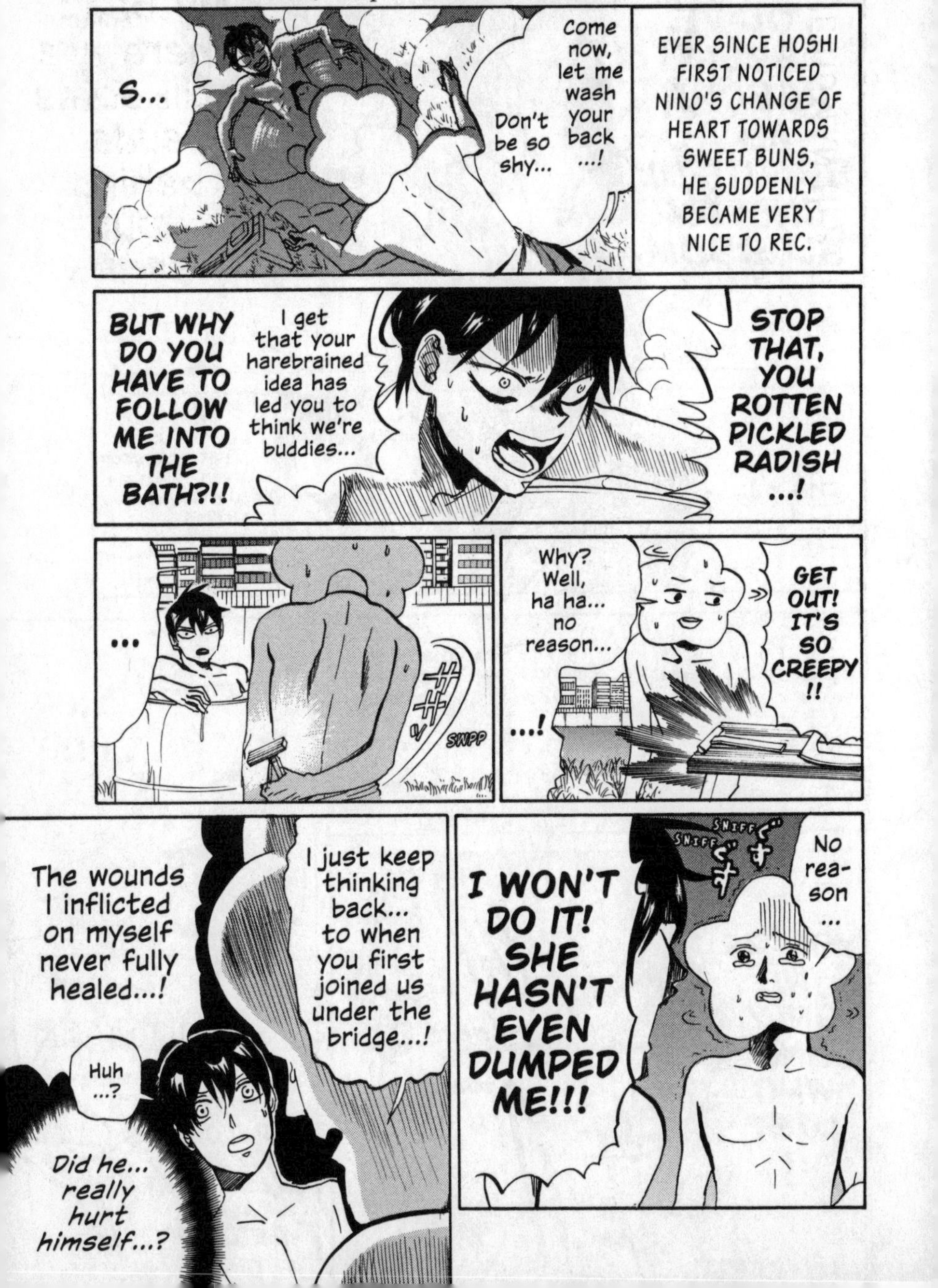
EVER SINCE HOSHI FIRST NOTICED NINO'S CHANGE OF HEART TOWARDS SWEET BUNS, HE SUDDENLY BECAME VERY NICE TO REC.
Come now, let me wash your back...!
Don't be so shy...
S...
STOP THAT, YOU ROTTEN PICKLED RADISH...!
I get that your harebrained idea has led you to think we're buddies...
BUT WHY DO YOU HAVE TO FOLLOW ME INTO THE BATH?!!
GET OUT! IT'S SO CREEPY!!
Why? Well, ha ha... no reason...
...!
SWPP
...
No rea-son...
SNIFF SNIFF
I WON'T DO IT! SHE HASN'T EVEN DUMPED ME!!!
I just keep thinking back... to when you first joined us under the bridge...!
The wounds I inflicted on myself never fully healed...!
Huh...?
Did he... really hurt himself...?

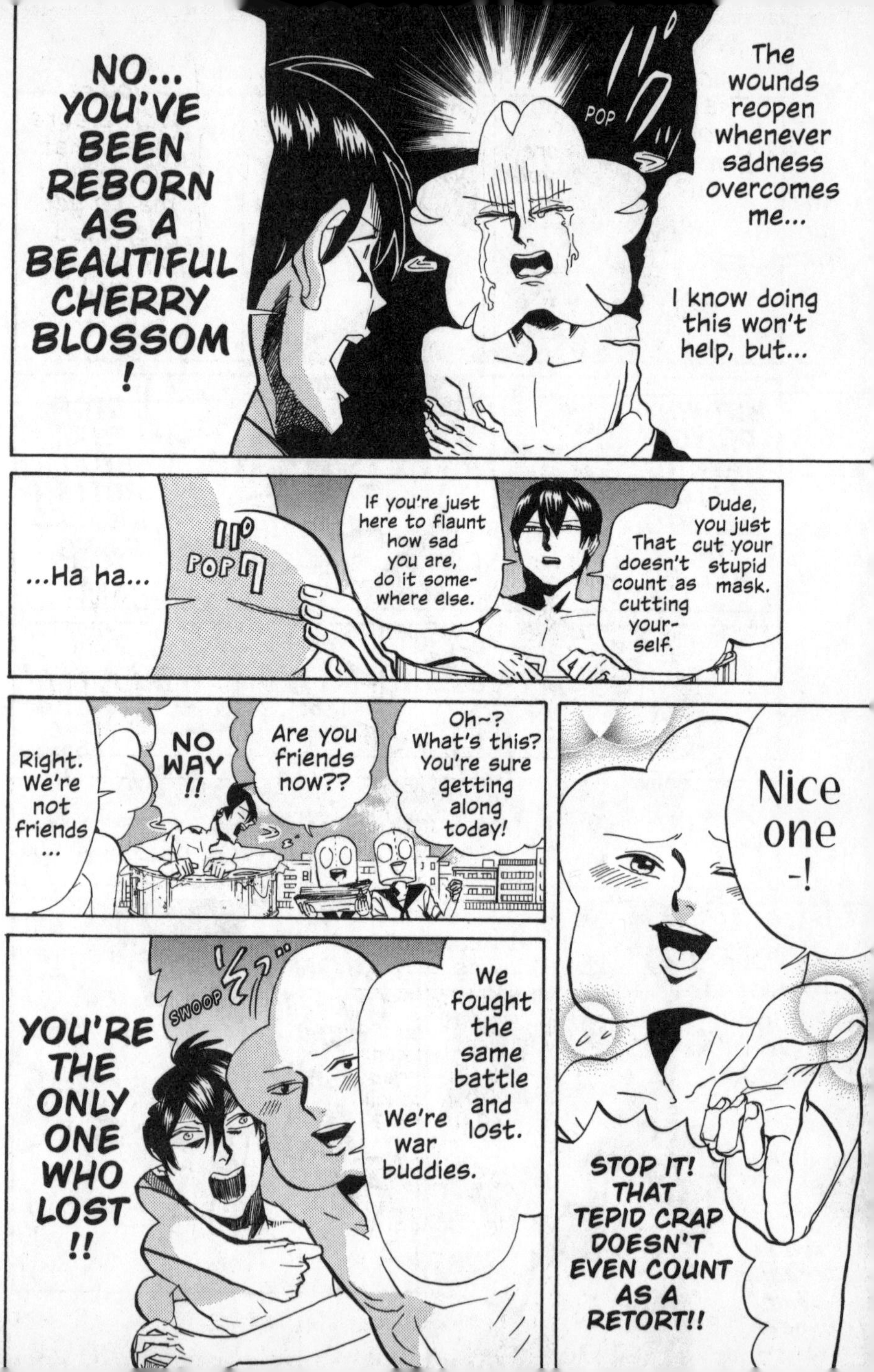
The wounds reopen whenever sadness overcomes me...
POP
I know doing this won't help, but...
NO... YOU'VE BEEN REBORN AS A BEAUTIFUL CHERRY BLOSSOM!
Dude, you just cut your stupid mask.
That doesn't count as cutting your-self.
If you're just here to flaunt how sad you are, do it some-where else.
POP
...Ha ha...
Nice one -!
STOP IT! THAT TEPID CRAP DOESN'T EVEN COUNT AS A RETORT!!
Oh~? What's this? You're sure getting along today!
Are you friends now??
NO WAY!!
Right. We're not friends...
SWOOP
We fought the same battle and lost.
We're war buddies.
YOU'RE THE ONLY ONE WHO LOST!!

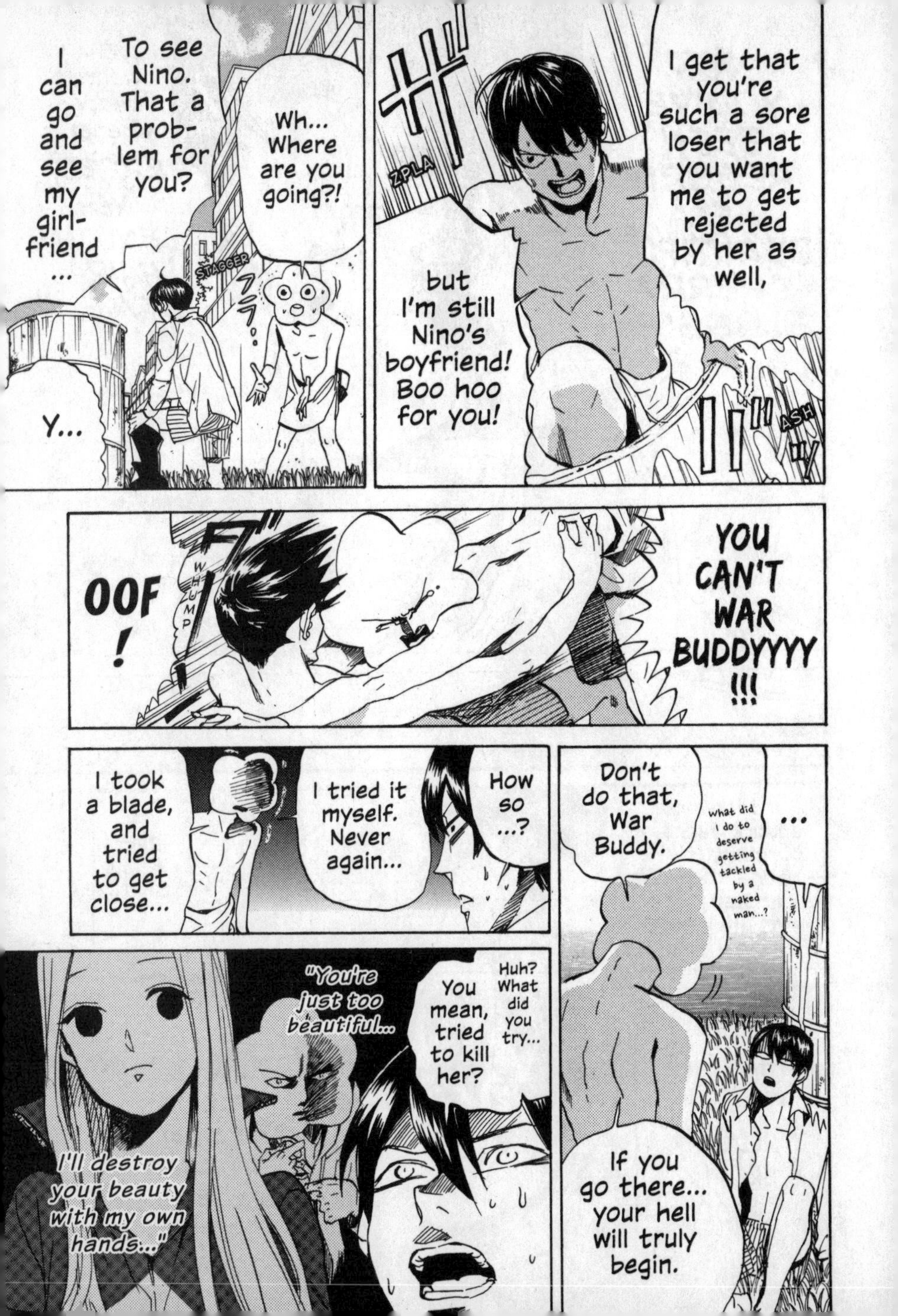
I get that you're such a sore loser that you want me to get rejected by her as well,
ZPLA
but I'm still Nino's boyfriend! Boo hoo for you!
ASH
Wh... Where are you going?!
To see Nino. That a prob-lem for you?
I can go and see my girl-friend...
STAGGER
Y...
YOU CAN'T WAR BUDDYYYY!!!
WHUMP
OOF!
...
What did I do to deserve getting tackled by a naked man...?
Don't do that, War Buddy.
If you go there... your hell will truly begin.
How so...?
I tried it myself. Never again...
I took a blade, and tried to get close...
Huh? What did you try...
You mean, tried to kill her?
"You're just too beautiful...
I'll destroy your beauty with my own hands..."

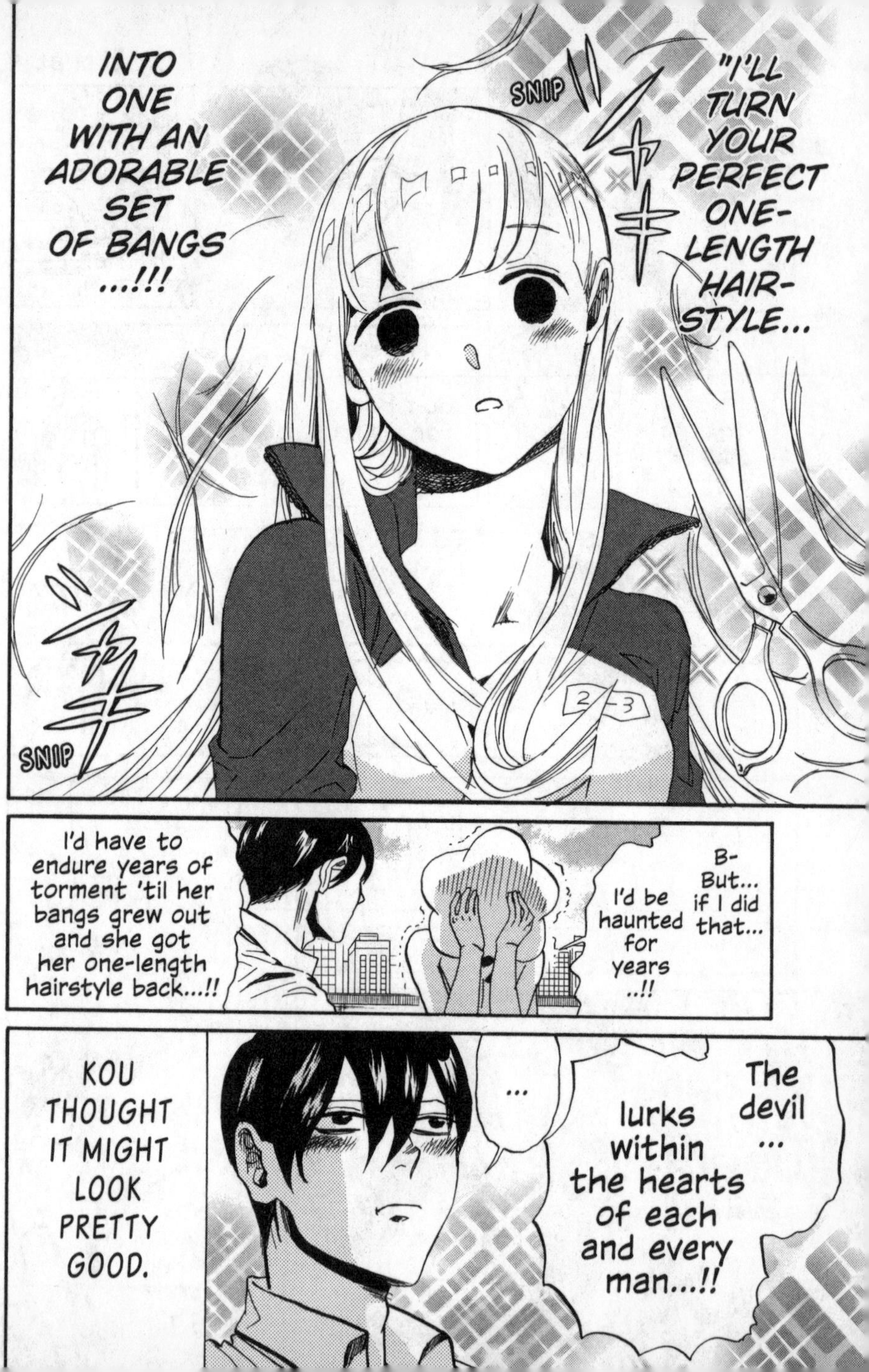
SNIP
"I'LL TURN YOUR PERFECT ONE-LENGTH HAIR-STYLE...
INTO ONE WITH AN ADORABLE SET OF BANGS ...!!!
SNIP
B-But... if I did that...
I'd be haunted for years ..!!
I'd have to endure years of torment 'til her bangs grew out and she got her one-length hairstyle back...!!
The devil ...
lurks within the hearts of each and every man...!!
...
KOU THOUGHT IT MIGHT LOOK PRETTY GOOD.

Chapter 379: Friendship

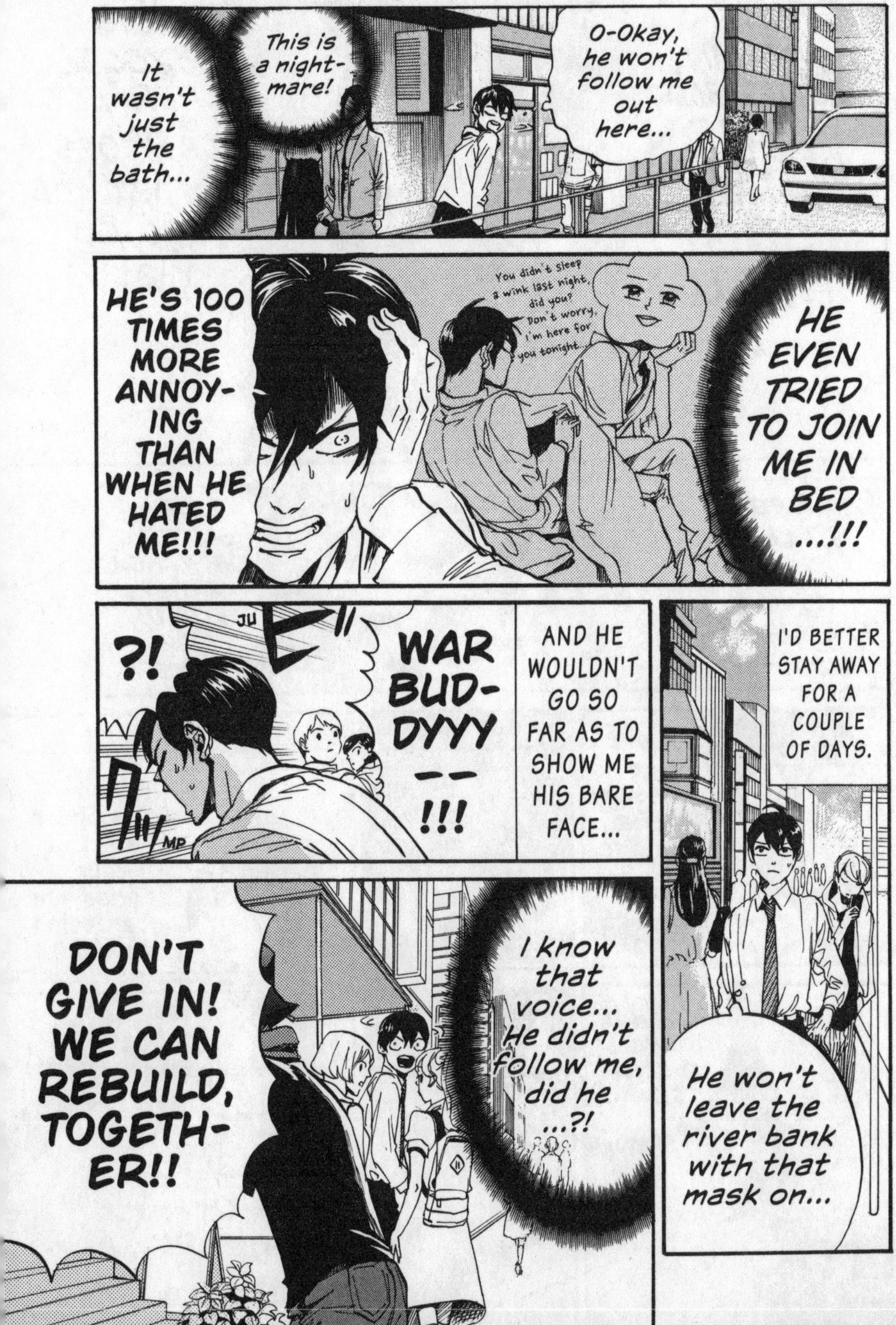
O-Okay, he won't follow me out here...
This is a nightmare!
It wasn't just the bath...
HE EVEN TRIED TO JOIN ME IN BED ...!!!
You didn't sleep a wink last night, did you? Don't worry, I'm here for you tonight.
HE'S 100 TIMES MORE ANNOYING THAN WHEN HE HATED ME!!!
I'D BETTER STAY AWAY FOR A COUPLE OF DAYS.
He won't leave the river bank with that mask on...
AND HE WOULDN'T GO SO FAR AS TO SHOW ME HIS BARE FACE...
WAR BUDDYYY --!!!
JU
?!
MP
I know that voice... He didn't follow me, did he ...?!
DON'T GIVE IN! WE CAN REBUILD, TOGETHER!!

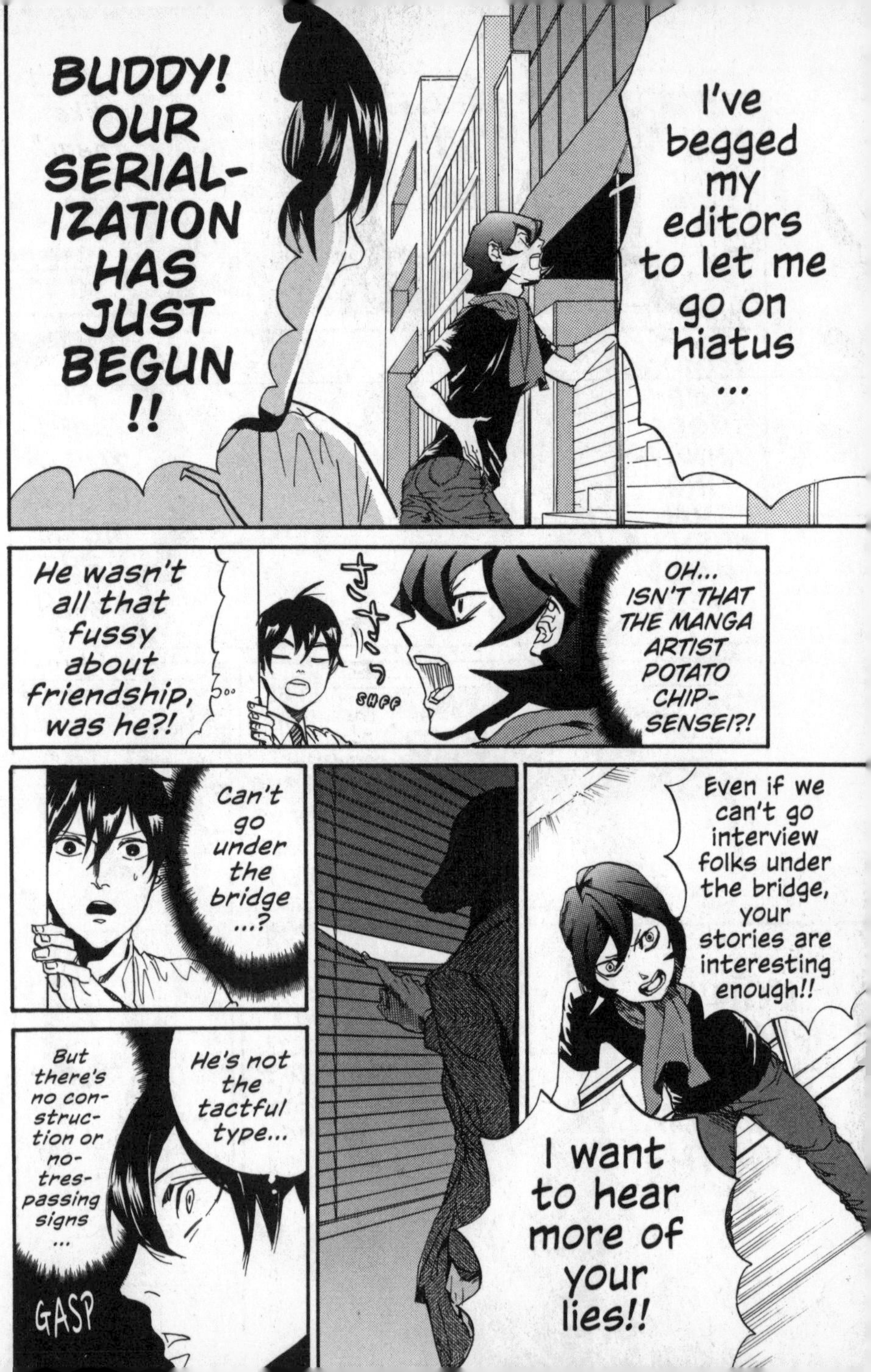
I've begged my editors to let me go on hiatus ...
BUDDY! OUR SERIAL-IZATION HAS JUST BEGUN !!
OH... ISN'T THAT THE MANGA ARTIST POTATO CHIP-SENSEI?!
SHFF
He wasn't all that fussy about friendship, was he?!
Even if we can't go interview folks under the bridge, your stories are interesting enough!!
I want to hear more of your lies!!
Can't go under the bridge ...?
He's not the tactful type...
But there's no con-struc-tion or no-tres-passing signs ...
GASP

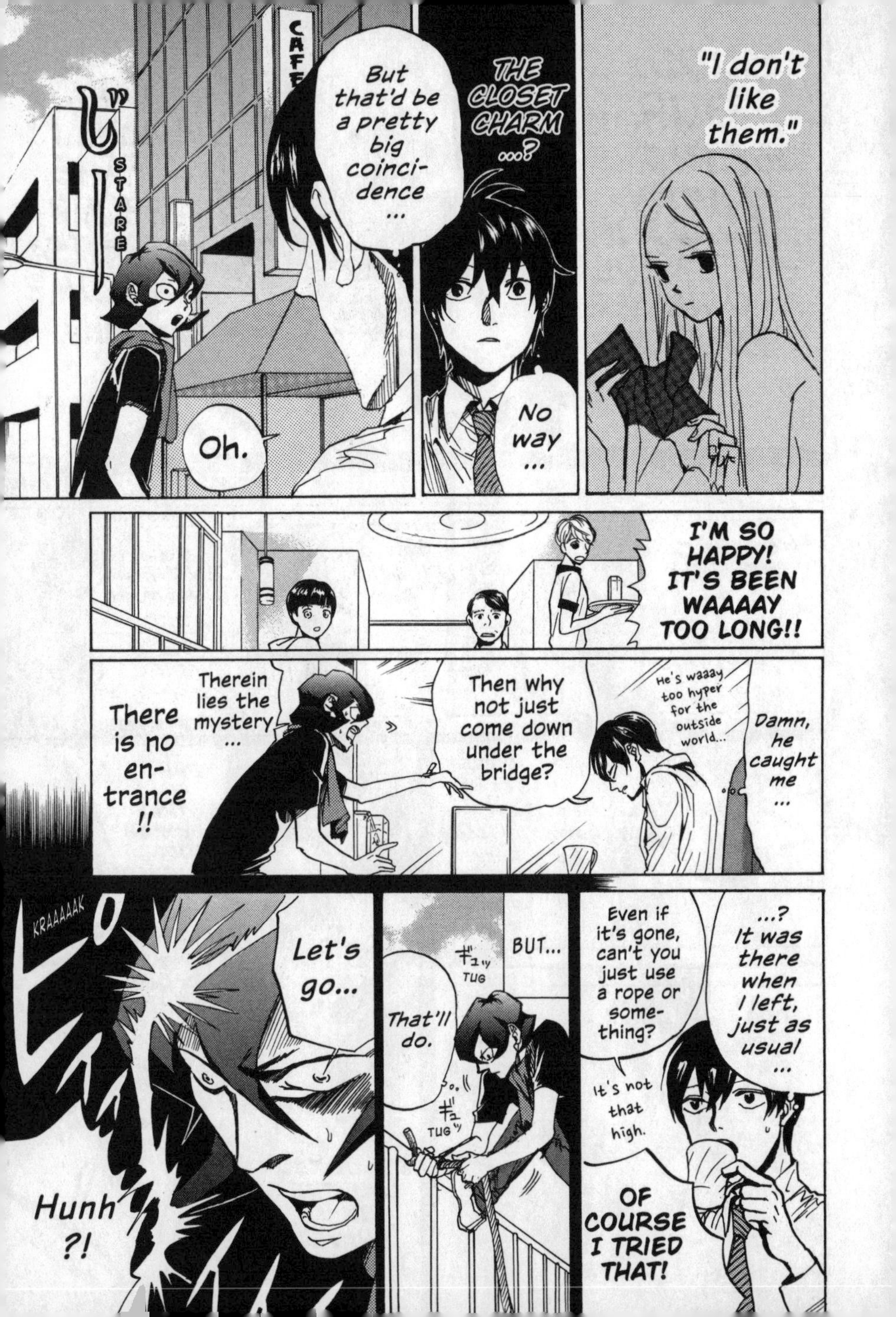
"I don't like them."
THE CLOSET CHARM ...?
No way ...
But that'd be a pretty big coincidence ...
STARE
Oh.
I'M SO HAPPY! IT'S BEEN WAAAAY TOO LONG!!
Damn, he caught me ...
He's waaay too hyper for the outside world...
Then why not just come down under the bridge?
Therein lies the mystery ...
There is no en-trance !!
...? It was there when I left, just as usual ...
Even if it's gone, can't you just use a rope or some-thing?
It's not that high.
OF COURSE I TRIED THAT!
BUT...
TUG
That'll do.
TUG
Let's go...
KRAAAAAK
Hunh ?!

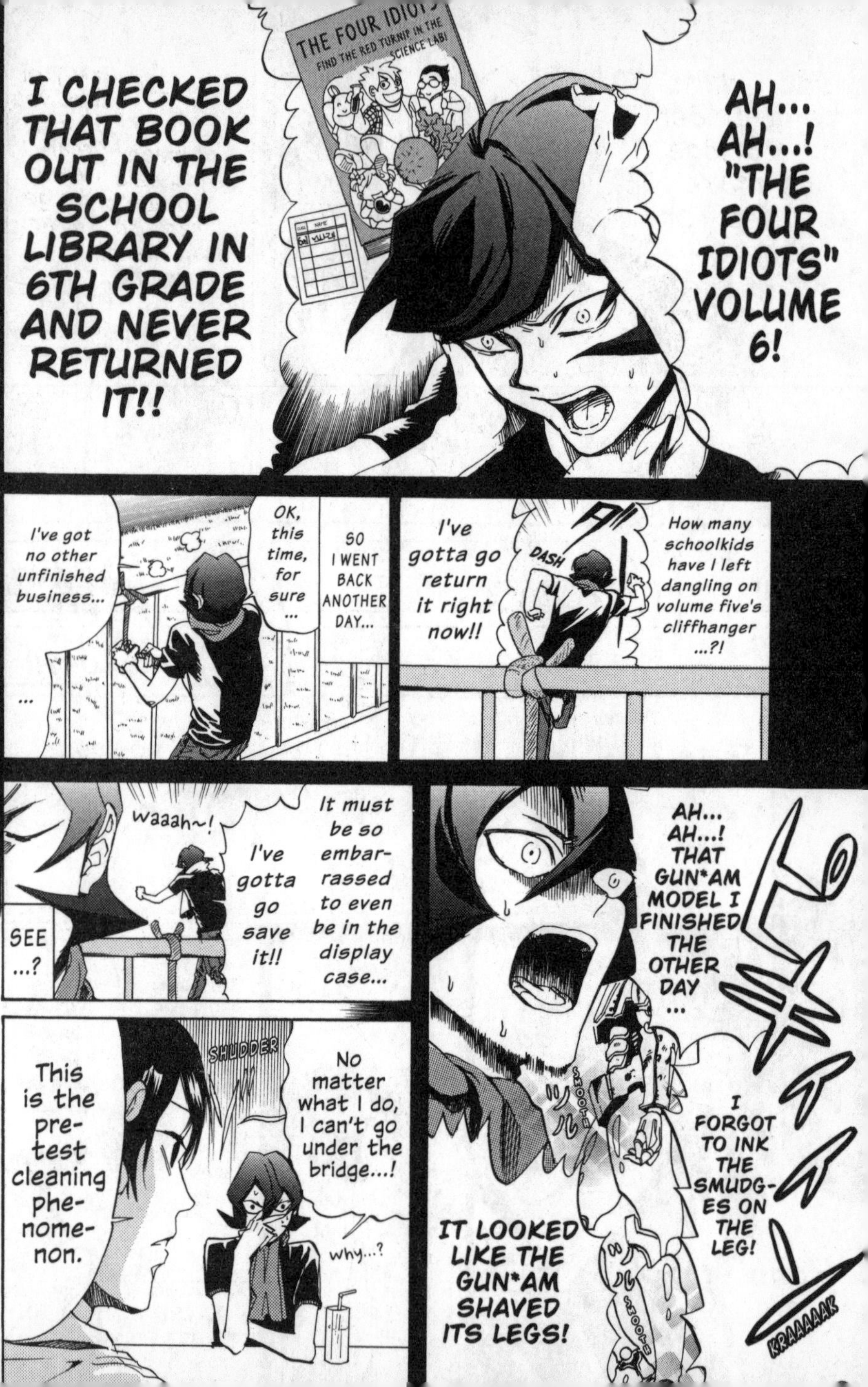
AH... AH...! "THE FOUR IDIOTS" VOLUME 6!
THE FOUR IDIOTS FIND THE RED TURNIP IN THE SCIENCE LAB!
I CHECKED THAT BOOK OUT IN THE SCHOOL LIBRARY IN 6TH GRADE AND NEVER RETURNED IT!!
How many schoolkids have I left dangling on volume five's cliffhanger ...?!
DASH
I've gotta go return it right now!!
SO I WENT BACK ANOTHER DAY...
OK, this time, for sure ...
I've got no other unfinished business...
...
AH... AH...! THAT GUN*AM MODEL I FINISHED THE OTHER DAY ...
I FORGOT TO INK THE SMUDGES ON THE LEG!
SMOOTH
SMOOTH
IT LOOKED LIKE THE GUN*AM SHAVED ITS LEGS!
KRAAAAAK
It must be so embarrassed to even be in the display case...
I've gotta go save it!!
waaah~!
SEE ...?
No matter what I do, I can't go under the bridge...!
SHUDDER
This is the pre-test cleaning phenomenon.
why...?

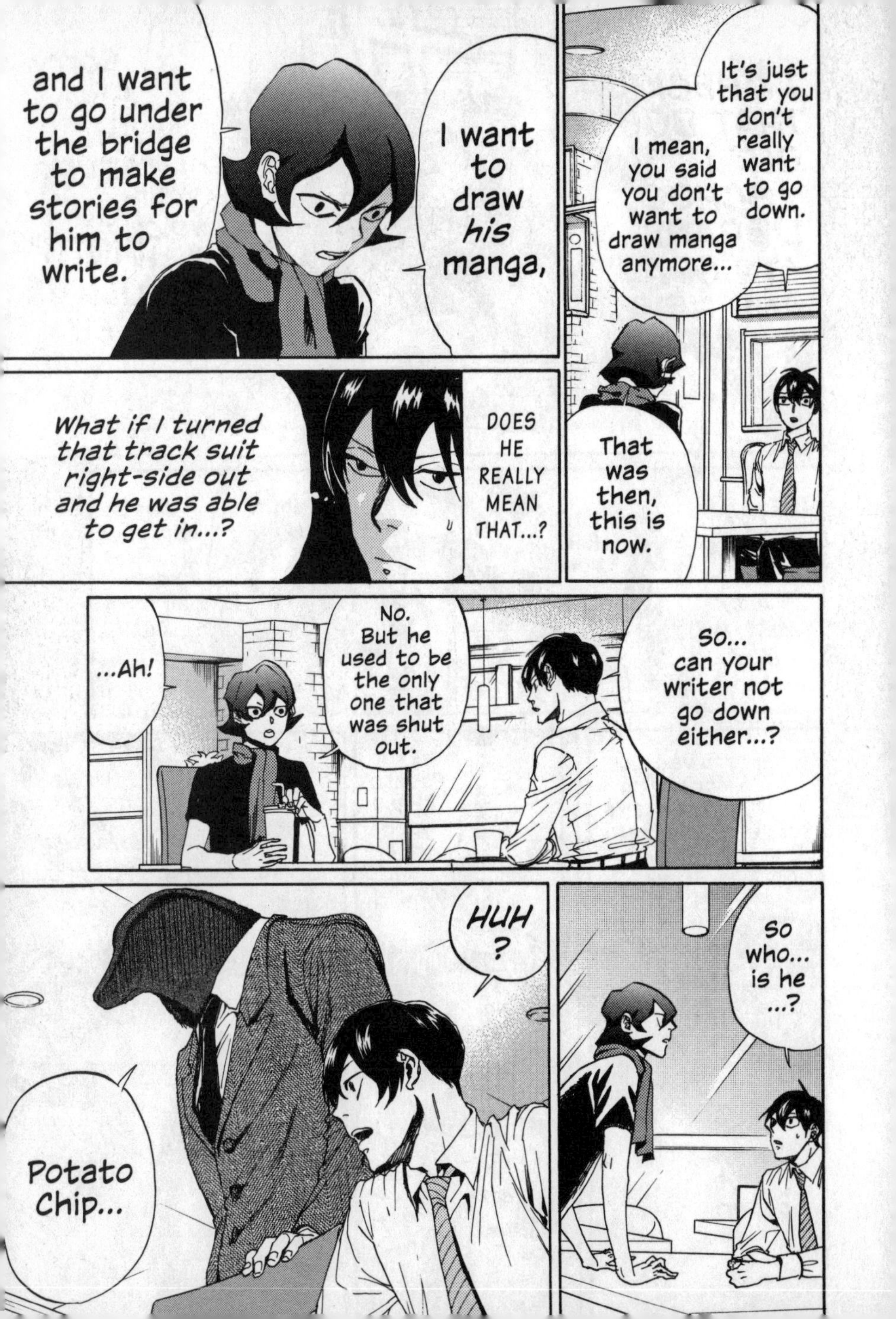
It's just that you don't really want to go down.
I mean, you said you don't want to draw manga anymore...
That was then, this is now.
I want to draw *his* manga,
and I want to go under the bridge to make stories for him to write.
DOES HE REALLY MEAN THAT...?
What if I turned that track suit right-side out and he was able to get in...?
So... can your writer not go down either...?
No. But he used to be the only one that was shut out.
...Ah!
So who... is he ...?
HUH?
Potato Chip...

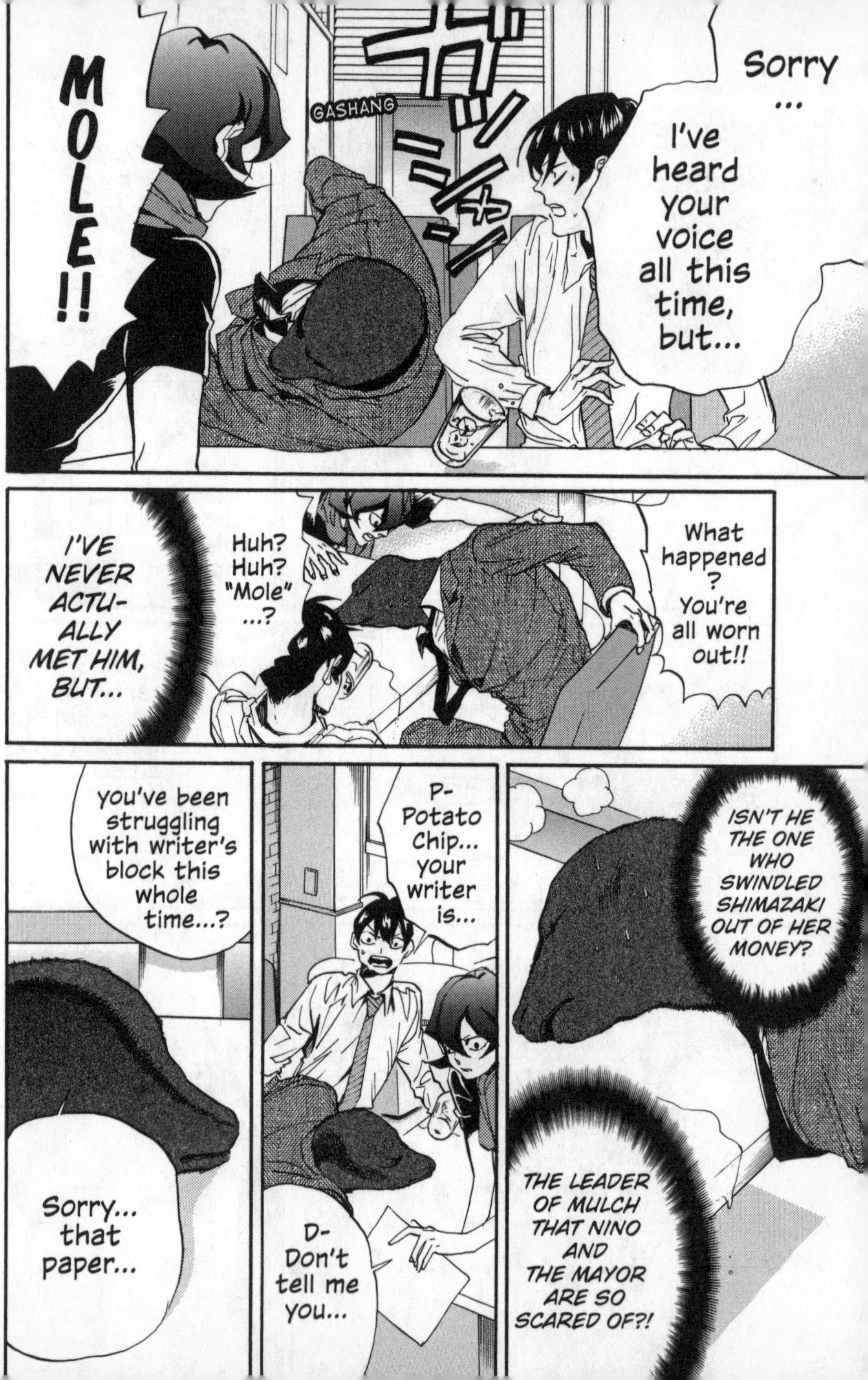
Sorry ... I've heard your voice all this time, but...
GASHANG
MOLE!!
What happened? You're all worn out!!
Huh? Huh? "Mole" ...?
I'VE NEVER ACTU-ALLY MET HIM, BUT...
ISN'T HE THE ONE WHO SWINDLED SHIMAZAKI OUT OF HER MONEY?
THE LEADER OF MULCH THAT NINO AND THE MAYOR ARE SO SCARED OF?!
P-Potato Chip... your writer is...
D-Don't tell me you...
you've been struggling with writer's block this whole time...?
Sorry... that paper...

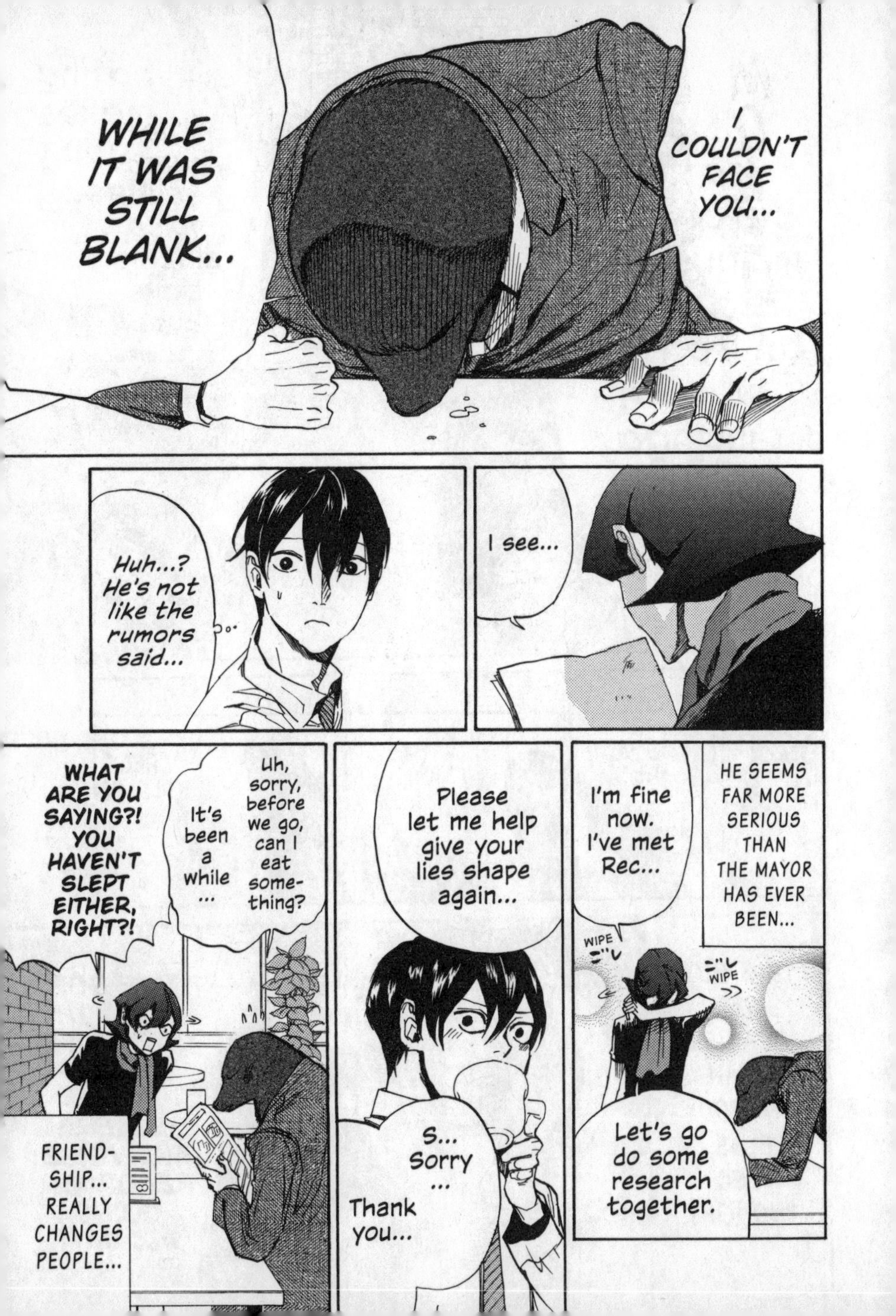
I COULDN'T FACE YOU...
WHILE IT WAS STILL BLANK...
I see...
Huh...? He's not like the rumors said...
HE SEEMS FAR MORE SERIOUS THAN THE MAYOR HAS EVER BEEN...
I'm fine now. I've met Rec...
WIPE
WIPE
Let's go do some research together.
Please let me help give your lies shape again...
S... Sorry ...
Thank you...
Uh, sorry, before we go, can I eat some-thing?
It's been a while ...
WHAT ARE YOU SAYING?! YOU HAVEN'T SLEPT EITHER, RIGHT?!
FRIEND-SHIP... REALLY CHANGES PEOPLE...

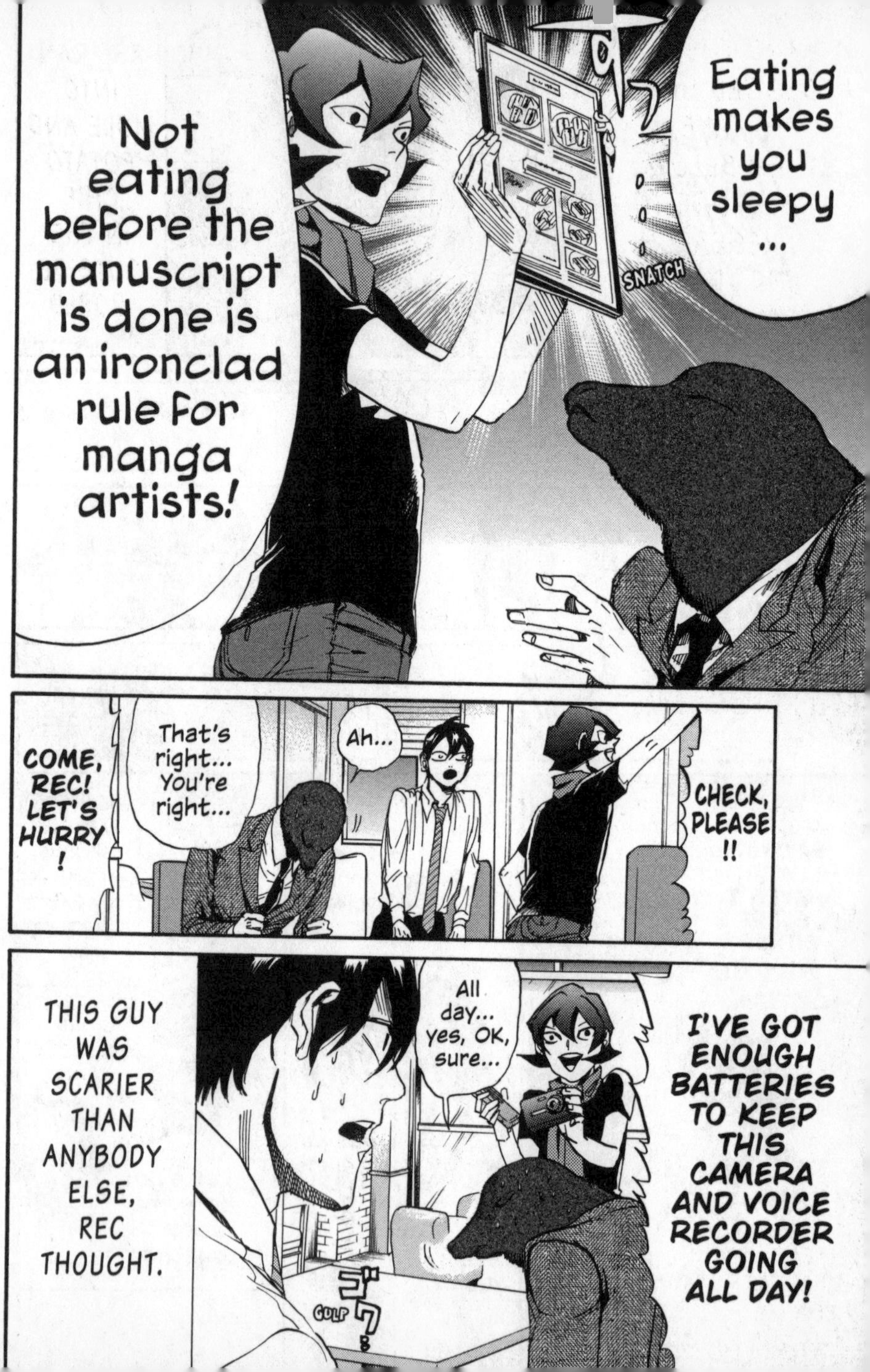
Eating makes you sleepy ...
SNATCH
Not eating before the manuscript is done is an ironclad rule for manga artists!
CHECK, PLEASE !!
Ah...
That's right... You're right...
COME, REC! LET'S HURRY!
I'VE GOT ENOUGH BATTERIES TO KEEP THIS CAMERA AND VOICE RECORDER GOING ALL DAY!
All day... yes, OK, sure...
ゴク
GULP
THIS GUY WAS SCARIER THAN ANYBODY ELSE, REC THOUGHT.

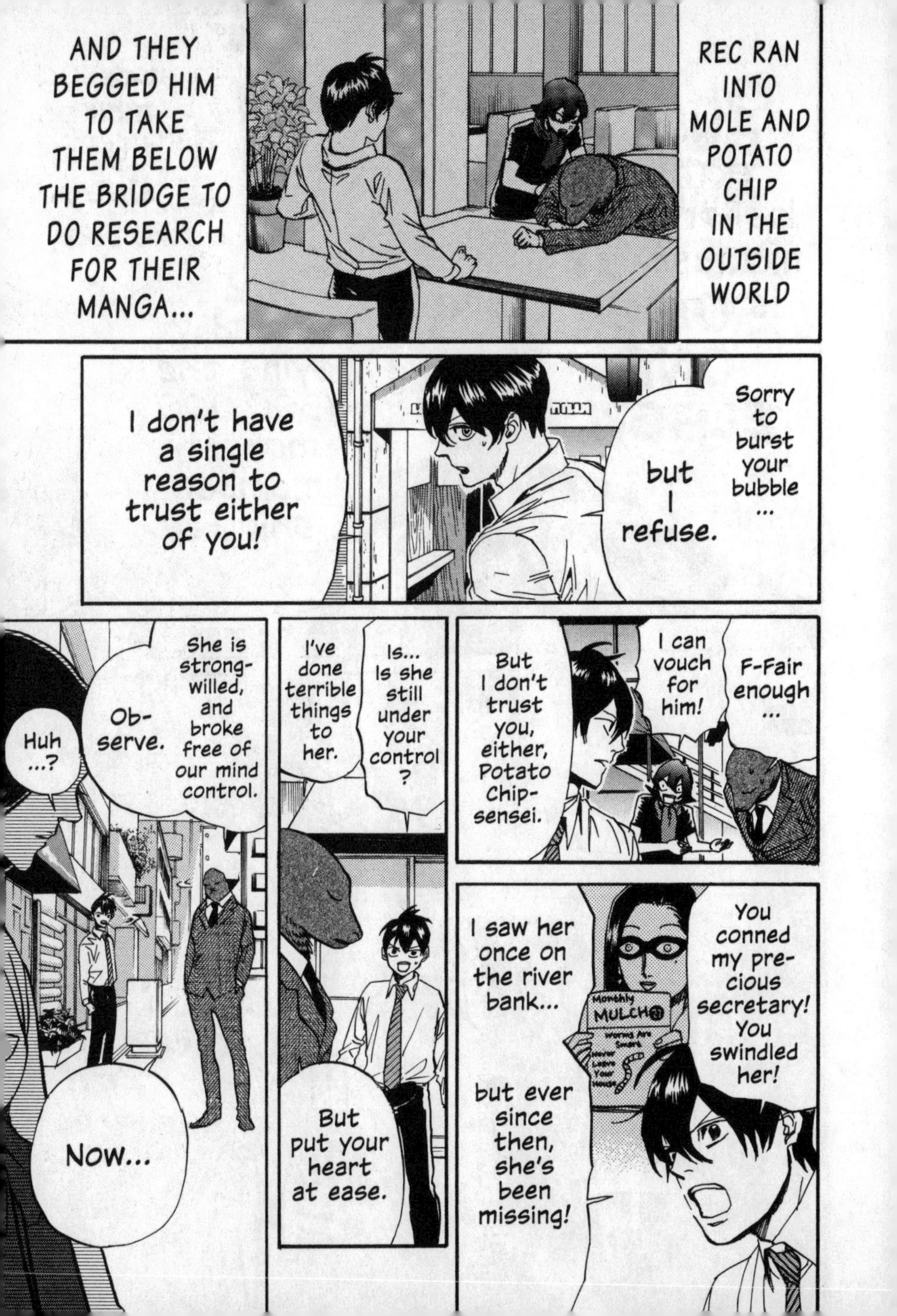
REC RAN INTO MOLE AND POTATO CHIP IN THE OUTSIDE WORLD
AND THEY BEGGED HIM TO TAKE THEM BELOW THE BRIDGE TO DO RESEARCH FOR THEIR MANGA...
Sorry to burst your bubble...
but I refuse.
I don't have a single reason to trust either of you!
F-Fair enough...
I can vouch for him!
But I don't trust you, either, Potato Chip-sensei.
You conned my precious secretary! You swindled her!
I saw her once on the river bank...
Monthly MULCH
but ever since then, she's been missing!
Is... Is she still under your control?
I've done terrible things to her.
But put your heart at ease.
She is strong-willed, and broke free of our mind control.
Ob-serve.
Huh...?
Now...

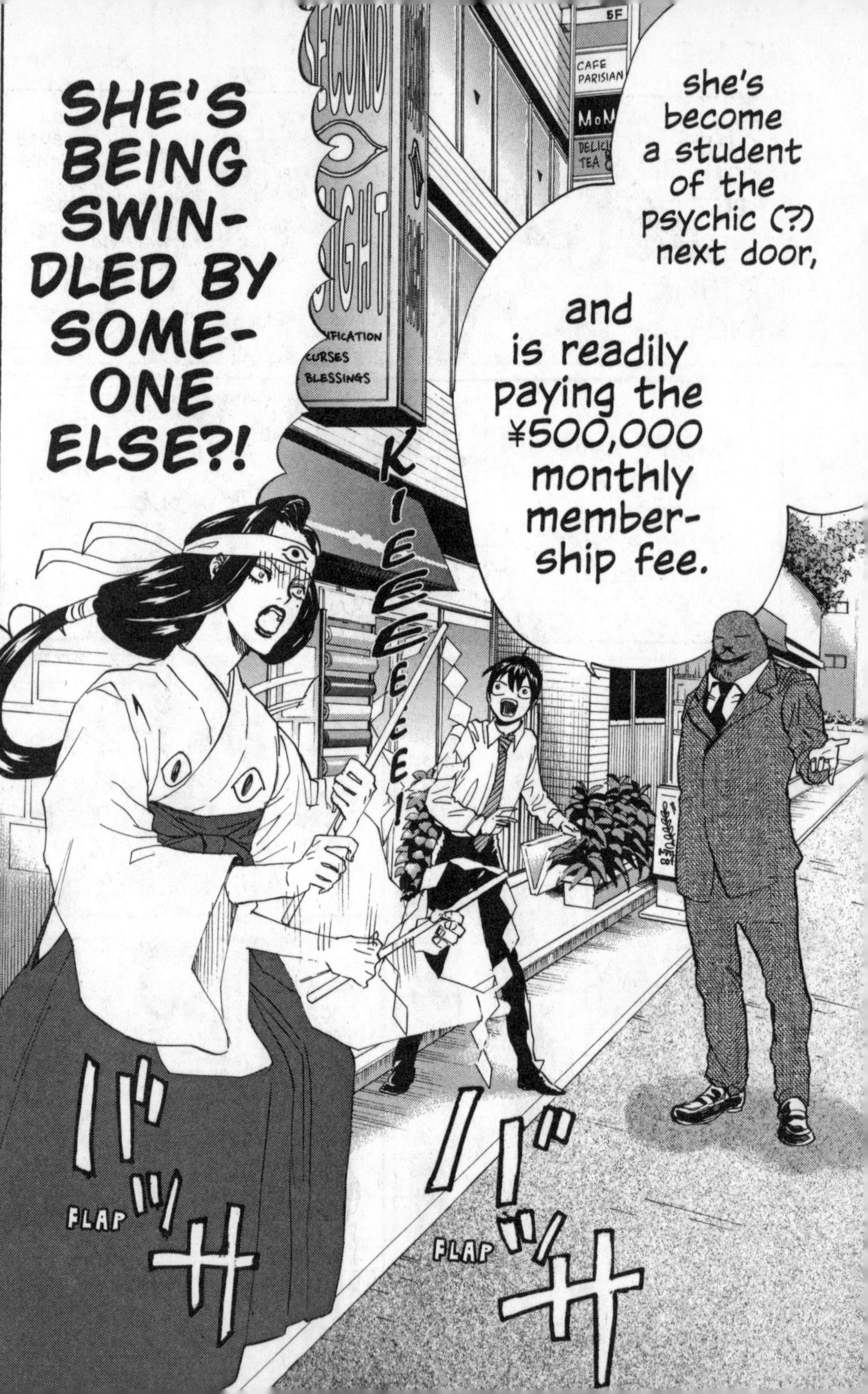
5F
CAFE PARISIAN
she's become a student of the psychic (?) next door,
and is readily paying the ¥500,000 monthly member-ship fee.
KIEEEEEEE!
SHE'S BEING SWIN-DLED BY SOME-ONE ELSE?!
CURSES
BLESSINGS
FLAP
FLAP

Chapter 380: Strong Spirit

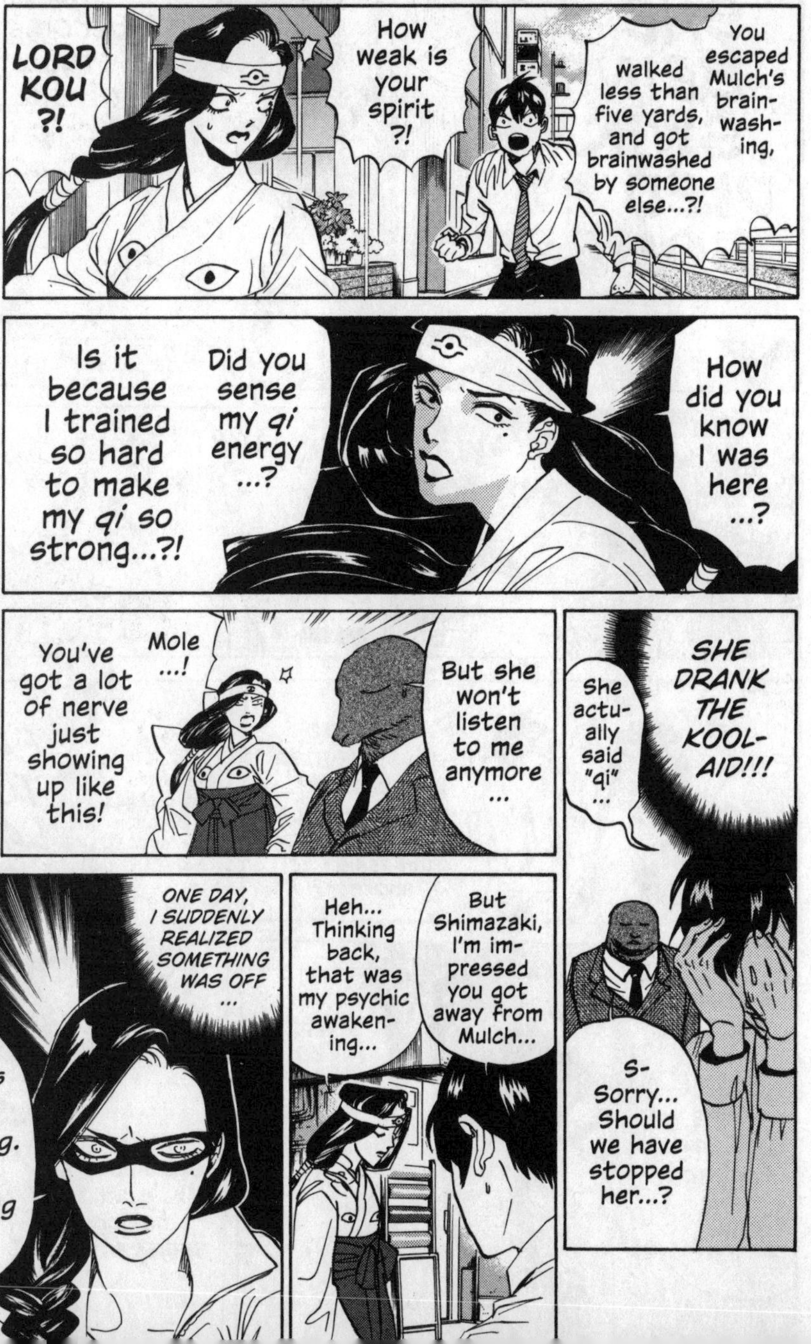
You escaped Mulch's brainwashing,
walked less than five yards, and got brainwashed by someone else...?!
How weak is your spirit?!
LORD KOU?!
How did you know I was here...?
Did you sense my *qi* energy...?
Is it because I trained so hard to make my *qi* so strong...?!
SHE DRANK THE KOOL-AID!!!
She actually said "qi"...
S-Sorry... Should we have stopped her...?
But she won't listen to me anymore...
Mole...!
You've got a lot of nerve just showing up like this!
But Shimazaki, I'm impressed you got away from Mulch...
Heh... Thinking back, that was my psychic awakening...
ONE DAY, I SUDDENLY REALIZED SOMETHING WAS OFF...
FLASH
This is... wrong. All wrong...

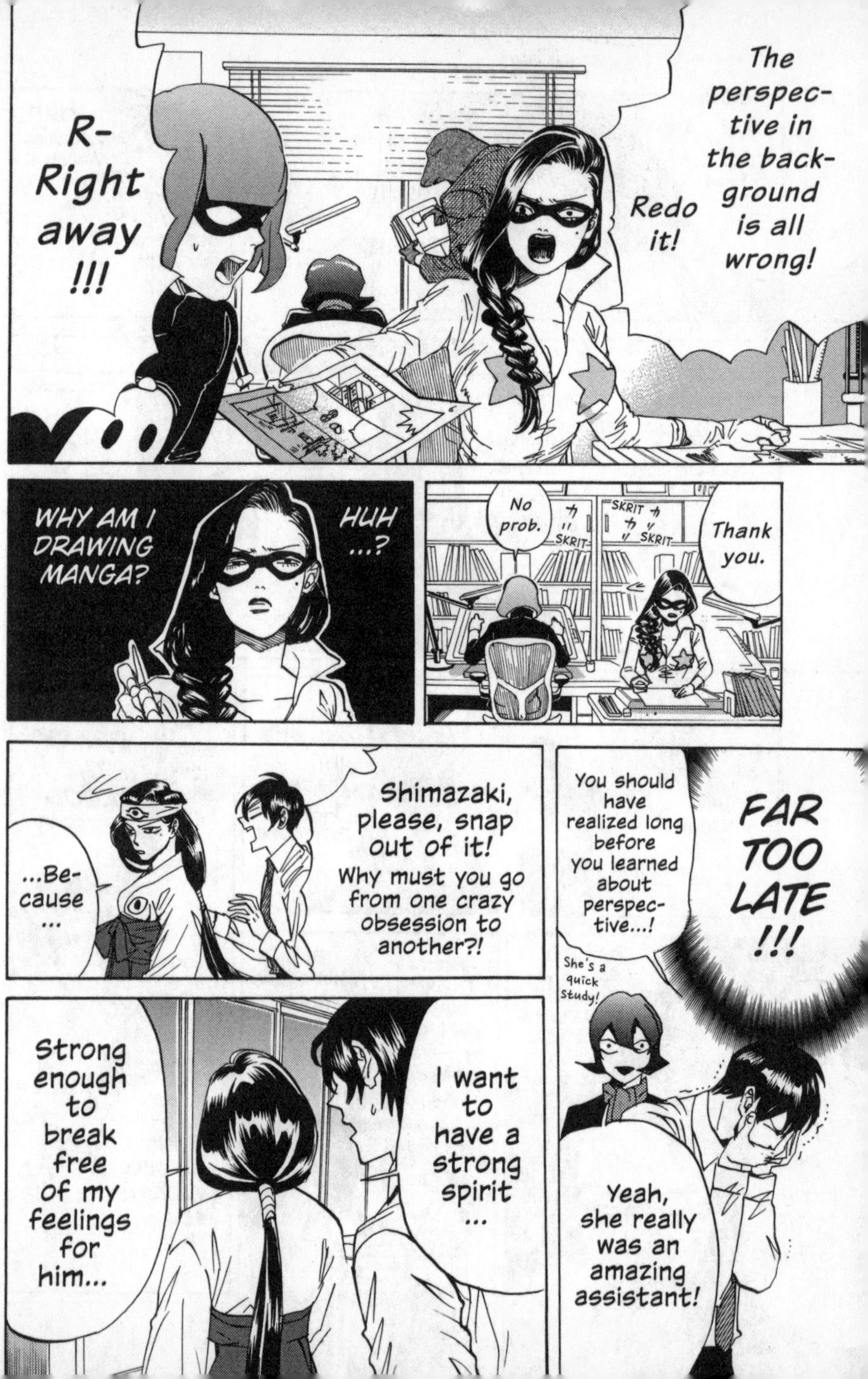
The perspective in the background is all wrong!
Redo it!
R-Right away!!!
Thank you.
SKRIT
SKRIT
SKRIT
No prob.
HUH...?
WHY AM I DRAWING MANGA?
FAR TOO LATE!!!
You should have realized long before you learned about perspective...!
She's a quick Study!
Yeah, she really was an amazing assistant!
Shimazaki, please, snap out of it! Why must you go from one crazy obsession to another?!
...Because...
I want to have a strong spirit...
Strong enough to break free of my feelings for him...

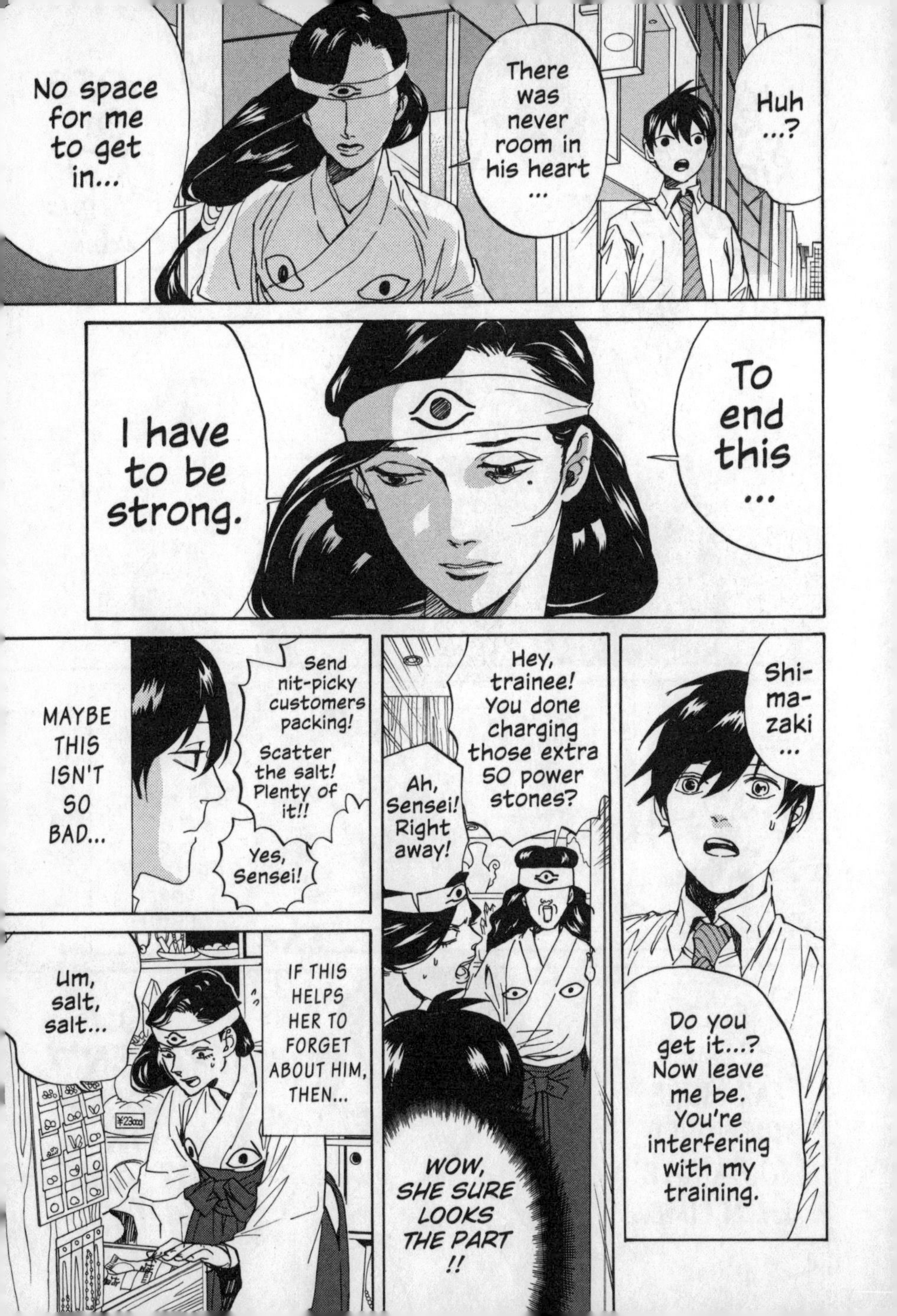
Huh ...?
There was never room in his heart ...
No space for me to get in...
To end this ...
I have to be strong.
Shi-ma-zaki ...
Do you get it...? Now leave me be. You're interfering with my training.
Hey, trainee! You done charging those extra 50 power stones?
Ah, Sensei! Right away!
WOW, SHE SURE LOOKS THE PART !!
Send nit-picky customers packing! Scatter the salt! Plenty of it!!
Yes, Sensei!
MAYBE THIS ISN'T SO BAD...
IF THIS HELPS HER TO FORGET ABOUT HIM, THEN...
Um, salt, salt...

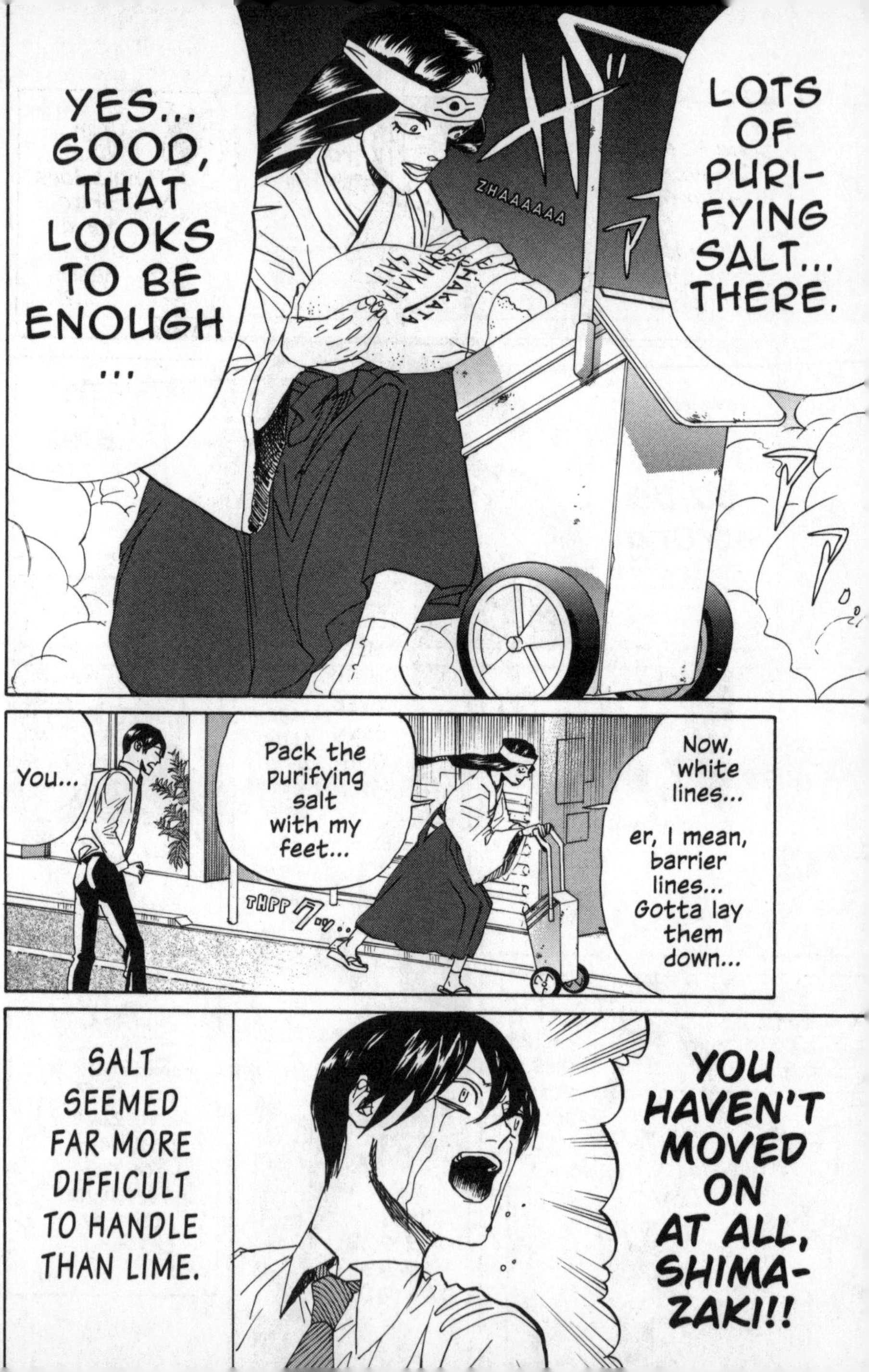
LOTS OF PURI-FYING SALT... THERE.
YES... GOOD, THAT LOOKS TO BE ENOUGH...
ZHAAAAAAA
SHAKATA SALT
Now, white lines...
er, I mean, barrier lines... Gotta lay them down...
Pack the purifying salt with my feet...
THPP
You...
YOU HAVEN'T MOVED ON AT ALL, SHIMA-ZAKI!!
SALT SEEMED FAR MORE DIFFICULT TO HANDLE THAN LIME.

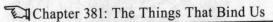

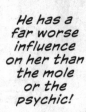

Chapter 381: The Things That Bind Us

Urgh... What hold does Shiro have on her heart ...?!
That man...
He has a far worse influence on her than the mole or the psychic!
Given that, I guess there's no reason to refuse them...
We just added that damn exhibitionist... Hm...?
"I'm scared."
HUH? THEN SHOULDN'T I...
BE WITH HER ON THE RIVER BANK RIGHT NOW...?
Ah!
NINOOOO!
I'M BAACK!
JOLT
WHAP
Ah ha ha, that takes me back!
I used to do that when I was a kid!
...Hm ...?

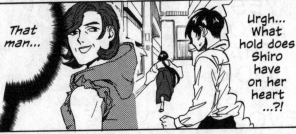

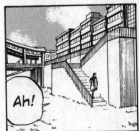

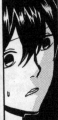

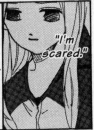

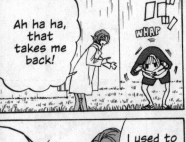

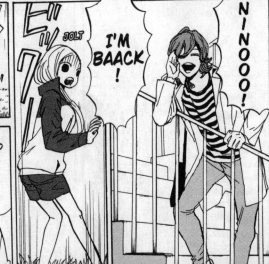

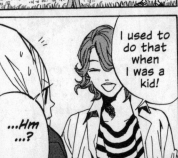

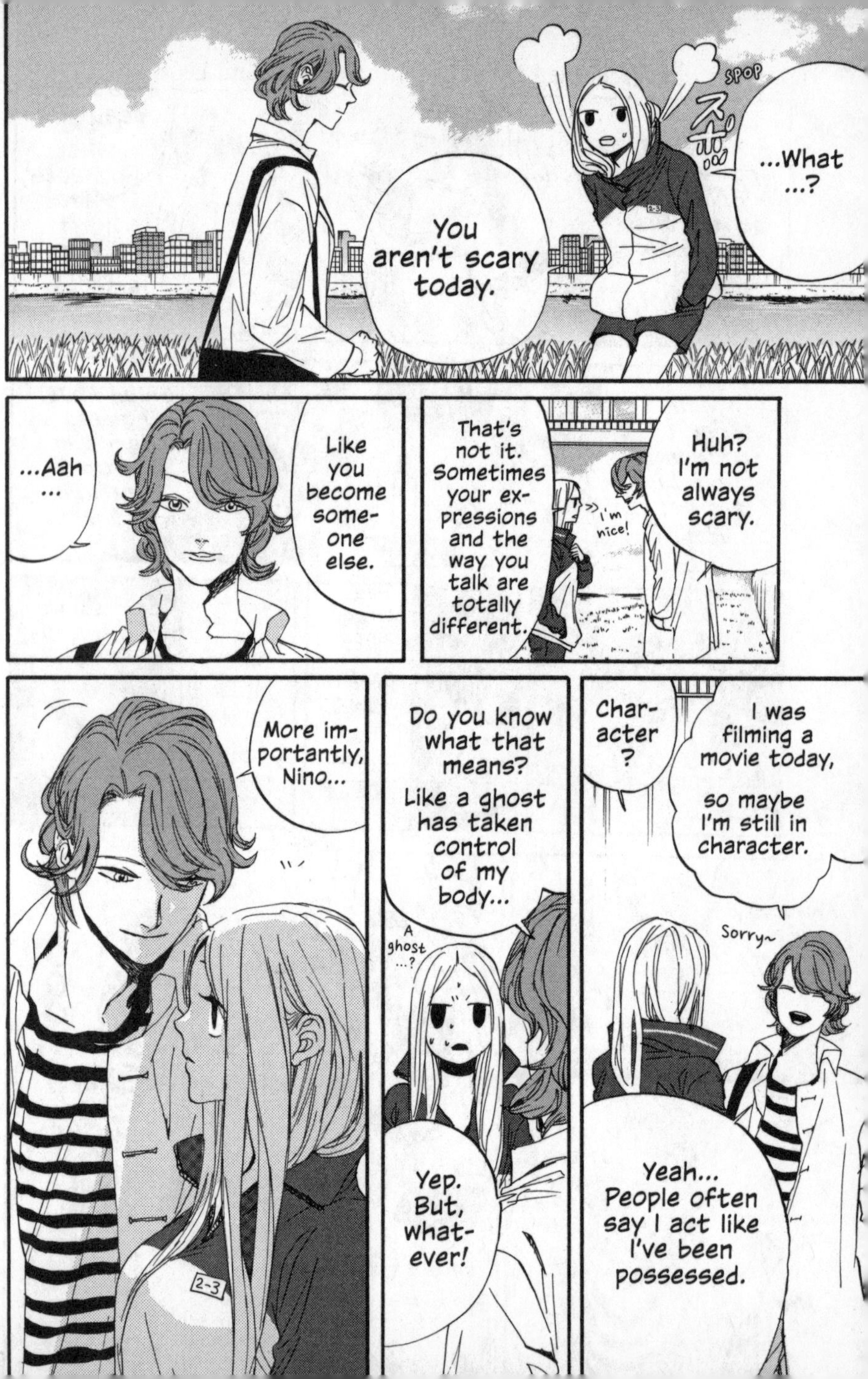
...What ...?
SPOP
スポッ
You aren't scary today.
Huh? I'm not always scary.
I'm nice!
That's not it. Sometimes your expressions and the way you talk are totally different.
Like you become some-one else.
...Aah ...
I was filming a movie today, so maybe I'm still in character.
Char-acter ?
Sorry~
Yeah... People often say I act like I've been possessed.
Do you know what that means? Like a ghost has taken control of my body...
A ghost ...?
Yep. But, what-ever!
More im-portantly, Nino...

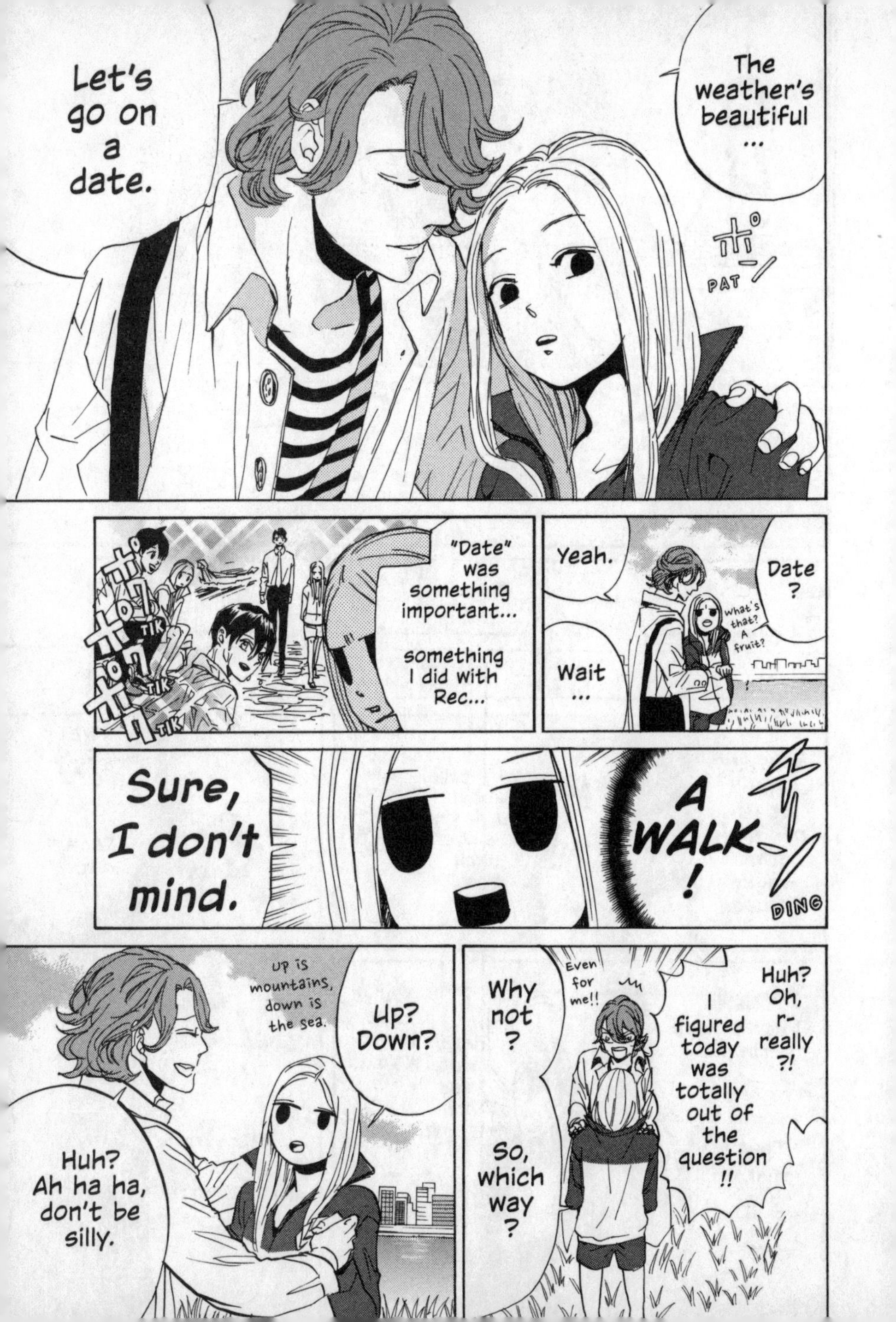
The weather's beautiful ...
Let's go on a date.
PAT
Date?
what's that? A fruit?
Yeah.
Wait ...
"Date" was something important...
something I did with Rec...
TIK
TIK
TIK
A WALK!
DING
Sure, I don't mind.
Huh? Oh, r-really?!
I figured today was totally out of the question!!
Even for me!!
Why not?
So, which way?
Up? Down?
Up is mountains, down is the sea.
Huh? Ah ha ha, don't be silly.

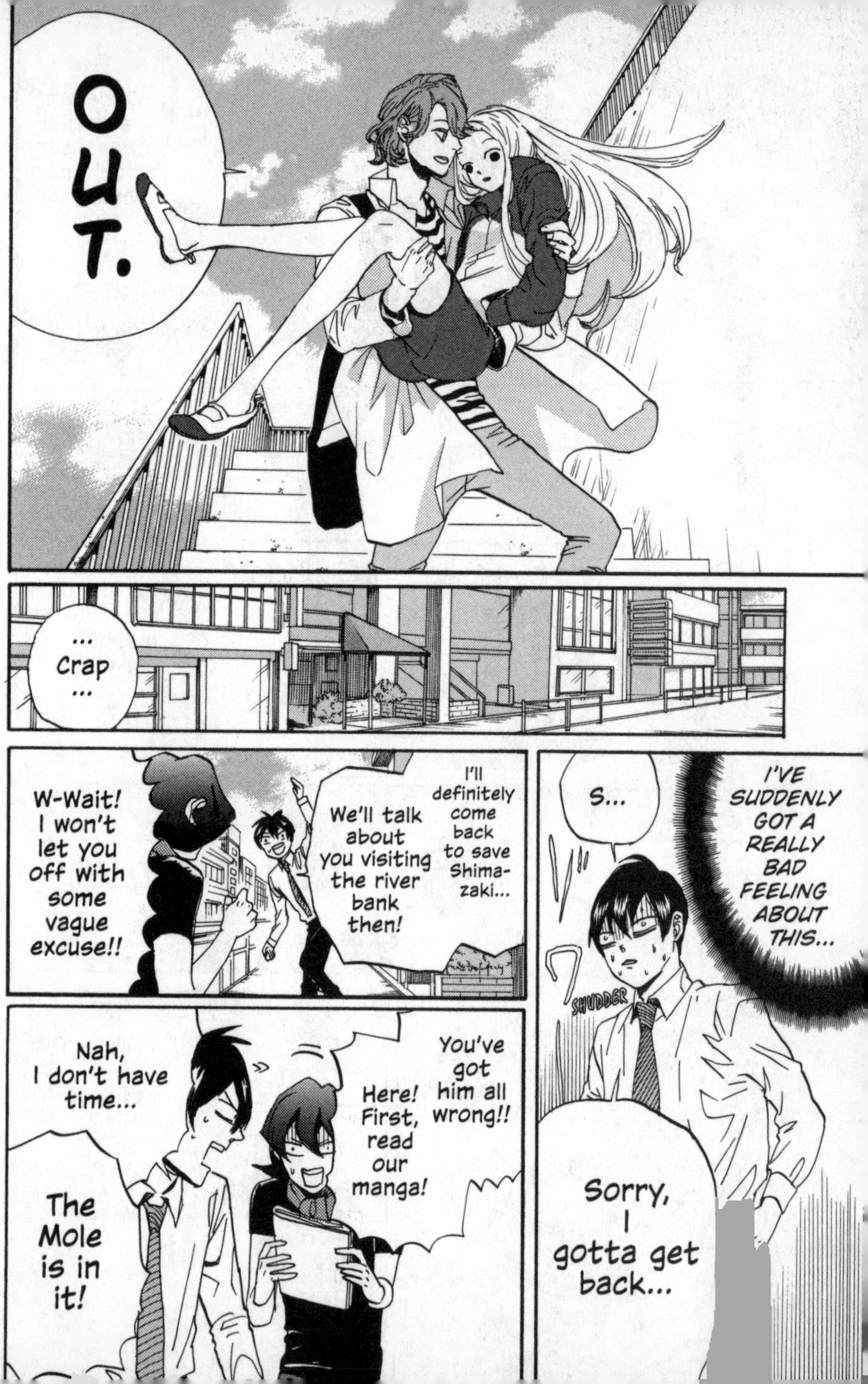
OUT.
... Crap ...
I'VE SUDDENLY GOT A REALLY BAD FEELING ABOUT THIS...
S...
SHUDDER
Sorry, I gotta get back...
I'll definitely come back to save Shimazaki...
We'll talk about you visiting the river bank then!
W-Wait! I won't let you off with some vague excuse!!
You've got him all wrong!!
Here! First, read our manga!
Nah, I don't have time...
The Mole is in it!

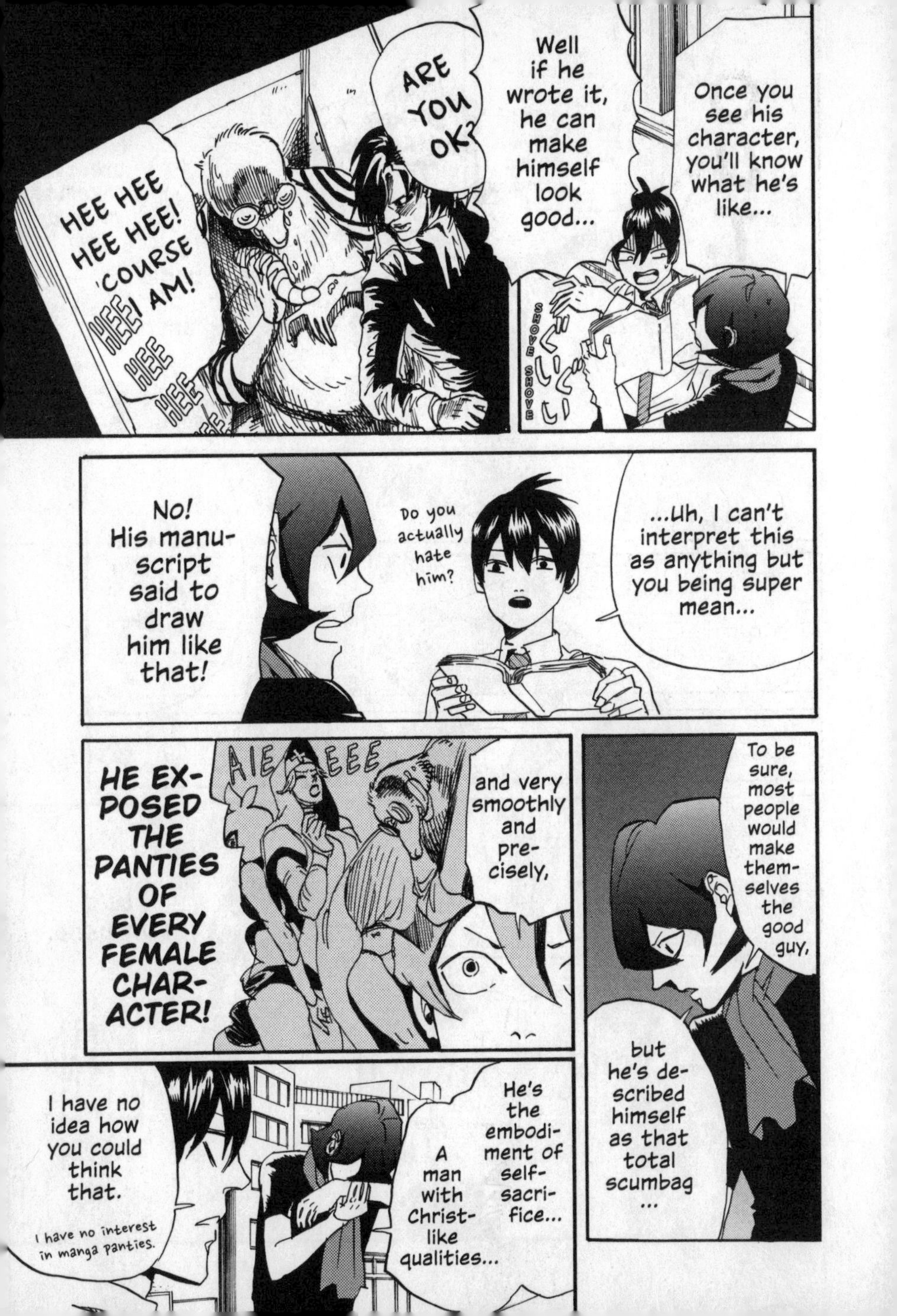
Once you see his character, you'll know what he's like...
Well if he wrote it, he can make himself look good...
SHOVE SHOVE
ARE YOU OK?
HEE HEE HEE HEE! 'COURSE I AM!
HEE HEE HEE
...Uh, I can't interpret this as anything but you being super mean...
Do you actually hate him?
No! His manu-script said to draw him like that!
To be sure, most people would make them-selves the good guy,
but he's de-scribed himself as that total scumbag...
and very smoothly and pre-cisely,
HE EX-POSED THE PANTIES OF EVERY FEMALE CHAR-ACTER!
AIEEEE
He's the embodi-ment of self-sacri-fice...
A man with Christ-like qualities...
I have no idea how you could think that.
I have no interest in manga panties.

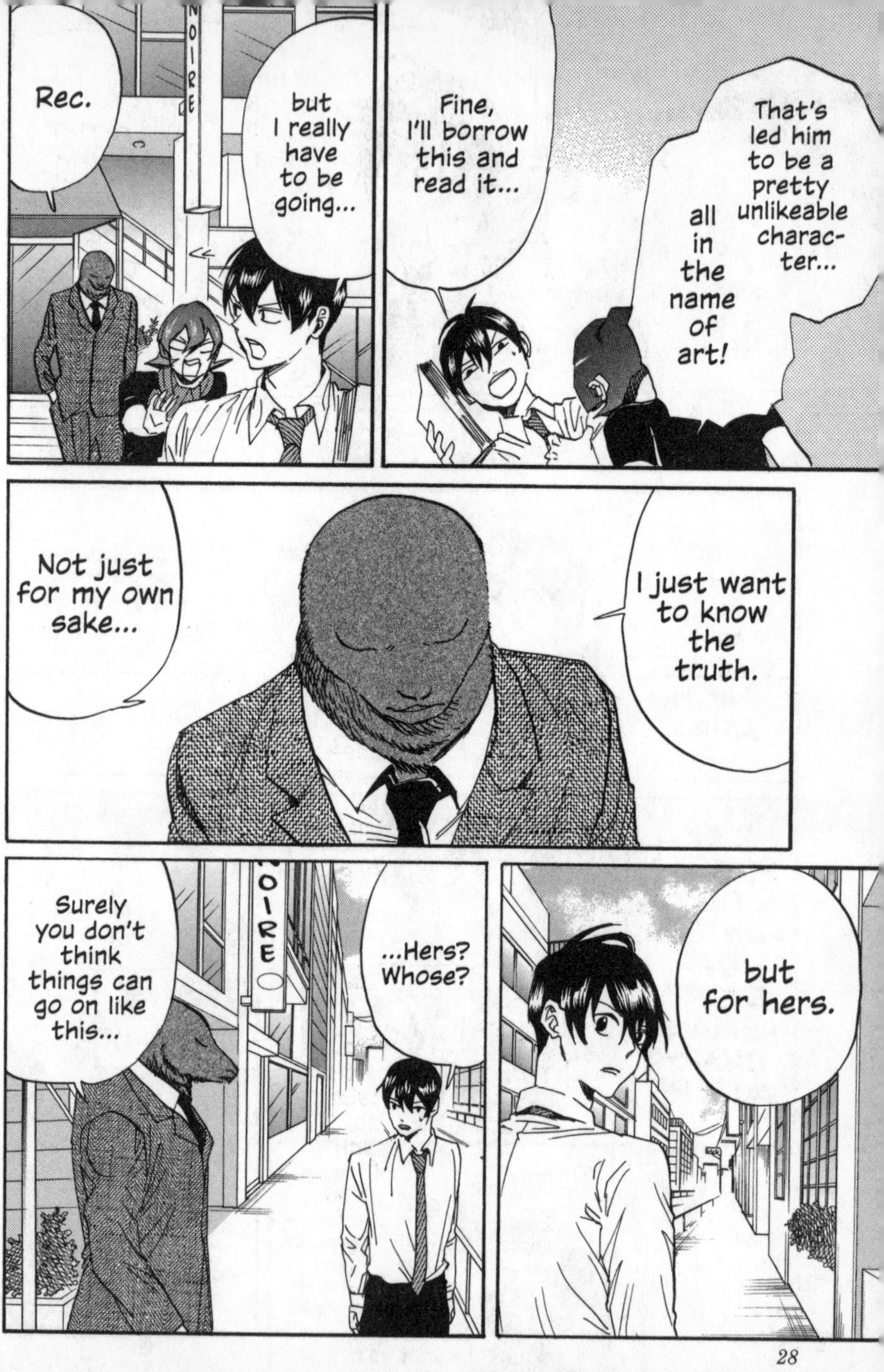
That's led him to be a pretty unlikeable character... all in the name of art!
Fine, I'll borrow this and read it...
but I really have to be going...
NOIRE
Rec.
I just want to know the truth.
Not just for my own sake...
but for hers.
...Hers? Whose?
NOIRE
Surely you don't think things can go on like this...

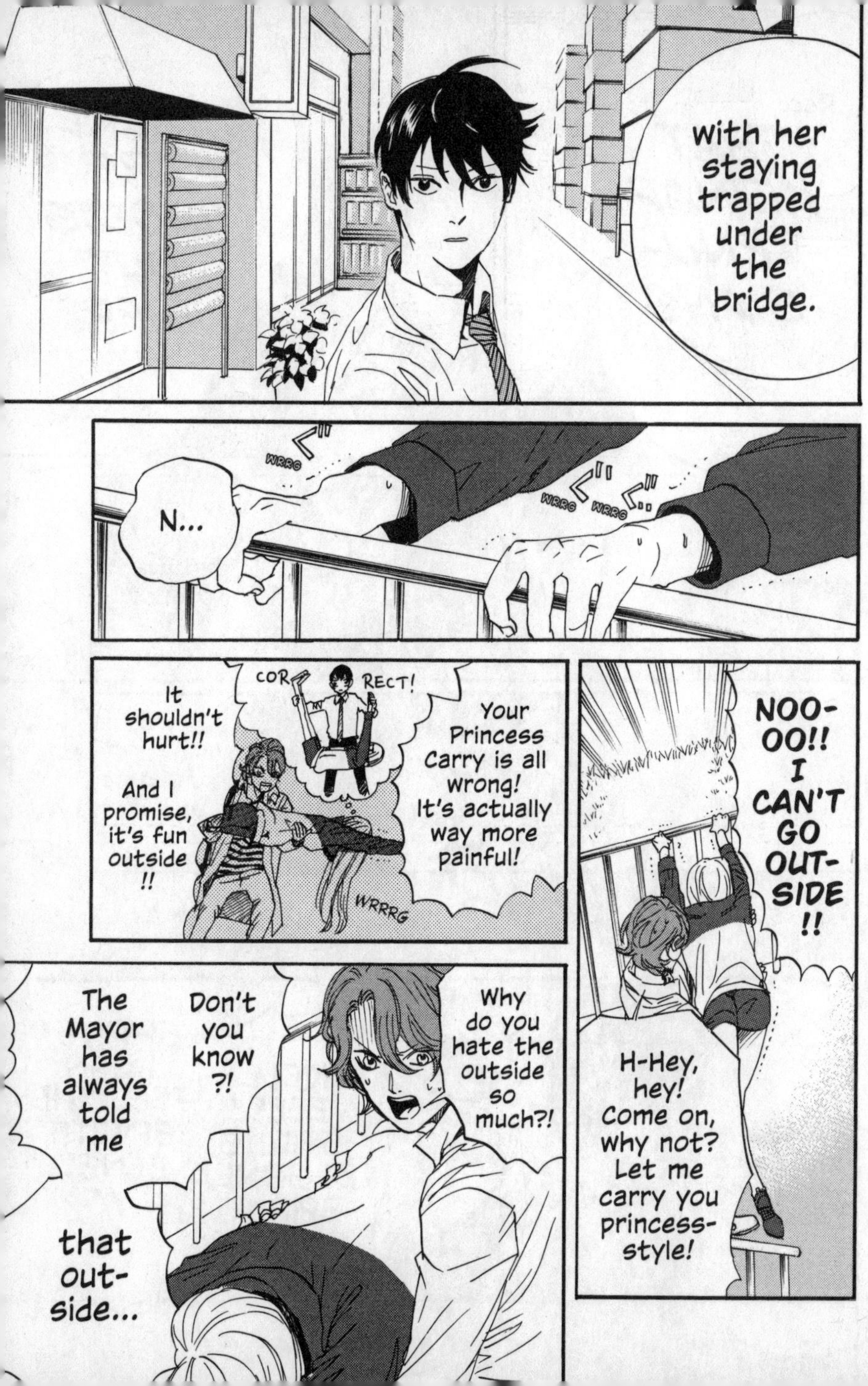
with her staying trapped under the bridge.
WRRG
N...
WRRG
WRRG
NOO-OO!! I CAN'T GO OUT-SIDE!!
H-Hey, hey! Come on, why not? Let me carry you princess-style!
COR
RECT!
Your Princess Carry is all wrong! It's actually way more painful!
It shouldn't hurt!!
And I promise, it's fun outside!!
WRRRG
Why do you hate the outside so much?!
Don't you know?!
The Mayor has always told me
that out-side...

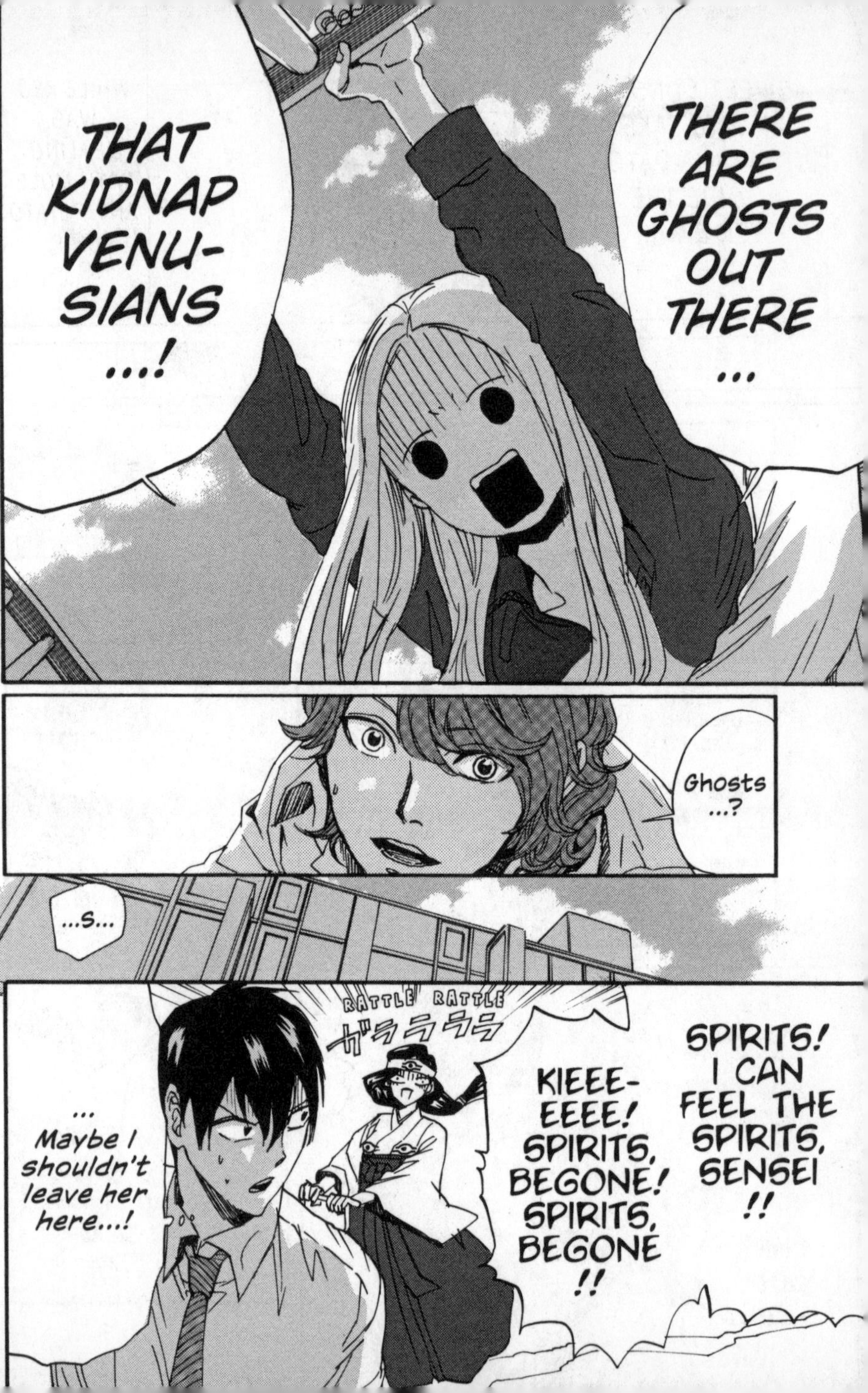
THERE ARE GHOSTS OUT THERE ...
THAT KIDNAP VENUSIANS ...!
Ghosts ...?
...S...
SPIRITS! I CAN FEEL THE SPIRITS, SENSEI !!
RATTLE RATTLE
ガララララ
KIEEEEEEE! SPIRITS, BEGONE! SPIRITS, BEGONE !!
... Maybe I shouldn't leave her here...!

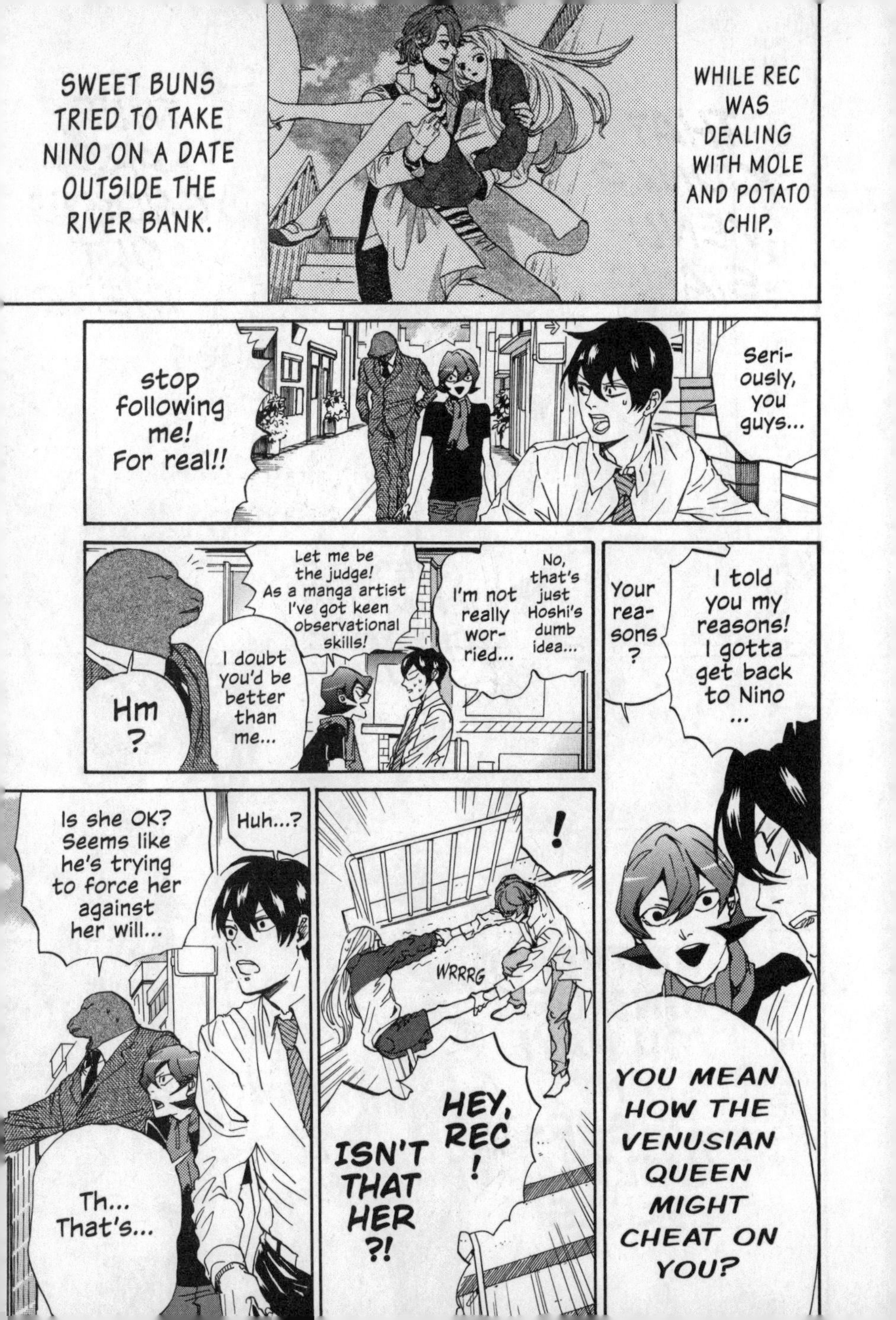
WHILE REC WAS DEALING WITH MOLE AND POTATO CHIP,
SWEET BUNS TRIED TO TAKE NINO ON A DATE OUTSIDE THE RIVER BANK.
Seri-ously, you guys...
stop following me! For real!!
I told you my reasons! I gotta get back to Nino ...
Your rea-sons ?
No, that's just Hoshi's dumb idea...
I'm not really wor-ried...
Let me be the judge! As a manga artist I've got keen observational skills!
I doubt you'd be better than me...
Hm ?
YOU MEAN HOW THE VENUSIAN QUEEN MIGHT CHEAT ON YOU?
!
HEY, REC !
ISN'T THAT HER ?!
WRRRG
Huh...?
Is she OK? Seems like he's trying to force her against her will...
Th... That's...

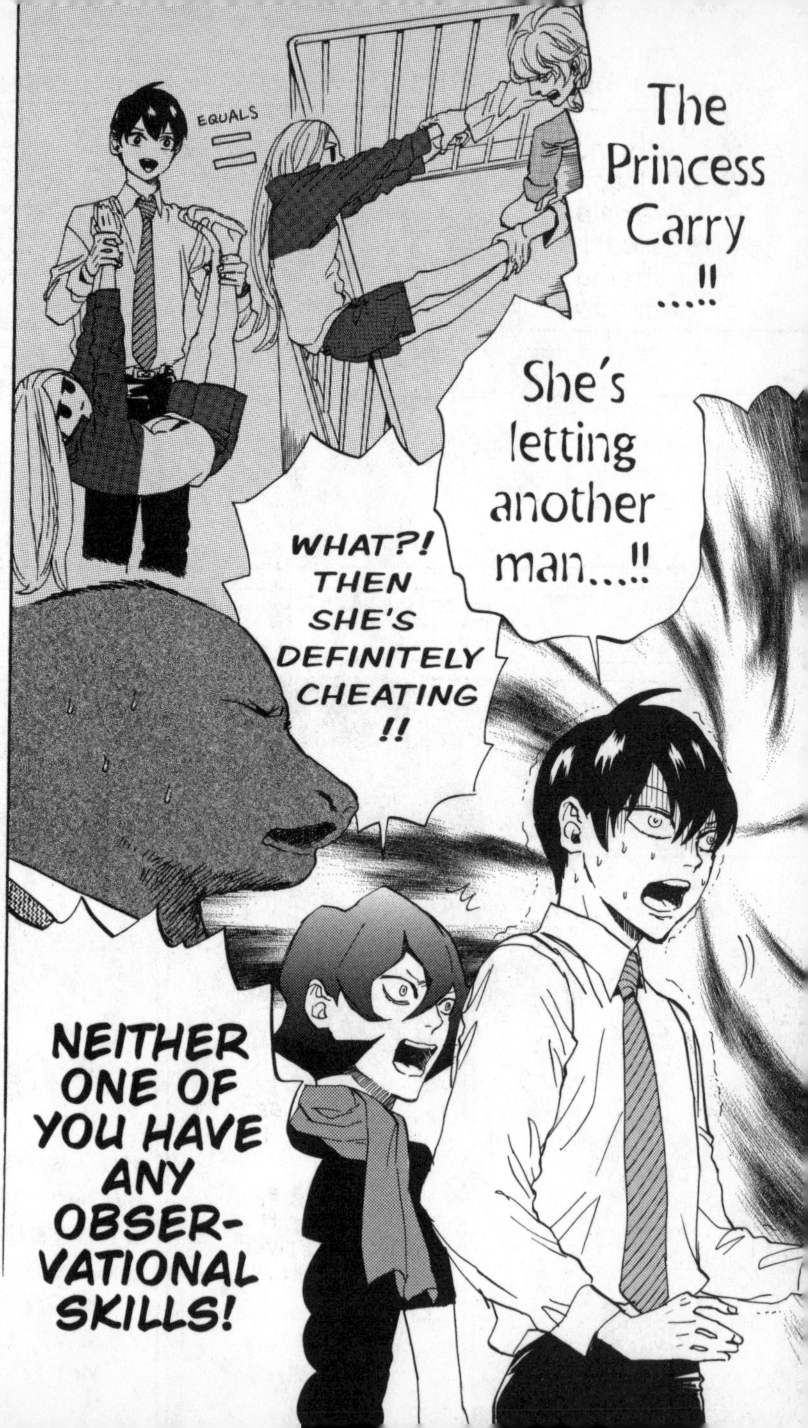
The Princess Carry ...!!
She's letting another man...!!
WHAT?! THEN SHE'S DEFINITELY CHEATING !!
EQUALS
NEITHER ONE OF YOU HAVE ANY OBSER-VATIONAL SKILLS!

REC NOW FIRMLY BELIEVED THE PRINCESS CARRY IS AS DEPICTED TO THE RIGHT.

Chapter 382: The Nature of the Spirit

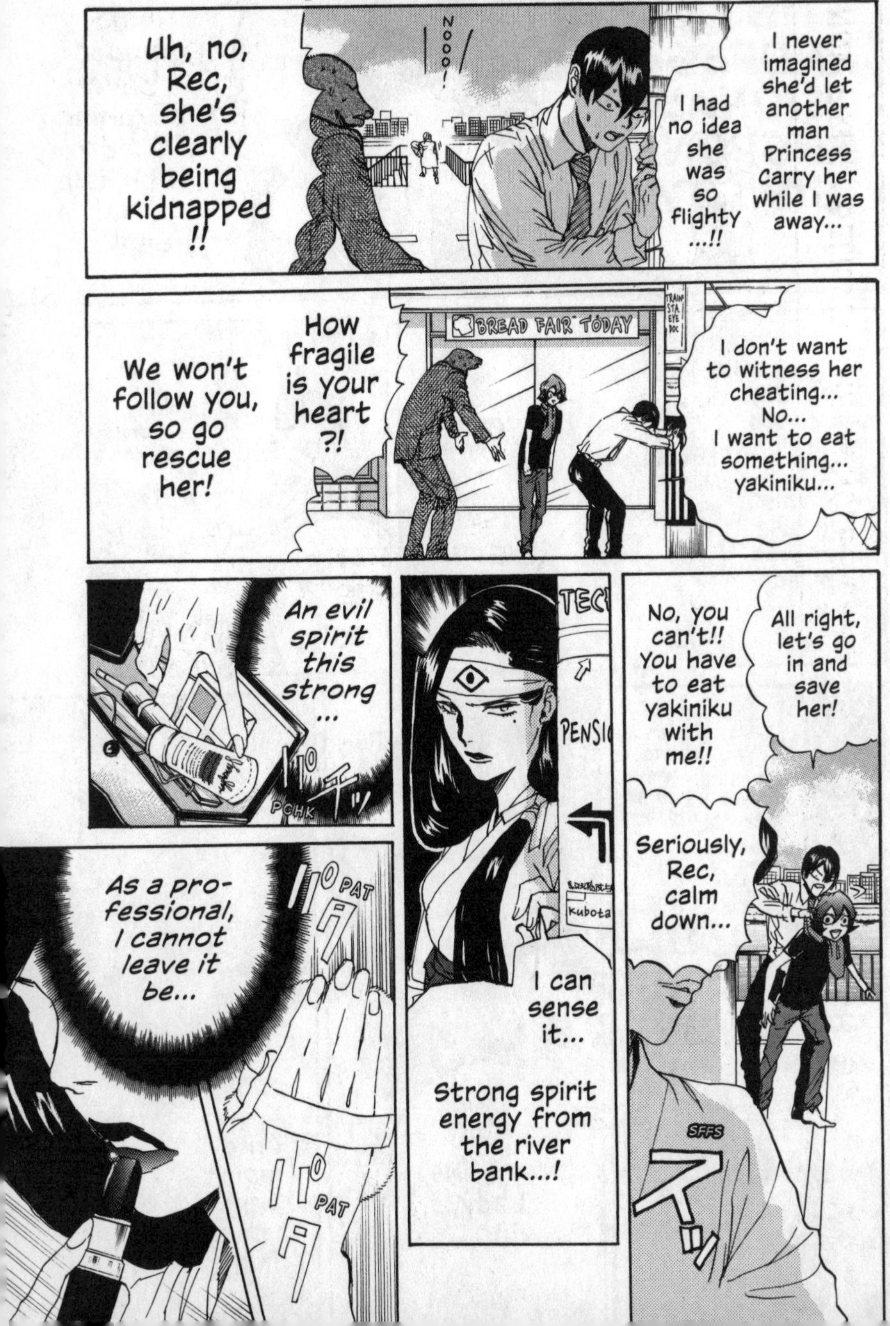
I never imagined she'd let another man Princess Carry her while I was away...
I had no idea she was so flighty ...!!
NOOO!
Uh, no, Rec, she's clearly being kidnapped!!
TRAIN STA. EYE DOC
I don't want to witness her cheating... No... I want to eat something... yakiniku...
BREAD FAIR TODAY
How fragile is your heart?!
We won't follow you, so go rescue her!
All right, let's go in and save her!
No, you can't!! You have to eat yakiniku with me!!
Seriously, Rec, calm down...
SFFS
kubota
I can sense it...
Strong spirit energy from the river bank...!
An evil spirit this strong...
PCHK
As a professional, I cannot leave it be...
PAT
PAT

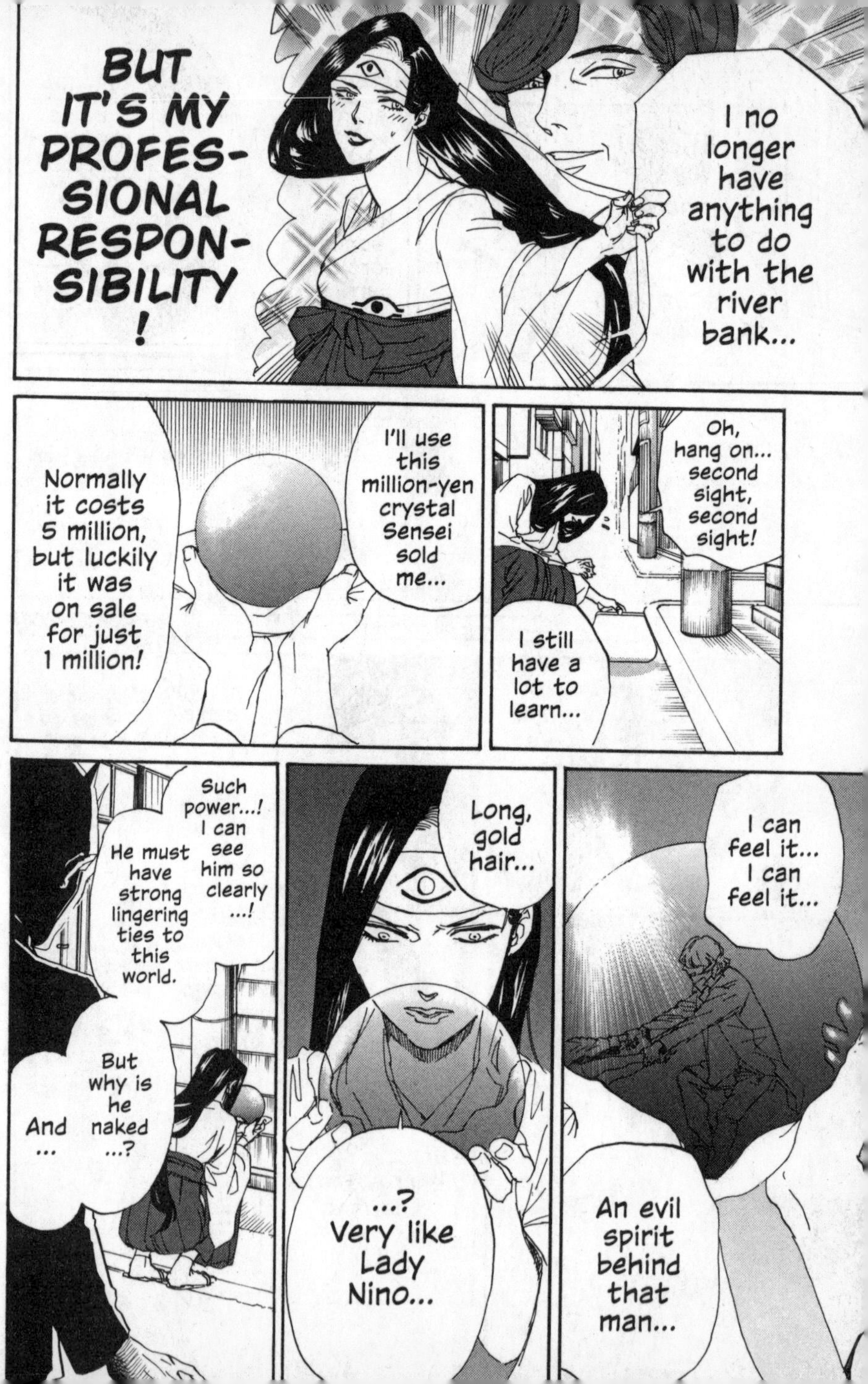
I no longer have anything to do with the river bank...
BUT IT'S MY PROFESSIONAL RESPONSIBILITY!
Oh, hang on... second sight, second sight!
I still have a lot to learn...
I'll use this million-yen crystal Sensei sold me...
Normally it costs 5 million, but luckily it was on sale for just 1 million!
I can feel it... I can feel it...
An evil spirit behind that man...
Long, gold hair...
...? Very like Lady Nino...
Such power...! I can see him so clearly ...!
He must have strong lingering ties to this world.
But why is he naked ...?
And ...

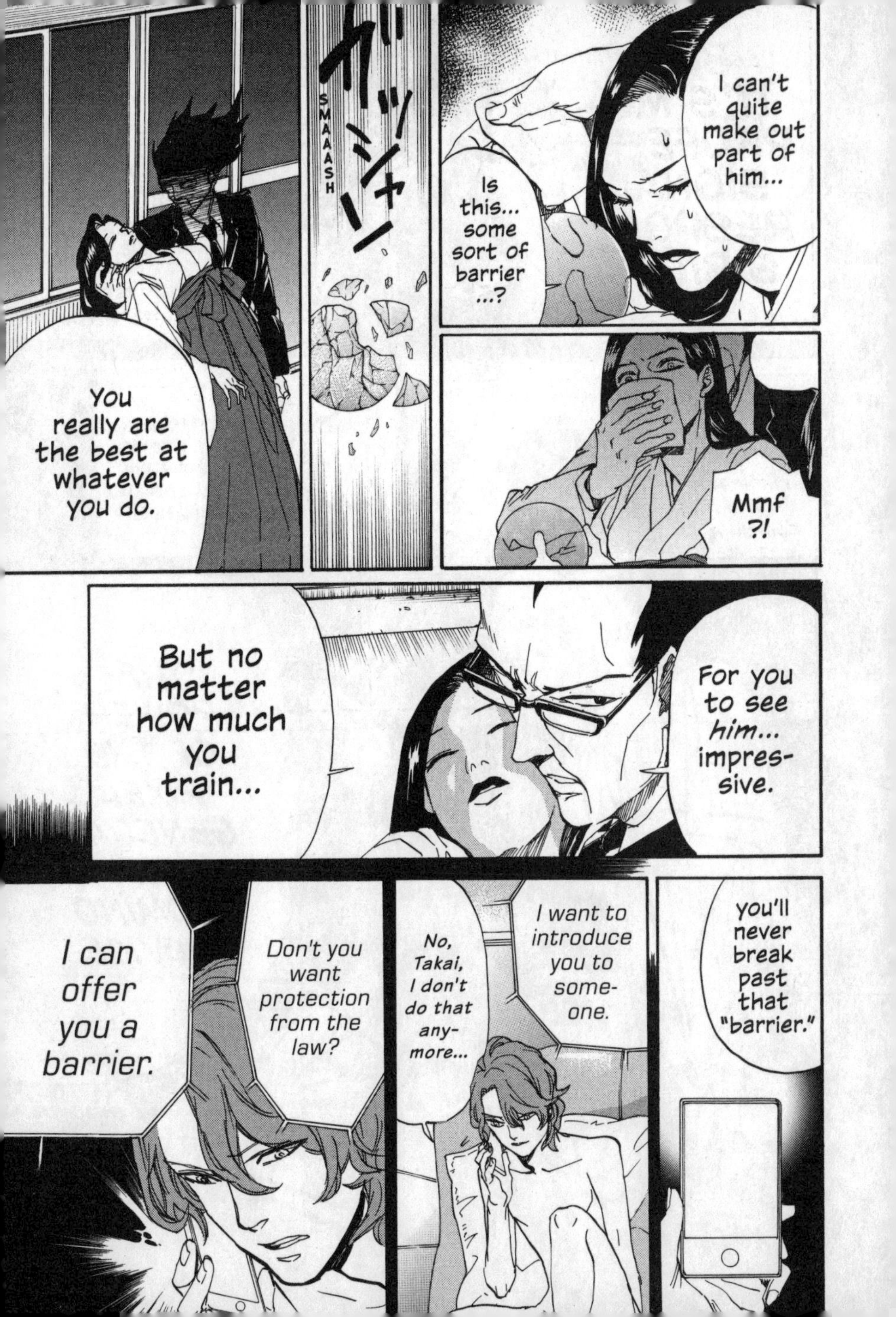
I can't quite make out part of him...
Is this... some sort of barrier ...?
Mmf ?!
SMAAASH
You really are the best at whatever you do.
For you to see *him*... impressive.
But no matter how much you train...
you'll never break past that "barrier."
I want to introduce you to someone.
No, Takai, I don't do that anymore...
Don't you want protection from the law?
I can offer you a barrier.

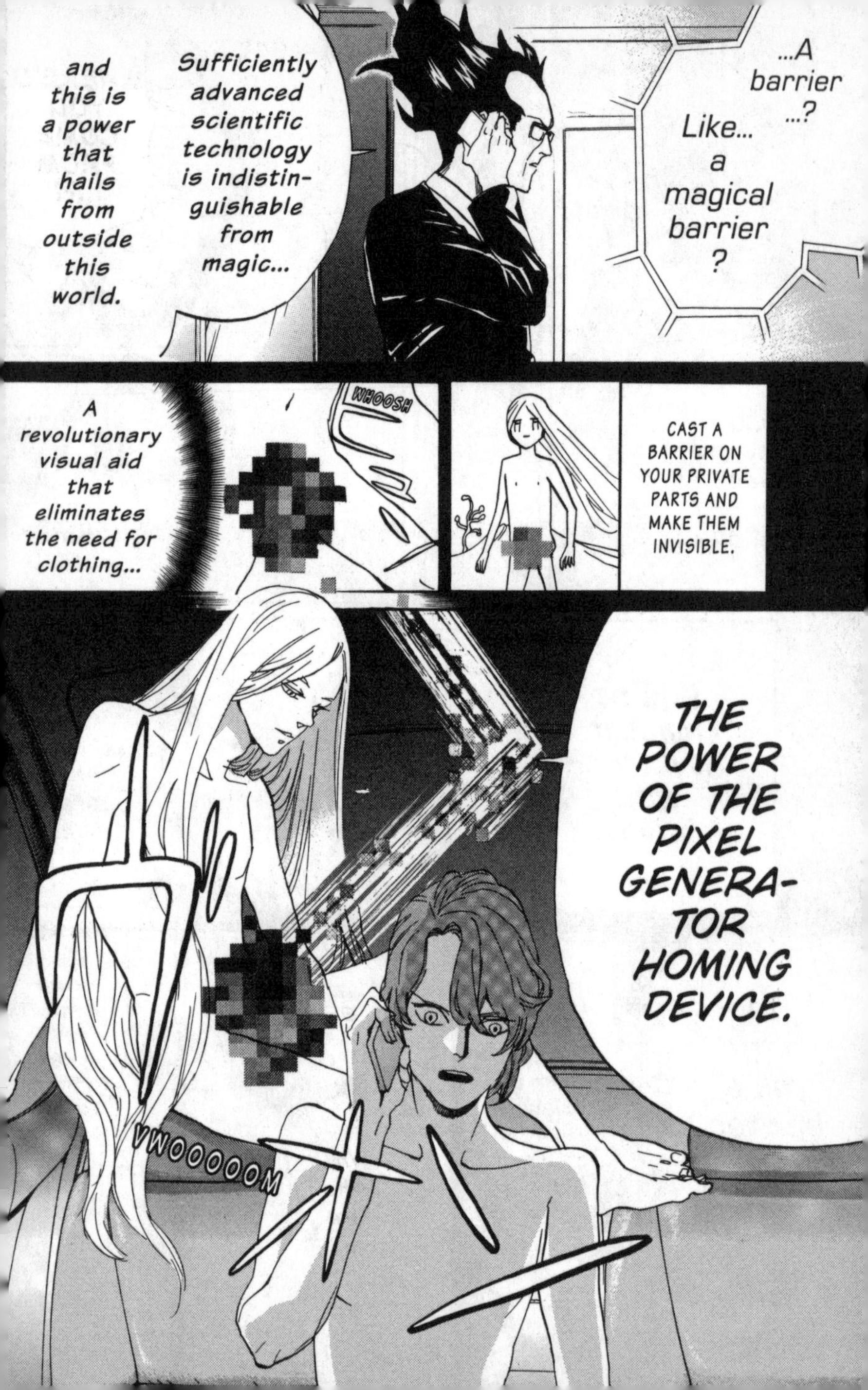
...A barrier ...?
Like... a magical barrier ?
Sufficiently advanced scientific technology is indistinguishable from magic...
and this is a power that hails from outside this world.
CAST A BARRIER ON YOUR PRIVATE PARTS AND MAKE THEM INVISIBLE.
WHOOSH
A revolutionary visual aid that eliminates the need for clothing...
THE POWER OF THE PIXEL GENERATOR HOMING DEVICE.
VWOOOOOOM

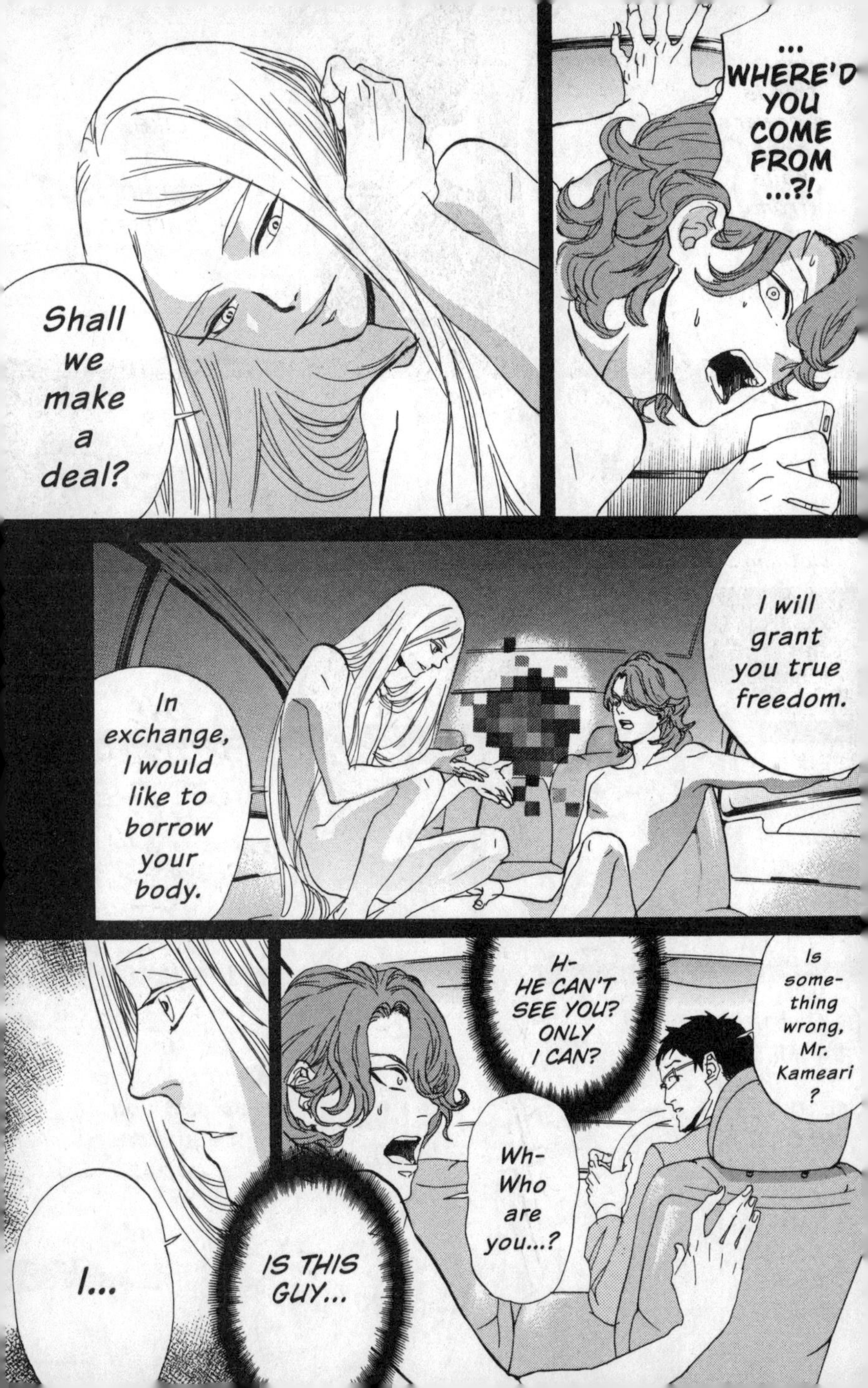
... WHERE'D YOU COME FROM ...?!
Shall we make a deal?
I will grant you true freedom.
In exchange, I would like to borrow your body.
Is something wrong, Mr. Kameari?
H- HE CAN'T SEE YOU? ONLY I CAN?
Wh- Who are you...?
IS THIS GUY...
I...

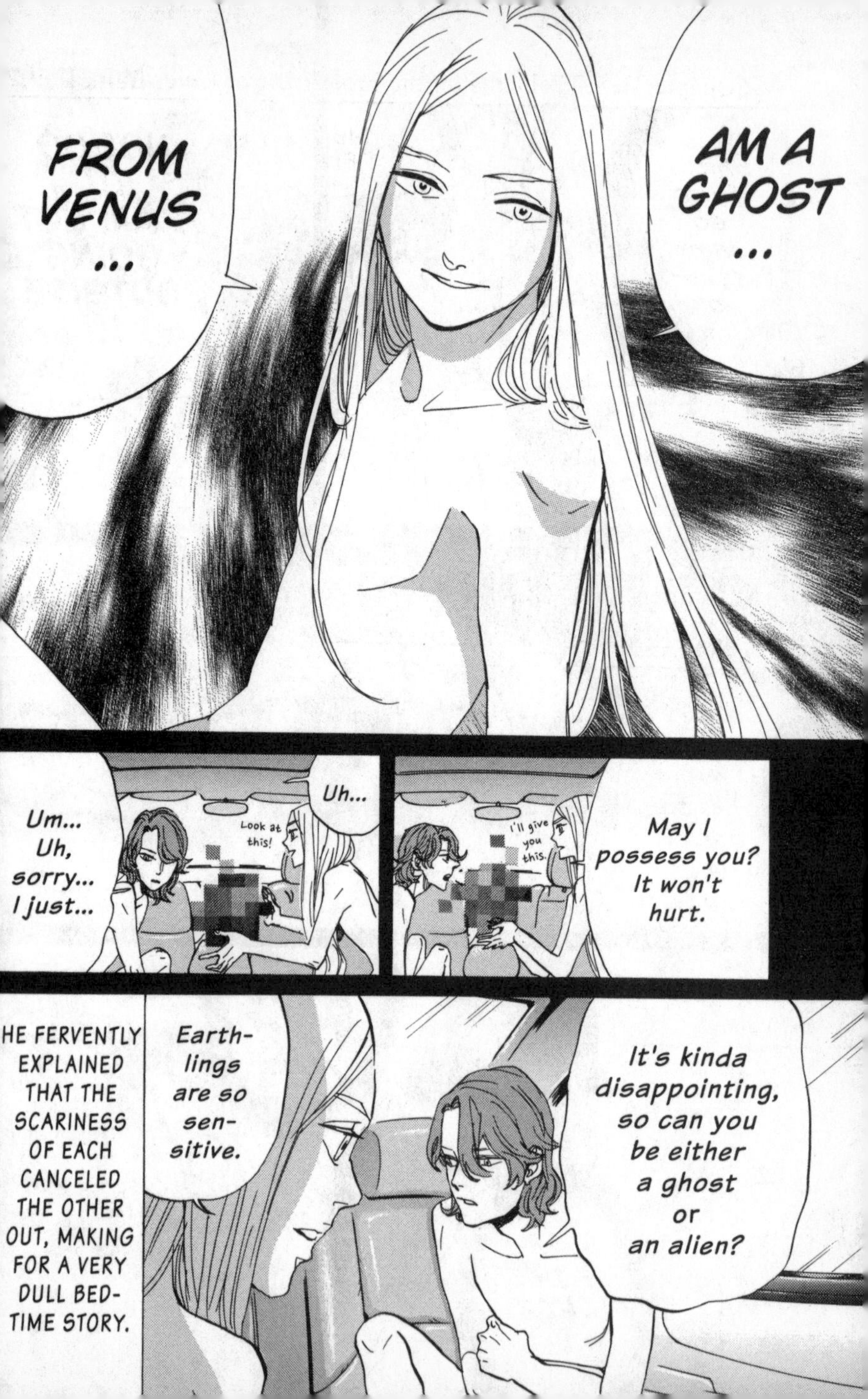
AM A GHOST ...
FROM VENUS ...
May I possess you? It won't hurt.
I'll give you this.
Uh...
Look at this!
Um... Uh, sorry... I just...
It's kinda disappointing, so can you be either a ghost or an alien?
Earth-lings are so sen-sitive.
HE FERVENTLY EXPLAINED THAT THE SCARINESS OF EACH CANCELED THE OTHER OUT, MAKING FOR A VERY DULL BED-TIME STORY.

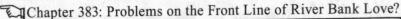

Chapter 383: Problems on the Front Line of River Bank Love?

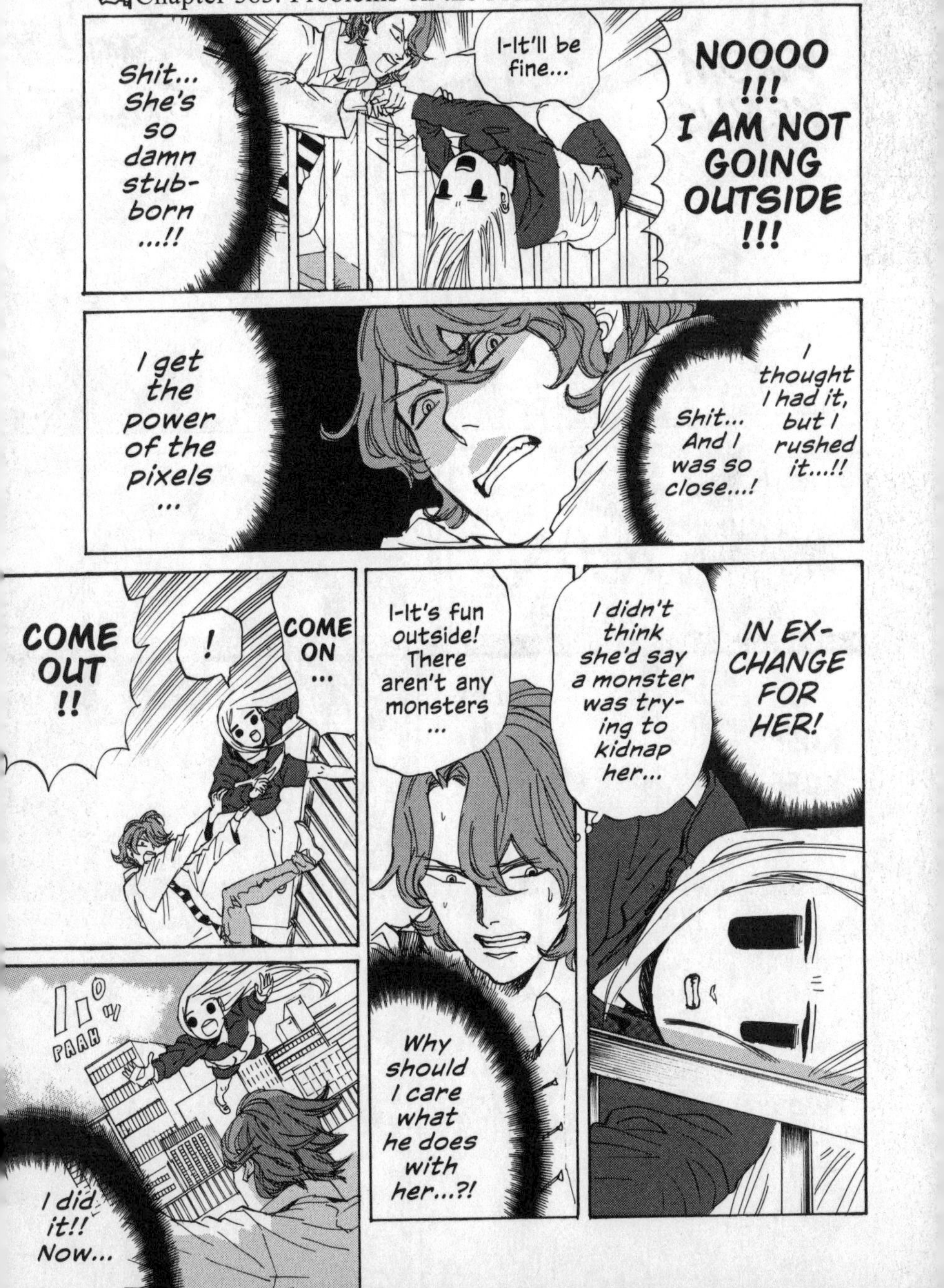
NOOOO!!! I AM NOT GOING OUTSIDE!!!
I-It'll be fine...
Shit... She's so damn stubborn...!!
I thought I had it, but I rushed it...!!
Shit... And I was so close...!
I get the power of the pixels...
IN EX-CHANGE FOR HER!
I didn't think she'd say a monster was try-ing to kidnap her...
I-It's fun outside! There aren't any monsters...
Why should I care what he does with her...?!
COME ON...
!
COME OUT!!
PAAH
I did it!! Now...

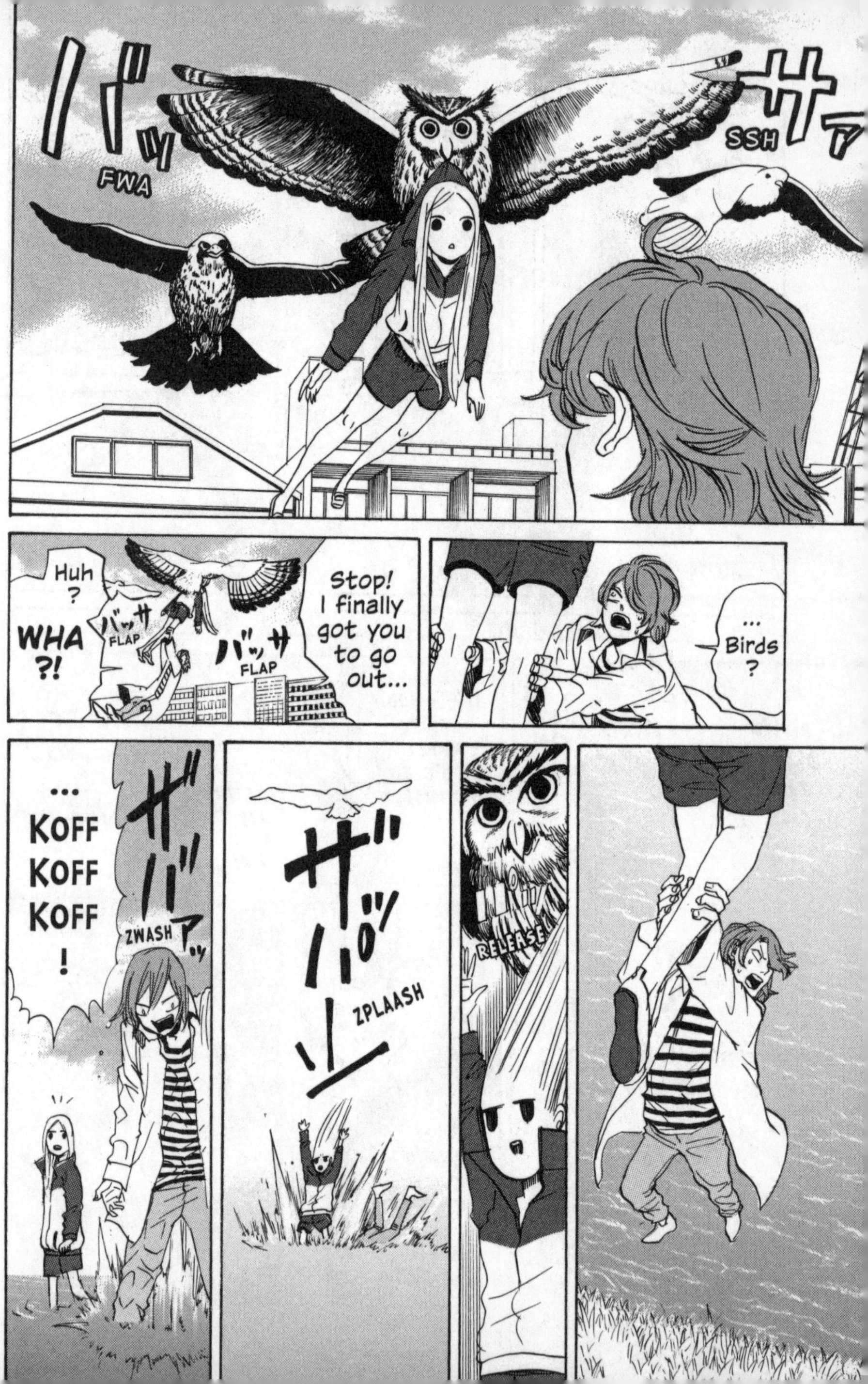
サァ
SSH
パッ
FWA
... Birds ?
Stop! I finally got you to go out...
Huh ?
WHA ?!
バッサ
FLAP
バッサ
FLAP
RELEASE
ザッバーン
ZPLAASH
ザバァッ
ZWASH
... KOFF KOFF KOFF !

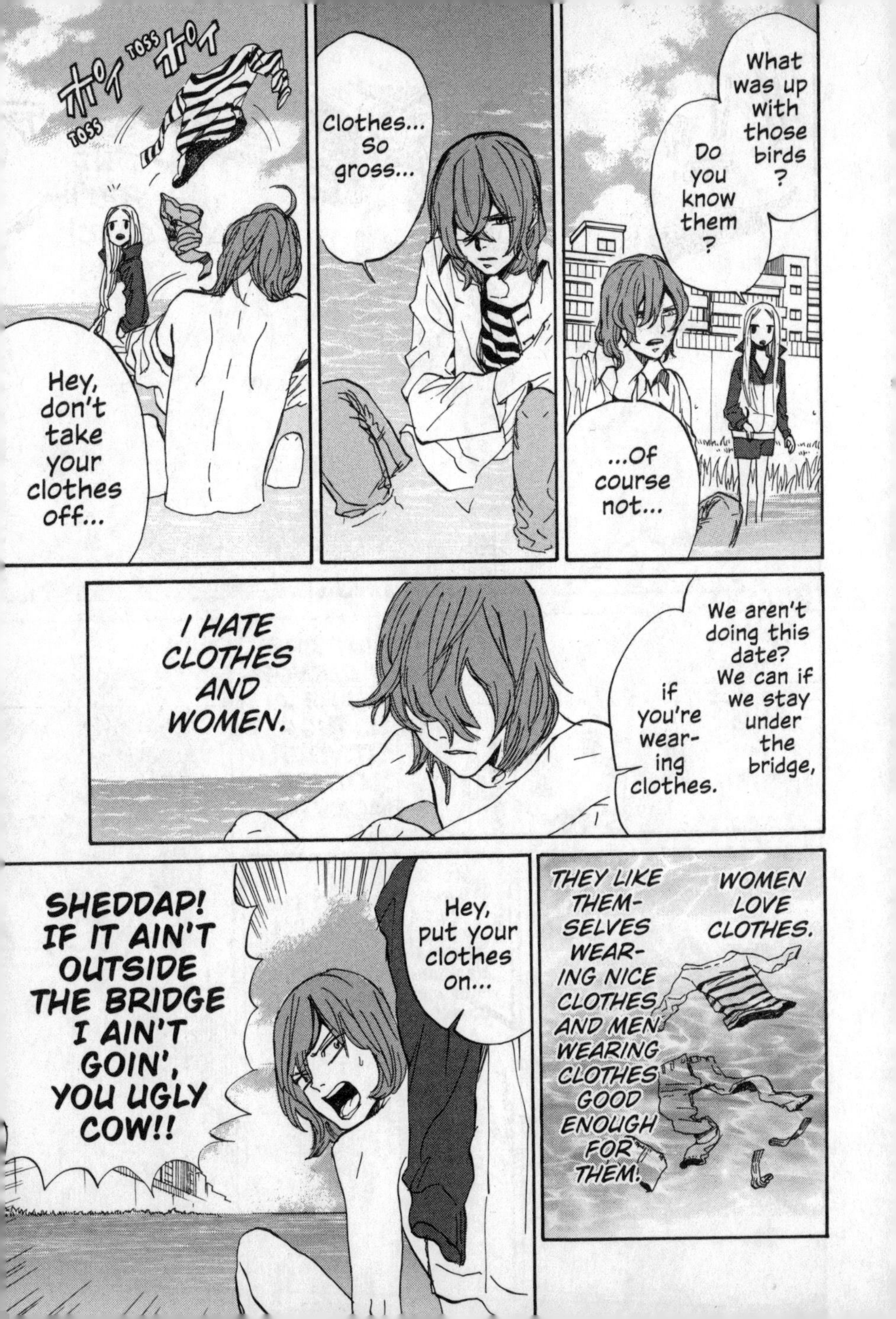
What was up with those birds?
Do you know them?
...Of course not...
Clothes... So gross...
ホイ TOSS
ホイ TOSS
Hey, don't take your clothes off...
We aren't doing this date? We can if we stay under the bridge,
if you're wear-ing clothes.
I HATE CLOTHES AND WOMEN.
WOMEN LOVE CLOTHES.
THEY LIKE THEM-SELVES WEAR-ING NICE CLOTHES AND MEN WEARING CLOTHES GOOD ENOUGH FOR THEM.
Hey, put your clothes on...
SHEDDAP! IF IT AIN'T OUTSIDE THE BRIDGE I AIN'T GOIN', YOU UGLY COW!!

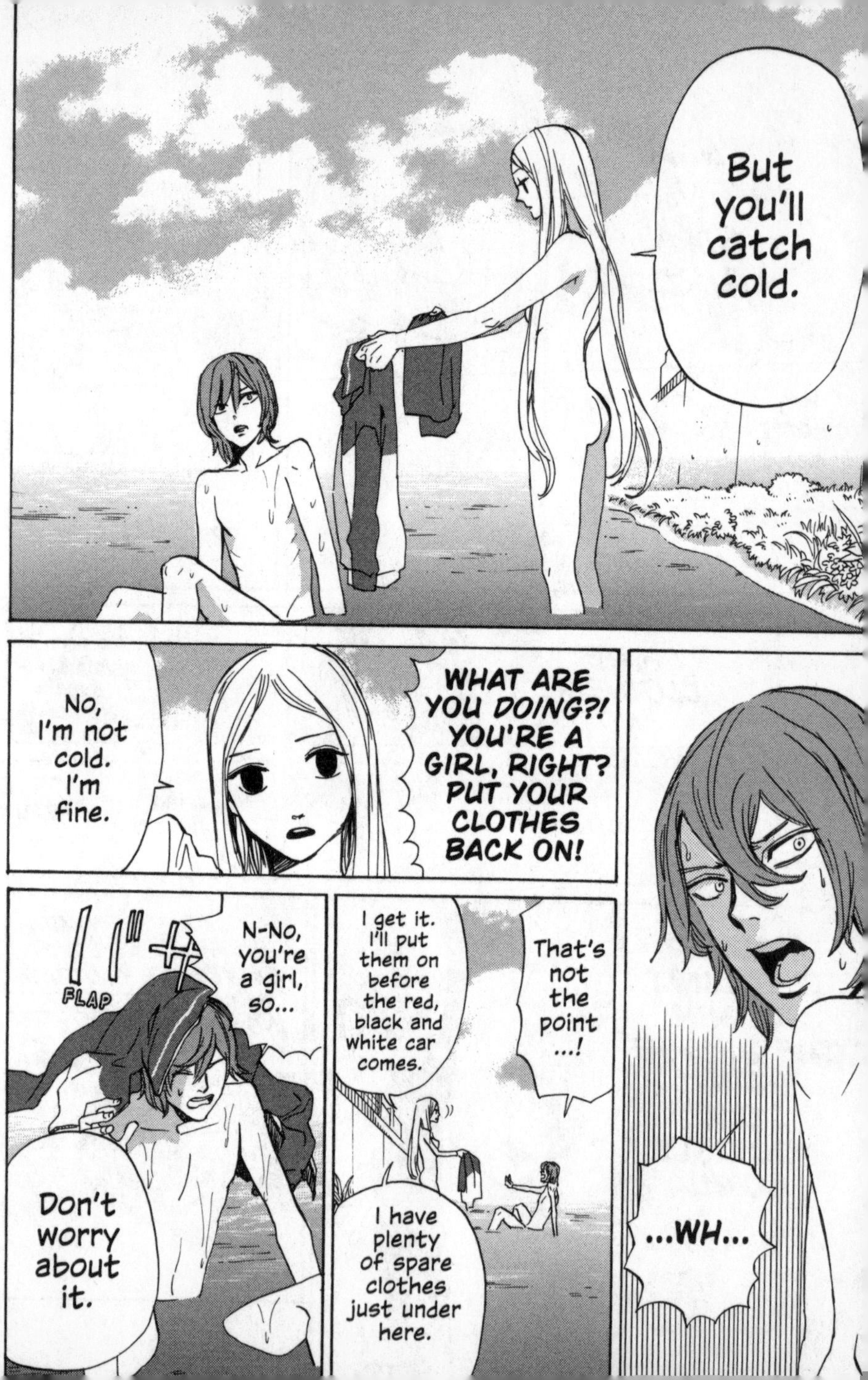
But you'll catch cold.
...WH...
WHAT ARE YOU DOING?! YOU'RE A GIRL, RIGHT? PUT YOUR CLOTHES BACK ON!
No, I'm not cold. I'm fine.
That's not the point ...!
I get it. I'll put them on before the red, black and white car comes.
I have plenty of spare clothes just under here.
N-No, you're a girl, so...
FLAP
Don't worry about it.

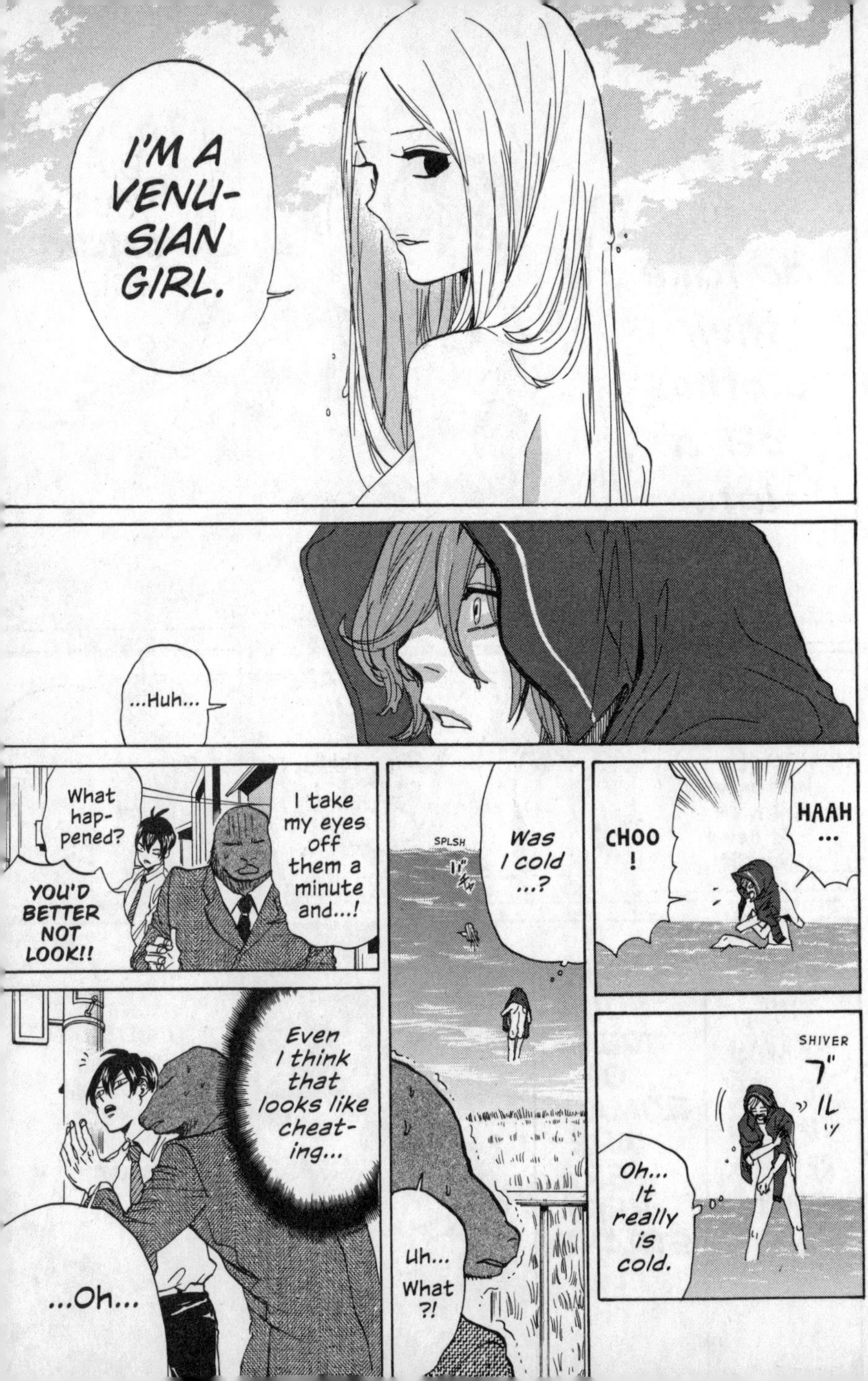
I'M A VENUSIAN GIRL.
...Huh...
HAAH ...
CHOO !
SHIVER
ブルッ
Oh... It really is cold.
SPLSH
Was I cold ...?
Uh... What ?!
I take my eyes off them a minute and...!
What hap- pened?
YOU'D BETTER NOT LOOK!!
Even I think that looks like cheat- ing...
...Oh...

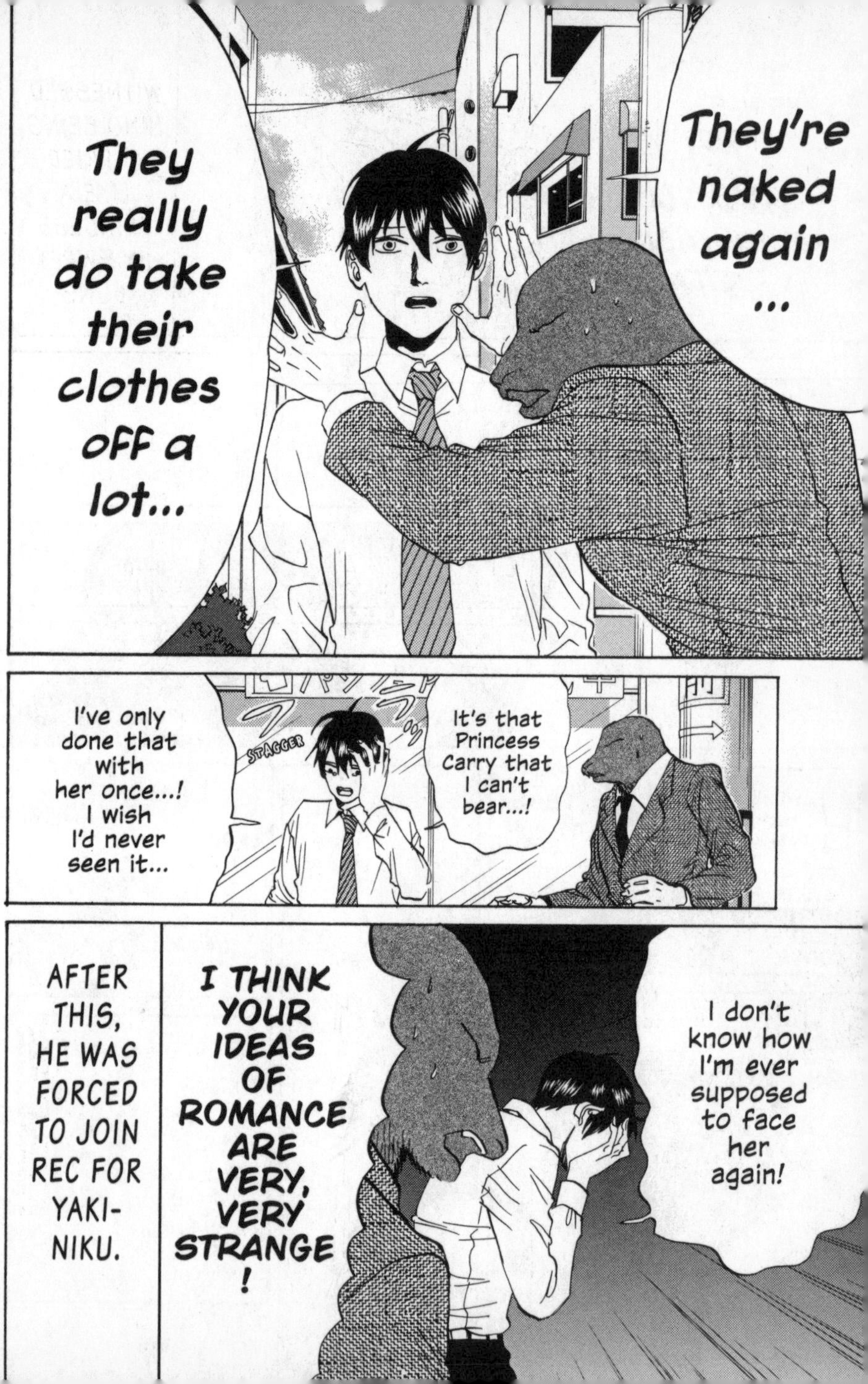
They're naked again ...
They really do take their clothes off a lot...
It's that Princess Carry that I can't bear...!
I've only done that with her once...! I wish I'd never seen it...
STAGGER
I don't know how I'm ever supposed to face her again!
I THINK YOUR IDEAS OF ROMANCE ARE VERY, VERY STRANGE!
AFTER THIS, HE WAS FORCED TO JOIN REC FOR YAKI-NIKU.

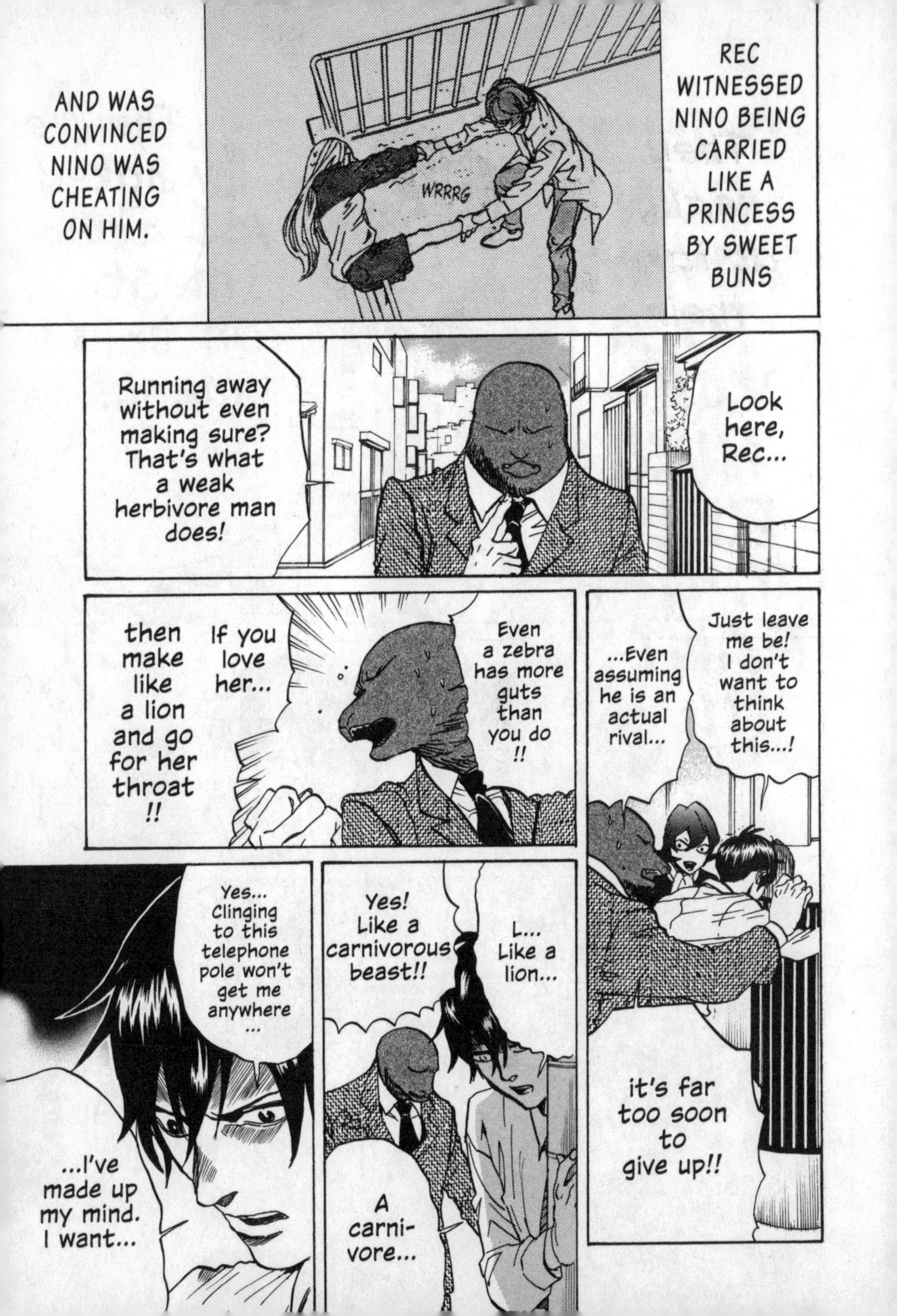
REC WITNESSED NINO BEING CARRIED LIKE A PRINCESS BY SWEET BUNS
WRRRG
AND WAS CONVINCED NINO WAS CHEATING ON HIM.
Look here, Rec...
Running away without even making sure? That's what a weak herbivore man does!
Just leave me be! I don't want to think about this...!
...Even assuming he is an actual rival...
it's far too soon to give up!!
Even a zebra has more guts than you do !!
If you love her...
then make like a lion and go for her throat !!
L... Like a lion...
Yes! Like a carnivorous beast!!
A carni-vore...
Yes... Clinging to this telephone pole won't get me anywhere ...
...I've made up my mind. I want...

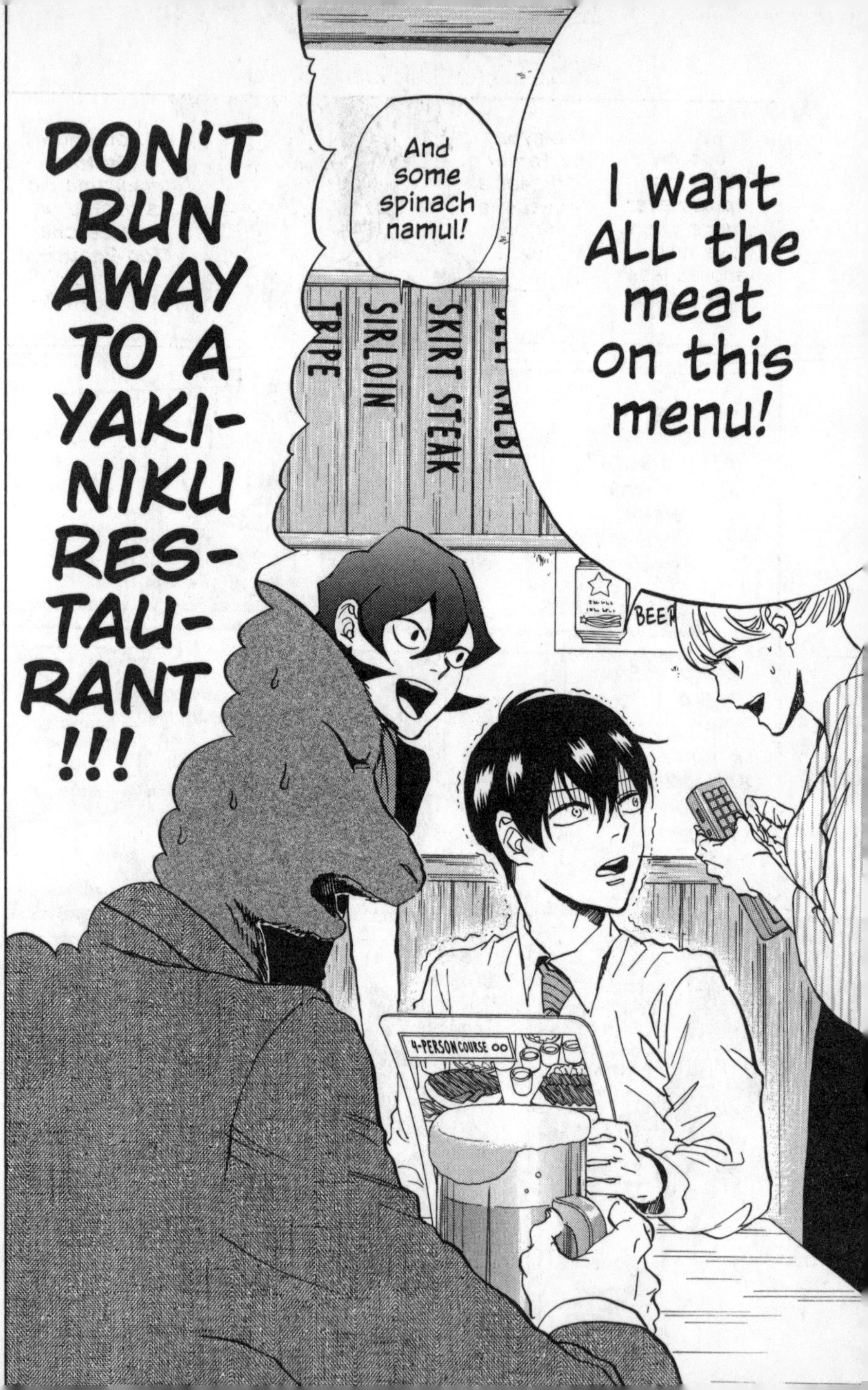
I want ALL the meat on this menu!
And some spinach namul!
SKIRT STEAK
SIRLOIN
TRIPE
BEER
4-PERSON COURSE 00
DON'T RUN AWAY TO A YAKI-NIKU RES-TAU-RANT!!!

Chapter 384: Prime Kalbi

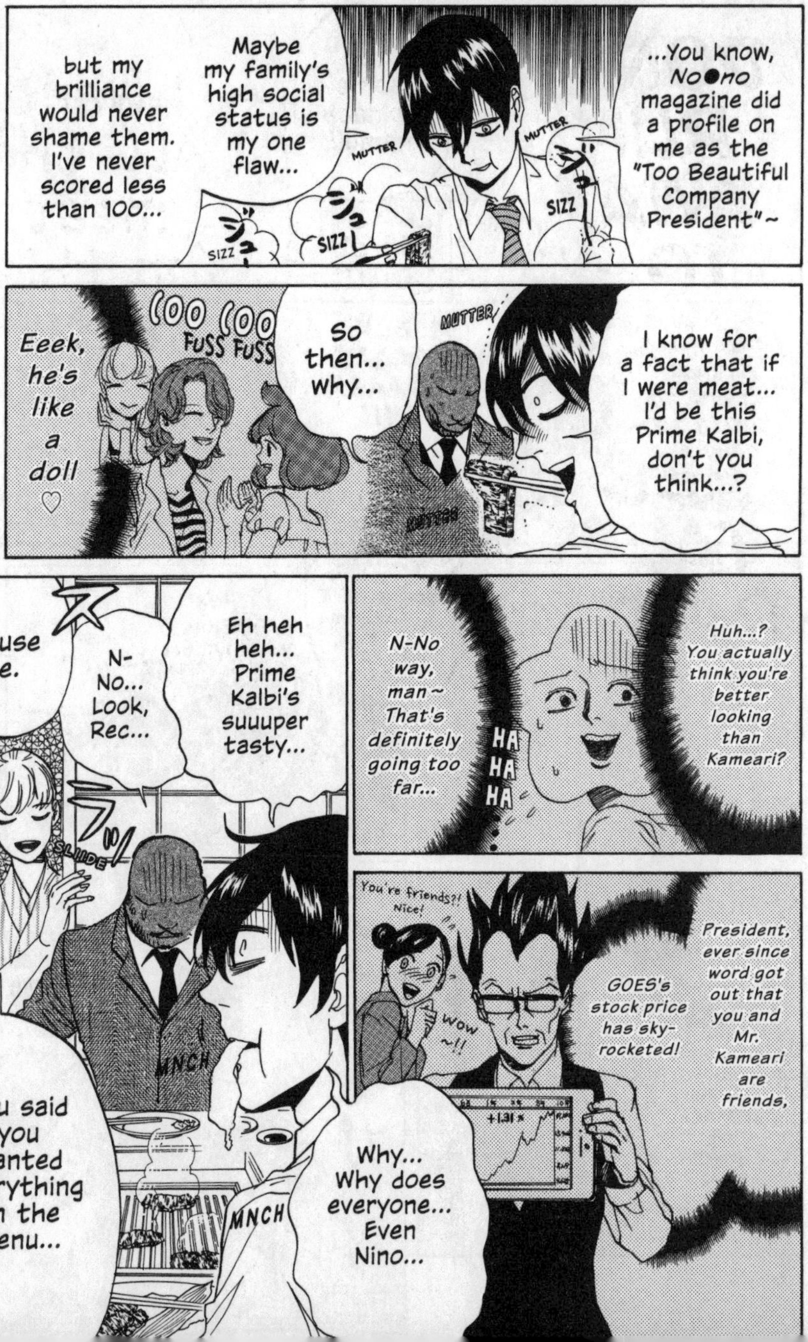
...You know, No●no magazine did a profile on me as the "Too Beautiful Company President"~
MUTTER
SIZZ
Maybe my family's high social status is my one flaw...
MUTTER
but my brilliance would never shame them. I've never scored less than 100...
SIZZ
SIZZ
I know for a fact that if I were meat... I'd be this Prime Kalbi, don't you think...?
MUTTER
So then... why...
COO COO
FUSS FUSS
Eeek, he's like a doll ♡
Huh...? You actually think you're better looking than Kameari?
HA HA HA
N-No way, man~ That's definitely going too far...
President, ever since word got out that you and Mr. Kameari are friends,
GOES's stock price has sky-rocketed!
You're friends?! Nice!
Wow ~!!
Why... Why does everyone... Even Nino...
Eh heh heh... Prime Kalbi's suuuper tasty...
N- No... Look, Rec...
Excuse me.
SLIIDE
MNCH
MNCH
You said you wanted everything on the menu...

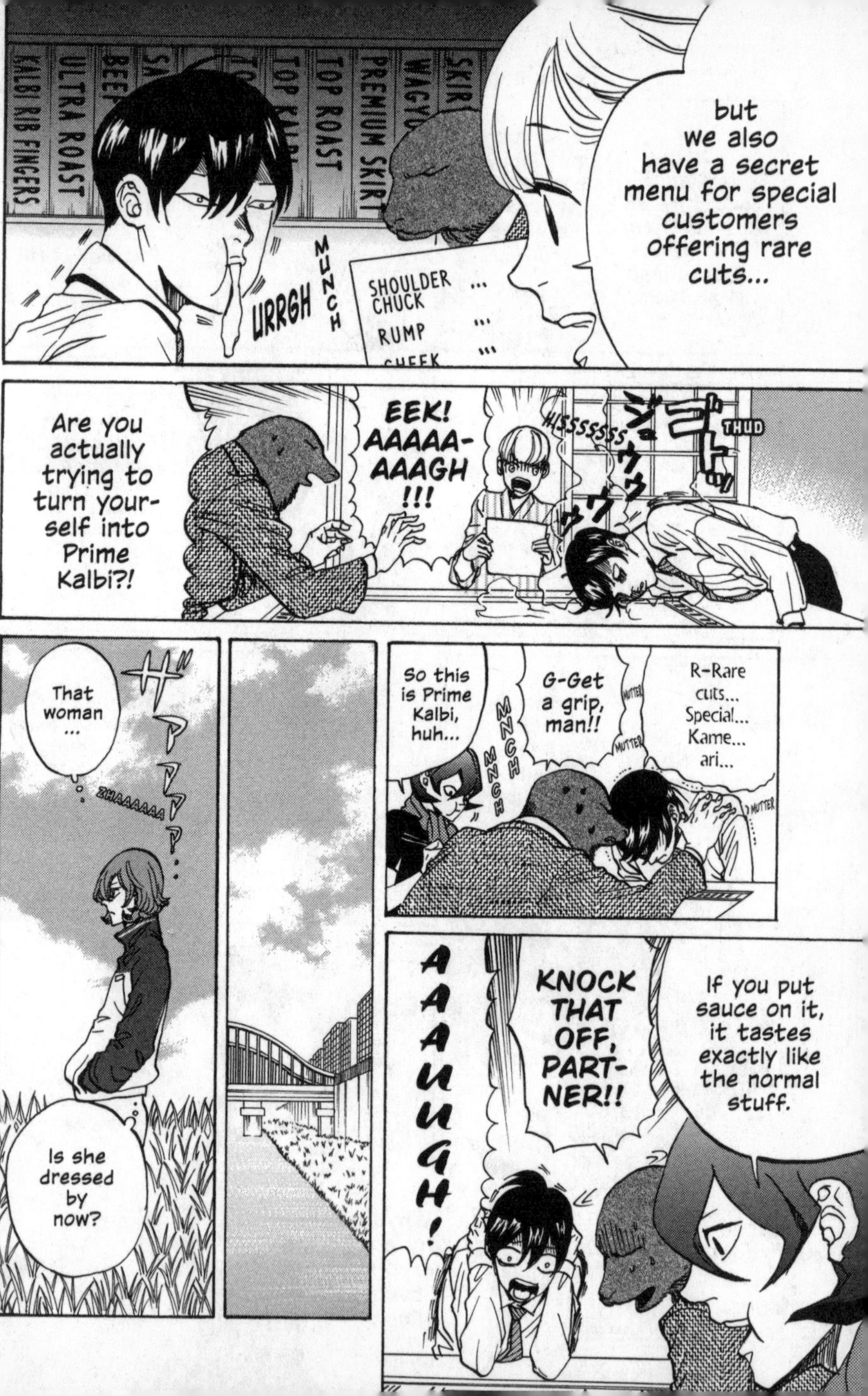
but we also have a secret menu for special customers offering rare cuts...
PREMIUM SKIRT
TOP ROAST
ULTRA ROAST
KALBI RIB FINGERS
SHOULDER CHUCK ...
RUMP ...
MUNCH
URRGH
THUD
HISSSSSSS
EEK! AAAAA-AAAGH!!!
Are you actually trying to turn yourself into Prime Kalbi?!
R-Rare cuts... Special... Kame... ari...
MUTTER
MUTTER
MUTTER
G-Get a grip, man!!
MNCH
MNCH
So this is Prime Kalbi, huh...
If you put sauce on it, it tastes exactly like the normal stuff.
KNOCK THAT OFF, PARTNER!!
AAAAUUGH!
ZHAAAAAAA
That woman ...
Is she dressed by now?

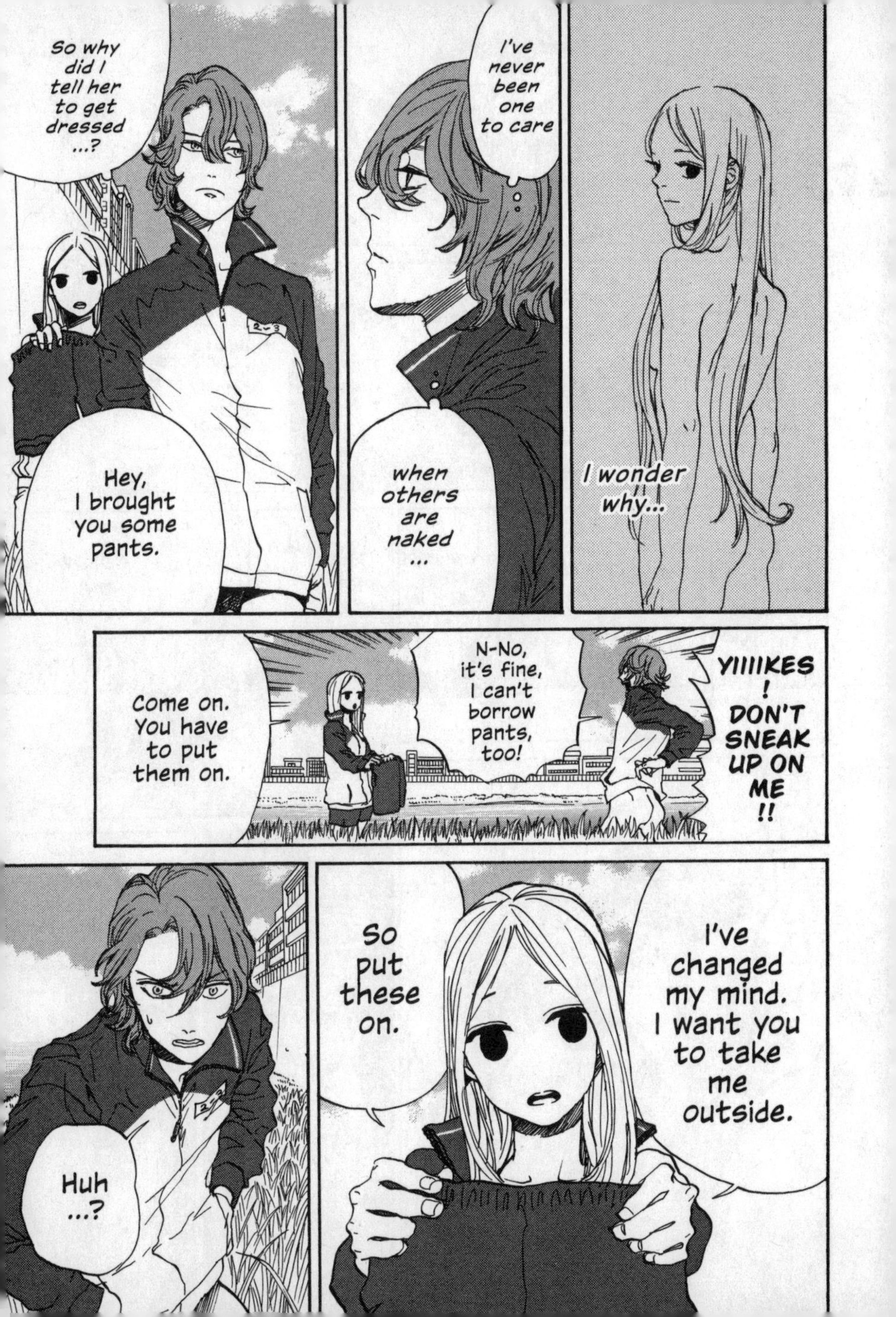
I wonder why...
I've never been one to care
when others are naked ...
So why did I tell her to get dressed ...?
Hey, I brought you some pants.
YIIIIKES ! DON'T SNEAK UP ON ME !!
N-No, it's fine, I can't borrow pants, too!
Come on. You have to put them on.
I've changed my mind. I want you to take me outside.
So put these on.
Huh ...?

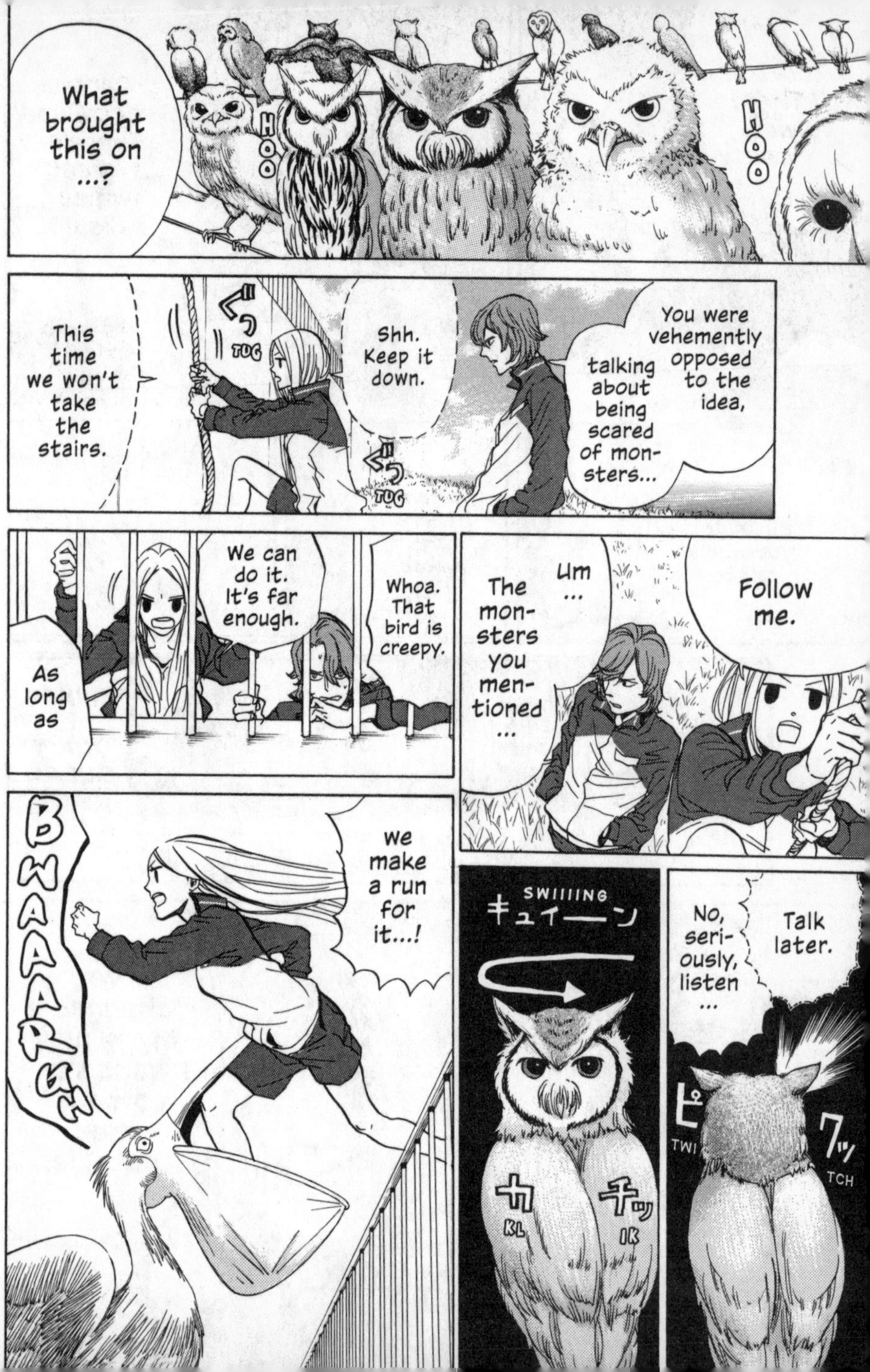
What brought this on ...?
HOO
HOO
You were vehemently opposed to the idea,
talking about being scared of monsters...
Shh. Keep it down.
TUG
TUG
This time we won't take the stairs.
Follow me.
Um ...
The monsters you mentioned ...
Whoa. That bird is creepy.
We can do it. It's far enough.
As long as
Talk later.
No, seriously, listen ...
TWITCH
SWIIIING
KLIK
we make a run for it...!
BWAAAARUH

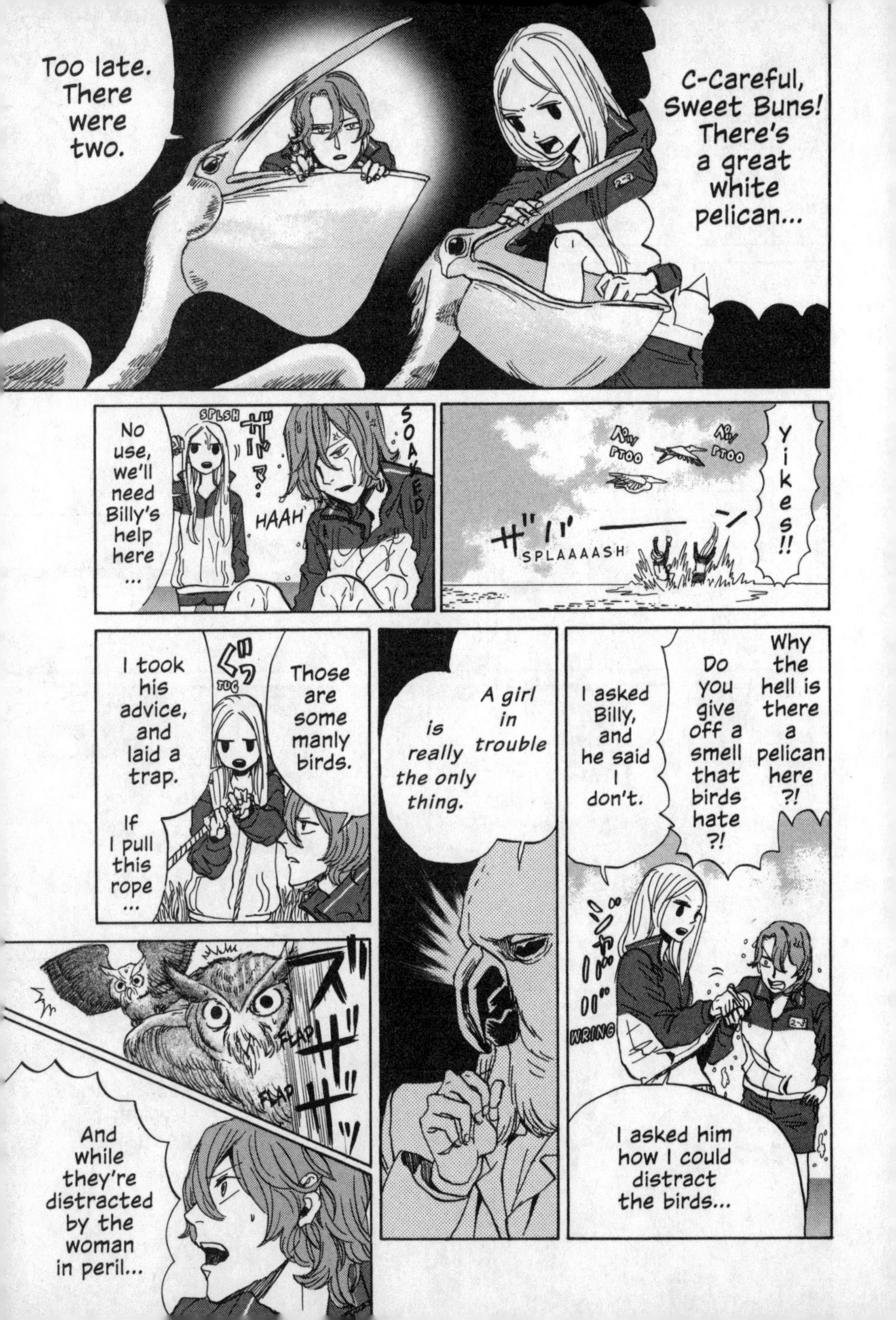
C-Careful, Sweet Buns! There's a great white pelican...
Too late. There were two.
Yikes!!
PTOO
PTOO
SPLAAAASH
SPLSH
SOAKED
HAAH
No use, we'll need Billy's help here ...
Why the hell is there a pelican here ?!
Do you give off a smell that birds hate ?!
I asked Billy, and he said I don't.
WRING
I asked him how I could distract the birds...
A girl in trouble is really the only thing.
Those are some manly birds.
TUG
I took his advice, and laid a trap.
If I pull this rope ...
FLAP
FLAP
And while they're distracted by the woman in peril...

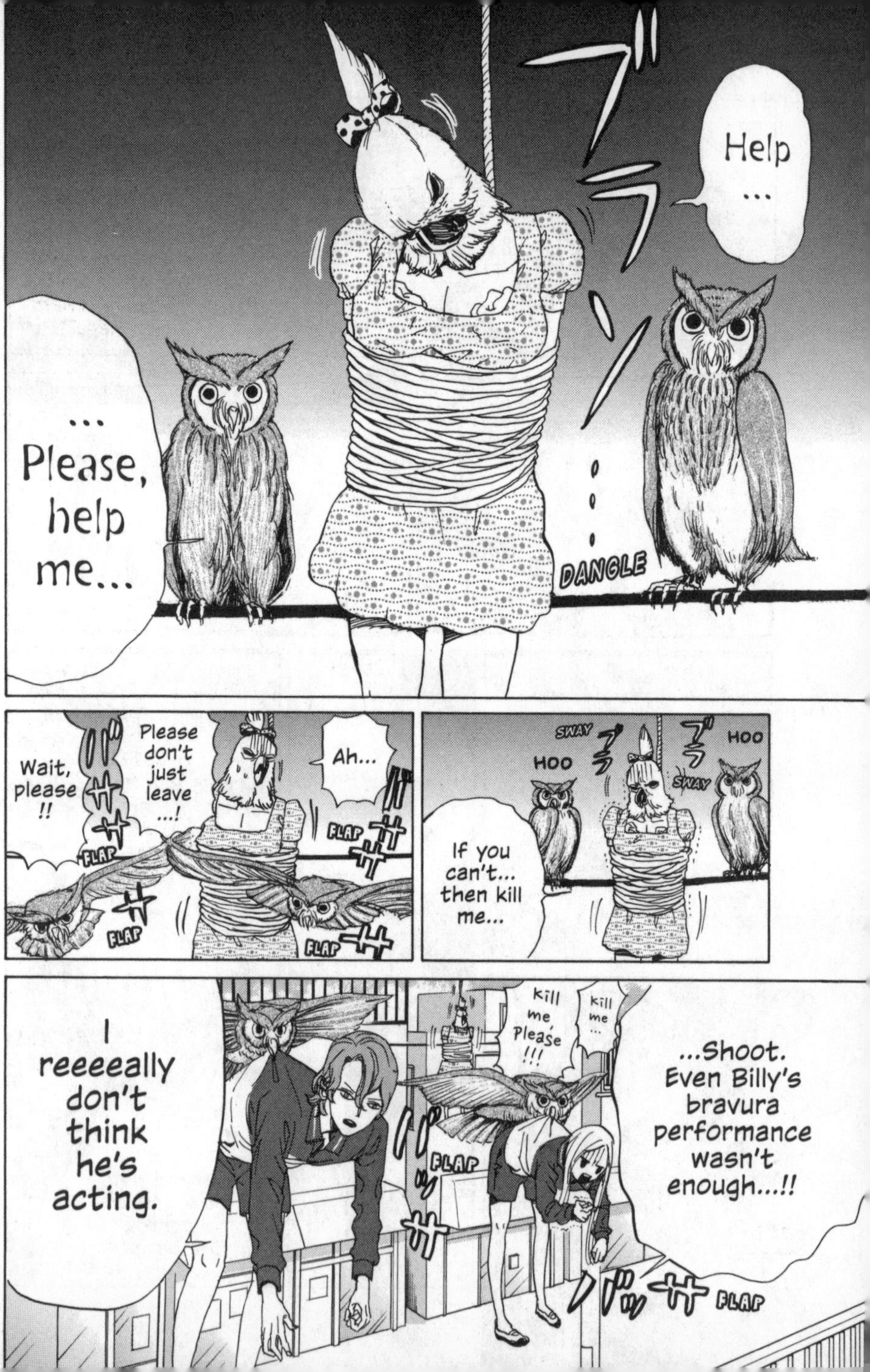

Help ...
DANGLE
... Please, help me...
Ah...
Please don't just leave ...!
Wait, please !!
FLAP
FLAP
FLAP
FLAP
HOO
SWAY
SWAY
HOO
If you can't... then kill me...
...Shoot. Even Billy's bravura performance wasn't enough...!!
Kill me ...
Kill me, Please !!!
I reeeeally don't think he's acting.
FLAP
FLAP

Chapter 385: Immutable Evidence

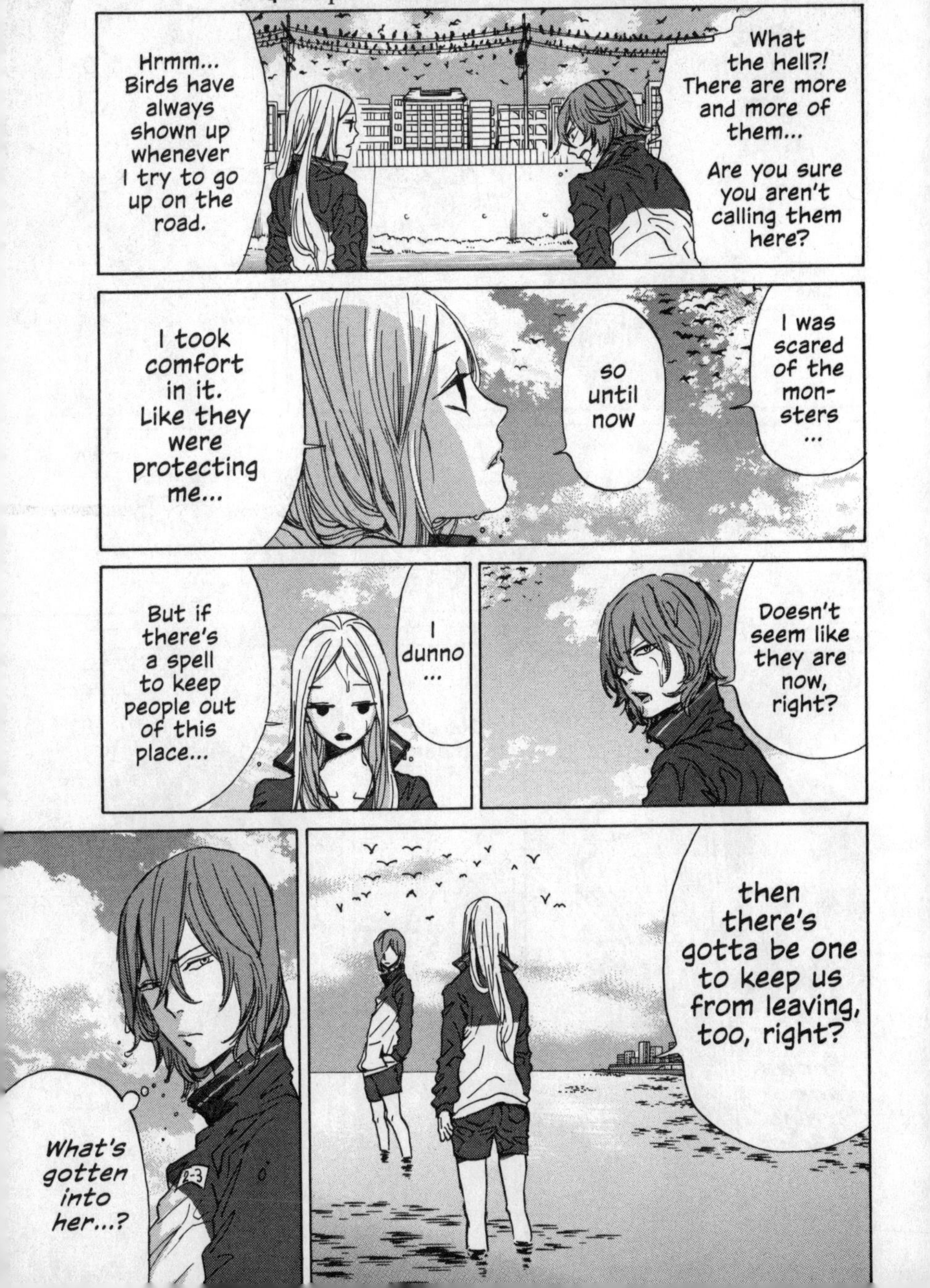
What the hell?! There are more and more of them...
Are you sure you aren't calling them here?
Hrmm... Birds have always shown up whenever I try to go up on the road.
I was scared of the monsters...
so until now
I took comfort in it. Like they were protecting me...
Doesn't seem like they are now, right?
I dunno...
But if there's a spell to keep people out of this place...
then there's gotta be one to keep us from leaving, too, right?
What's gotten into her...?

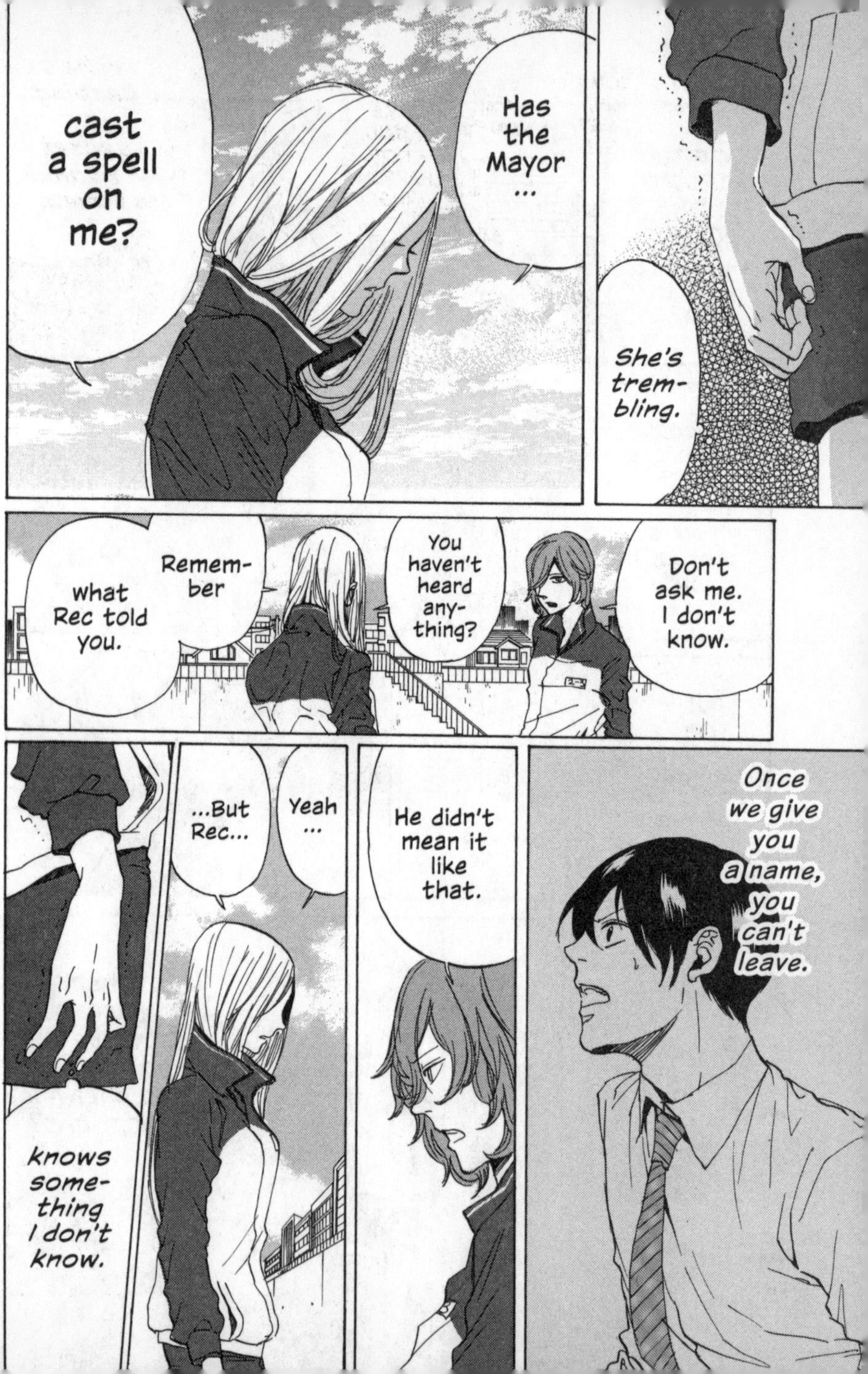
She's trem-bling.
Has the Mayor ...
cast a spell on me?
Don't ask me. I don't know.
You haven't heard any-thing?
Remem-ber
what Rec told you.
Once we give you a name, you can't leave.
He didn't mean it like that.
Yeah ...
...But Rec...
knows some-thing I don't know.

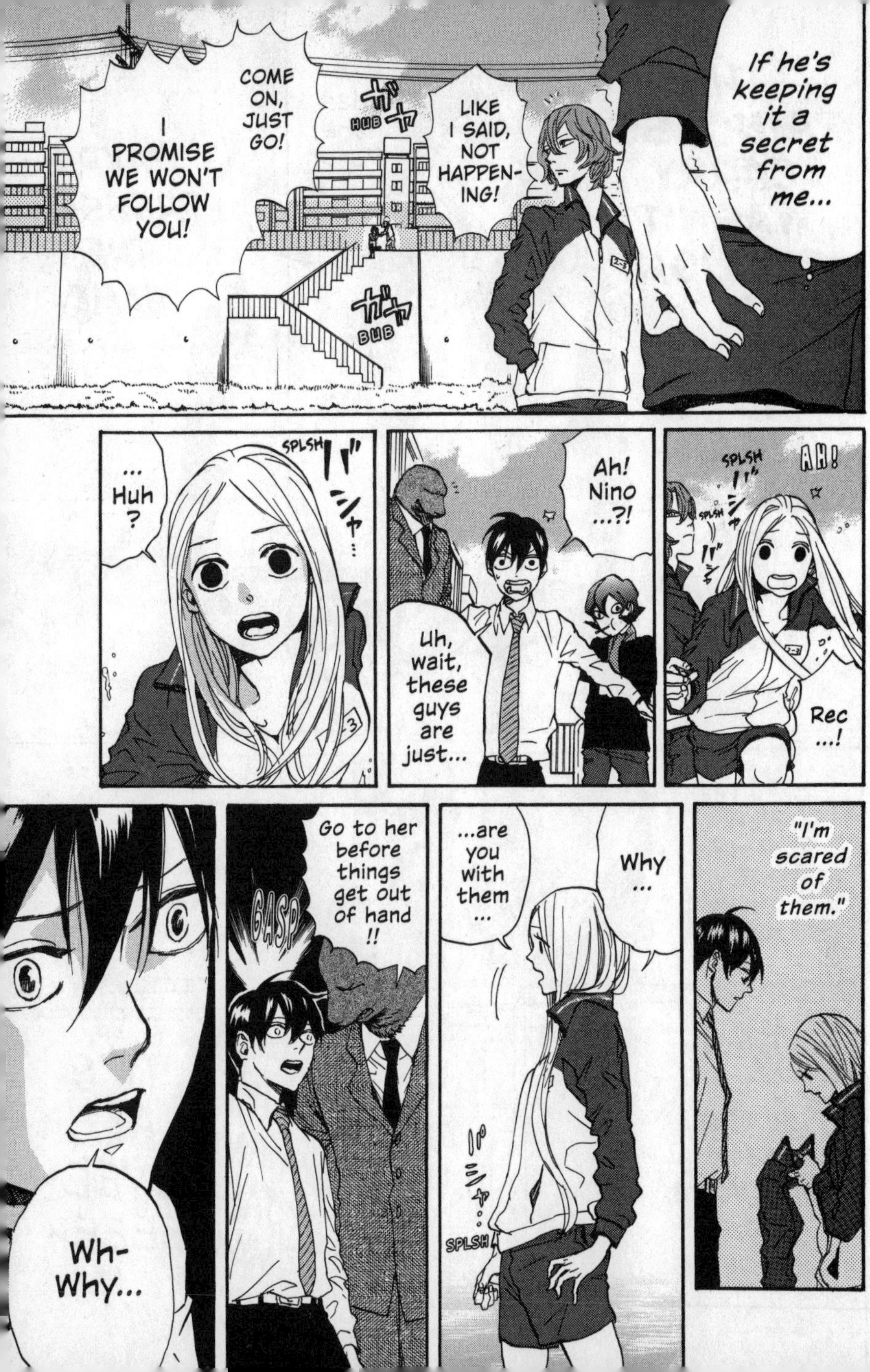
If he's keeping it a secret from me...
LIKE I SAID, NOT HAPPENING!
HUB
COME ON, JUST GO!
I PROMISE WE WON'T FOLLOW YOU!
BUB
AH!
SPLSH
SPLSH
Rec ...!
Ah! Nino ...?!
Uh, wait, these guys are just...
SPLSH
... Huh ?
"I'm scared of them."
Why ...
...are you with them ...
SPLSH
Go to her before things get out of hand !!
GASP
Wh- Why...

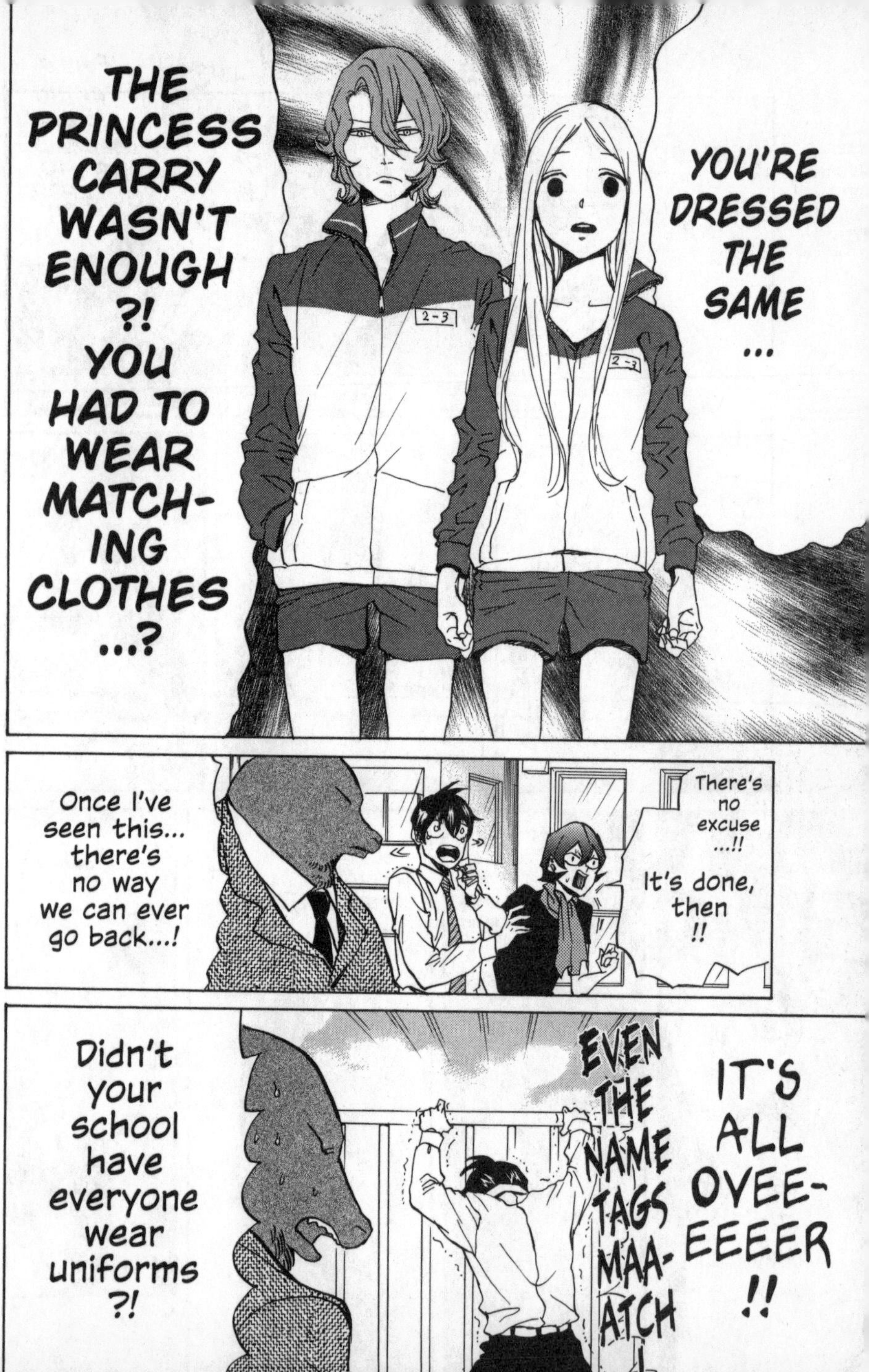
YOU'RE DRESSED THE SAME ...
THE PRINCESS CARRY WASN'T ENOUGH?! YOU HAD TO WEAR MATCH-ING CLOTHES ...?
There's no excuse ...!!
It's done, then !!
Once I've seen this... there's no way we can ever go back...!
IT'S ALL OVEE-EEEER !!
EVEN THE NAME TAGS MAA-ATCH
Didn't your school have everyone wear uniforms ?!

Chapter 386: Between Rec and Nino is...?

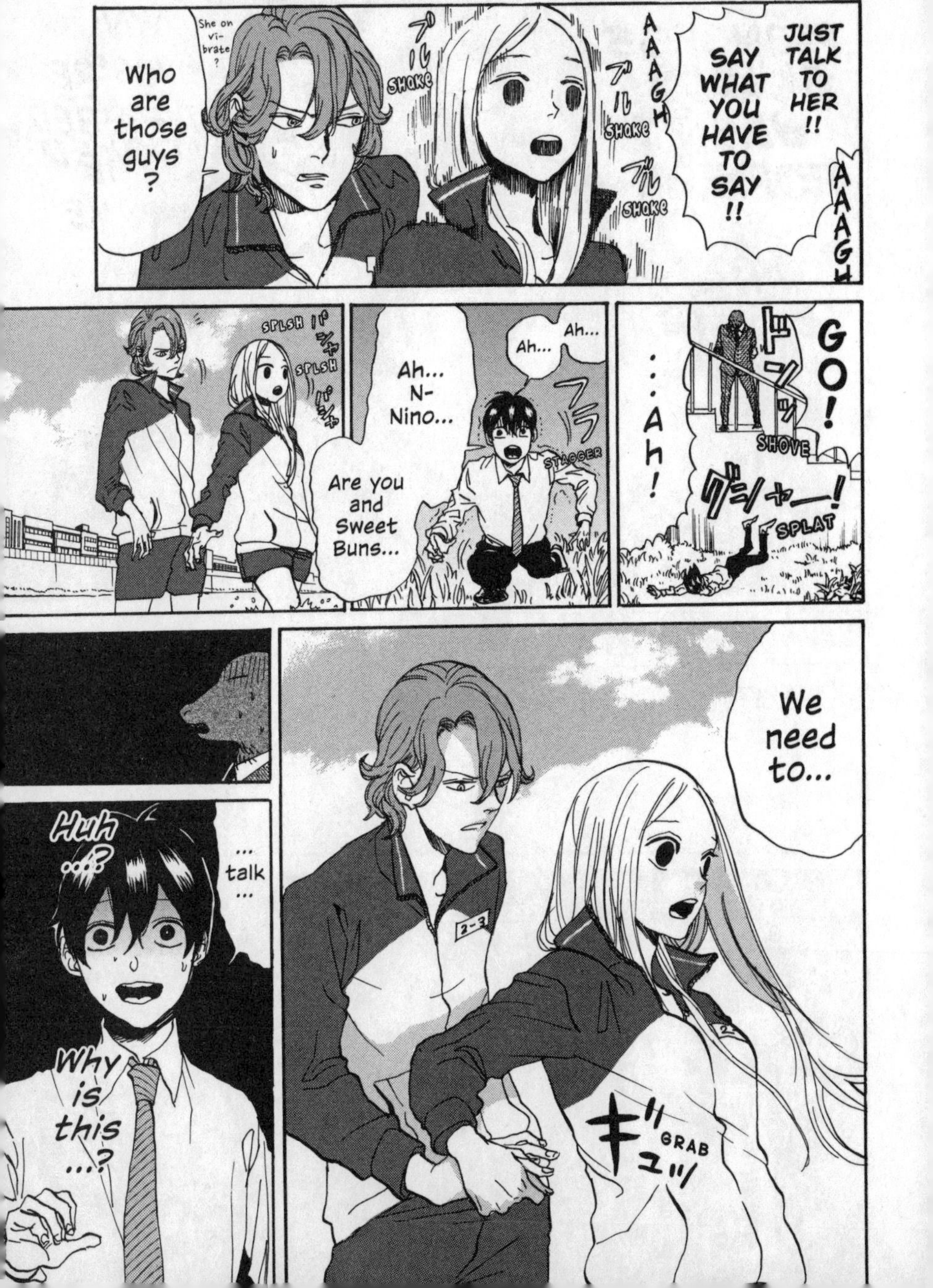

AAAAGH
JUST TALK TO HER!!
SAY WHAT YOU HAVE TO SAY!!
AAAAGH
SHAKE
SHAKE
SHAKE
She on vi-brate?
Who are those guys?
GO!
...Ah!
SHOVE
SPLAT
Ah...
Ah...
Ah... N-Nino...
STAGGER
Are you and Sweet Buns...
SPLSH
SPLSH
We need to...
GRAB
...talk...
Huh...?
Why is this...?

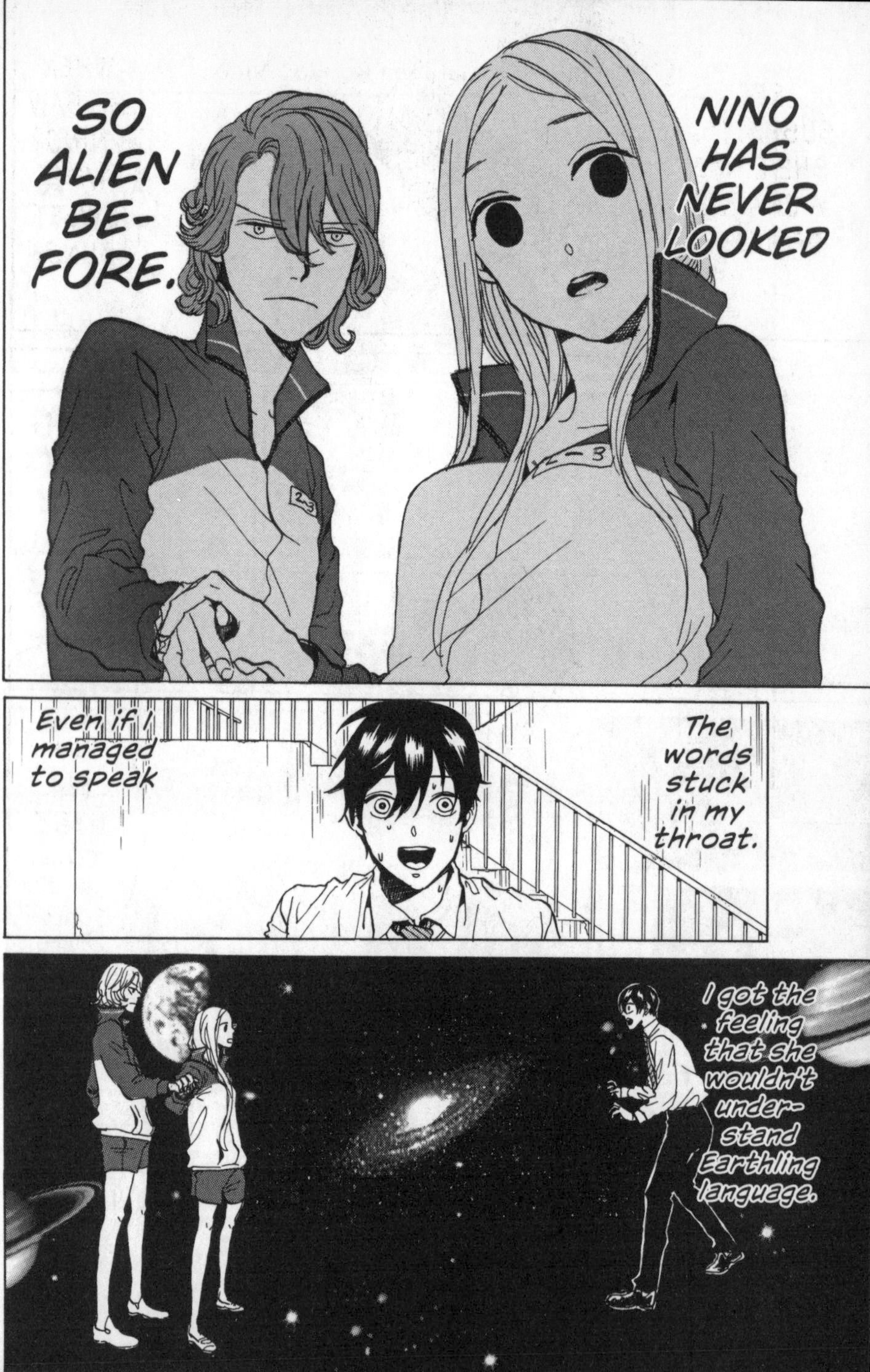
NINO HAS NEVER LOOKED
SO ALIEN BE-FORE.
The words stuck in my throat.
Even if I managed to speak
I got the feeling that she wouldn't under-stand Earthling language.

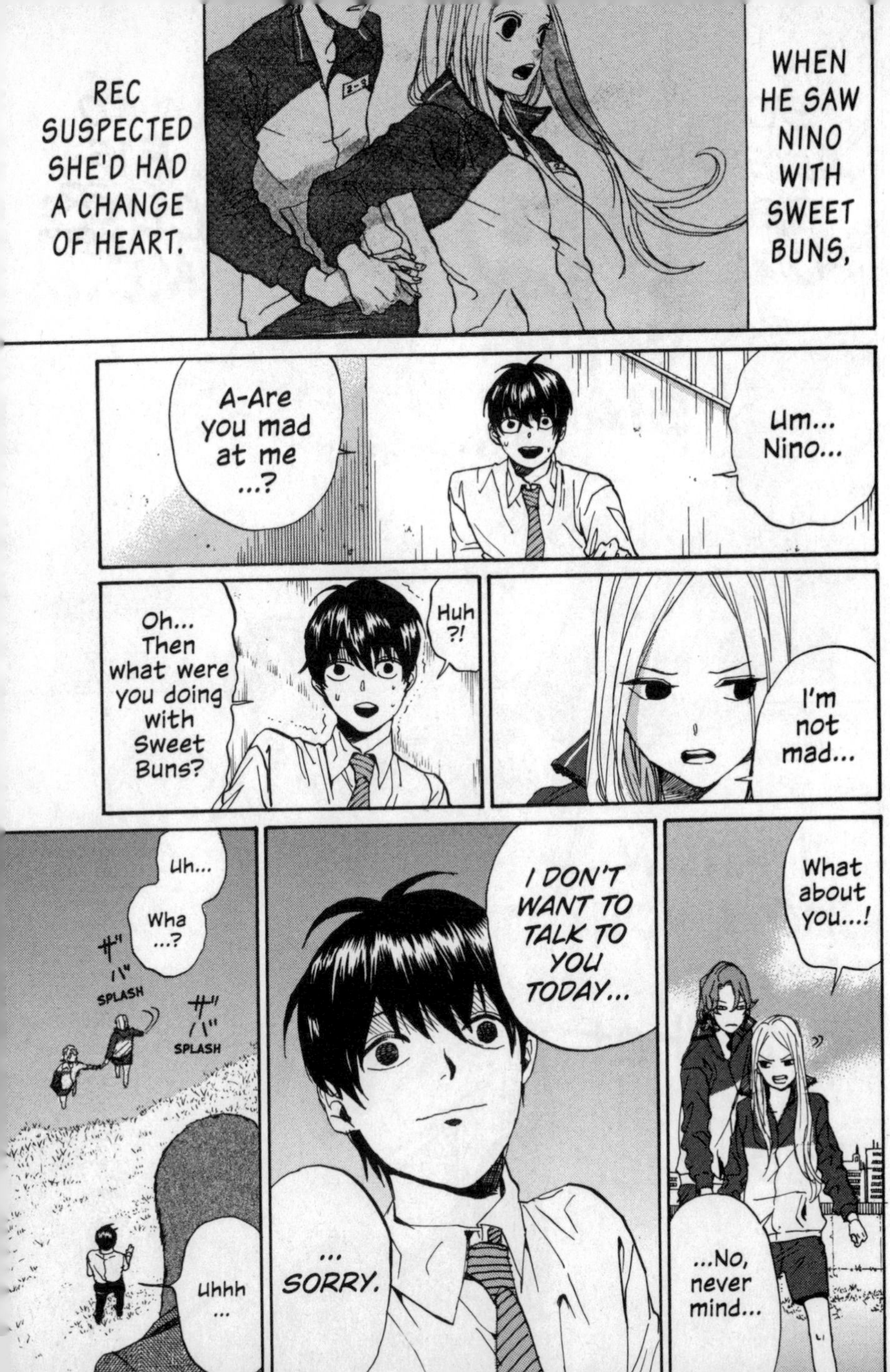
WHEN HE SAW NINO WITH SWEET BUNS,
REC SUSPECTED SHE'D HAD A CHANGE OF HEART.
Um... Nino...
A-Are you mad at me ...?
I'm not mad...
Huh ?!
Oh... Then what were you doing with Sweet Buns?
What about you...!
...No, never mind...
I DON'T WANT TO TALK TO YOU TODAY...
... SORRY.
Uh...
Wha ...?
SPLASH
SPLASH
Uhhh ...

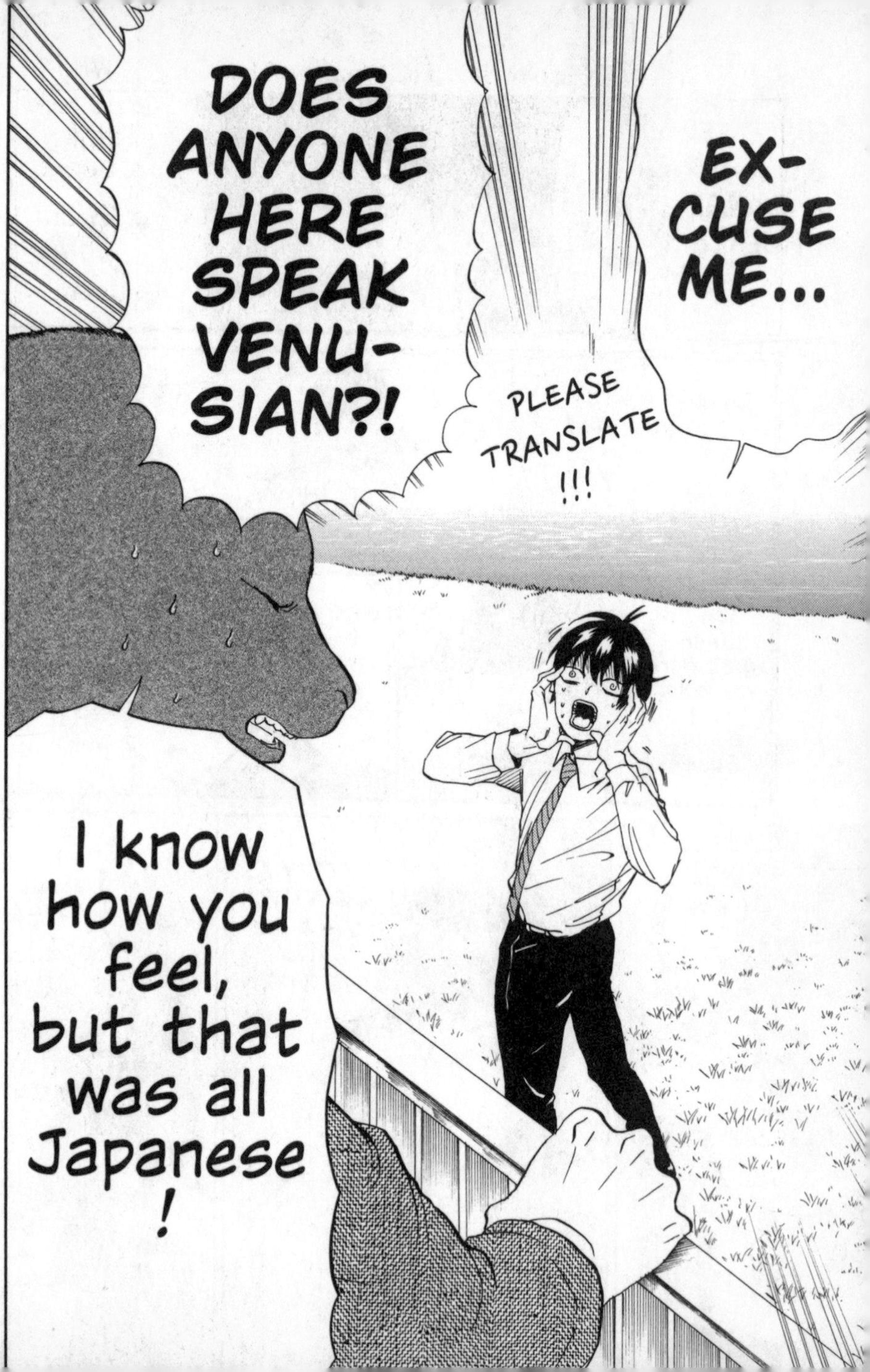
EX-CUSE ME...
PLEASE TRANSLATE !!!
DOES ANYONE HERE SPEAK VENU-SIAN?!
I know how you feel, but that was all Japanese!

Chapter 387: The Words of Maria

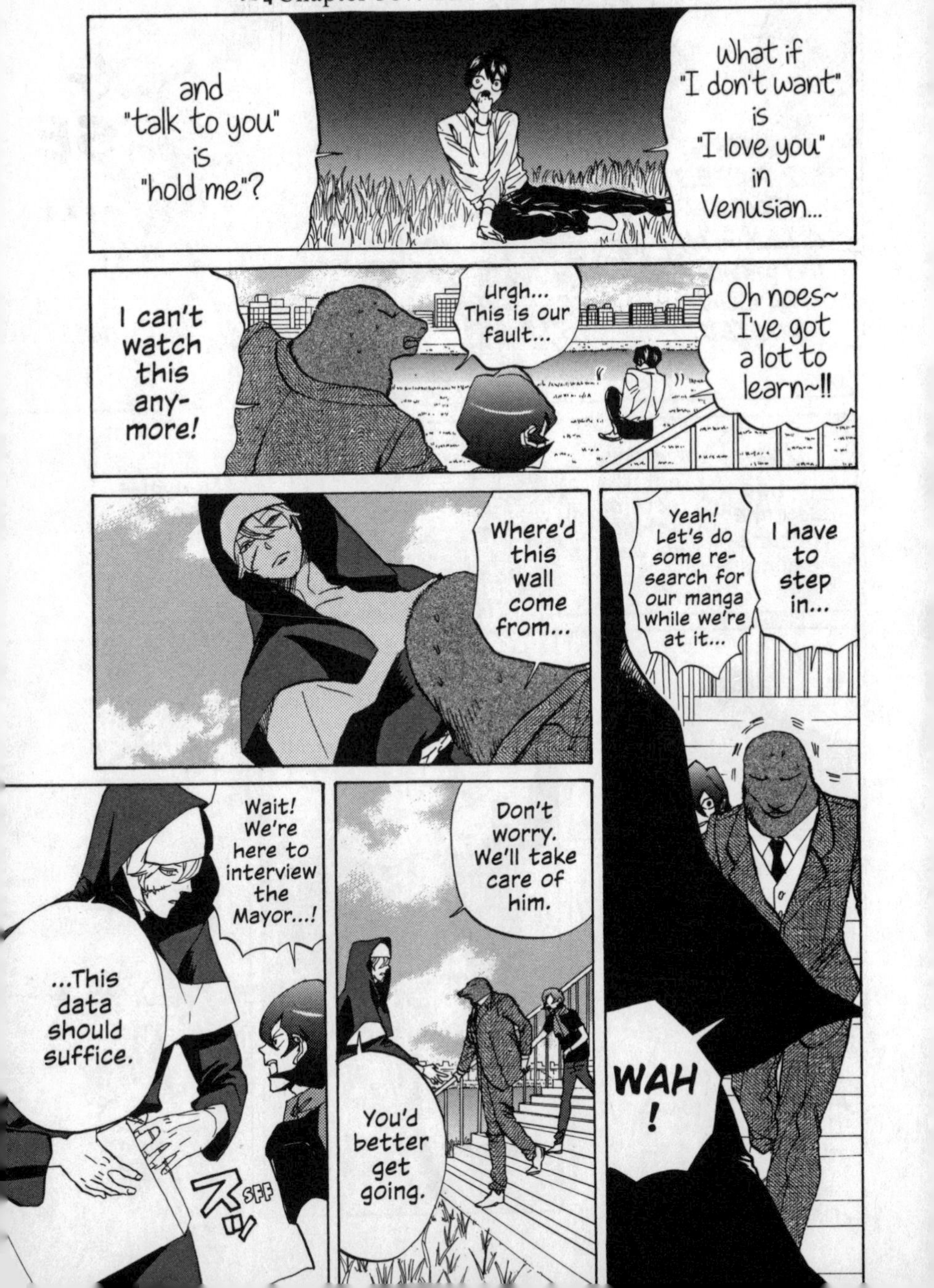
What if "I don't want" is "I love you" in Venusian...
and "talk to you" is "hold me"?
Oh noes~ I've got a lot to learn~!!
Urgh... This is our fault...
I can't watch this anymore!
I have to step in...
Yeah! Let's do some research for our manga while we're at it...
WAH!
Where'd this wall come from...
Don't worry. We'll take care of him.
You'd better get going.
Wait! We're here to interview the Mayor...!
...This data should suffice.
SFF

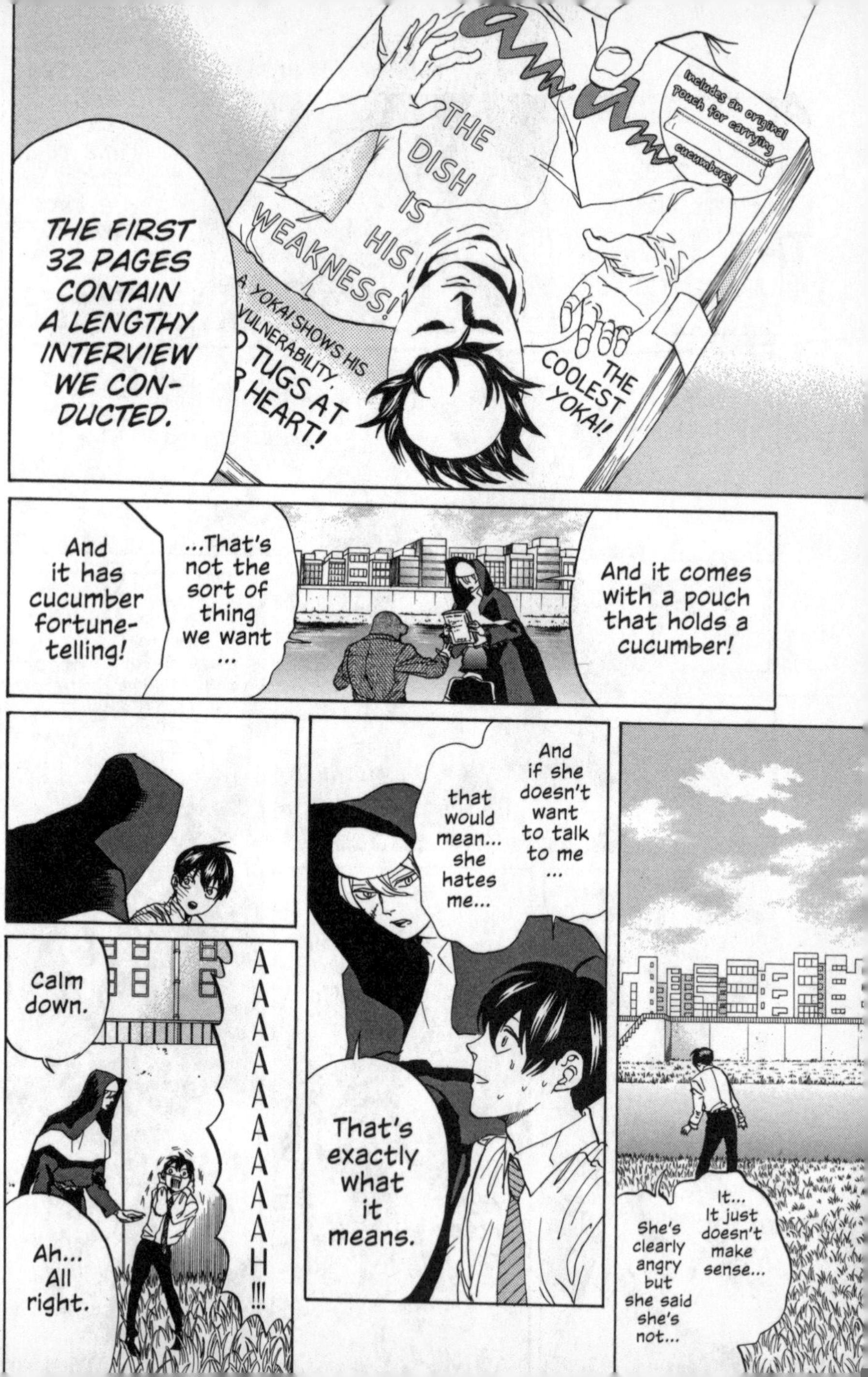

Includes an original pouch for carrying cucumbers!
THE DISH IS HIS WEAKNESS!
THE COOLEST YOKAI!
A YOKAI SHOWS HIS VULNERABILITY,
TUGS AT
HEART!
THE FIRST 32 PAGES CONTAIN A LENGTHY INTERVIEW WE CONDUCTED.
And it comes with a pouch that holds a cucumber!
...That's not the sort of thing we want ...
And it has cucumber fortune-telling!
It... It just doesn't make sense...
She's clearly angry but she said she's not...
And if she doesn't want to talk to me ...
that would mean... she hates me...
That's exactly what it means.
AAAAAAAAAAAAH!!!
Calm down.
Ah... All right.

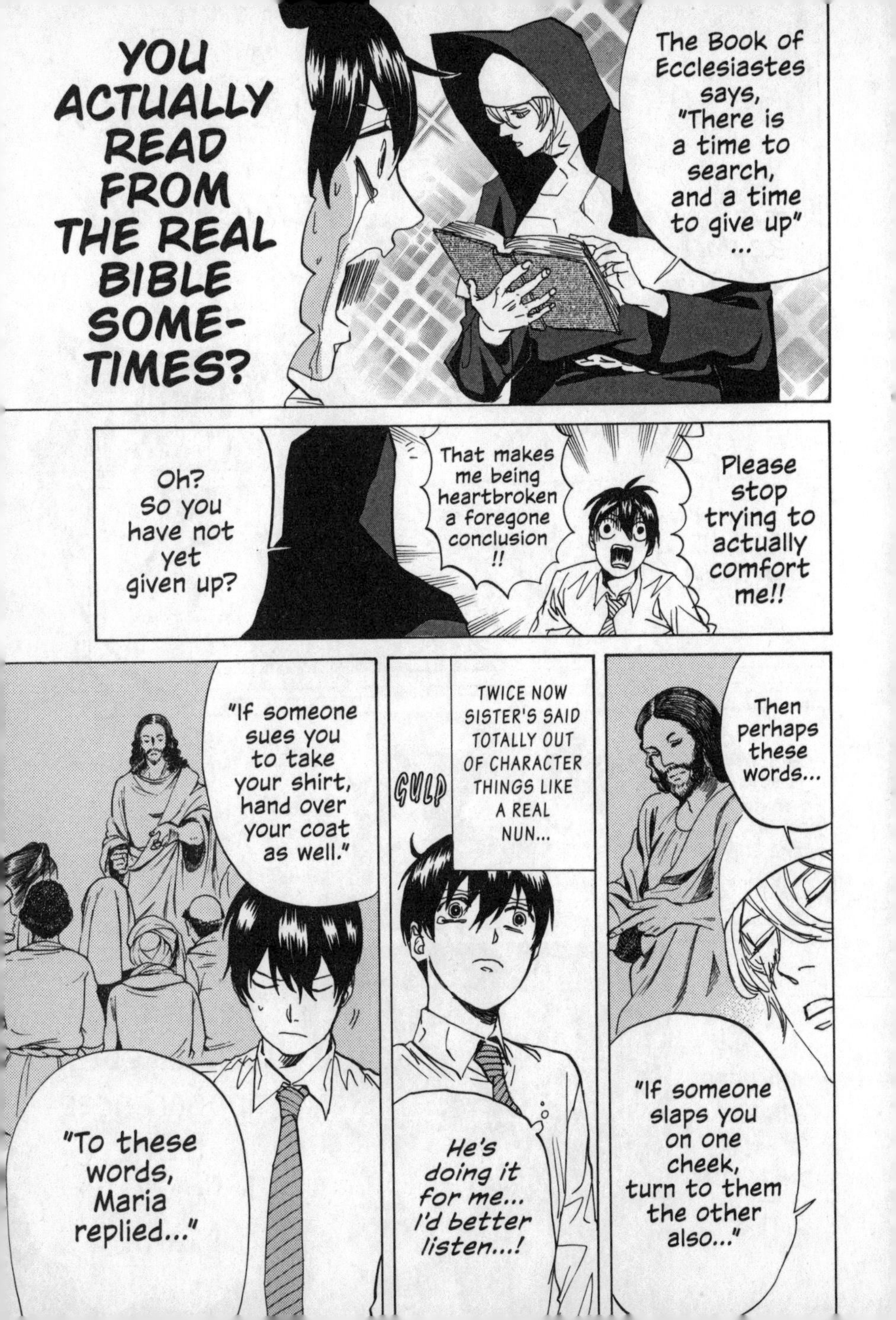
The Book of Ecclesiastes says, "There is a time to search, and a time to give up" ...
YOU ACTUALLY READ FROM THE REAL BIBLE SOME-TIMES?
Please stop trying to actually comfort me!!
That makes me being heartbroken a foregone conclusion !!
Oh? So you have not yet given up?
Then perhaps these words...
"If someone slaps you on one cheek, turn to them the other also..."
TWICE NOW SISTER'S SAID TOTALLY OUT OF CHARACTER THINGS LIKE A REAL NUN...
GULP
He's doing it for me... I'd better listen...!
"If someone sues you to take your shirt, hand over your coat as well."
"To these words, Maria replied..."

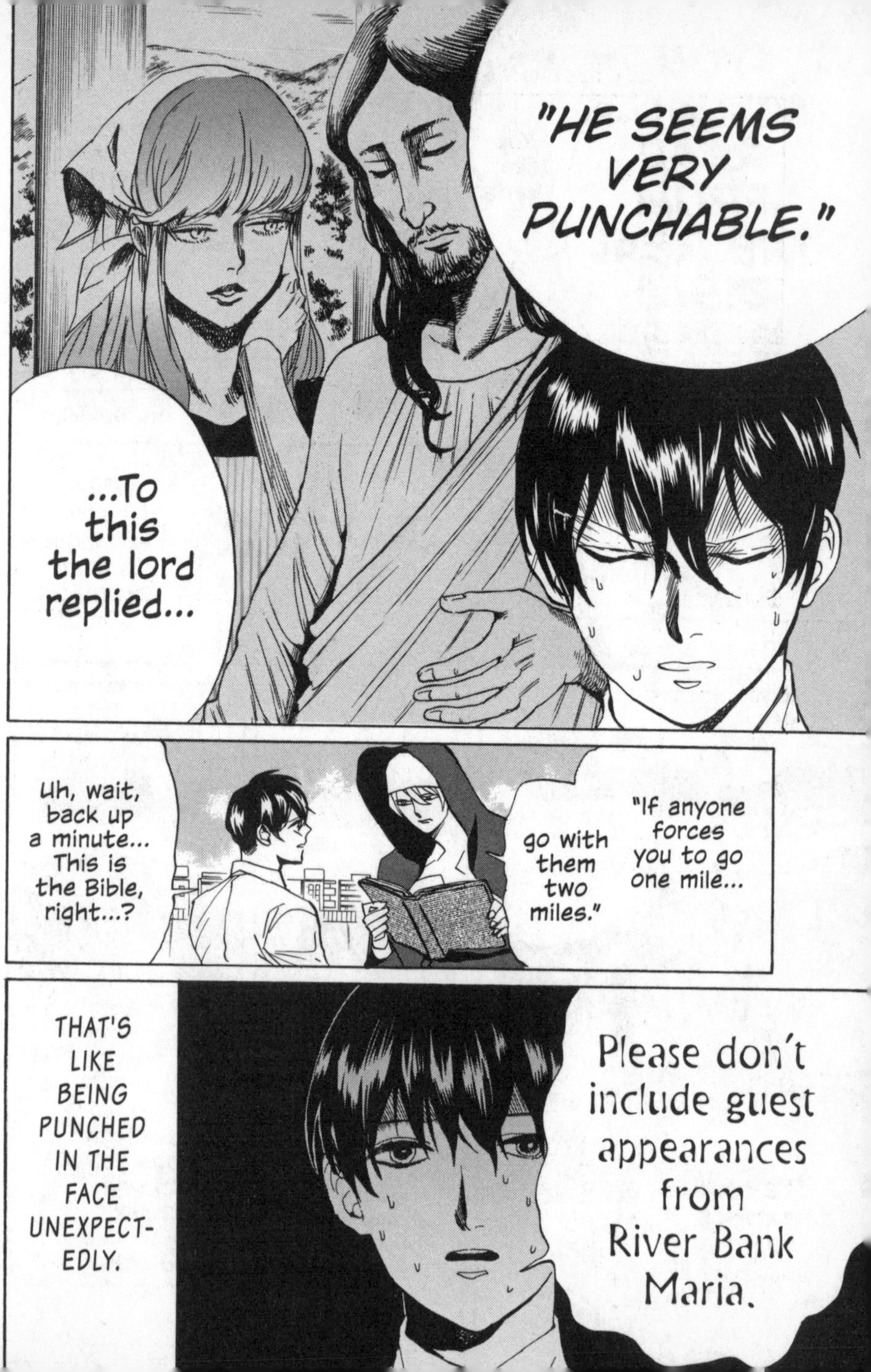
"HE SEEMS VERY PUNCHABLE."
...To this the lord replied...
"If anyone forces you to go one mile...
go with them two miles."
Uh, wait, back up a minute... This is the Bible, right...?
Please don't include guest appearances from River Bank Maria.
THAT'S LIKE BEING PUNCHED IN THE FACE UNEXPECT-EDLY.

☜ Chapter 388: Visit to the Holy Mother

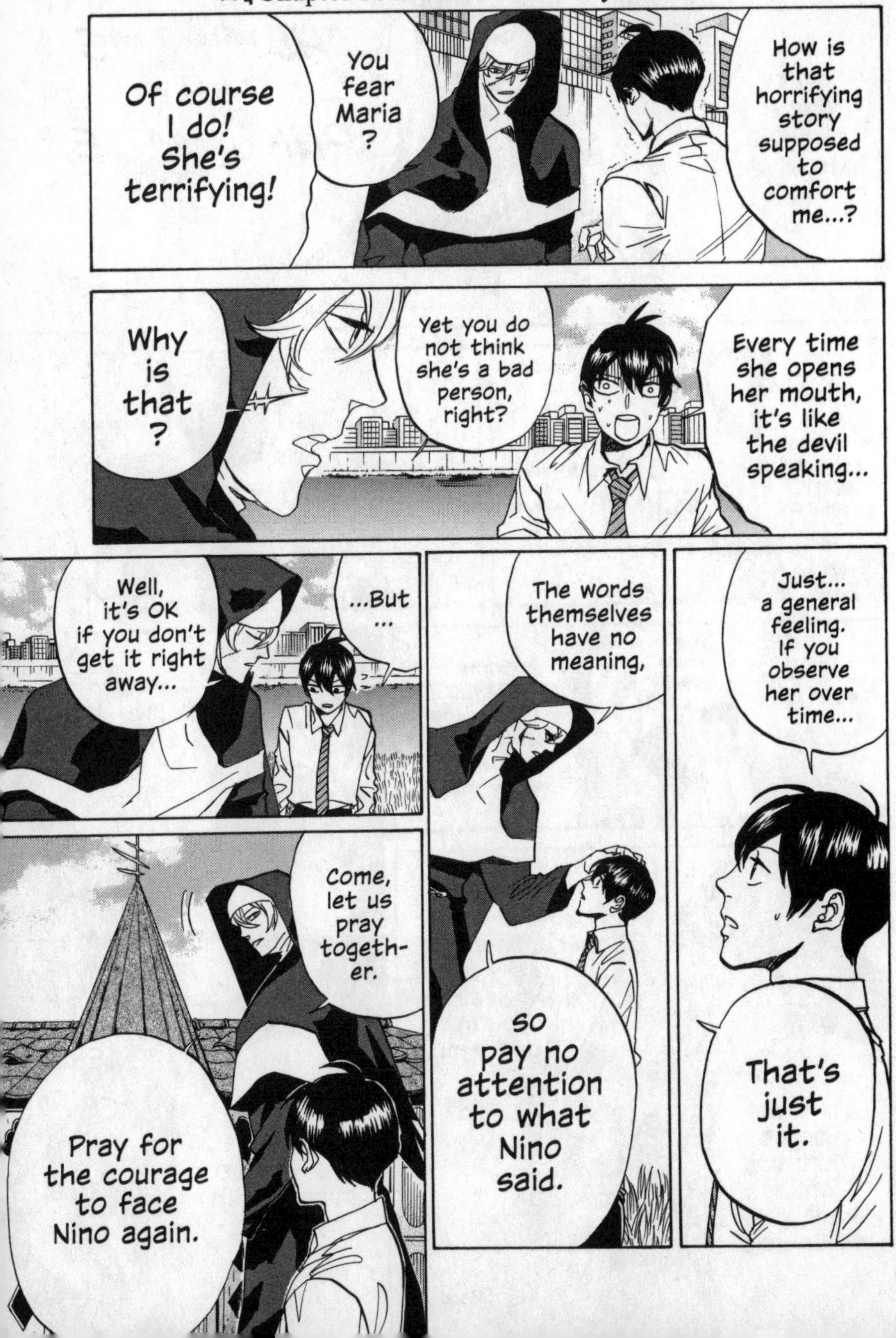
How is that horrifying story supposed to comfort me...?
You fear Maria?
Of course I do! She's terrifying!
Every time she opens her mouth, it's like the devil speaking...
Yet you do not think she's a bad person, right?
Why is that?
Just... a general feeling. If you observe her over time...
That's just it.
The words themselves have no meaning,
so pay no attention to what Nino said.
...But...
Well, it's OK if you don't get it right away...
Come, let us pray together.
Pray for the courage to face Nino again.

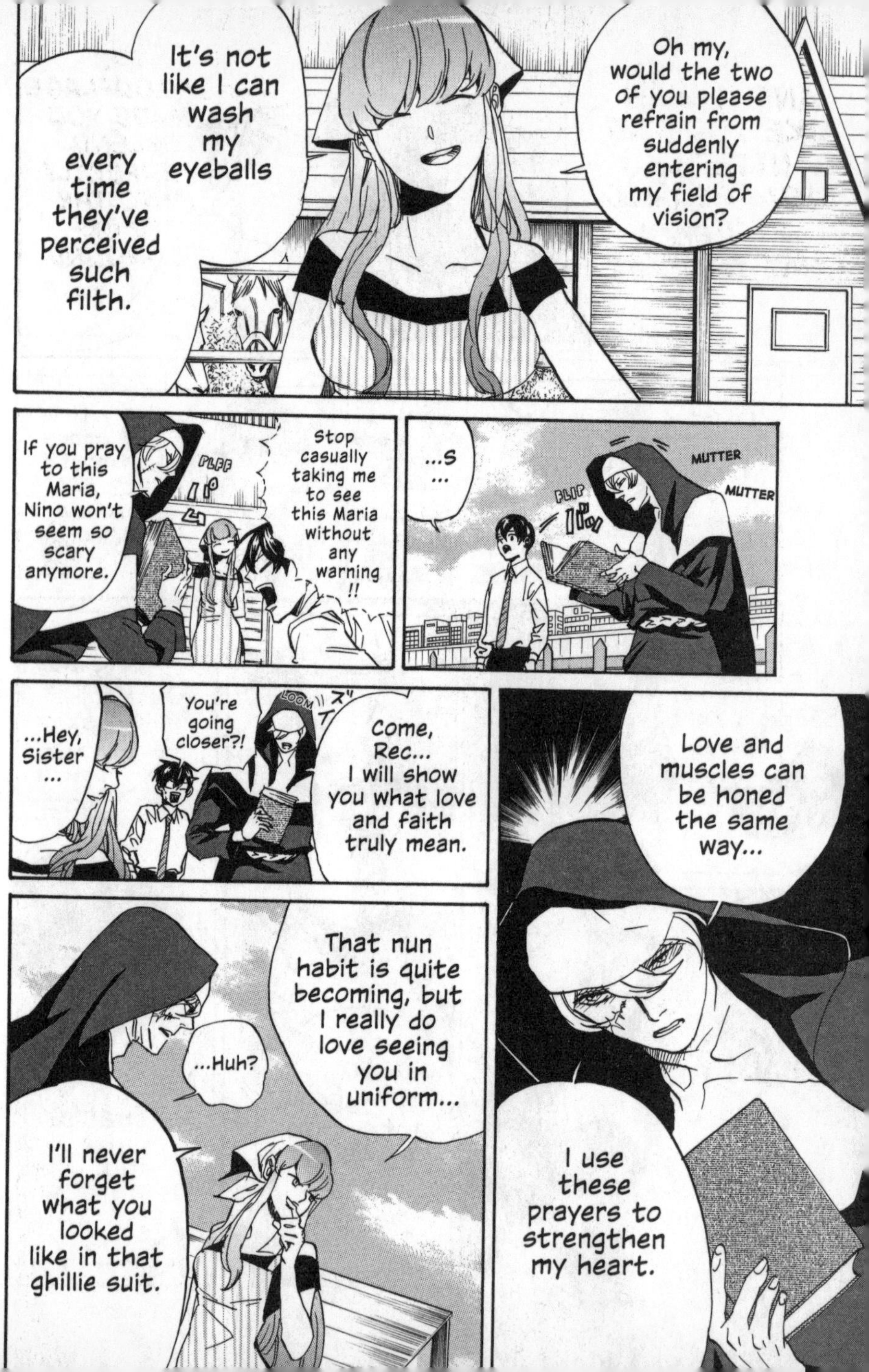

Oh my, would the two of you please refrain from suddenly entering my field of vision?
It's not like I can wash my eyeballs every time they've perceived such filth.
...S ...
MUTTER
MUTTER
FLIP
Stop casually taking me to see this Maria without any warning !!
If you pray to this Maria, Nino won't seem so scary anymore.
Love and muscles can be honed the same way...
I use these prayers to strengthen my heart.
Come, Rec... I will show you what love and faith truly mean.
LOOM
You're going closer?!
...Hey, Sister ...
That nun habit is quite becoming, but I really do love seeing you in uniform...
...Huh?
I'll never forget what you looked like in that ghillie suit.

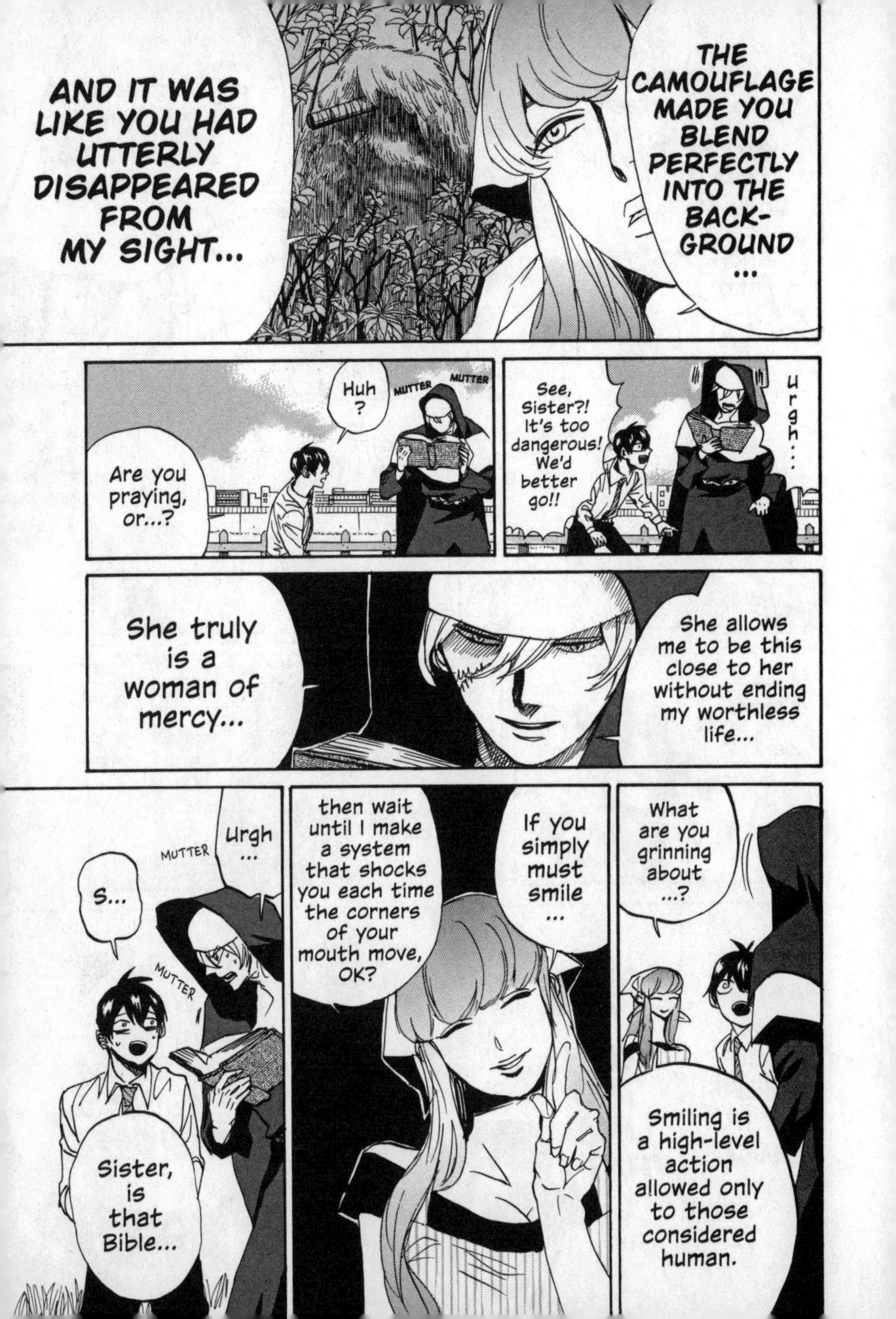
THE CAMOUFLAGE MADE YOU BLEND PERFECTLY INTO THE BACK-GROUND ...
AND IT WAS LIKE YOU HAD UTTERLY DISAPPEARED FROM MY SIGHT...
Urgh...
See, Sister?! It's too dangerous! We'd better go!!
MUTTER MUTTER
Huh?
Are you praying, or...?
She allows me to be this close to her without ending my worthless life...
She truly is a woman of mercy...
What are you grinning about ...?
Smiling is a high-level action allowed only to those considered human.
If you simply must smile ...
then wait until I make a system that shocks you each time the corners of your mouth move, OK?
Urgh ...
MUTTER
S...
MUTTER
Sister, is that Bible...

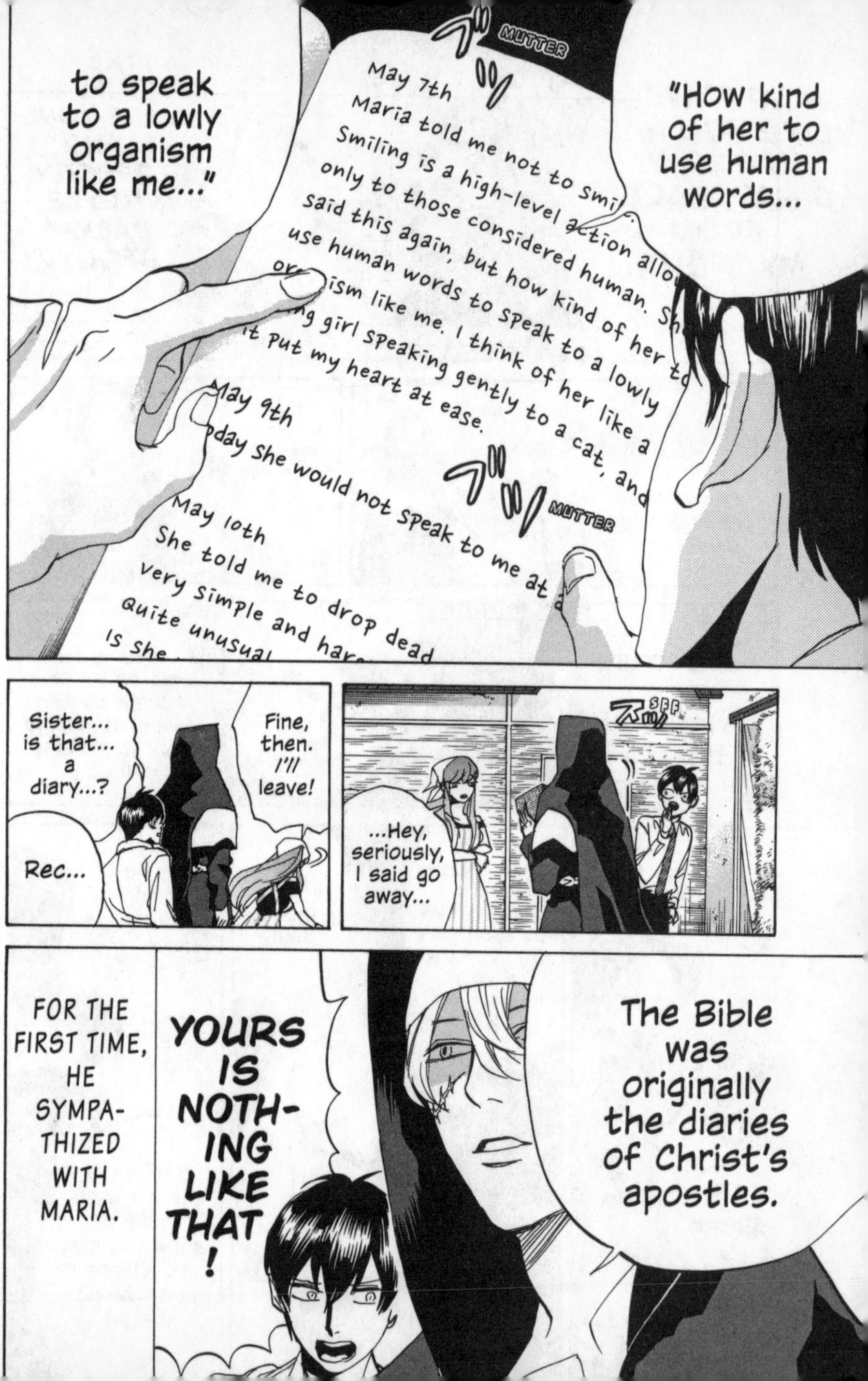
MUTTER
"How kind of her to use human words...
May 7th
Maria told me not to smi
Smiling is a high-level action allo
only to those considered human. Sh
said this again, but how kind of her to
use human words to speak to a lowly
or ism like me. I think of her like a
g girl speaking gently to a cat, and
it put my heart at ease.
May 9th
day She would not speak to me at
May 10th
She told me to drop dead
very simple and har
Quite unusual
Is she
MUTTER
to speak to a lowly organism like me..."
SFF
...Hey, seriously, I said go away...
Fine, then. I'll leave!
Sister... is that... a diary...?
Rec...
The Bible was originally the diaries of Christ's apostles.
YOURS IS NOTHING LIKE THAT!
FOR THE FIRST TIME, HE SYMPATHIZED WITH MARIA.

Chapter 389: Lost Clothes

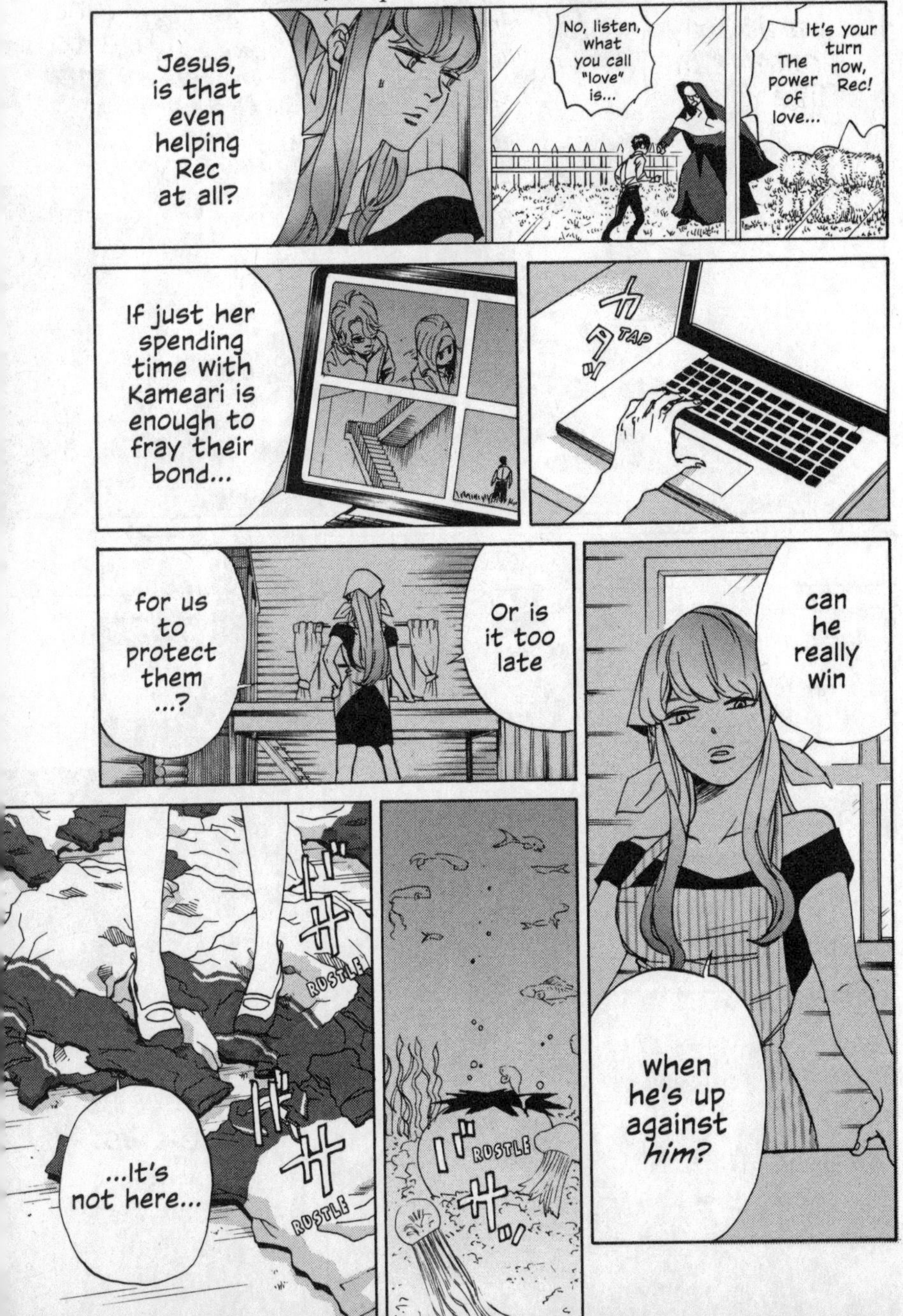
It's your turn now, Rec!
The power of love...
No, listen, what you call "love" is...
Jesus, is that even helping Rec at all?
TAP
If just her spending time with Kameari is enough to fray their bond...
can he really win
when he's up against *him*?
Or is it too late
for us to protect them ...?
RUSTLE
RUSTLE
...It's not here...
RUSTLE

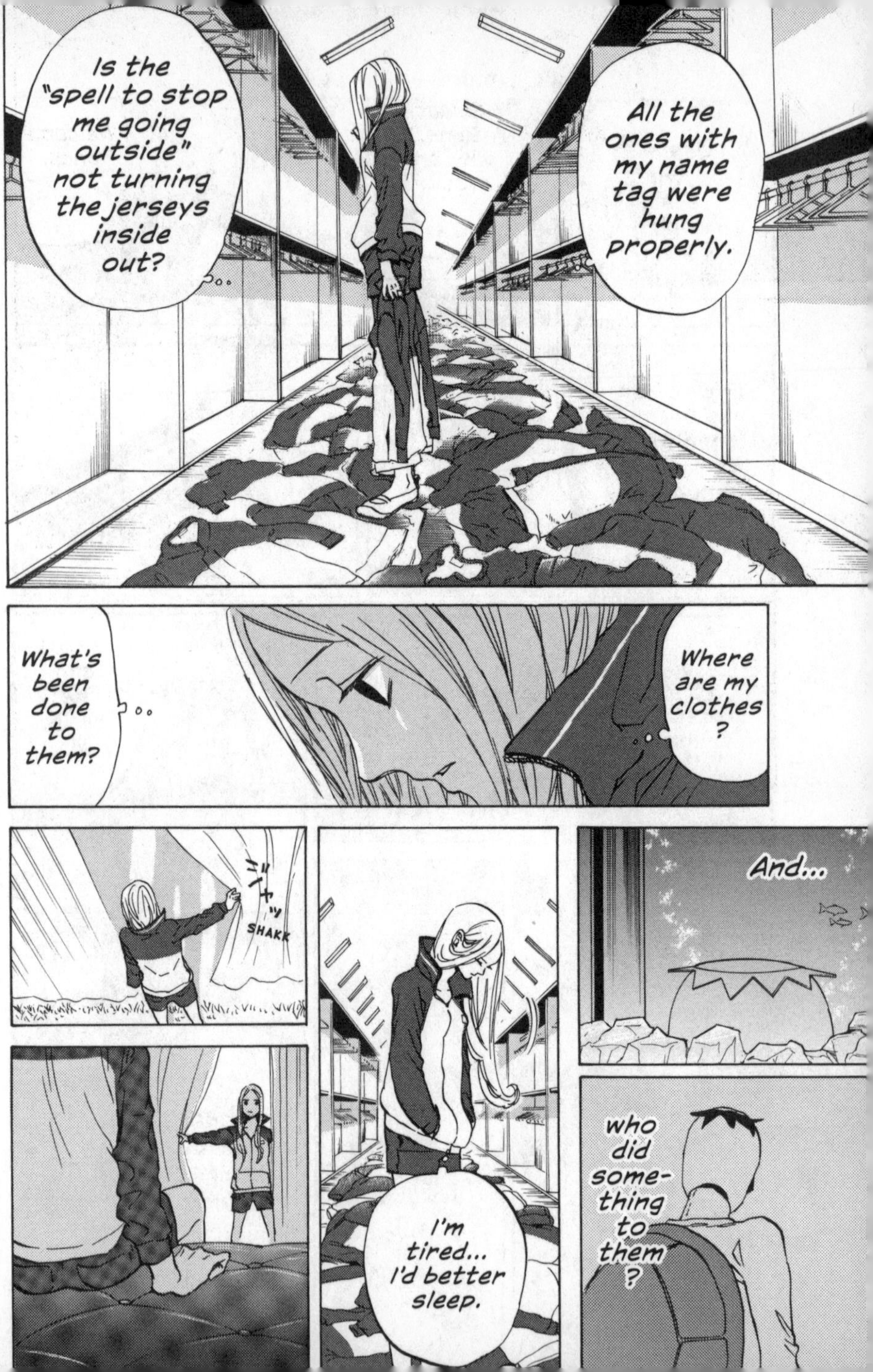
All the ones with my name tag were hung properly.
Is the "spell to stop me going outside" not turning the jerseys inside out?
Where are my clothes?
What's been done to them?
And...
who did some-thing to them?
I'm tired... I'd better sleep.
ジャッ
SHAKK

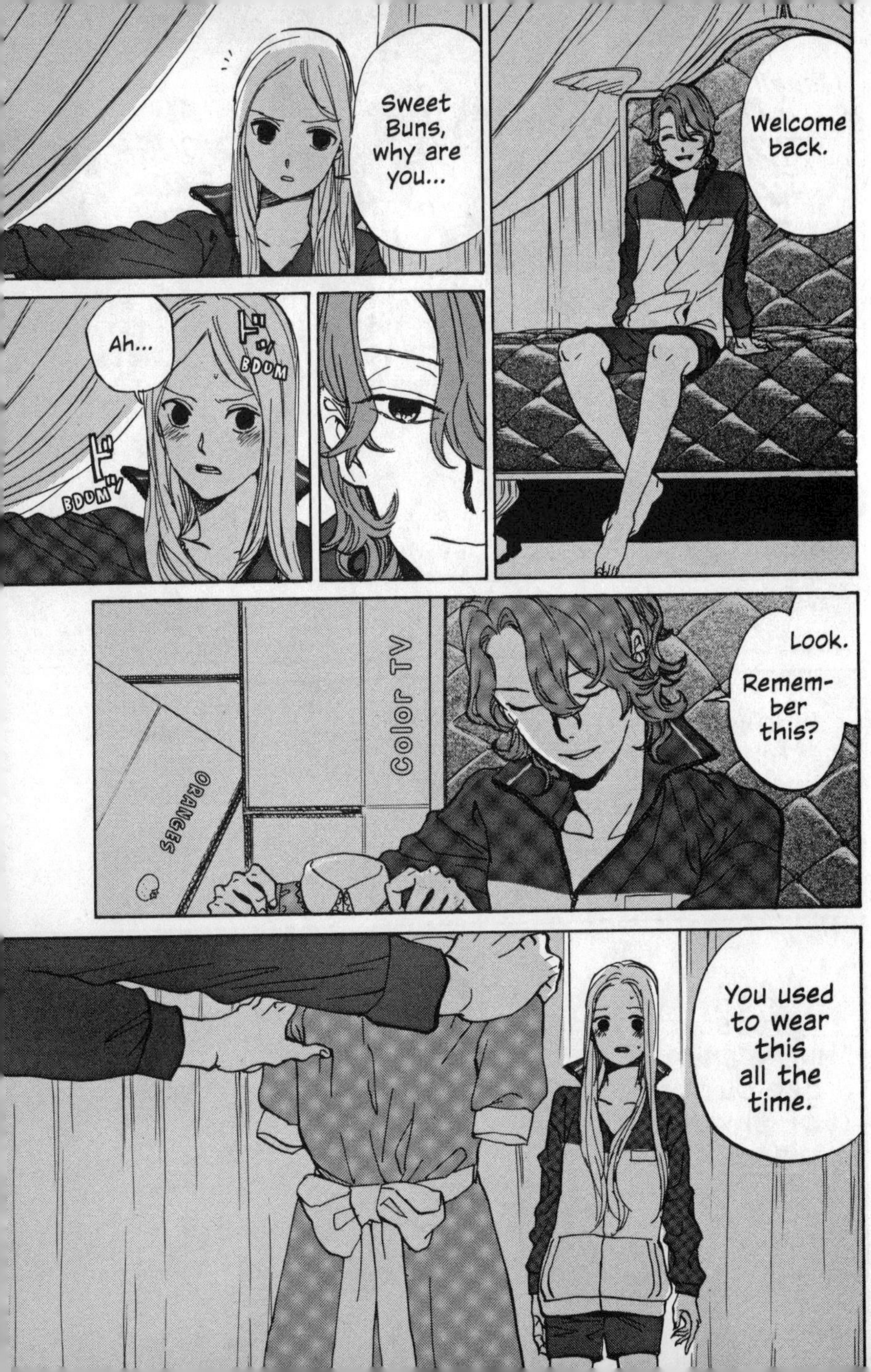
Welcome back.
Sweet Buns, why are you...
Ah...
BDUM
BDUM
Look.
Remember this?
Color TV
ORANGES
You used to wear this all the time.

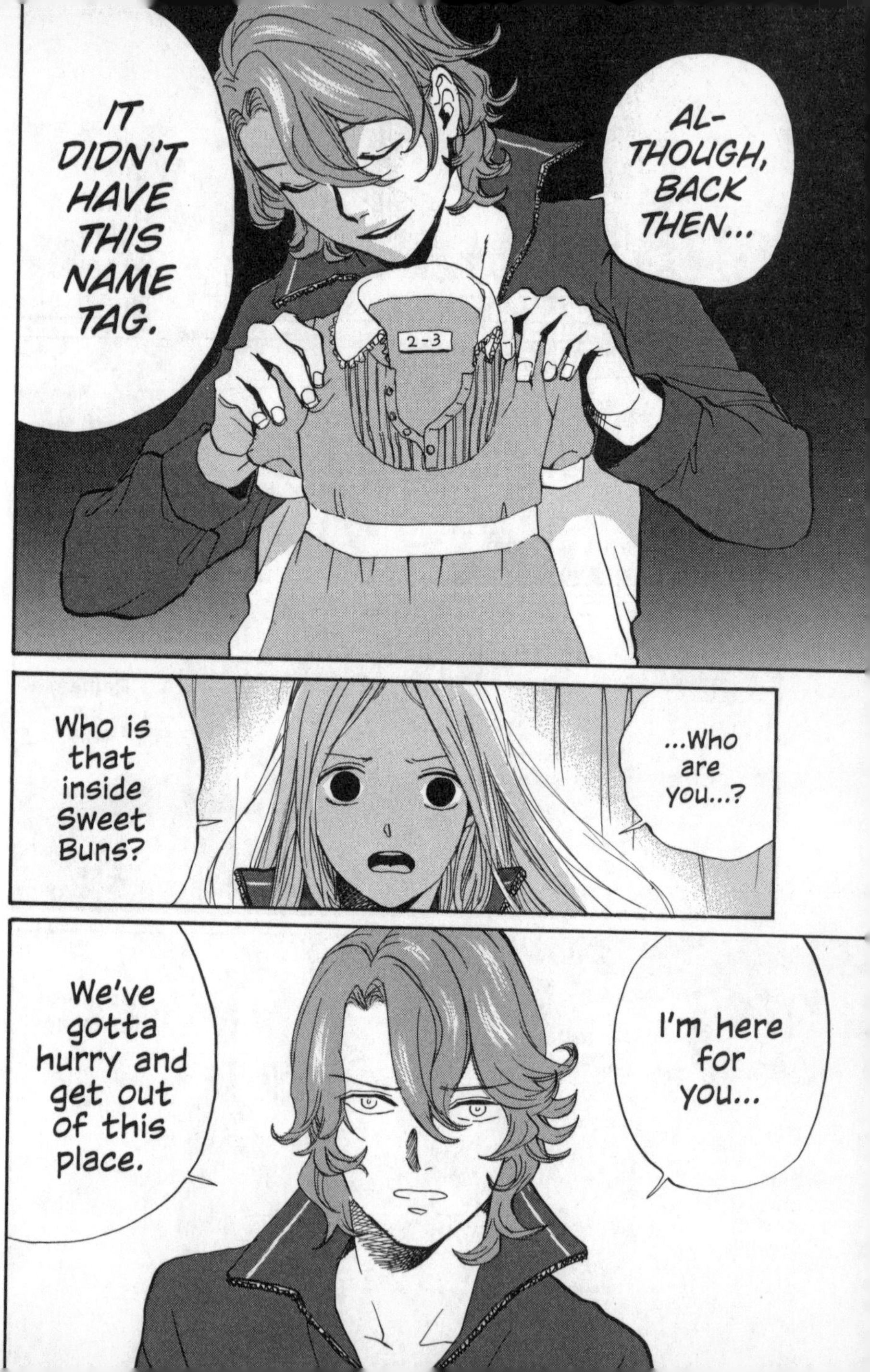
AL-THOUGH, BACK THEN...
IT DIDN'T HAVE THIS NAME TAG.
2-3
...Who are you...?
Who is that inside Sweet Buns?
I'm here for you...
We've gotta hurry and get out of this place.

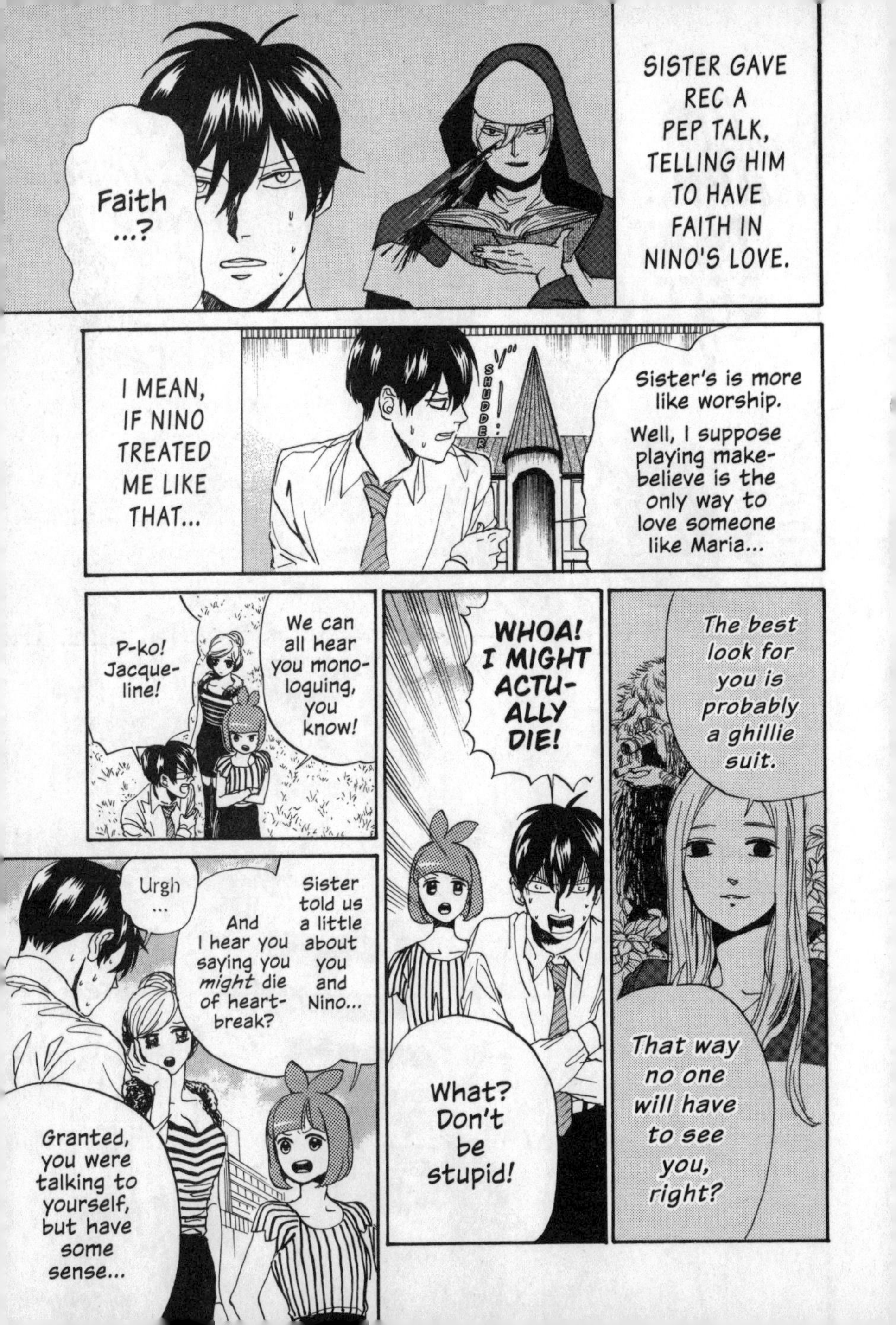
SISTER GAVE REC A PEP TALK, TELLING HIM TO HAVE FAITH IN NINO'S LOVE.
Faith ...?
Sister's is more like worship.
Well, I suppose playing make-believe is the only way to love someone like Maria...
SHUDDER
I MEAN, IF NINO TREATED ME LIKE THAT...
The best look for you is probably a ghillie suit.
That way no one will have to see you, right?
WHOA! I MIGHT ACTUALLY DIE!
What? Don't be stupid!
We can all hear you monologuing, you know!
P-ko! Jacqueline!
Sister told us a little about you and Nino...
And I hear you saying you *might* die of heartbreak?
Urgh ...
Granted, you were talking to yourself, but have some sense...

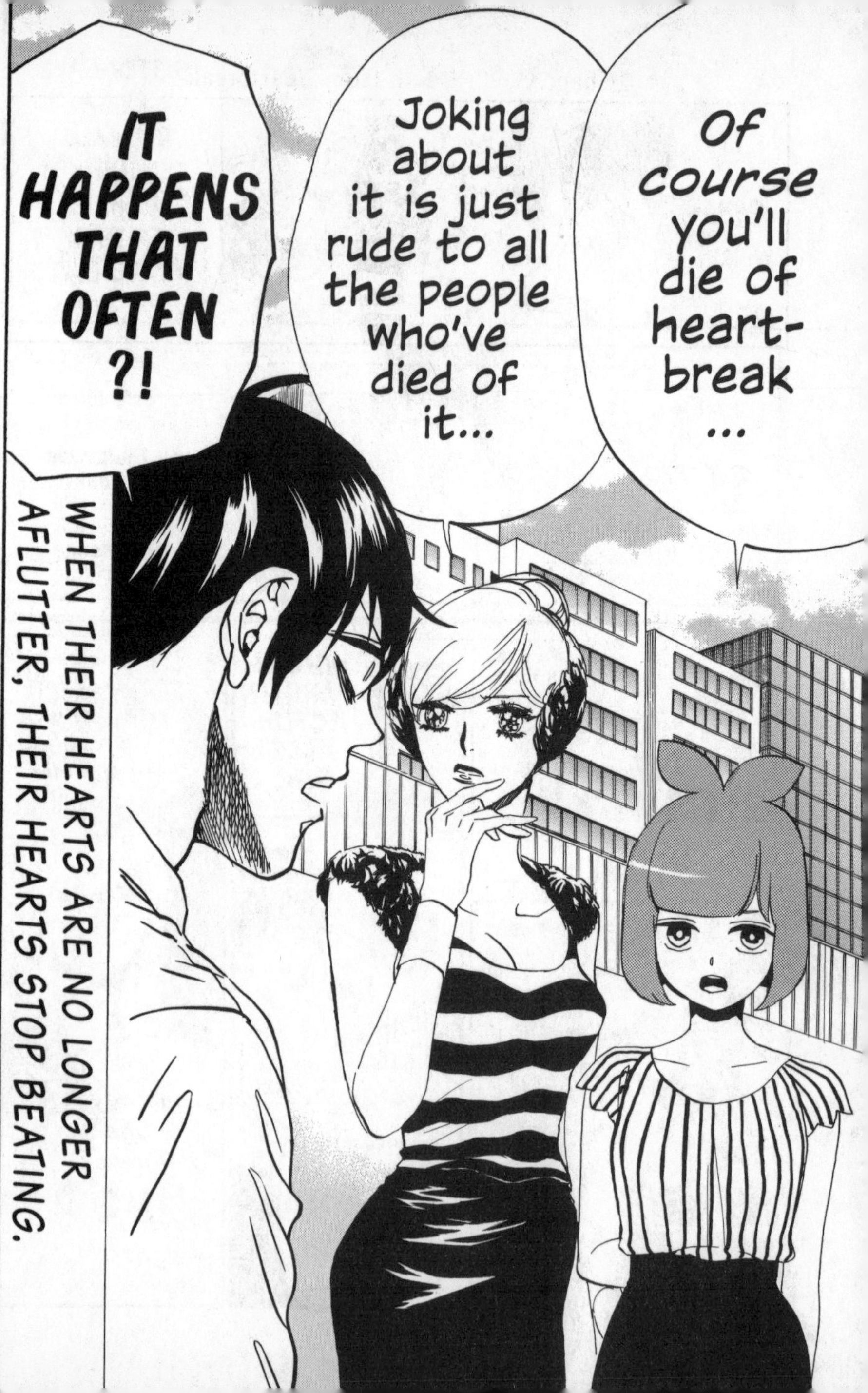
Of course you'll die of heart-break ...
Joking about it is just rude to all the people who've died of it...
IT HAPPENS THAT OFTEN ?!
WHEN THEIR HEARTS ARE NO LONGER AFLUTTER, THEIR HEARTS STOP BEATING.

Chapter 390: Death from Heartbreak

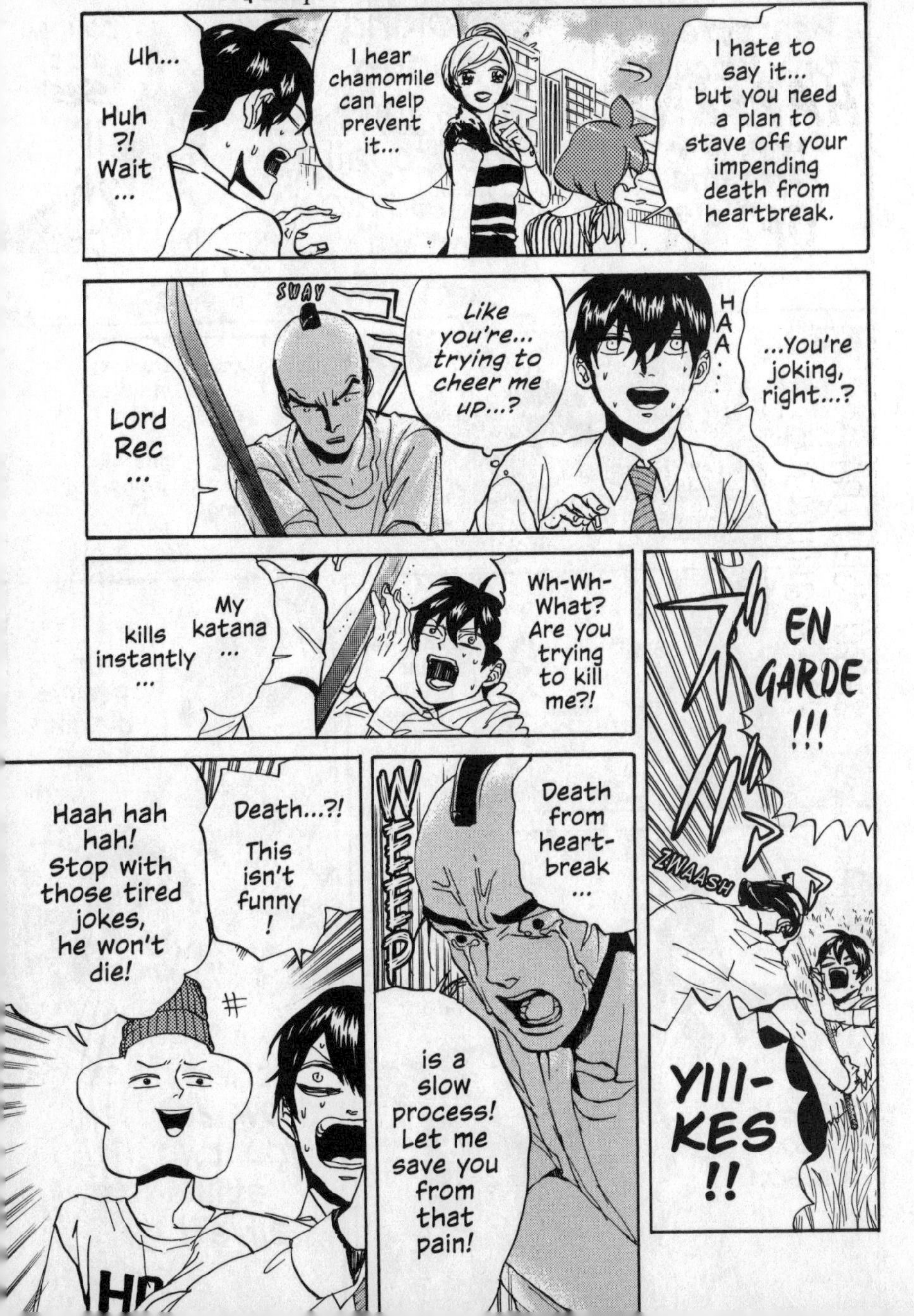
I hate to say it... but you need a plan to stave off your impending death from heartbreak.
I hear chamomile can help prevent it...
Uh...
Huh?! Wait...
...You're joking, right...?
HAA...
SWAY
Like you're... trying to cheer me up...?
Lord Rec...
EN GARDE!!!
ZWAASH
YIII-KES!!
Wh-Wh-What? Are you trying to kill me?!
My katana...
kills instantly...
Death from heart-break...
WEEEP
is a slow process! Let me save you from that pain!
Death...?!
This isn't funny!
Haah hah hah! Stop with those tired jokes, he won't die!

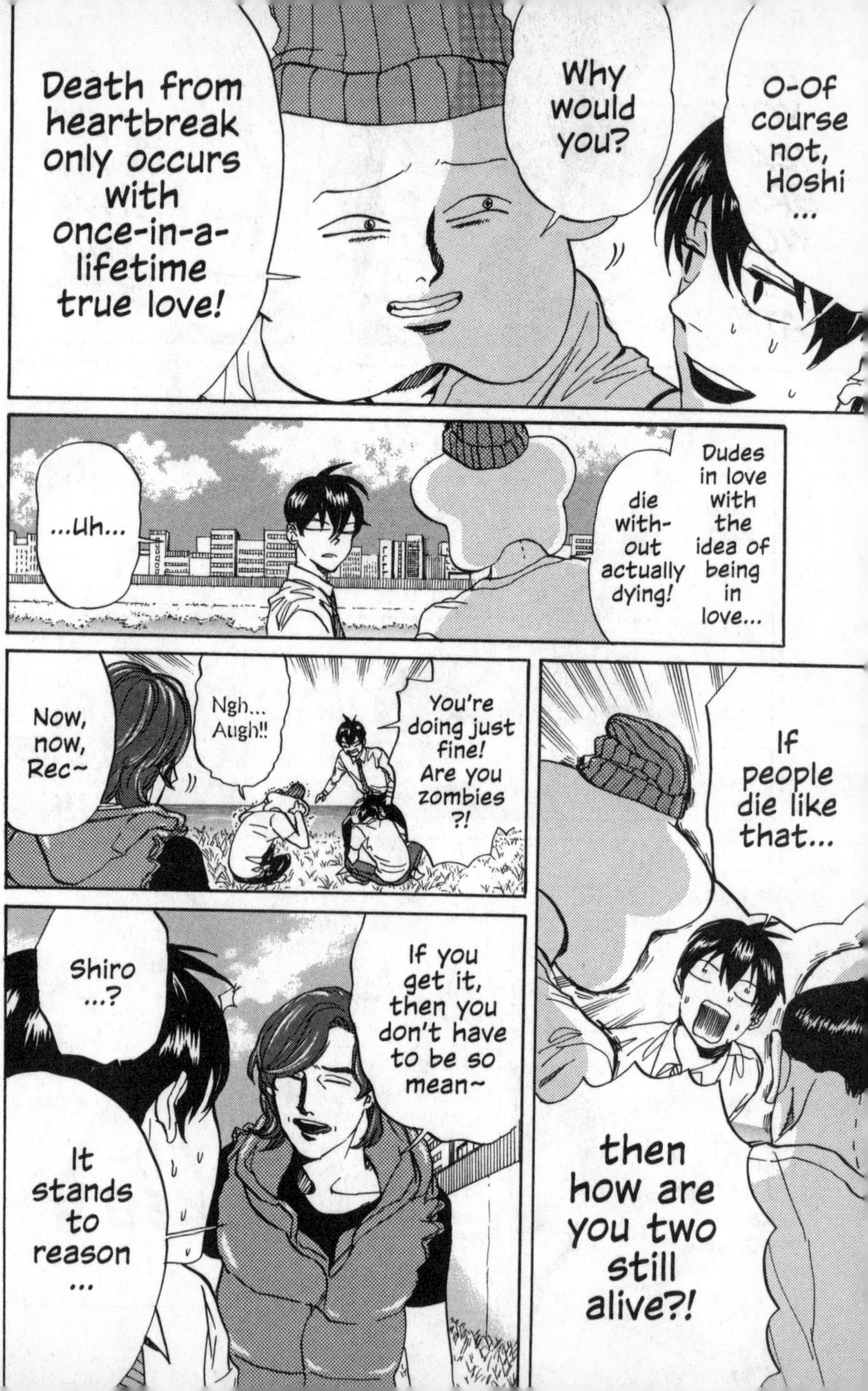
O-Of course not, Hoshi ...
Why would you?
Death from heartbreak only occurs with once-in-a-lifetime true love!
Dudes in love with the idea of being in love...
die with-out actually dying!
...Uh...
If people die like that...
then how are you two still alive?!
You're doing just fine! Are you zombies?!
Ngh... Augh!!
Now, now, Rec~
If you get it, then you don't have to be so mean~
Shiro ...?
It stands to reason ...

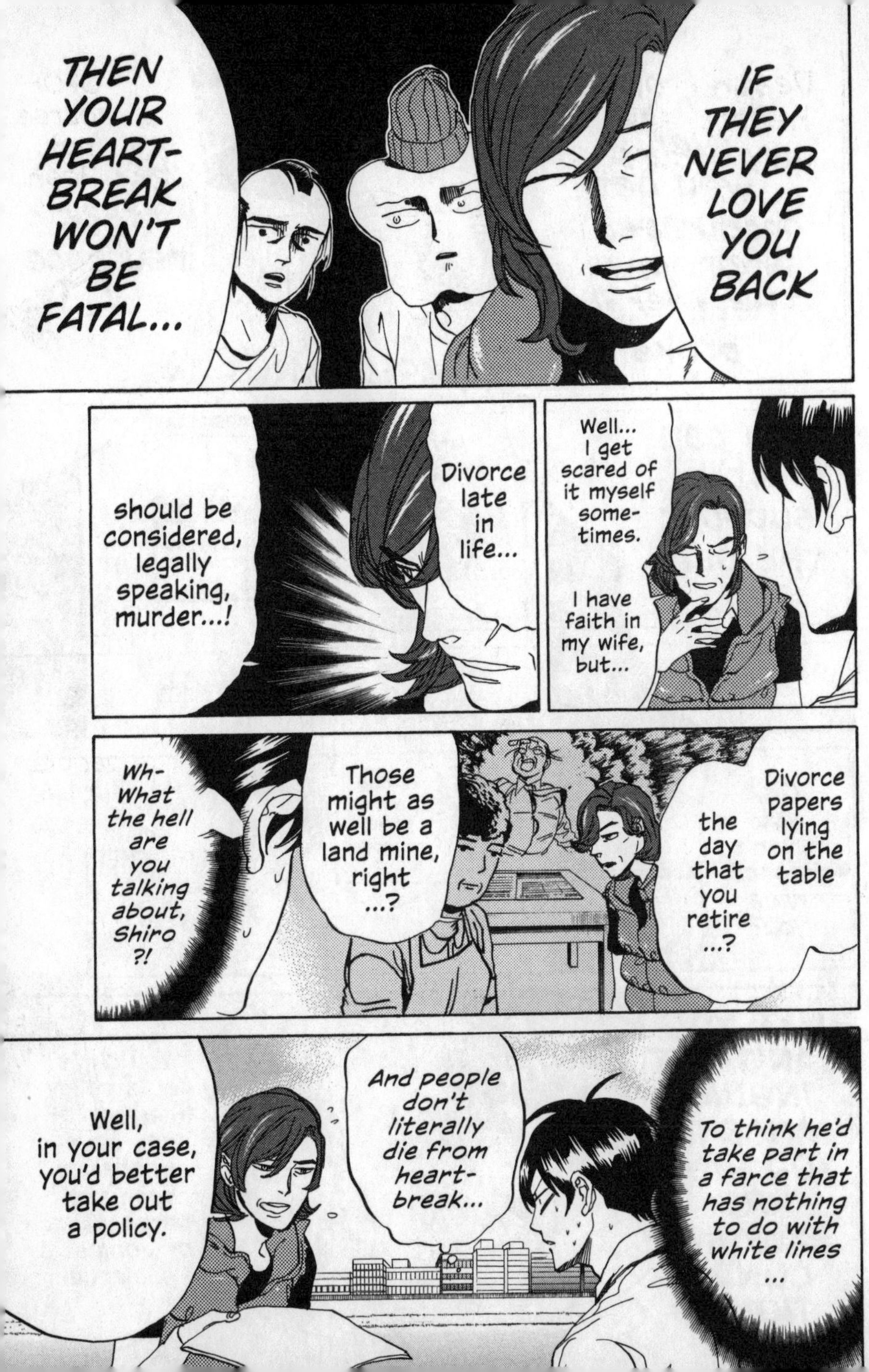
IF THEY NEVER LOVE YOU BACK
THEN YOUR HEART-BREAK WON'T BE FATAL...
Well... I get scared of it myself some-times.
I have faith in my wife, but...
Divorce late in life...
should be considered, legally speaking, murder...!
Divorce papers lying on the table the day that you retire ...?
Those might as well be a land mine, right ...?
Wh- What the hell are you talking about, Shiro ?!
To think he'd take part in a farce that has nothing to do with white lines ...
And people don't literally die from heart-break...
Well, in your case, you'd better take out a policy.

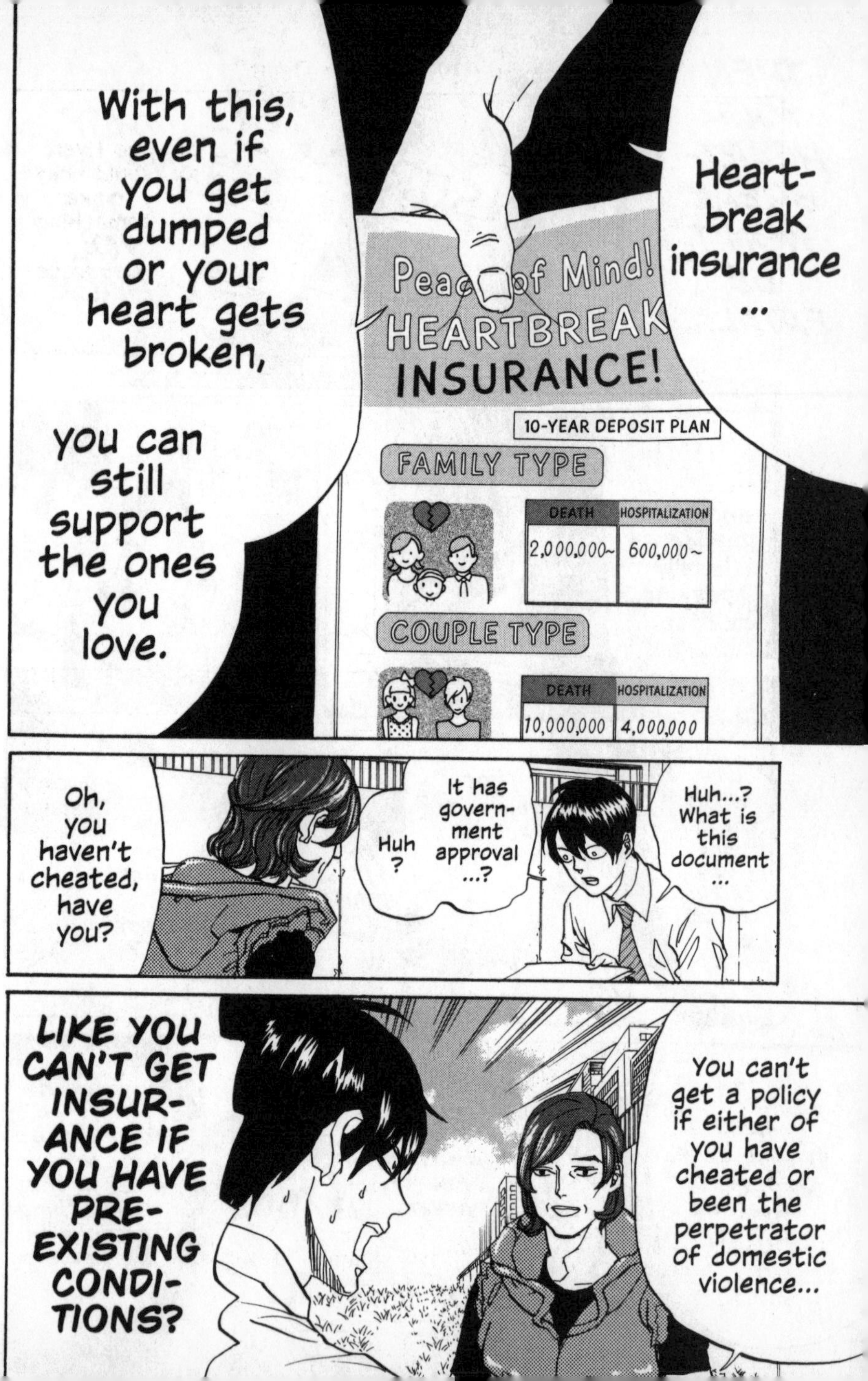

Heart-break insurance...
With this, even if you get dumped or your heart gets broken,
you can still support the ones you love.
Peac of Mind!
HEARTBREAK INSURANCE!
10-YEAR DEPOSIT PLAN
FAMILY TYPE
DEATH
HOSPITALIZATION
2,000,000~
600,000~
COUPLE TYPE
DEATH
HOSPITALIZATION
10,000,000
4,000,000
Huh...? What is this document...
It has government approval...?
Huh?
Oh, you haven't cheated, have you?
You can't get a policy if either of you have cheated or been the perpetrator of domestic violence...
LIKE YOU CAN'T GET INSURANCE IF YOU HAVE PRE-EXISTING CONDITIONS?

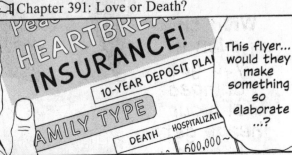

Chapter 391: Love or Death?

This flyer... would they make something so elaborate ...?
HEARTBREAK
INSURANCE!
10-YEAR DEPOSIT PLA
AMILY TYPE
DEATH
HOSPITALIZATI
600,000~
But I guess they are crazy enough to go this far...
Aw geez, this is just a tasteless practical joke!
Nobody would believe this crap!
SKRNCH
GULP...
But just in case...
I'd better ask Mr. Zoozle.
SCHK
SSFFF
Death from heartbreak
Cancel
ZOOZLE SEARCH
Death from heartbreak
Heartbreak insurance
BLIP
BLIP
Huh ...?
POP
Preventing Post-heartbreak Death
Can affect anyone; The secon most common cause of death Japan after accidents.
Are Japanese people unusually susceptible?
A common caus communication death before yo know it
how to solve
Calm down... It's just your imagination...
Or maybe the whole world is trying to trick me...
I... I have to be sure...
GOTTA ASK SOMEONE WHO WOULDN'T TAKE PART IN A PRANK...
SOMEONE WHO'D NEVER JOKE AROUND...!!!!

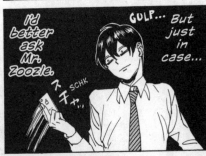

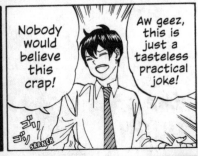

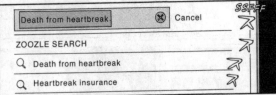

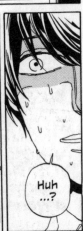

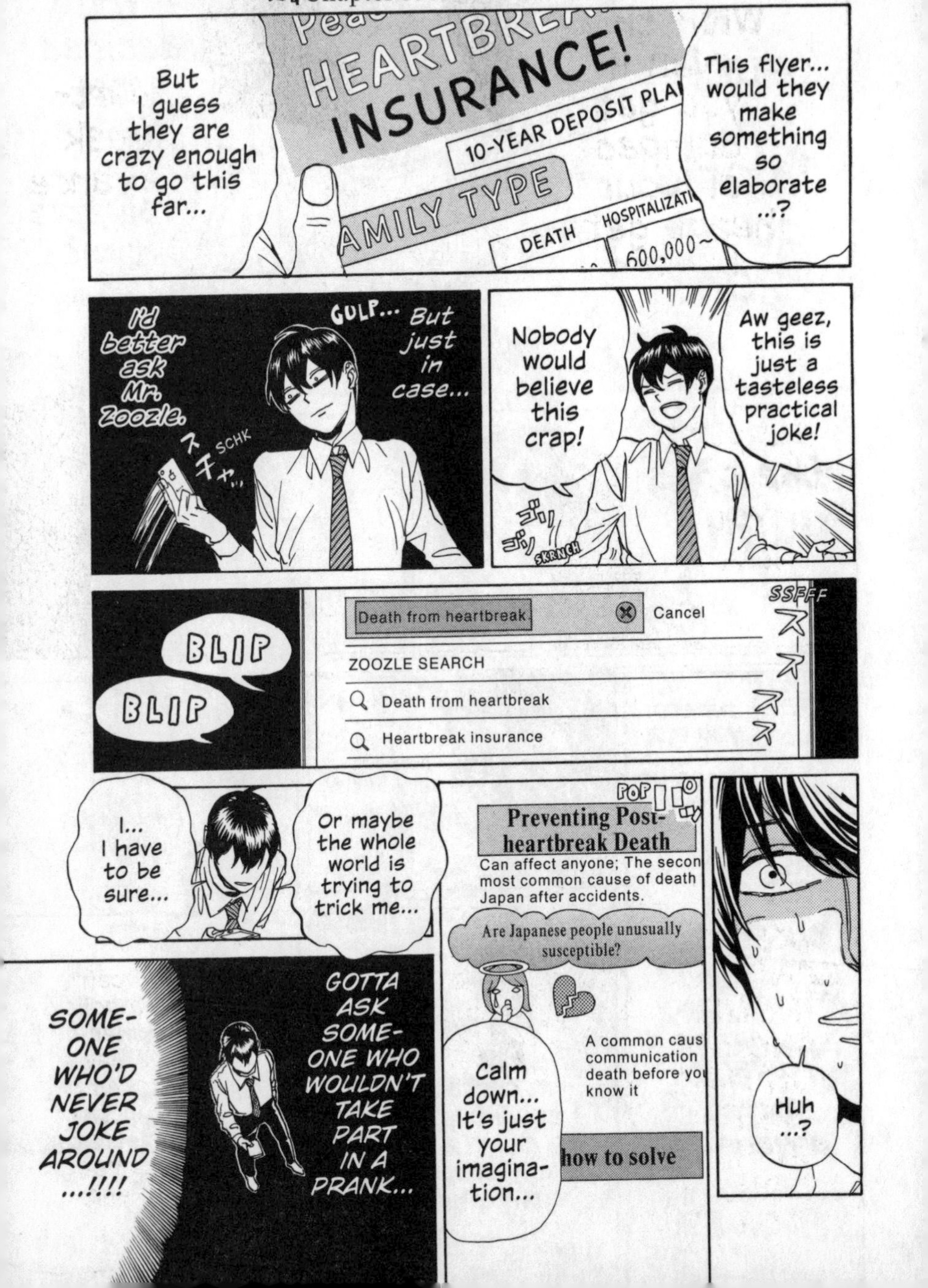

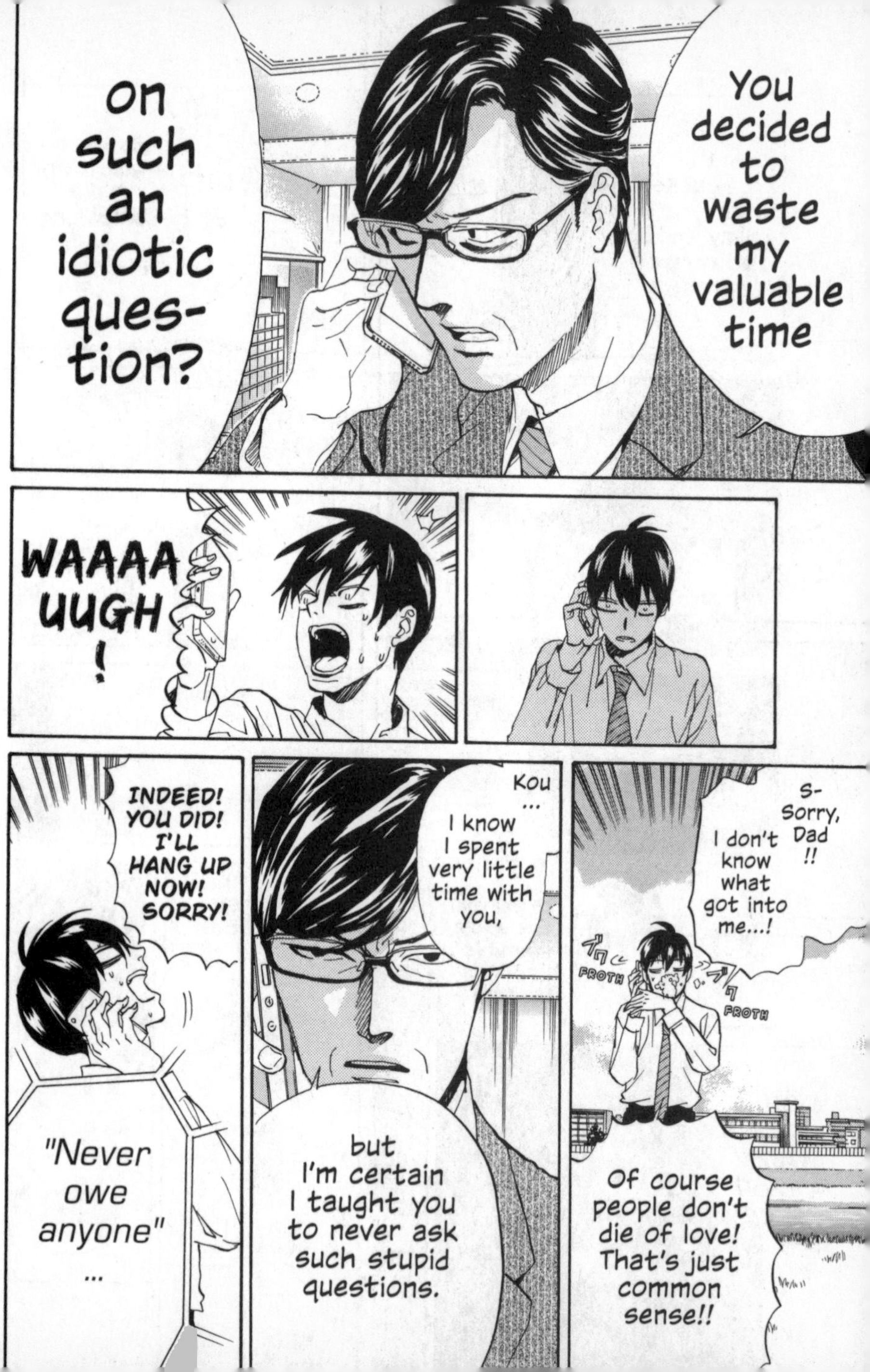
You decided to waste my valuable time
on such an idiotic ques-tion?
WAAAA UUGH !
S-Sorry, Dad !!
I don't know what got into me...!
FROTH
FROTH
Of course people don't die of love! That's just common sense!!
Kou ...
I know I spent very little time with you,
but I'm certain I taught you to never ask such stupid questions.
INDEED! YOU DID! I'LL HANG UP NOW! SORRY!
"Never owe anyone" ...

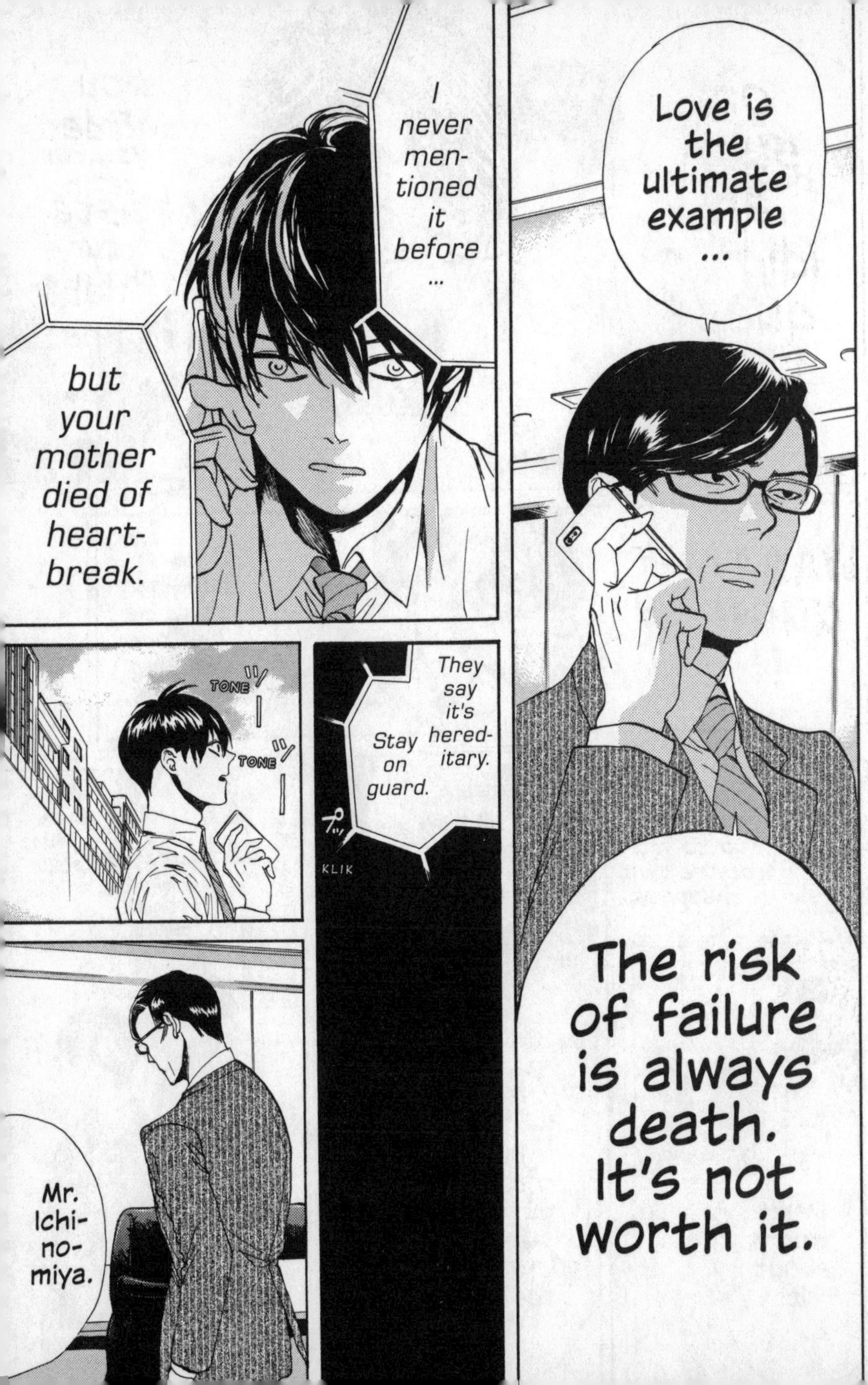
I never mentioned it before ...
but your mother died of heartbreak.
Love is the ultimate example ...
The risk of failure is always death. It's not worth it.
They say it's hereditary.
Stay on guard.
KLIK
TONE
TONE
Mr. Ichinomiya.

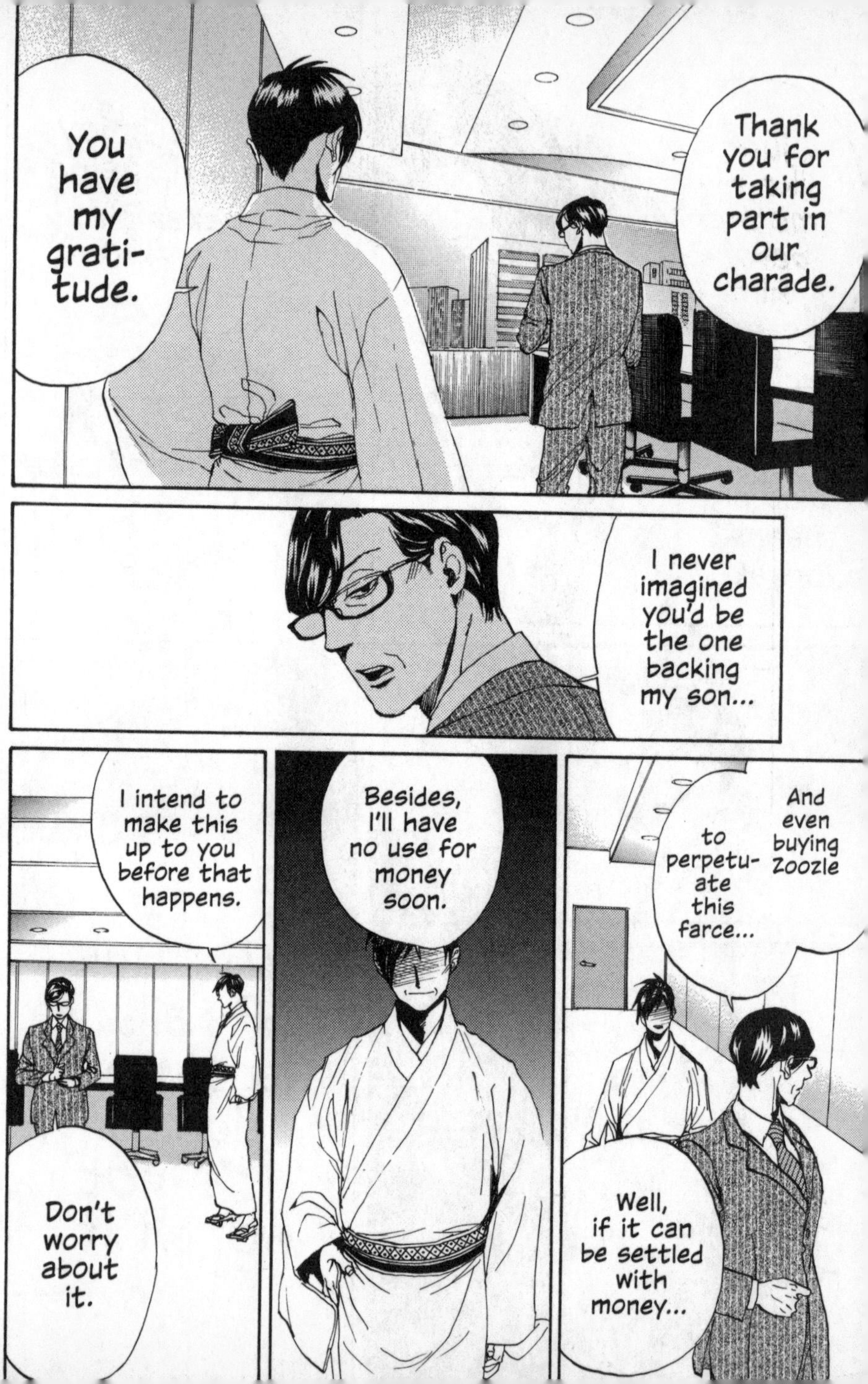
Thank you for taking part in our charade.
You have my gratitude.
I never imagined you'd be the one backing my son...
And even buying Zoozle
to perpetuate this farce...
Well, if it can be settled with money...
Besides, I'll have no use for money soon.
I intend to make this up to you before that happens.
Don't worry about it.

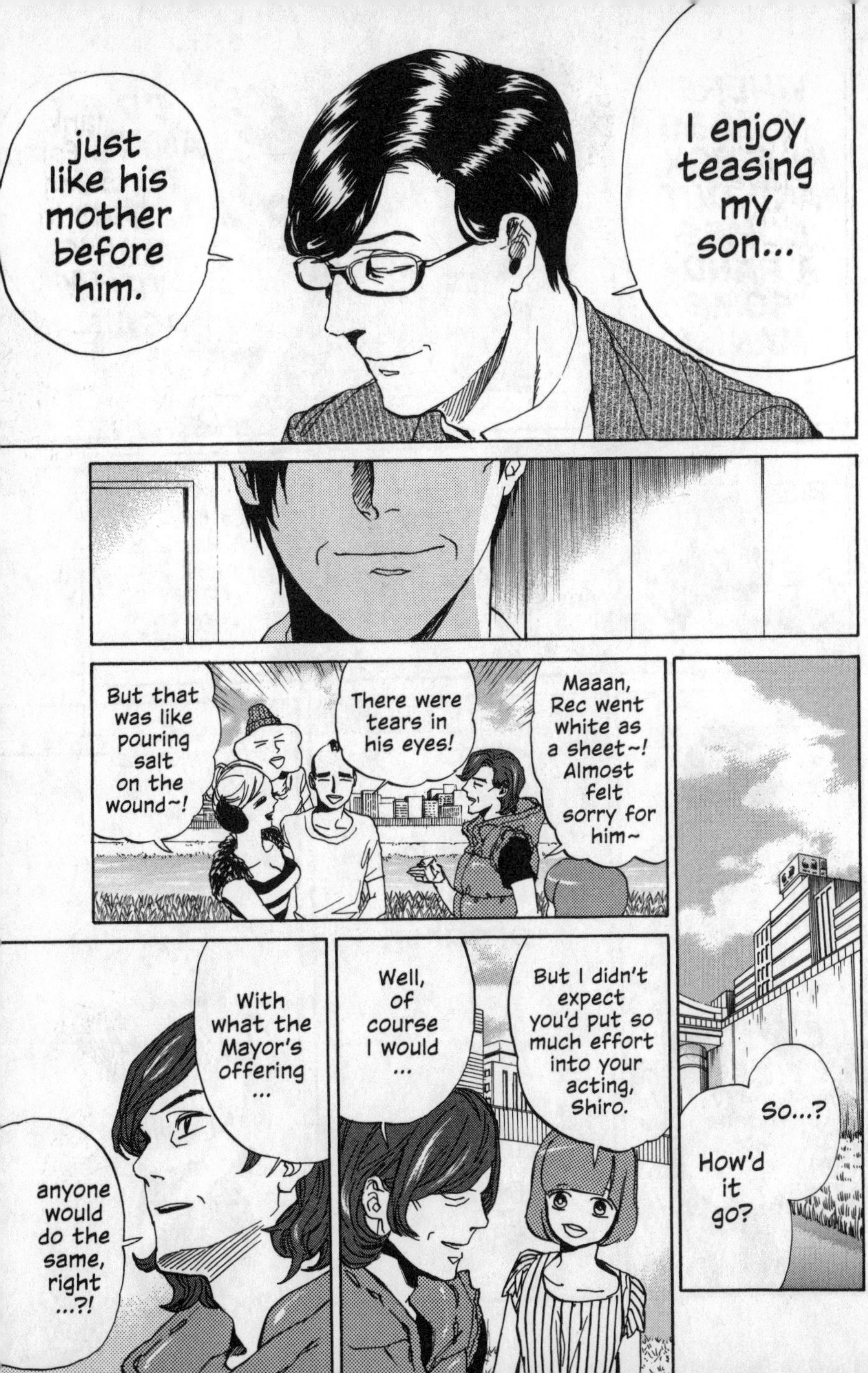
I enjoy teasing my son...
just like his mother before him.
So...?
How'd it go?
Maaan, Rec went white as a sheet~! Almost felt sorry for him~
There were tears in his eyes!
But that was like pouring salt on the wound~!
But I didn't expect you'd put so much effort into your acting, Shiro.
Well, of course I would ...
With what the Mayor's offering ...
anyone would do the same, right ...?!

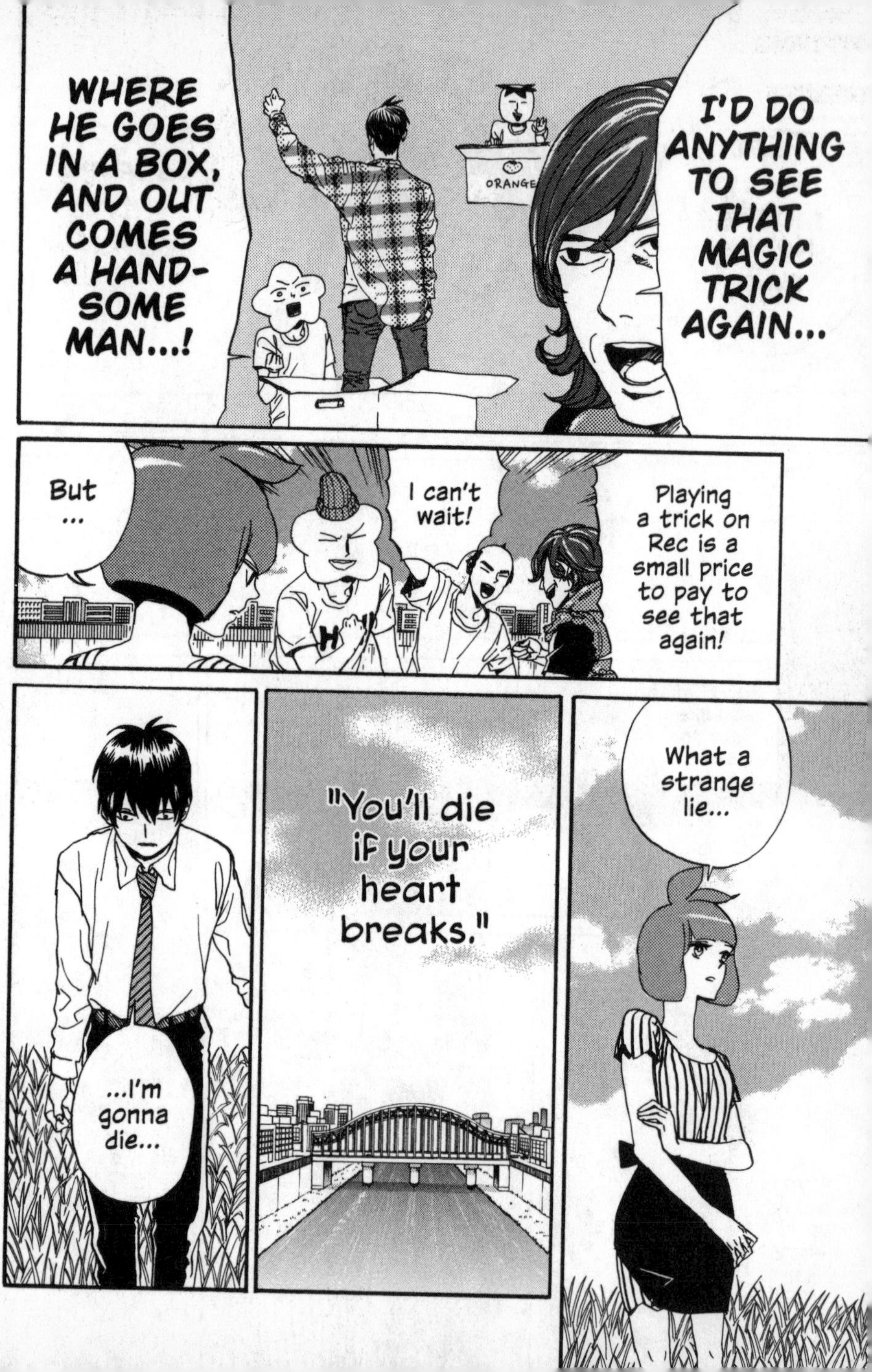
I'D DO ANYTHING TO SEE THAT MAGIC TRICK AGAIN...
ORANGE
WHERE HE GOES IN A BOX, AND OUT COMES A HAND-SOME MAN...!
Playing a trick on Rec is a small price to pay to see that again!
I can't wait!
But ...
What a strange lie...
"You'll die if your heart breaks."
...I'm gonna die...

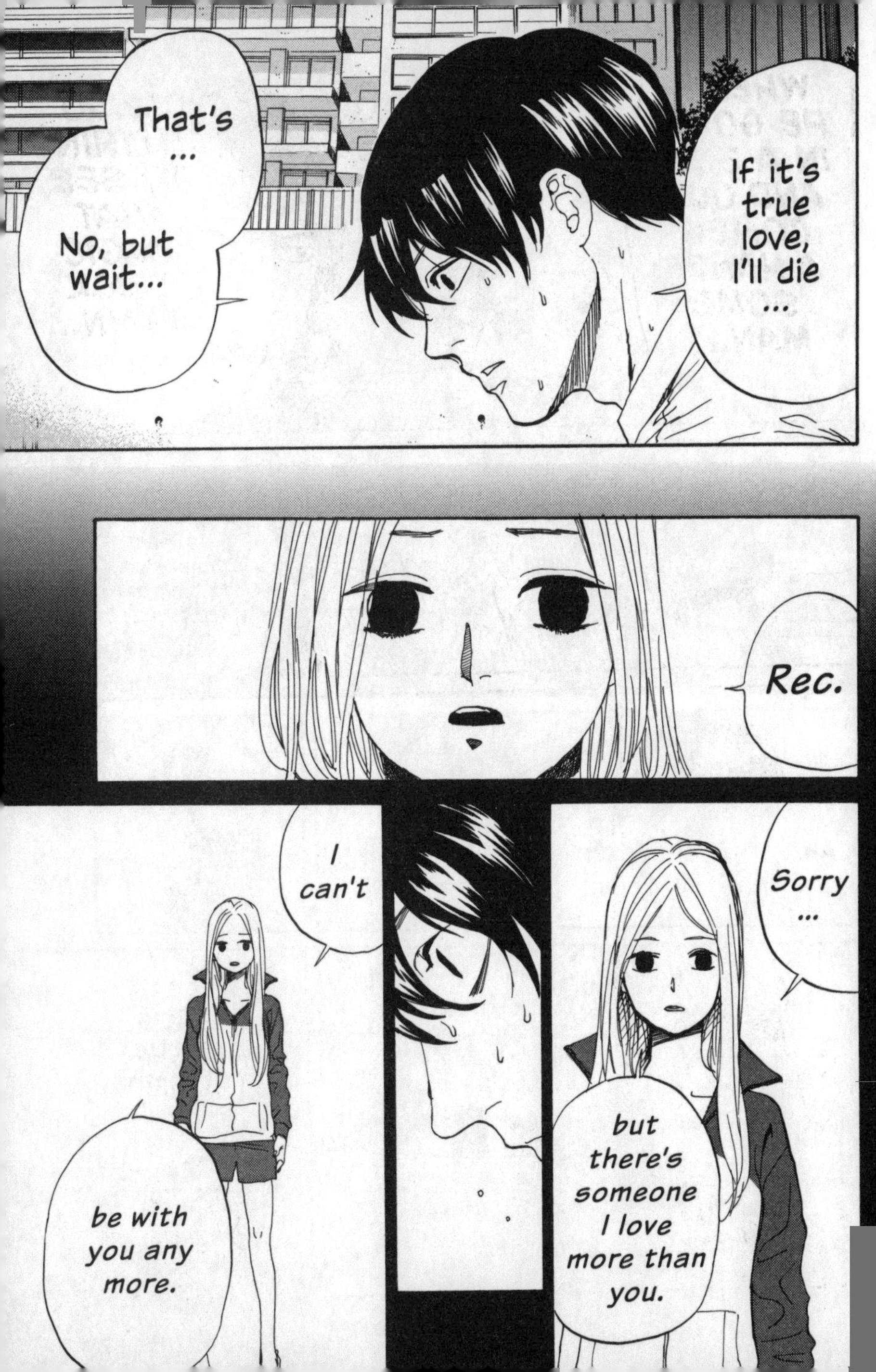
If it's true love, I'll die ...
That's ... No, but wait...
Rec.
Sorry ...
but there's someone I love more than you.
I can't
be with you any more.

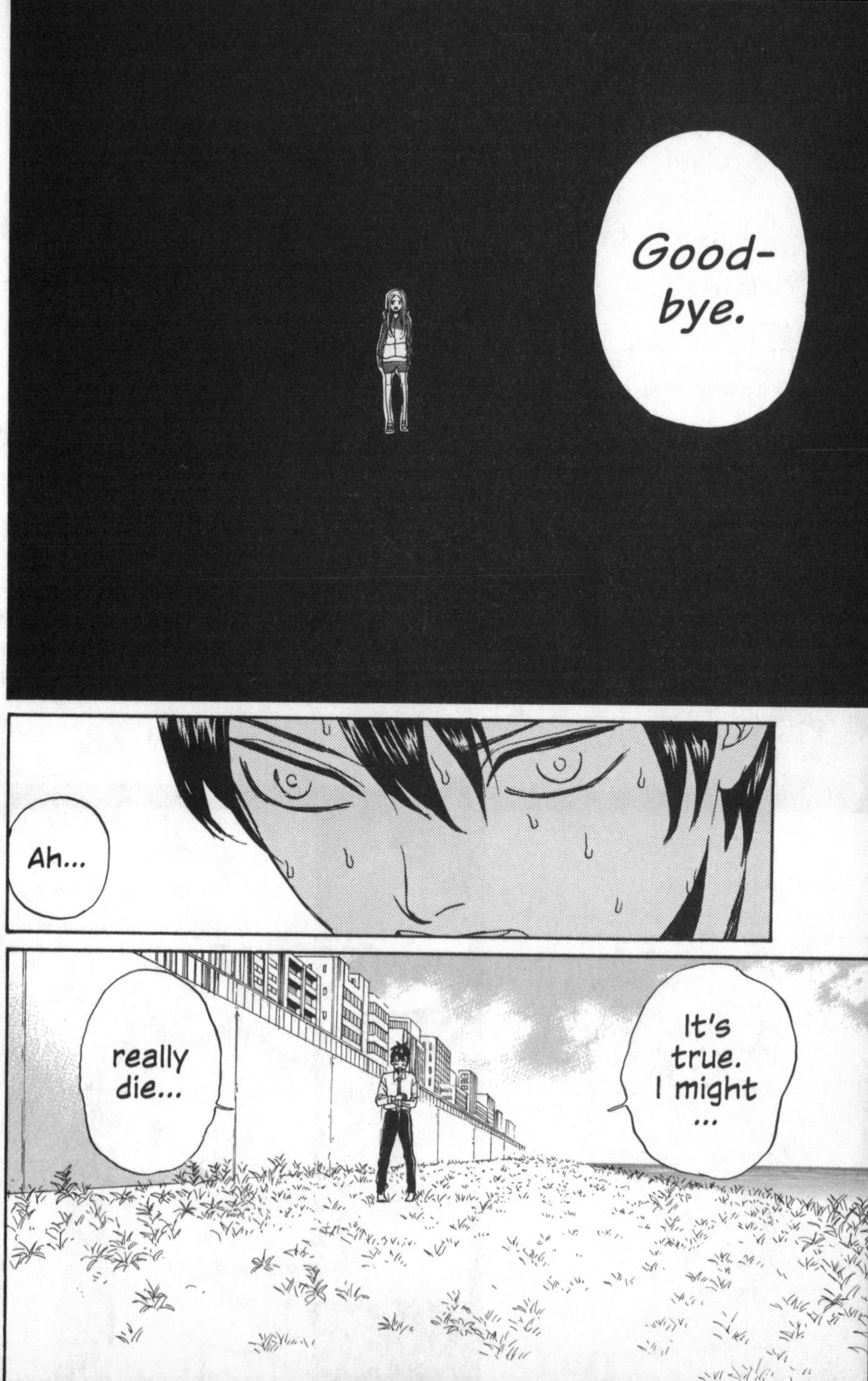
Good-bye.
Ah...
It's true. I might ...
really die...

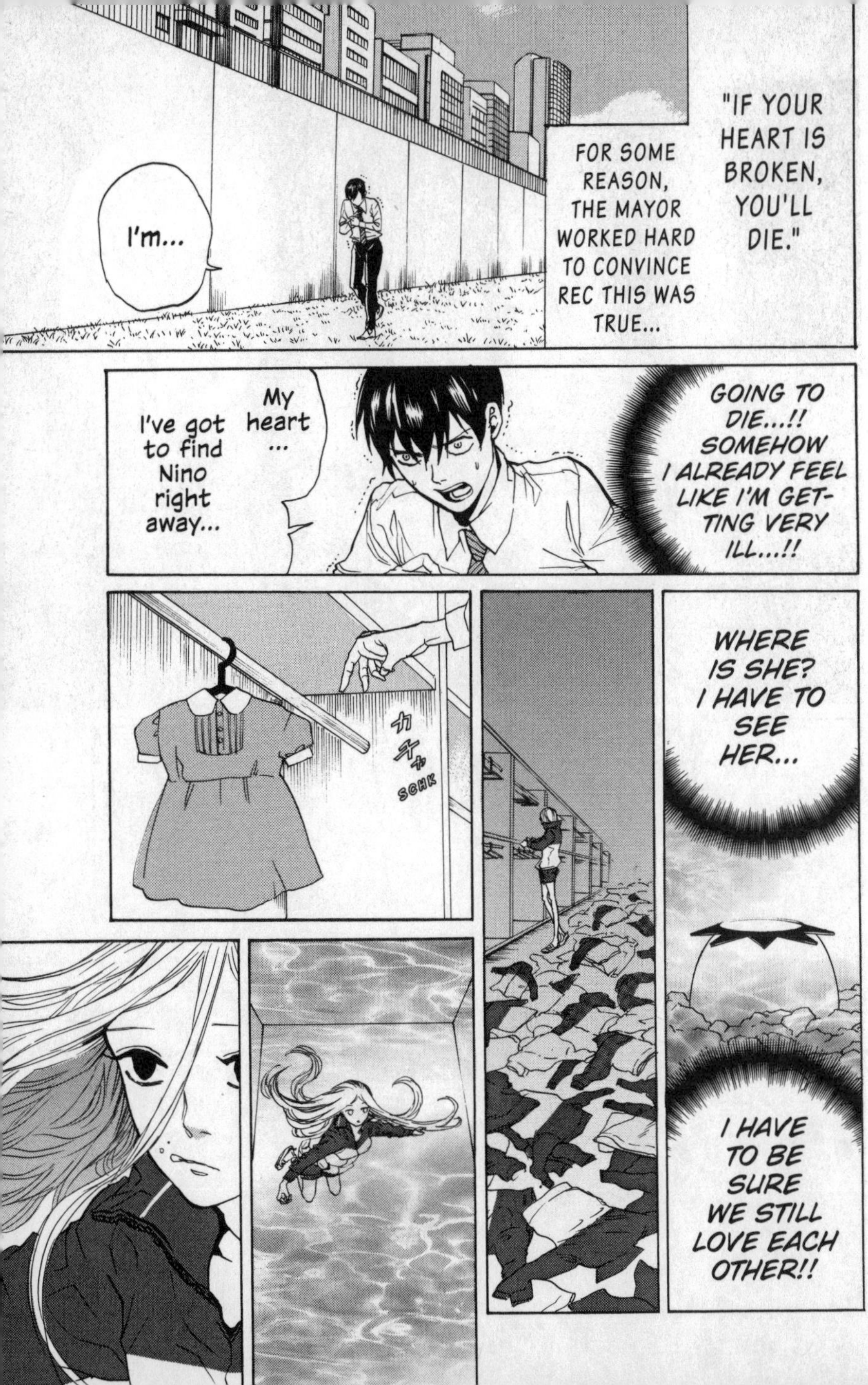
"IF YOUR HEART IS BROKEN, YOU'LL DIE."
FOR SOME REASON, THE MAYOR WORKED HARD TO CONVINCE REC THIS WAS TRUE...
I'm...
GOING TO DIE...!! SOMEHOW I ALREADY FEEL LIKE I'M GETTING VERY ILL...!!
My heart...
I've got to find Nino right away...
WHERE IS SHE? I HAVE TO SEE HER...
I HAVE TO BE SURE WE STILL LOVE EACH OTHER!!
カチャ
SCHK

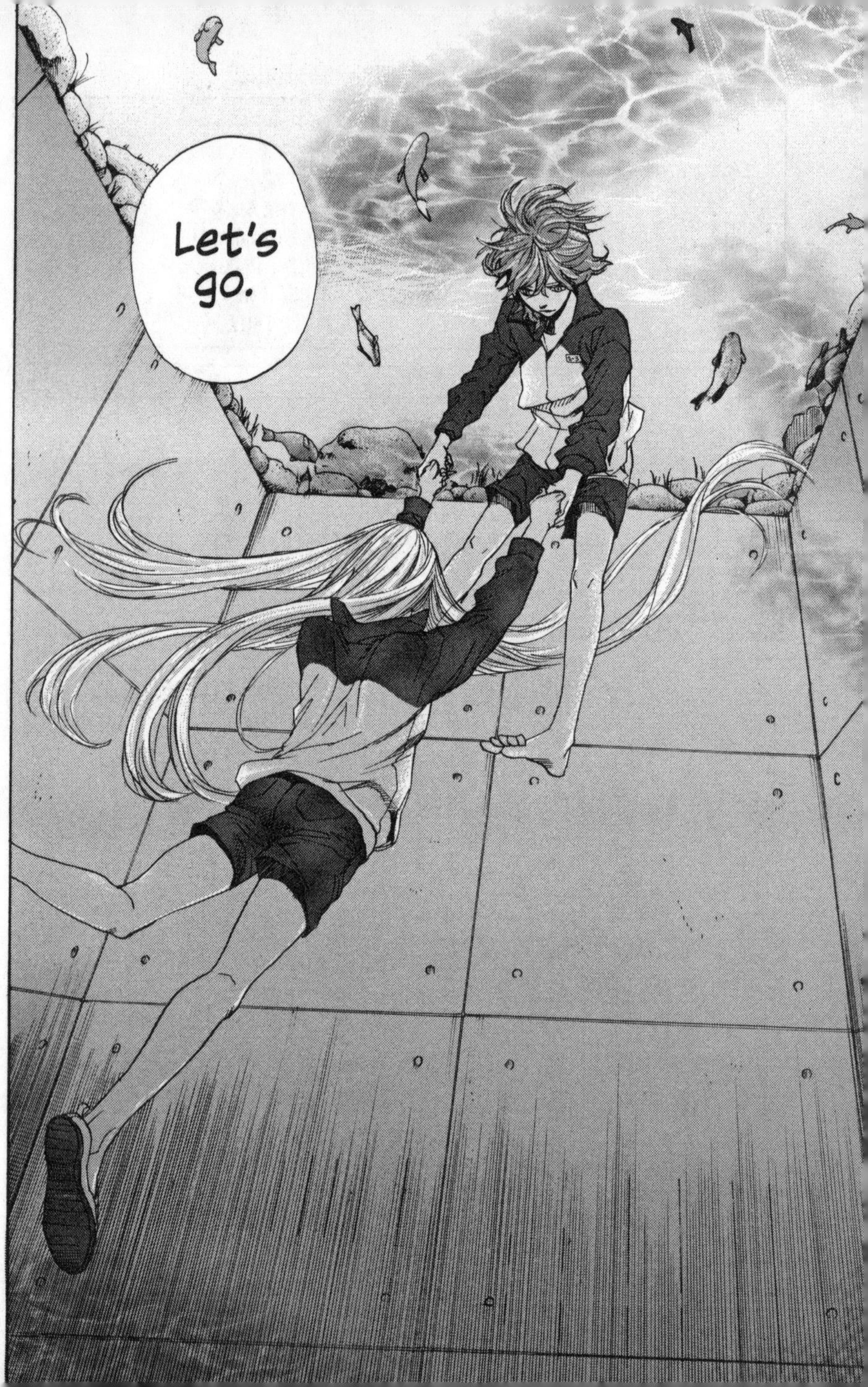
Let's go.

Chapter 392: Spirit, Begone!

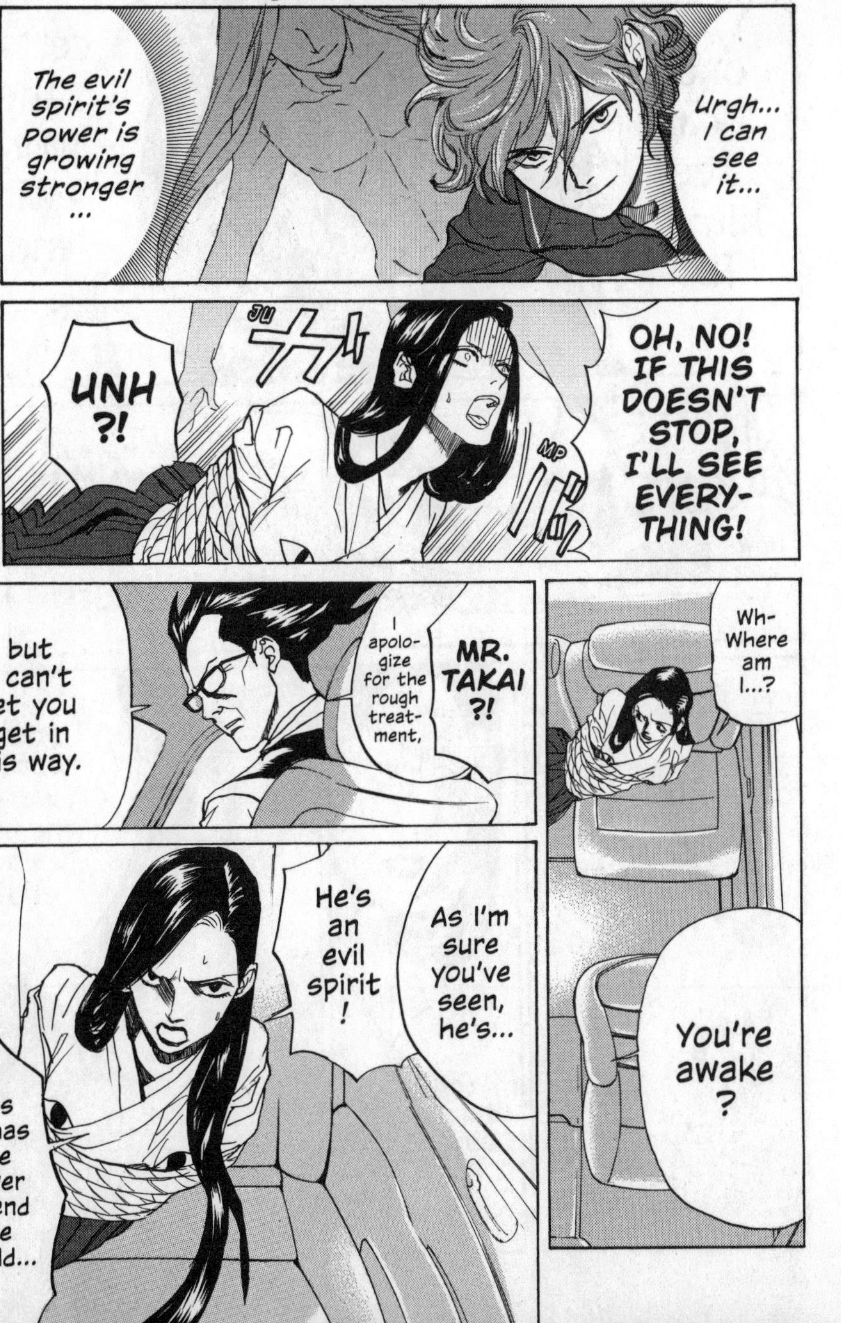
Urgh... I can see it...
The evil spirit's power is growing stronger ...
OH, NO! IF THIS DOESN'T STOP, I'LL SEE EVERYTHING!
MP
JU
UNH ?!
Wh- Where am I...?
You're awake ?
MR. TAKAI ?!
I apologize for the rough treatment,
but I can't let you get in his way.
As I'm sure you've seen, he's...
He's an evil spirit !
Plus he has the power to end the world...

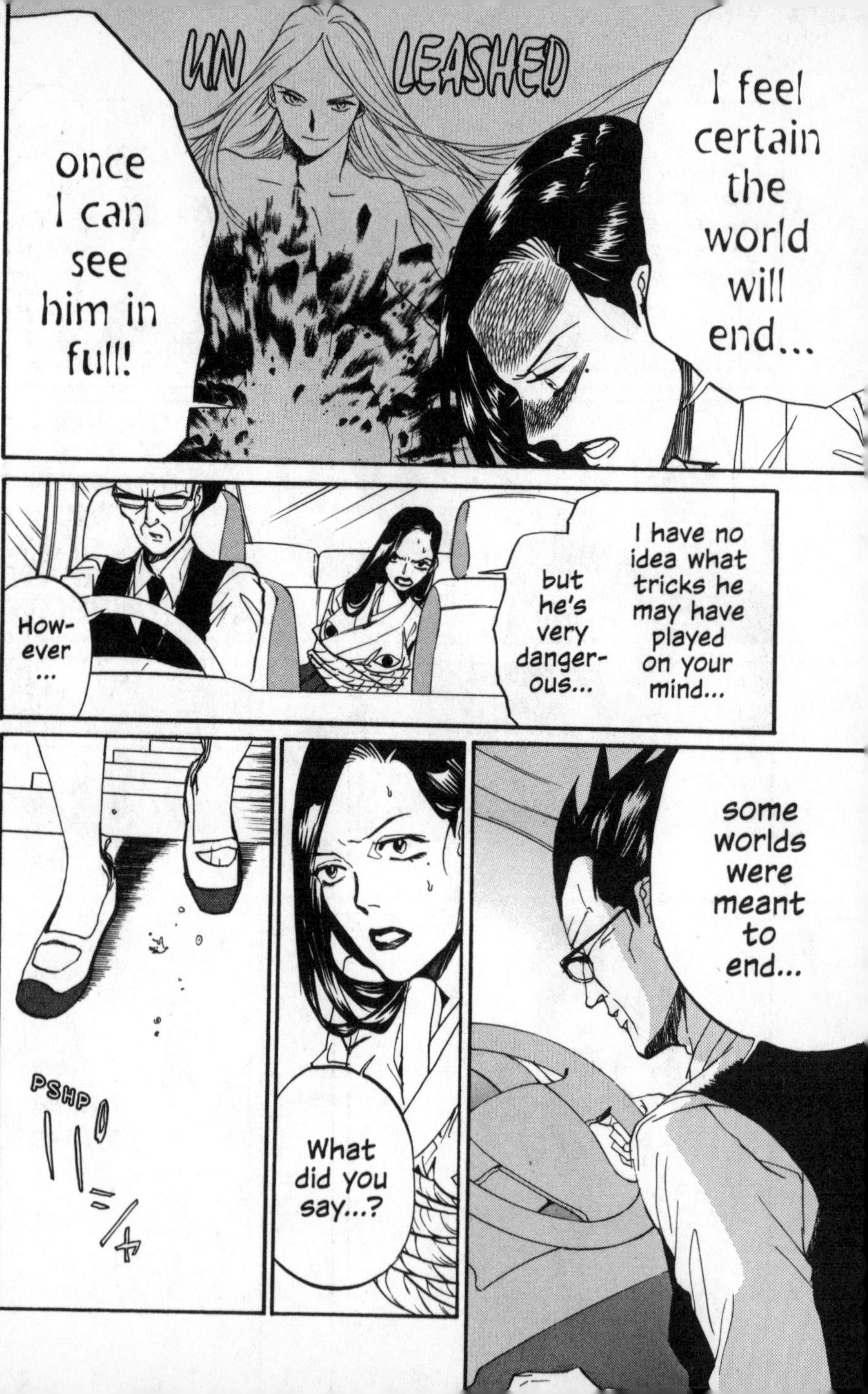
UN LEASHED
I feel certain the world will end...
once I can see him in full!
I have no idea what tricks he may have played on your mind...
but he's very danger-ous...
How-ever ...
some worlds were meant to end...
What did you say...?
PSHP

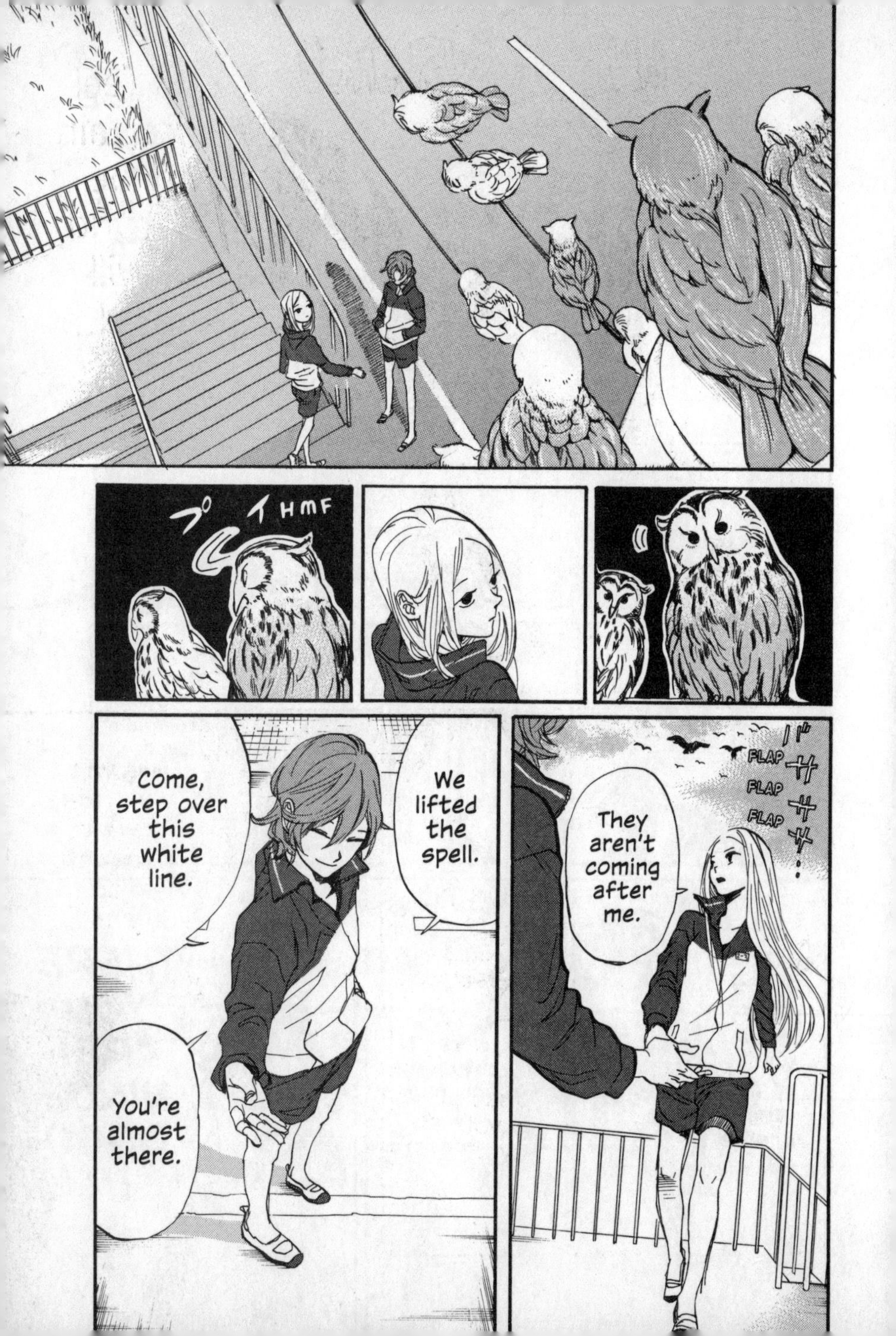

プイ HMF
FLAP
FLAP
FLAP
They aren't coming after me.
We lifted the spell.
Come, step over this white line.
You're almost there.

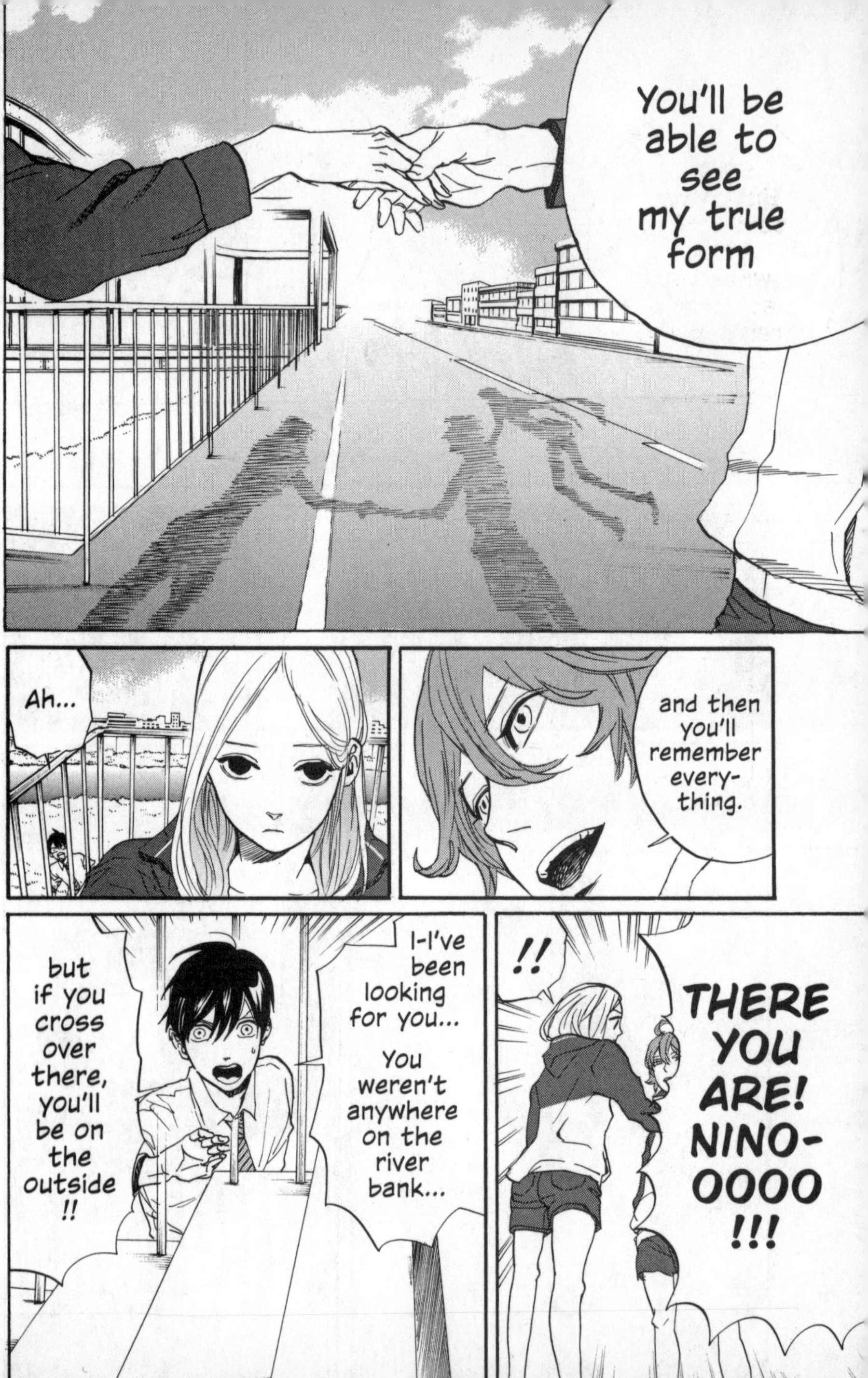
You'll be able to see my true form
and then you'll remember every-thing.
Ah...
!!
THERE YOU ARE! NINO-OOOO !!!
I-I've been looking for you...
You weren't anywhere on the river bank...
but if you cross over there, you'll be on the outside !!

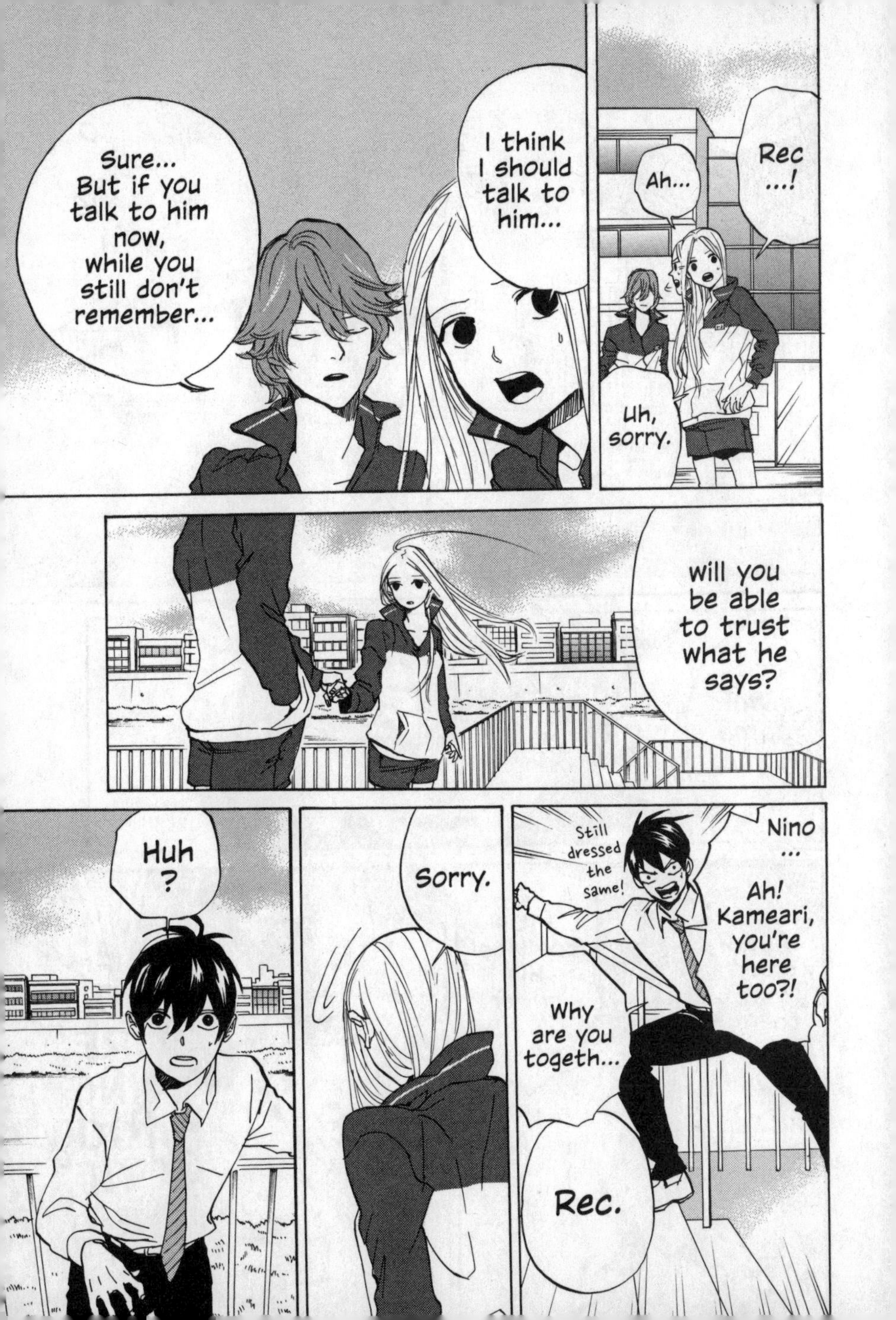
Rec ...!
Ah...
Uh, sorry.
I think I should talk to him...
Sure... But if you talk to him now, while you still don't remember...
will you be able to trust what he says?
Nino ...
Still dressed the same!
Ah! Kameari, you're here too?!
Why are you togeth...
Rec.
Sorry.
Huh ?

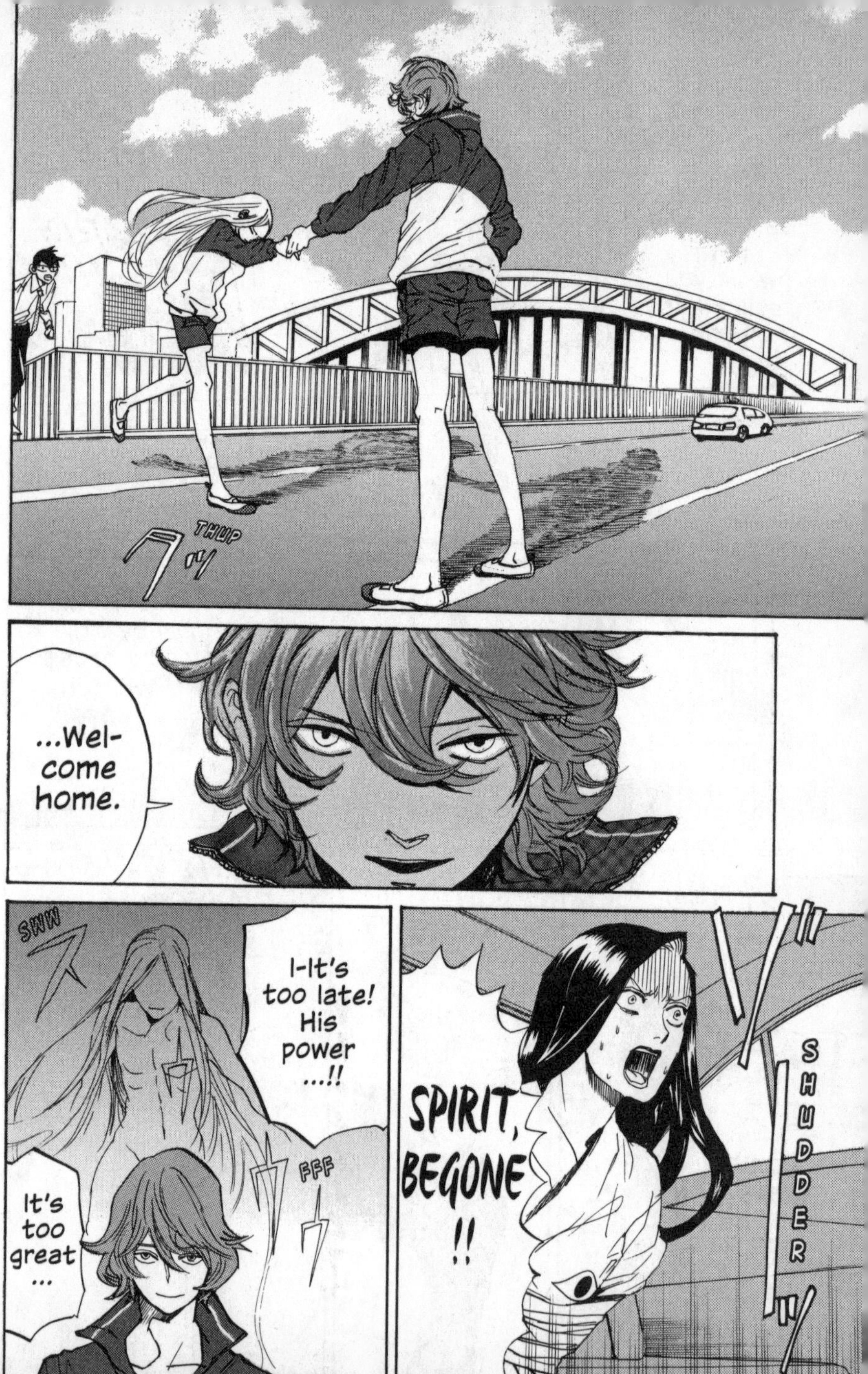
THUP
クッ
...Wel-come home.
SPIRIT, BEGONE!!
SHUDDER
SWW
I-It's too late! His power ...!!
FFF
It's too great ...

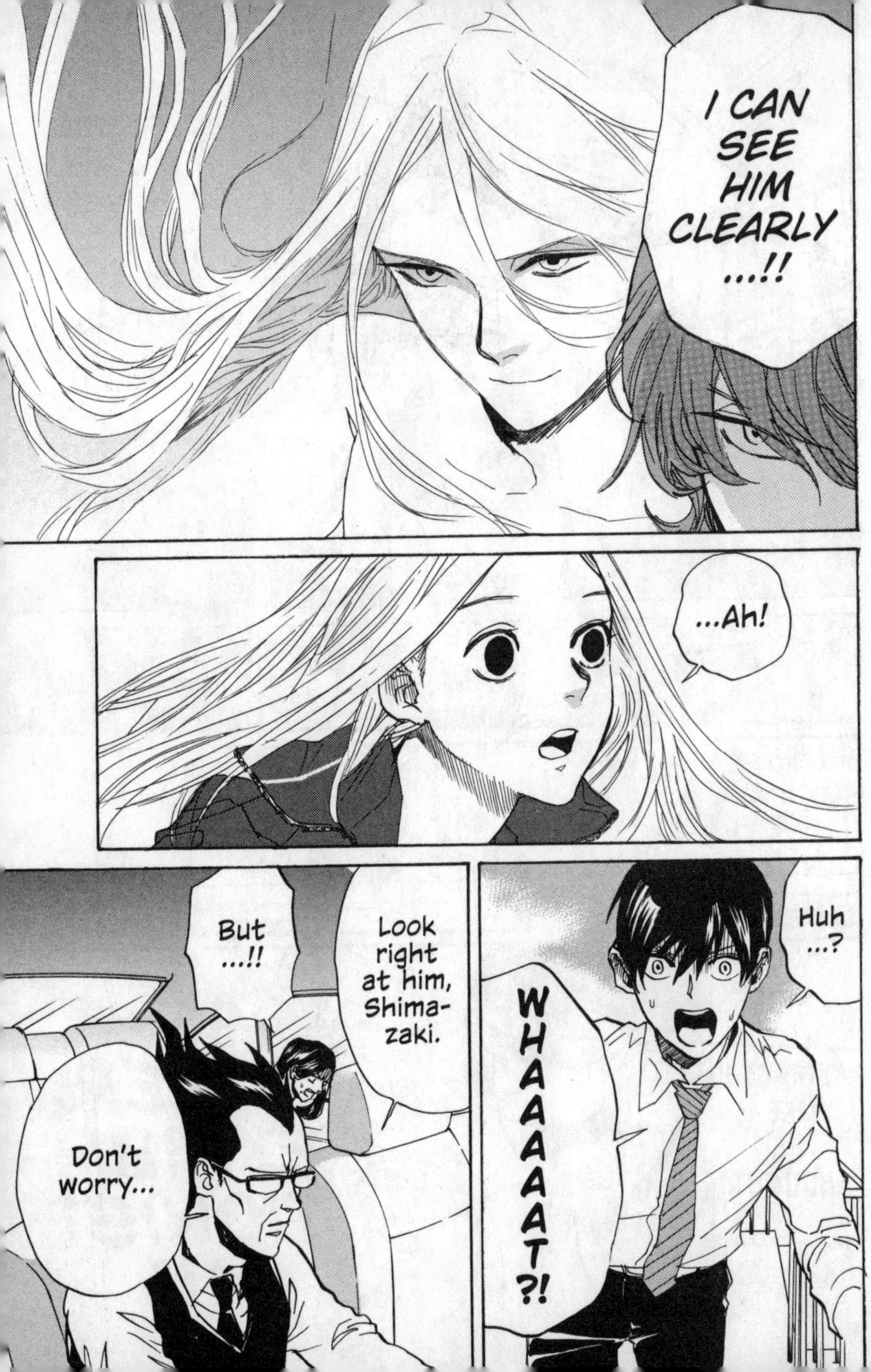
I CAN SEE HIM CLEARLY ...!!
...Ah!
Huh ...?
WHAAAAAT?!
Look right at him, Shimazaki.
But ...!!
Don't worry...

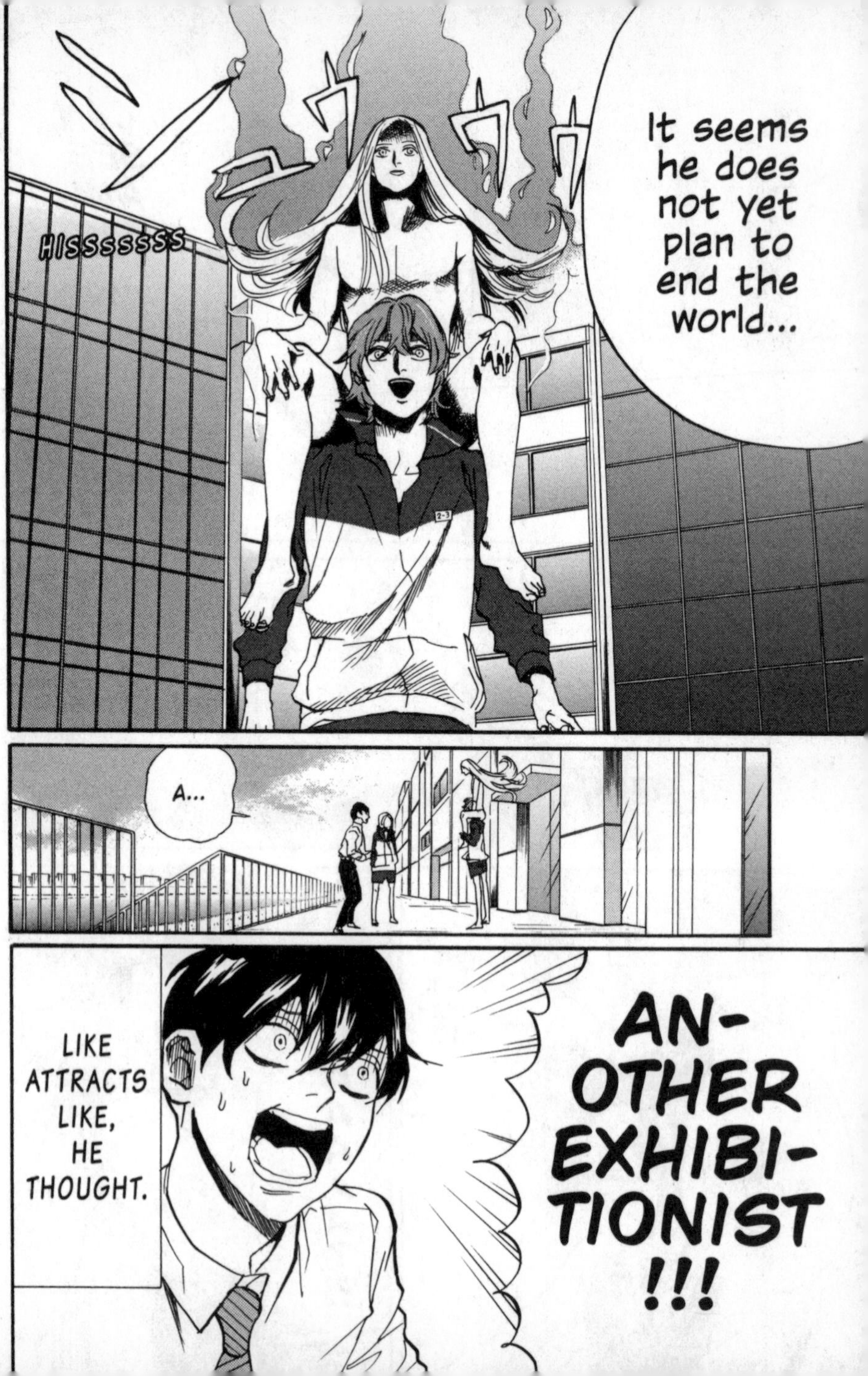
It seems he does not yet plan to end the world...
HISSSSSSS
A...
AN-OTHER EXHIBI-TIONIST!!!
LIKE ATTRACTS LIKE, HE THOUGHT.

Chapter 393: What Are You To Nino?

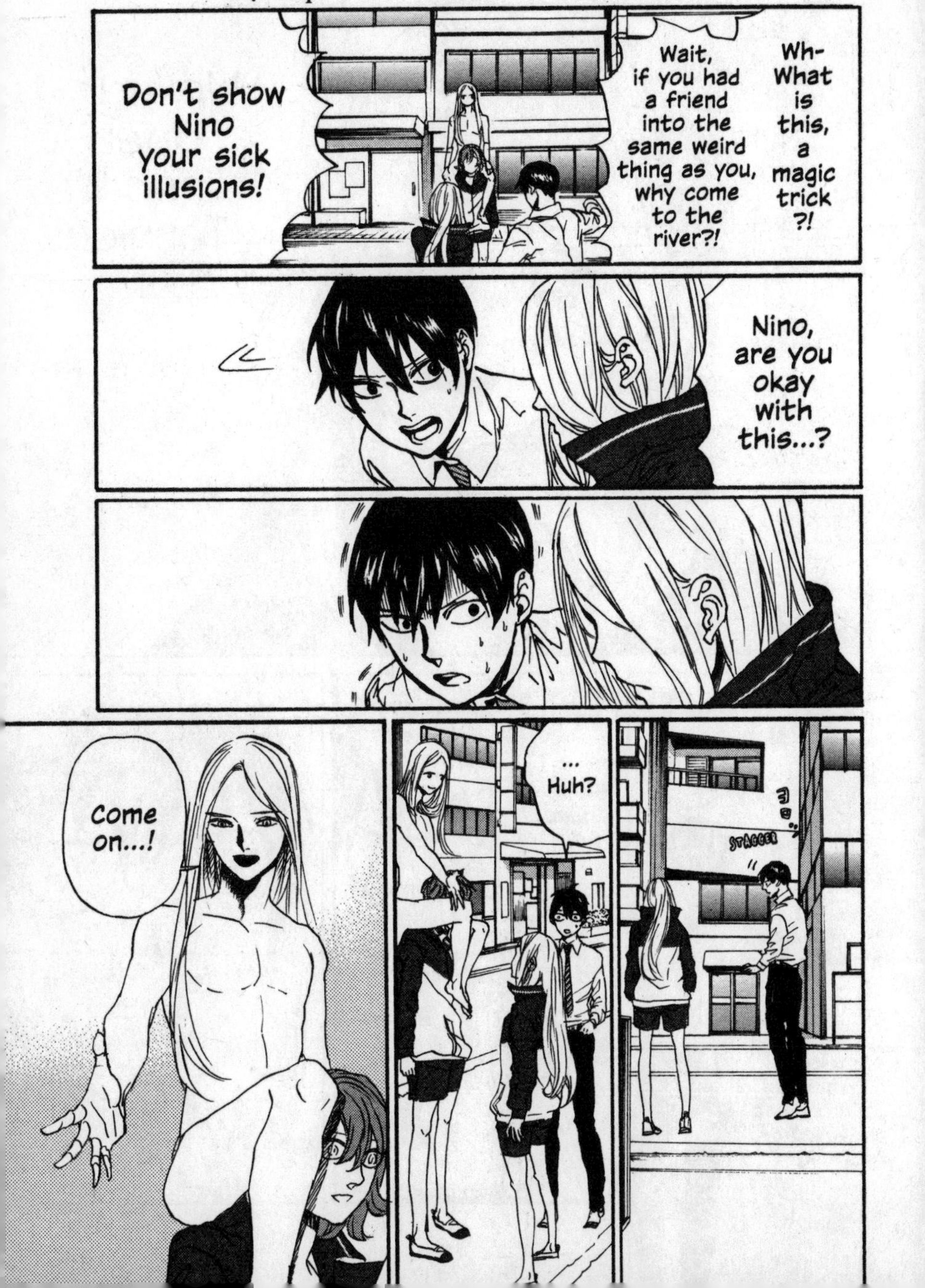
Wh- What is this, a magic trick?!
Wait, if you had a friend into the same weird thing as you, why come to the river?!
Don't show Nino your sick illusions!
Nino, are you okay with this...?
STAGGER
... Huh?
Come on...!

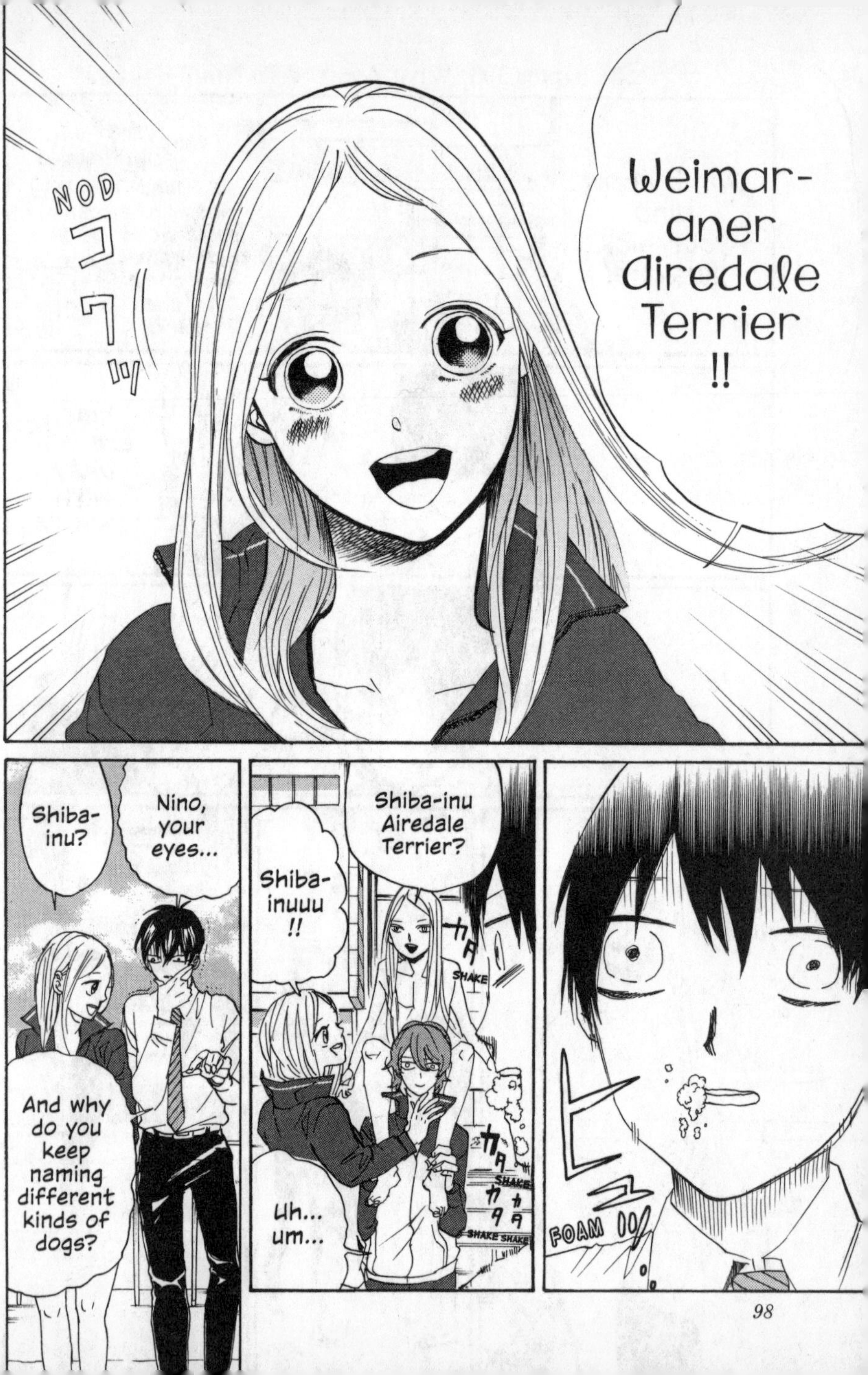
Weimar-aner Airedale Terrier !!
NOD
FOAM
Shiba-inu Airedale Terrier?
Shiba-inuuu !!
SHAKE
SHAKE
SHAKE SHAKE
Uh... um...
Nino, your eyes...
Shiba-inu?
And why do you keep naming different kinds of dogs?

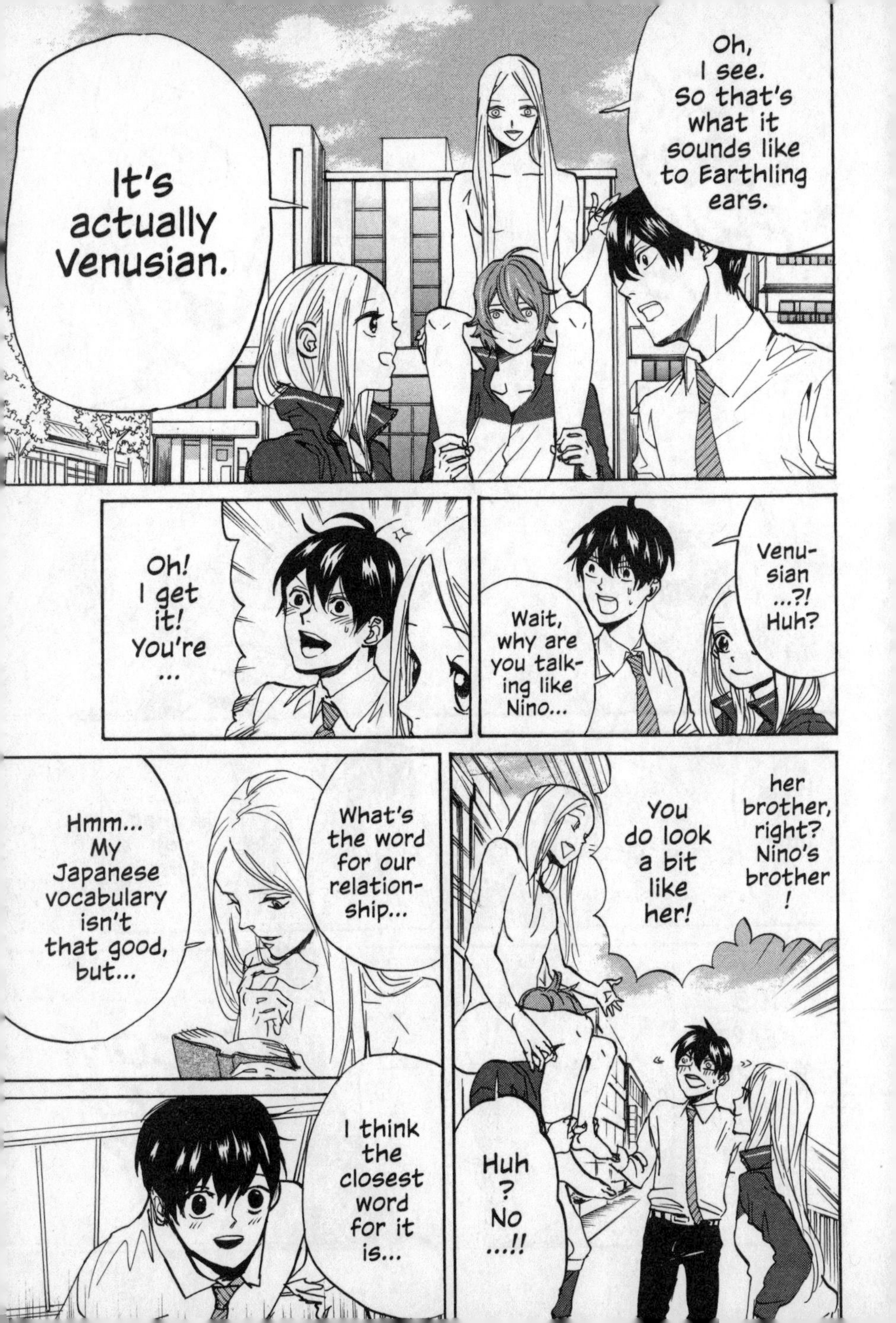

Oh, I see. So that's what it sounds like to Earthling ears.
It's actually Venusian.
Venu-sian ...?! Huh?
Wait, why are you talk-ing like Nino...
Oh! I get it! You're ...
her brother, right? Nino's brother!
You do look a bit like her!
Huh? No ...!!
What's the word for our relation-ship...
Hmm... My Japanese vocabulary isn't that good, but...
I think the closest word for it is...

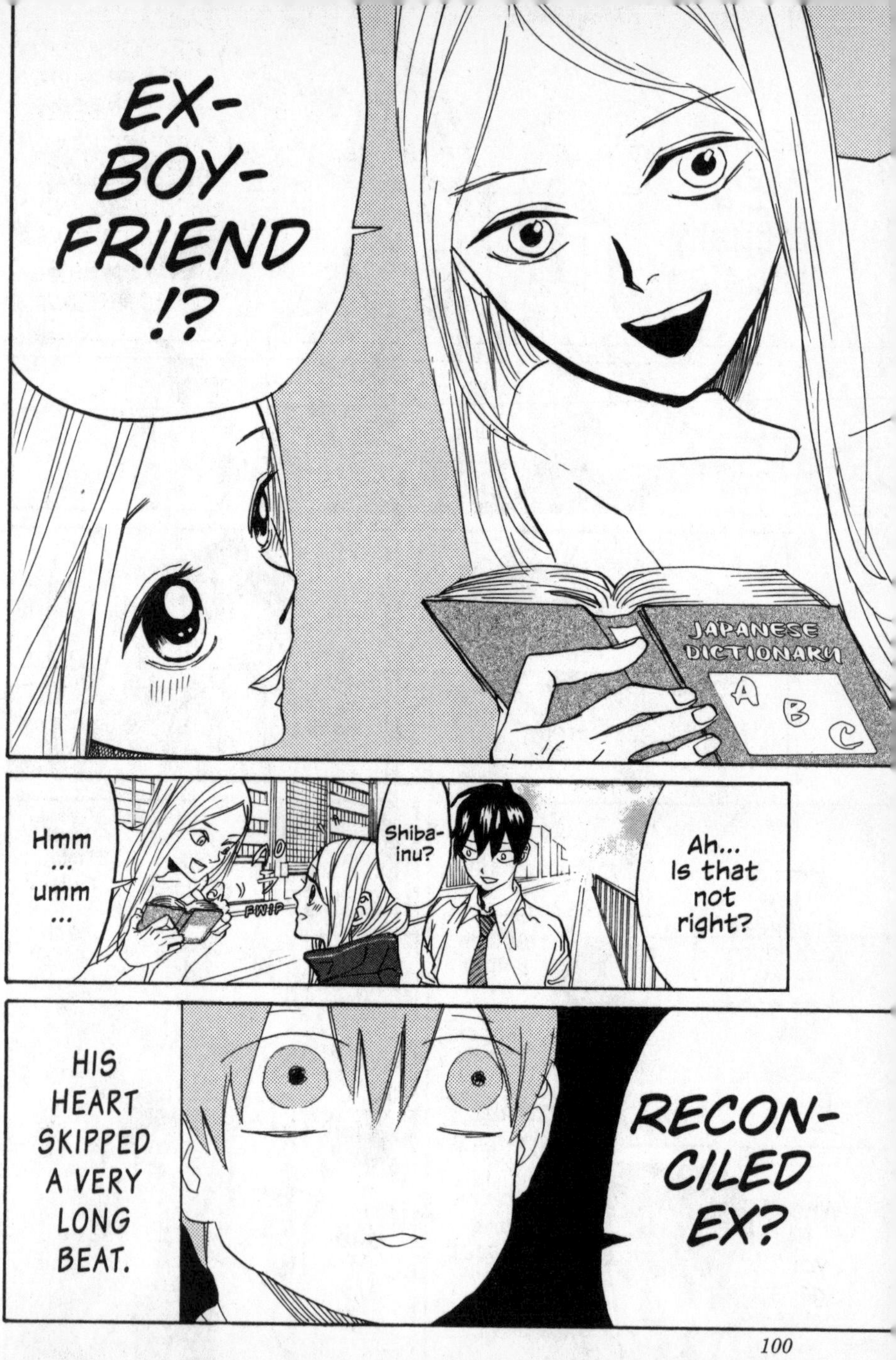
EX-BOY-FRIEND!?
JAPANESE DICTIONARY
A B C
Ah... Is that not right?
Shiba-inu?
Hmm... umm...
FWIP
RECON-CILED EX?
HIS HEART SKIPPED A VERY LONG BEAT.

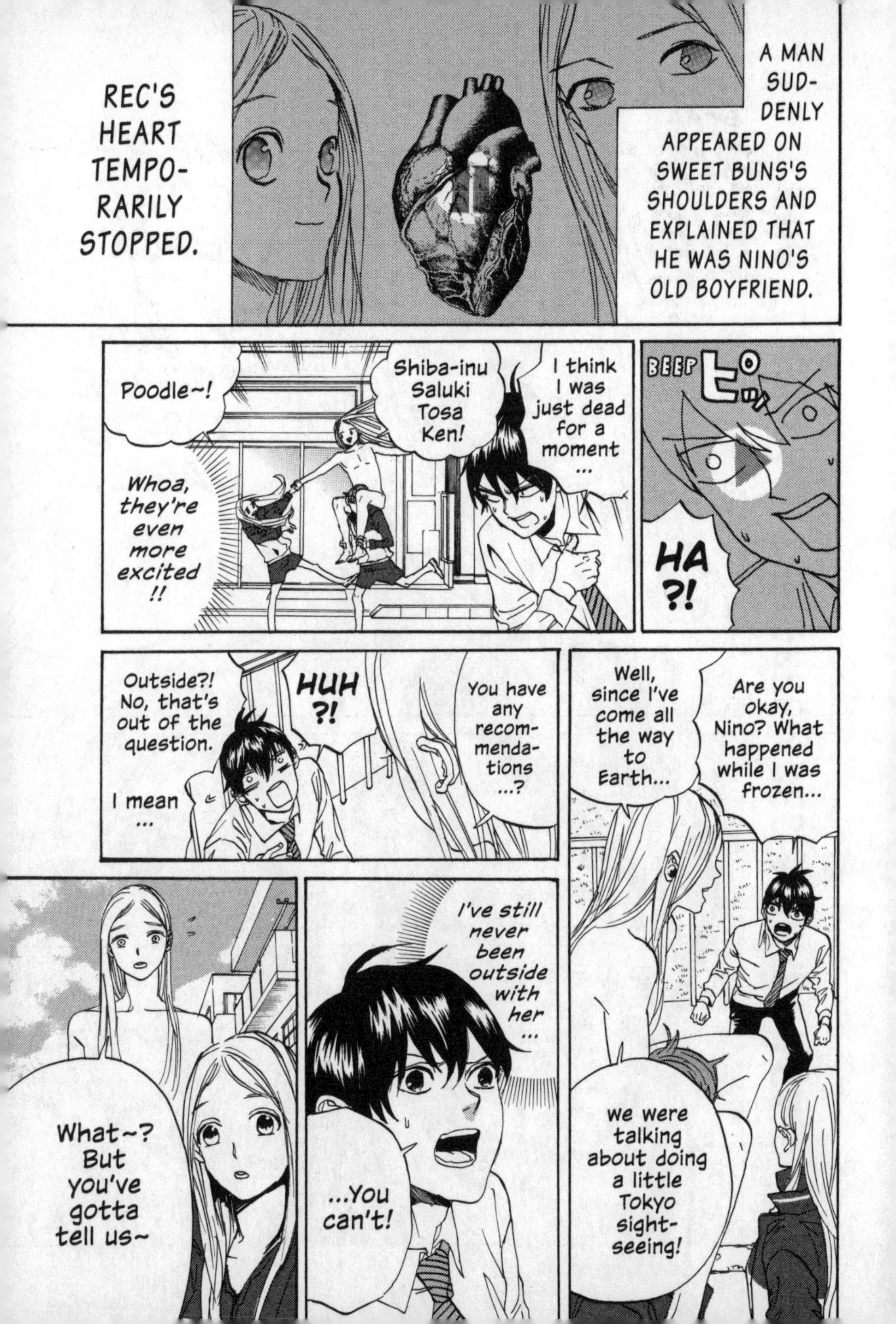
A MAN SUDDENLY APPEARED ON SWEET BUNS'S SHOULDERS AND EXPLAINED THAT HE WAS NINO'S OLD BOYFRIEND.
REC'S HEART TEMPORARILY STOPPED.
BEEP
HA ?!
I think I was just dead for a moment ...
Shiba-inu Saluki Tosa Ken!
Poodle~!
Whoa, they're even more excited !!
Are you okay, Nino? What happened while I was frozen...
Well, since I've come all the way to Earth...
we were talking about doing a little Tokyo sightseeing!
You have any recommendations ...?
HUH ?!
Outside?! No, that's out of the question.
I mean ...
I've still never been outside with her ...
...You can't!
What~? But you've gotta tell us~

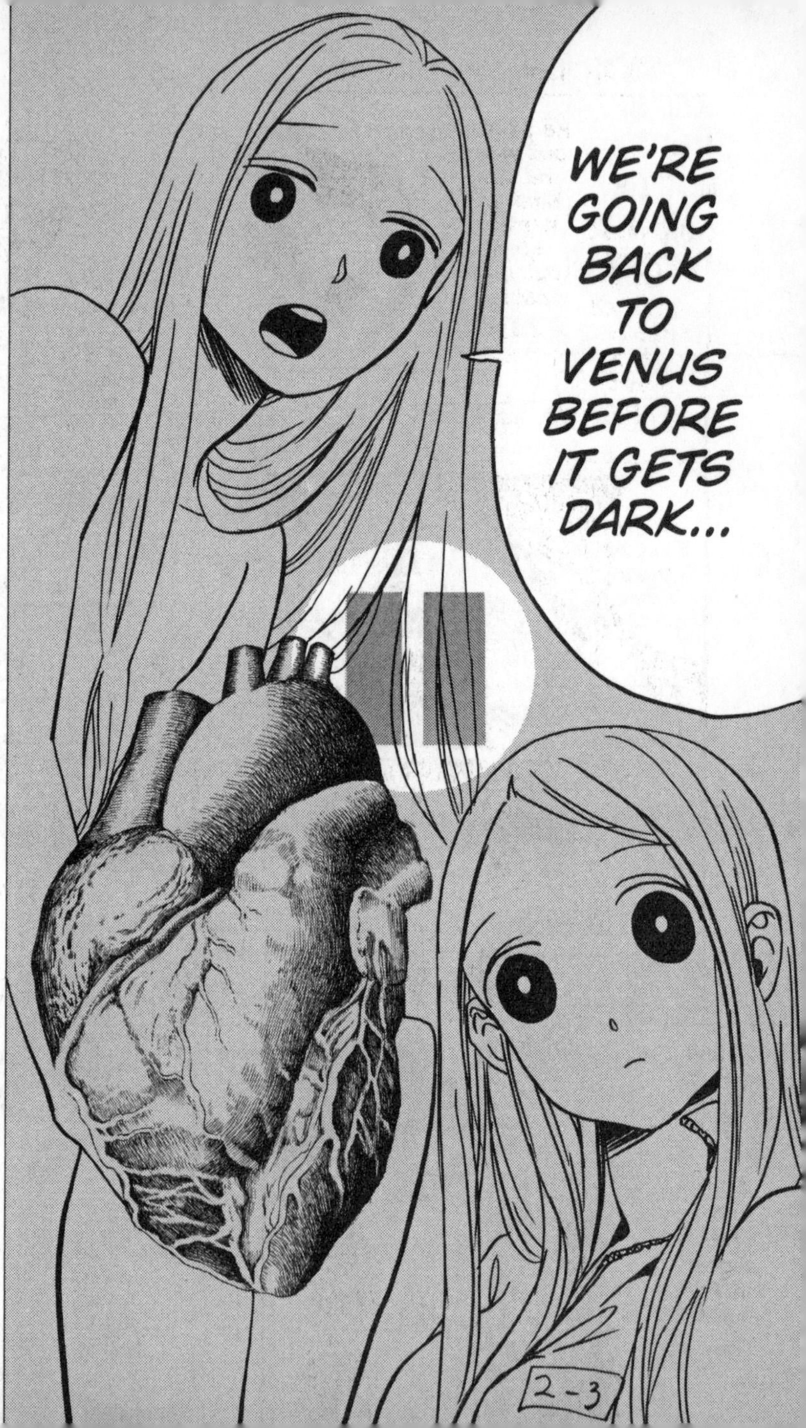

THIS TEMPORARILY STOPPED REC'S HEART AGAIN.

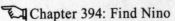

Chapter 394: Find Nino

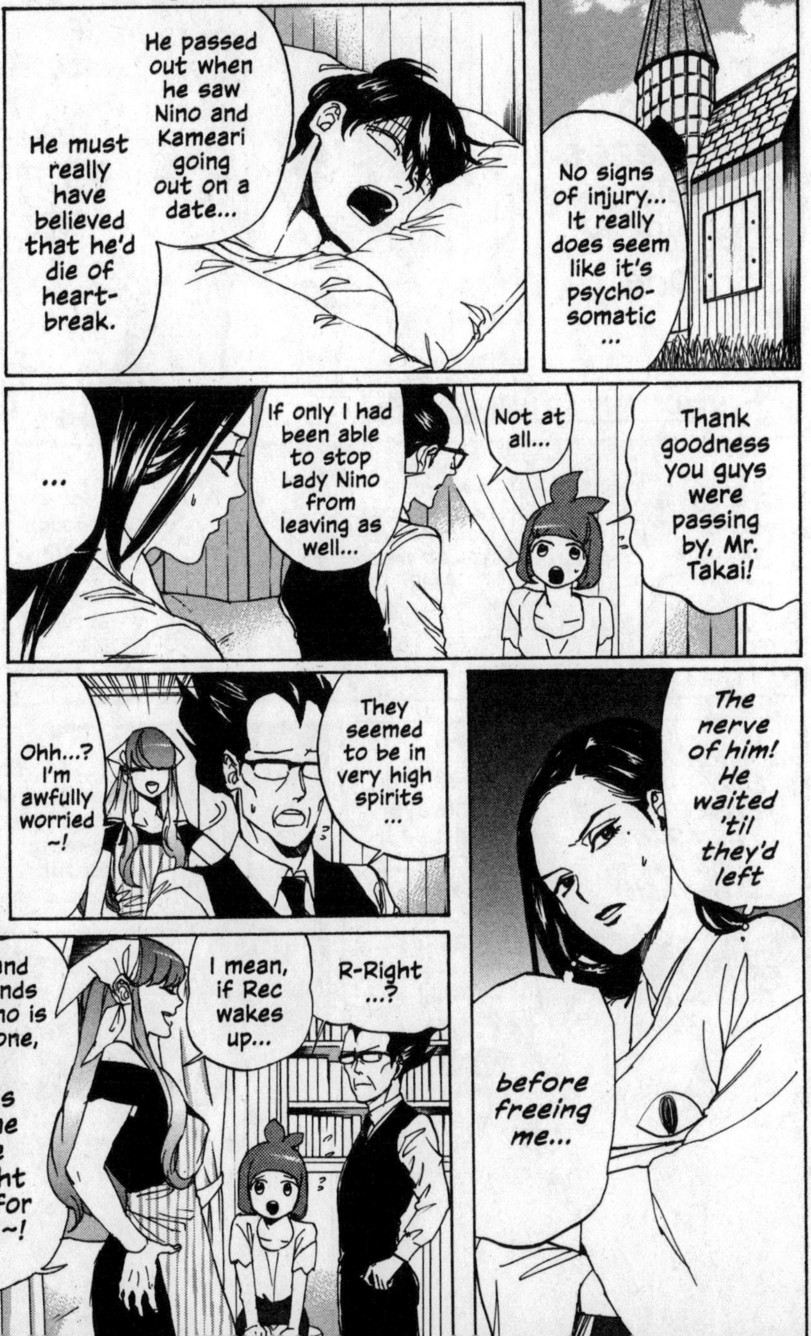
No signs of injury... It really does seem like it's psycho-somatic ...
He passed out when he saw Nino and Kameari going out on a date...
He must really have believed that he'd die of heart-break.
Thank goodness you guys were passing by, Mr. Takai!
Not at all...
If only I had been able to stop Lady Nino from leaving as well...
...
The nerve of him! He waited 'til they'd left
before freeing me...
They seemed to be in very high spirits ...
Ohh...? I'm awfully worried ~!
I mean, if Rec wakes up...
and finds Nino is gone,
this time he might die for real~!
R-Right ...?

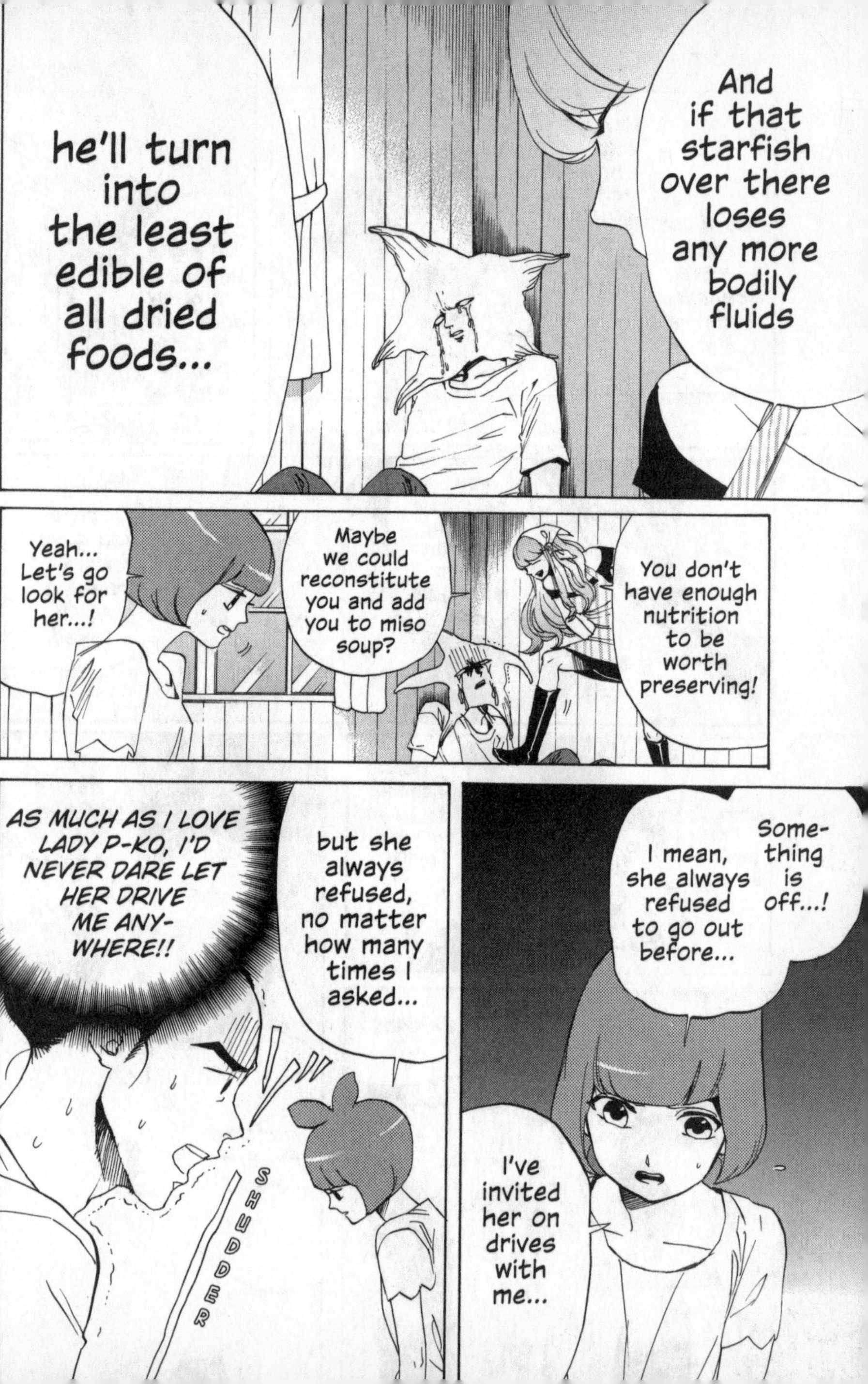
And if that starfish over there loses any more bodily fluids
he'll turn into the least edible of all dried foods...
You don't have enough nutrition to be worth preserving!
Maybe we could reconstitute you and add you to miso soup?
Yeah... Let's go look for her...!
Something is off...!
I mean, she always refused to go out before...
I've invited her on drives with me...
but she always refused, no matter how many times I asked...
AS MUCH AS I LOVE LADY P-KO, I'D NEVER DARE LET HER DRIVE ME ANY-WHERE!!
SHUDDER

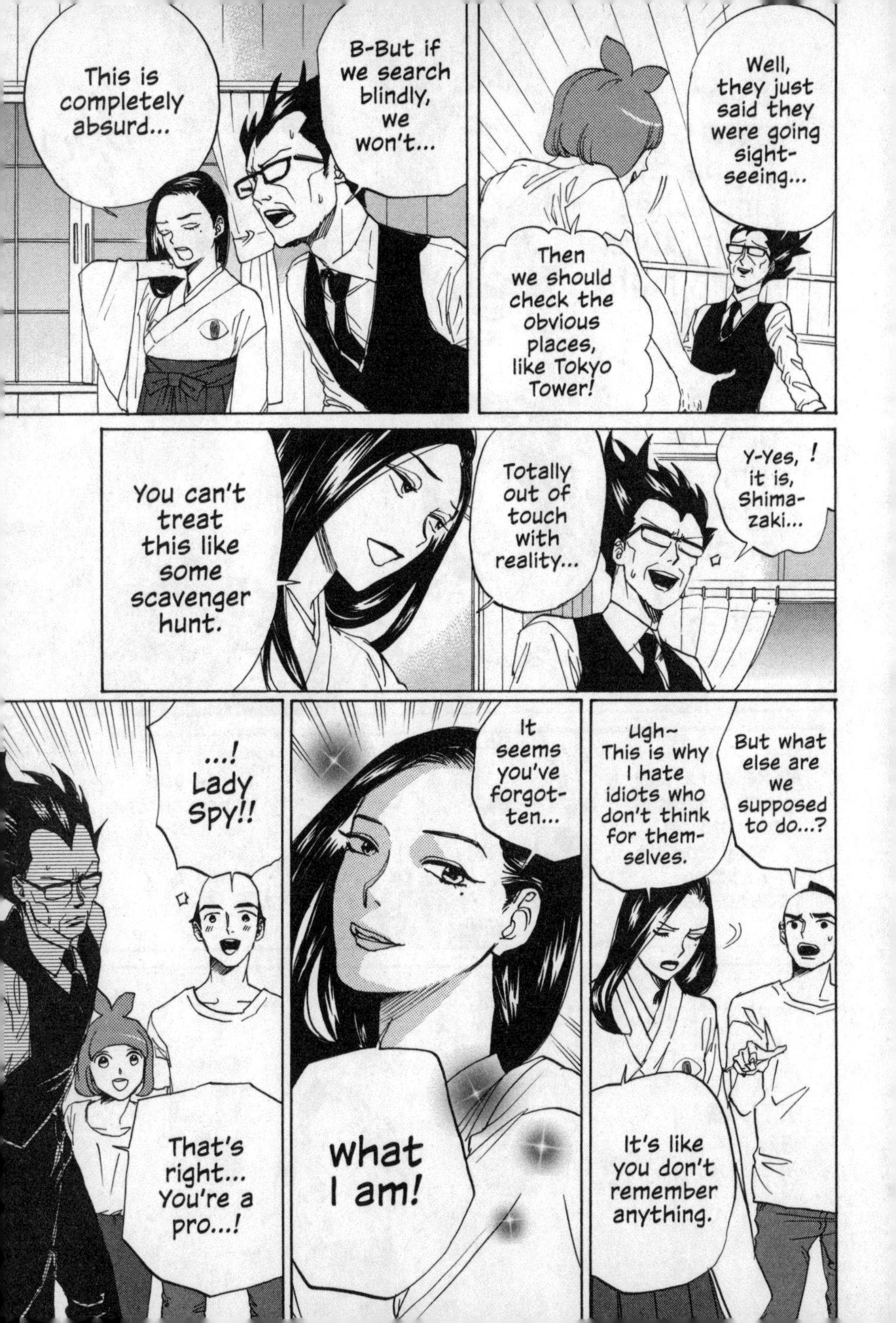
Well, they just said they were going sight-seeing...
Then we should check the obvious places, like Tokyo Tower!
B-But if we search blindly, we won't...
This is completely absurd...
Y-Yes, it is, Shima-zaki...
Totally out of touch with reality...
You can't treat this like some scavenger hunt.
But what else are we supposed to do...?
Ugh~ This is why I hate idiots who don't think for them-selves.
It's like you don't remember anything.
It seems you've forgot-ten...
what I am!
...! Lady Spy!!
That's right... You're a pro...!

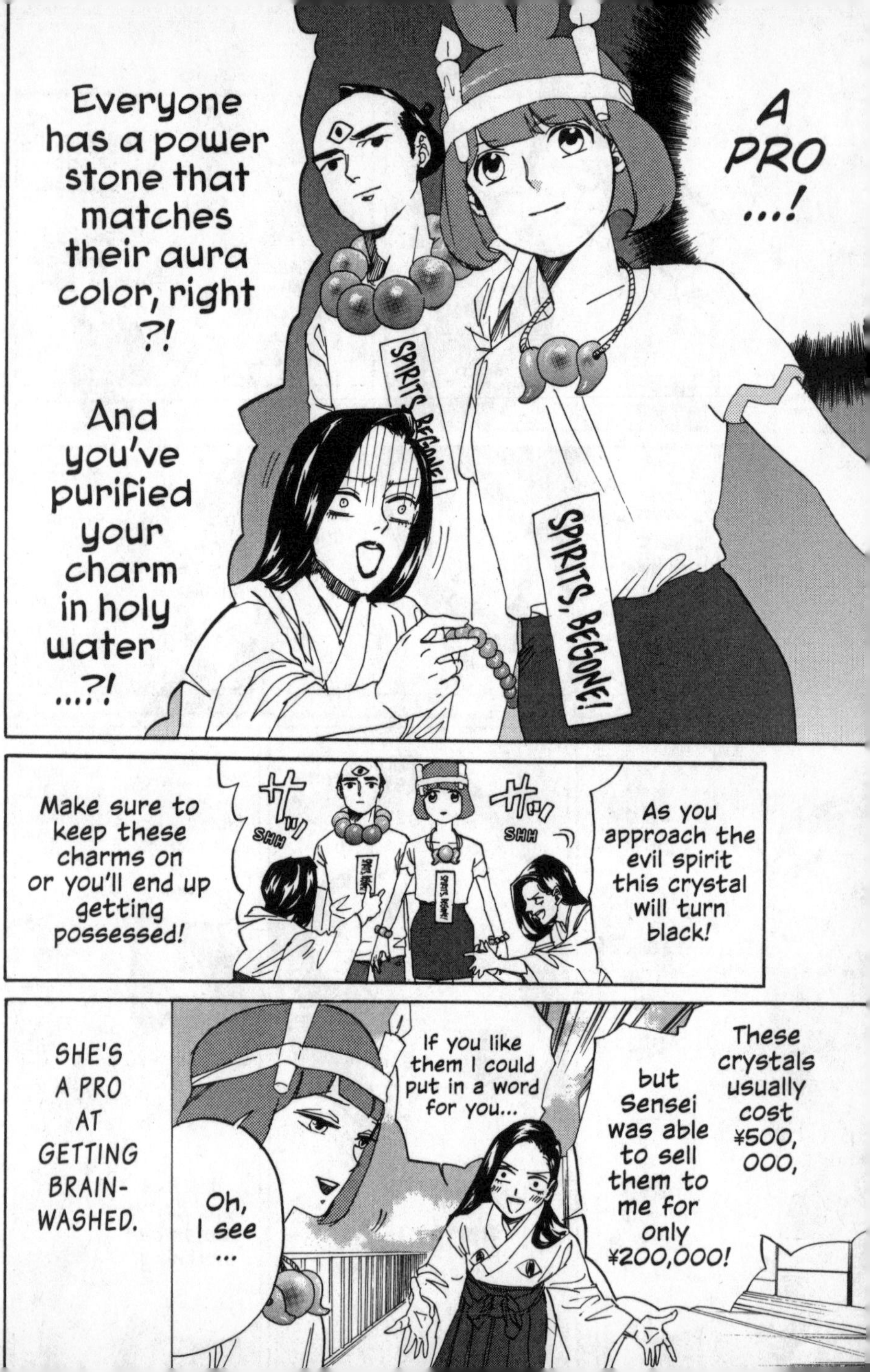
A PRO ...!
Everyone has a power stone that matches their aura color, right ?!
SPIRITS, BEGONE!
SPIRITS, BEGONE!
And you've purified your charm in holy water ...?!
As you approach the evil spirit this crystal will turn black!
SHH
SHH
Make sure to keep these charms on or you'll end up getting possessed!
These crystals usually cost ¥500, 000,
but Sensei was able to sell them to me for only ¥200,000!
If you like them I could put in a word for you...
Oh, I see ...
SHE'S A PRO AT GETTING BRAIN-WASHED.

Chapter 395: Where She Wants To Go

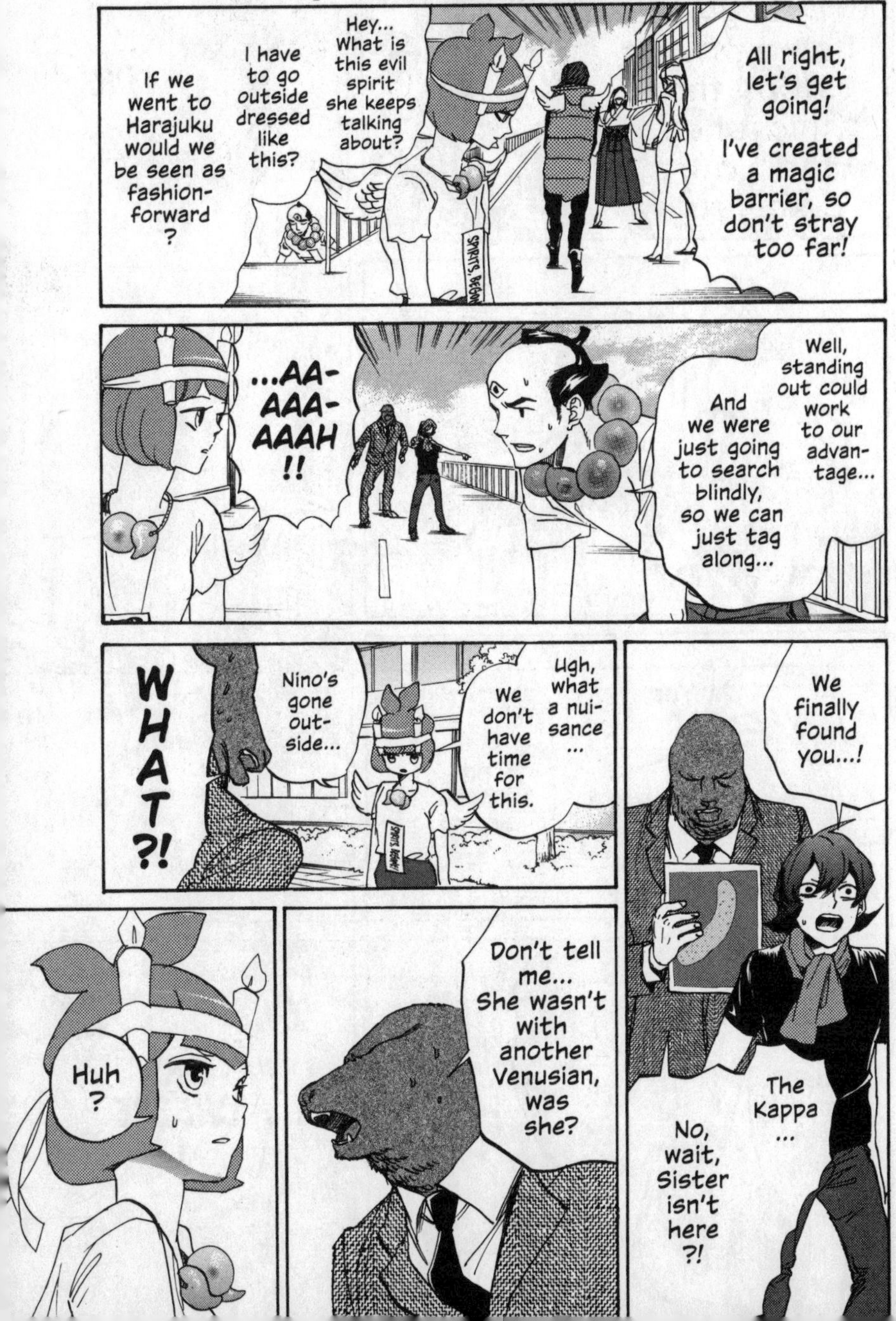
All right, let's get going!
I've created a magic barrier, so don't stray too far!
Hey... What is this evil spirit she keeps talking about?
I have to go outside dressed like this?
If we went to Harajuku would we be seen as fashion-forward?
Well, standing out could work to our advantage...
And we were just going to search blindly, so we can just tag along...
...AA-AAA-AAAH!!
We finally found you...!
The Kappa...
No, wait, Sister isn't here?!
Ugh, what a nui-sance...
We don't have time for this.
Nino's gone out-side...
WHAT?!
Don't tell me... She wasn't with another Venusian, was she?
Huh?

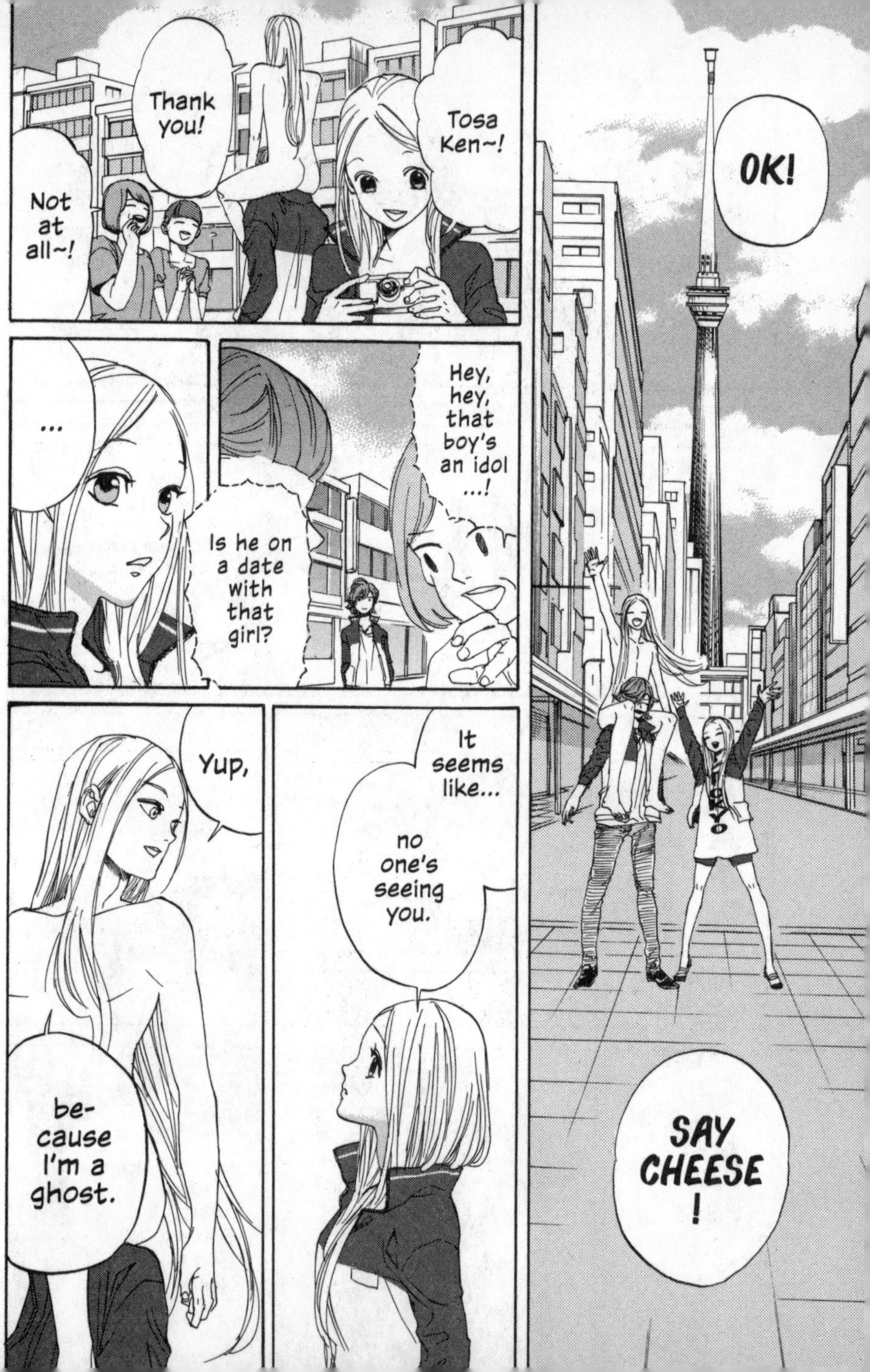
OK!
SAY CHEESE !
Tosa Ken~!
Thank you!
Not at all~!
Hey, hey, that boy's an idol ...!
Is he on a date with that girl?
...
It seems like...
no one's seeing you.
Yup,
be-cause I'm a ghost.

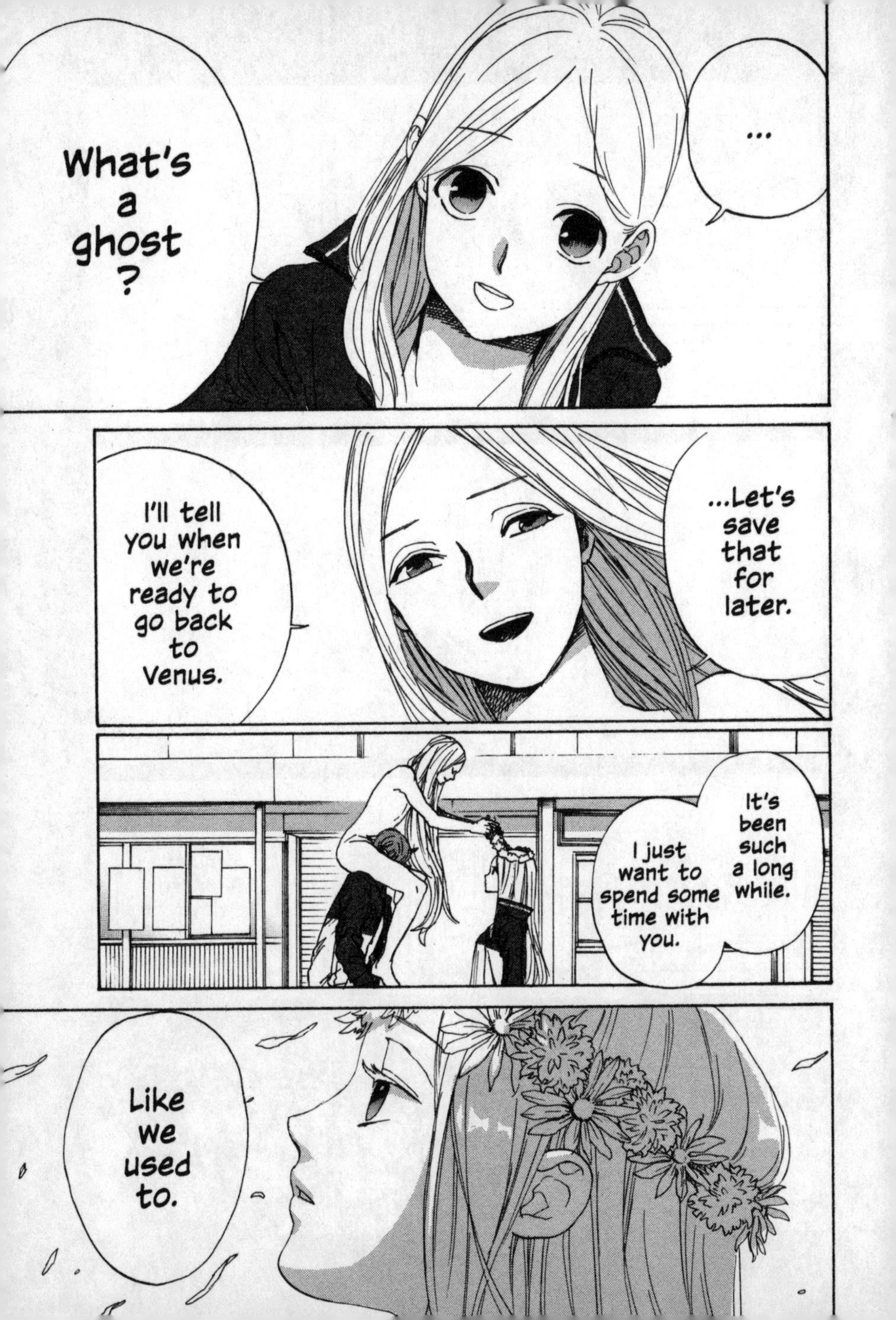
...
What's a ghost?
...Let's save that for later.
I'll tell you when we're ready to go back to Venus.
It's been such a long while.
I just want to spend some time with you.
Like we used to.

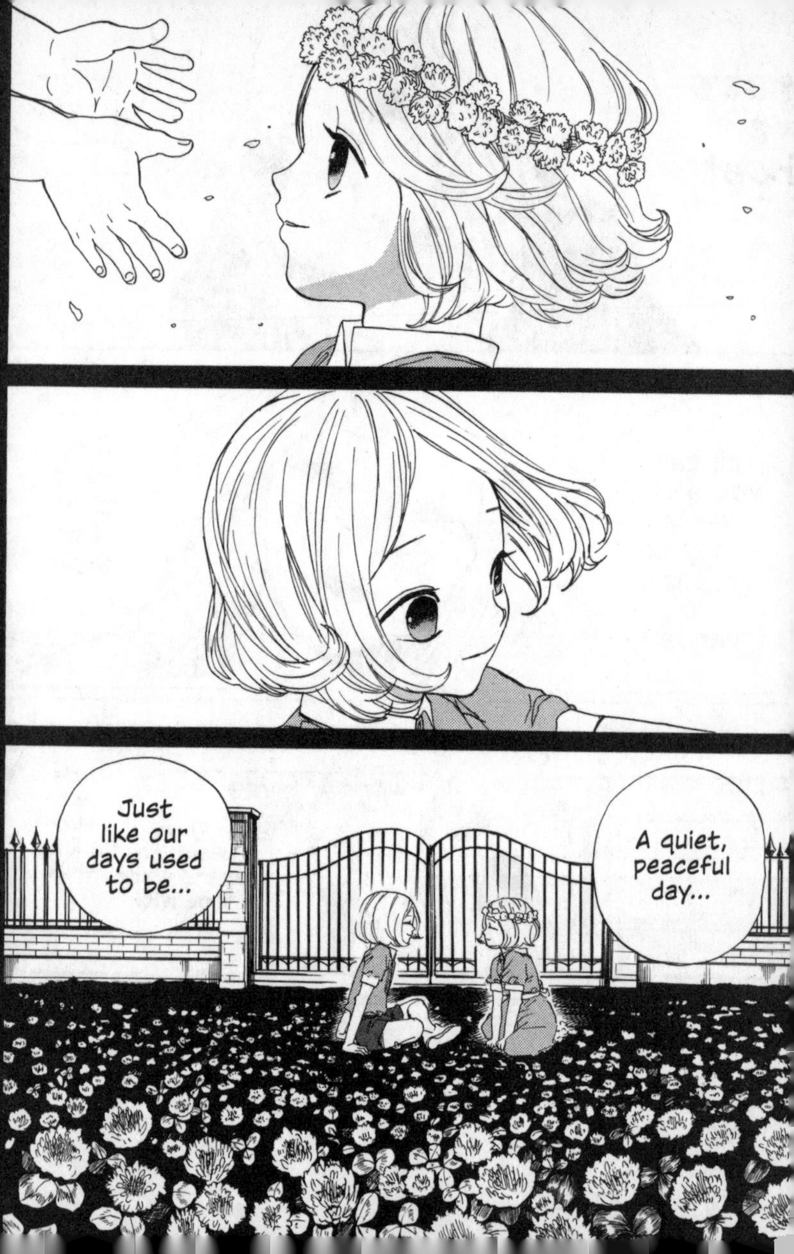
A quiet, peaceful day...
Just like our days used to be...

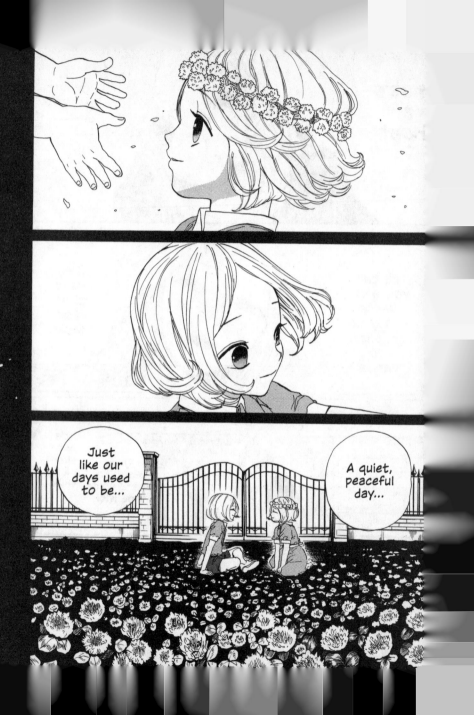

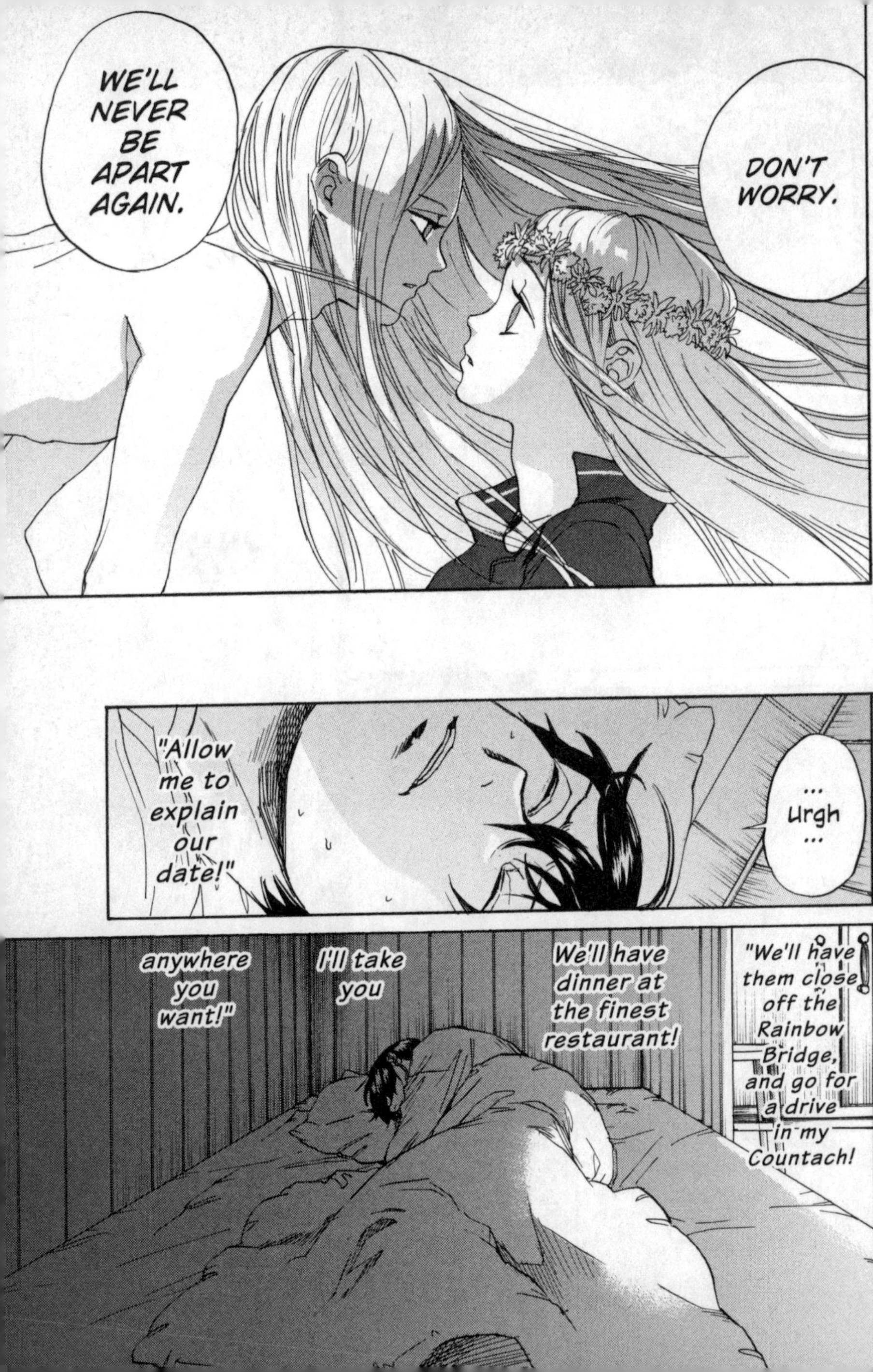
DON'T WORRY.
WE'LL NEVER BE APART AGAIN.
... Urgh ...
"Allow me to explain our date!"
"We'll have them close off the Rainbow Bridge, and go for a drive in my Countach!
We'll have dinner at the finest restaurant!
I'll take you
anywhere you want!"

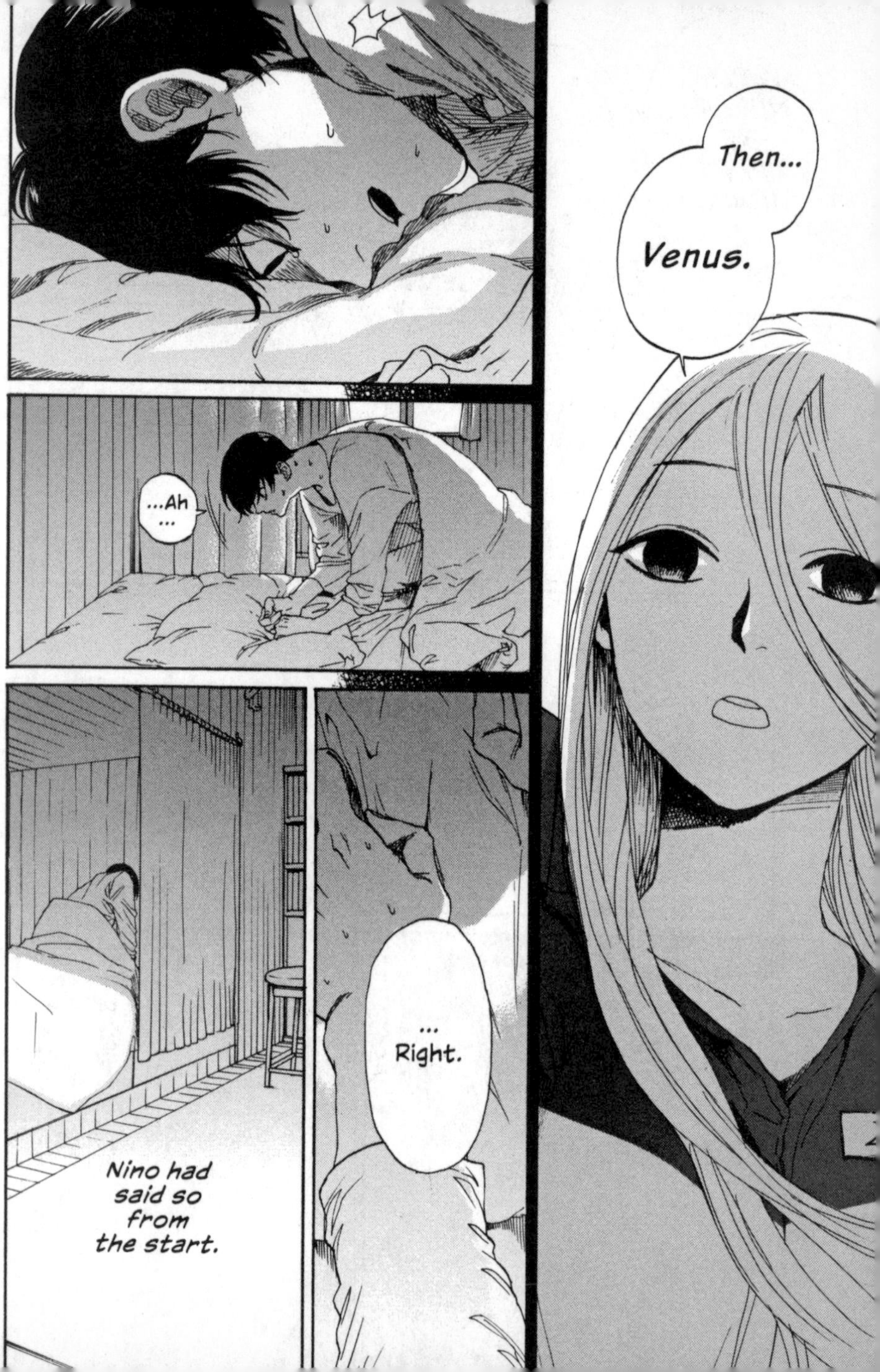
Then... Venus.
...Ah ...
... Right.
Nino had said so from the start.

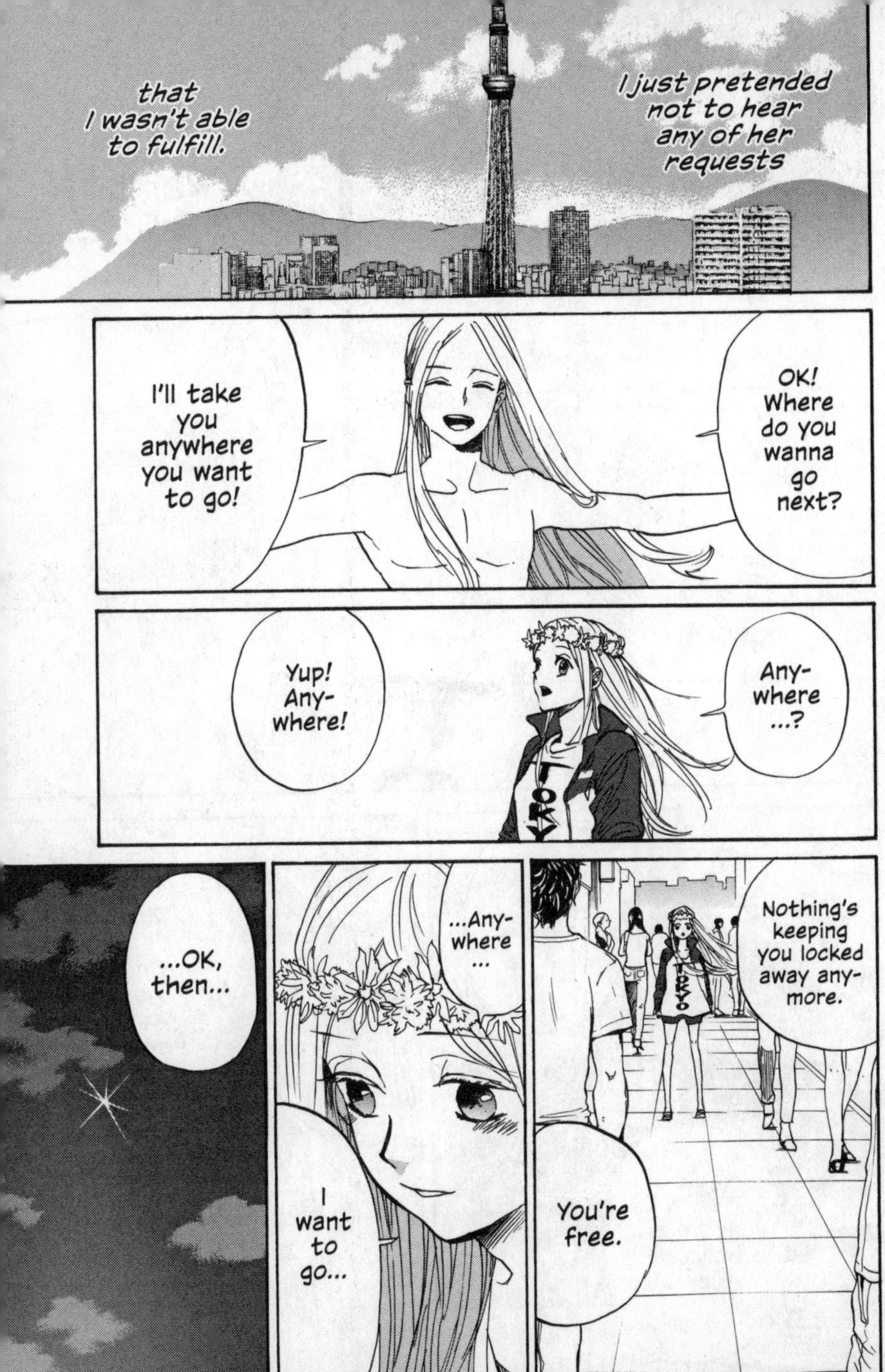
I just pretended not to hear any of her requests
that I wasn't able to fulfill.
OK! Where do you wanna go next?
I'll take you anywhere you want to go!
Any-where ...?
Yup! Any-where!
Nothing's keeping you locked away any-more.
You're free.
...Any-where ...
I want to go...
...OK, then...

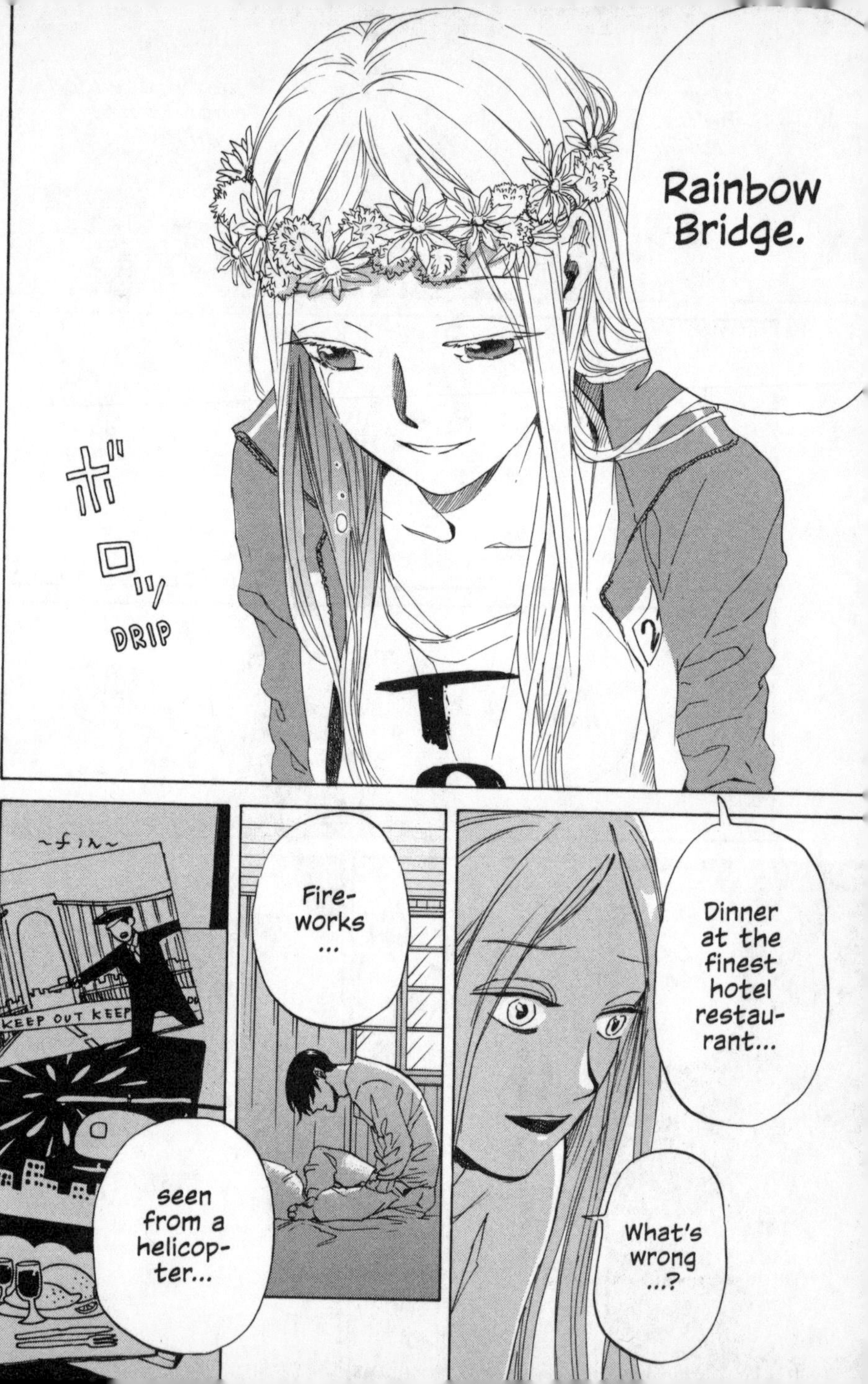
Rainbow Bridge.
ボロッ
DRIP
Dinner at the finest hotel restaurant...
What's wrong ...?
Fire-works ...
seen from a helicop-ter...
KEEP OUT KEEP

ARAKAWA
UNDER
THE BRIDGE

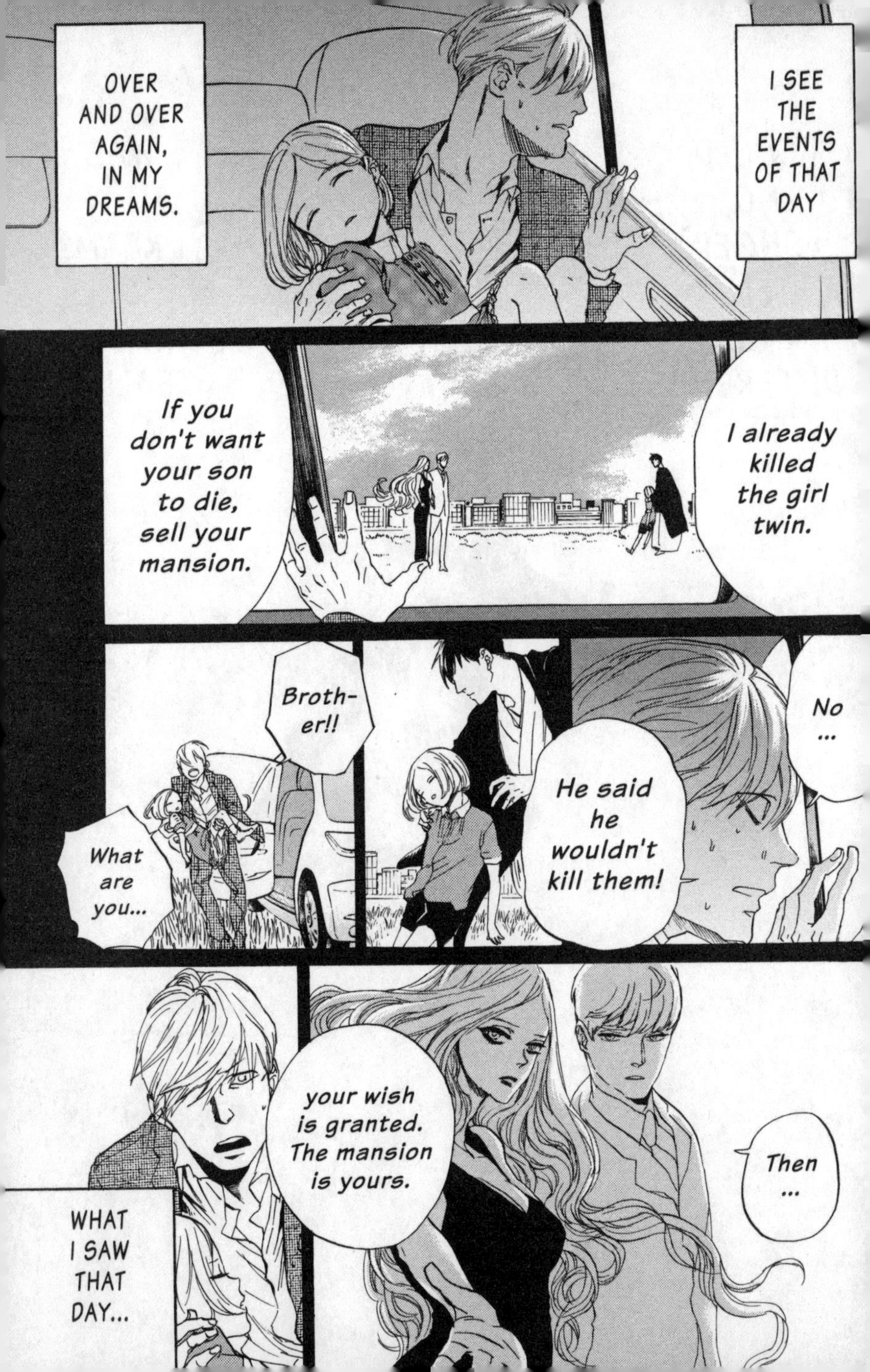
I SEE THE EVENTS OF THAT DAY
OVER AND OVER AGAIN, IN MY DREAMS.
I already killed the girl twin.
If you don't want your son to die, sell your mansion.
No ...
He said he wouldn't kill them!
Broth-er!!
What are you...
Then ...
your wish is granted. The mansion is yours.
WHAT I SAW THAT DAY...

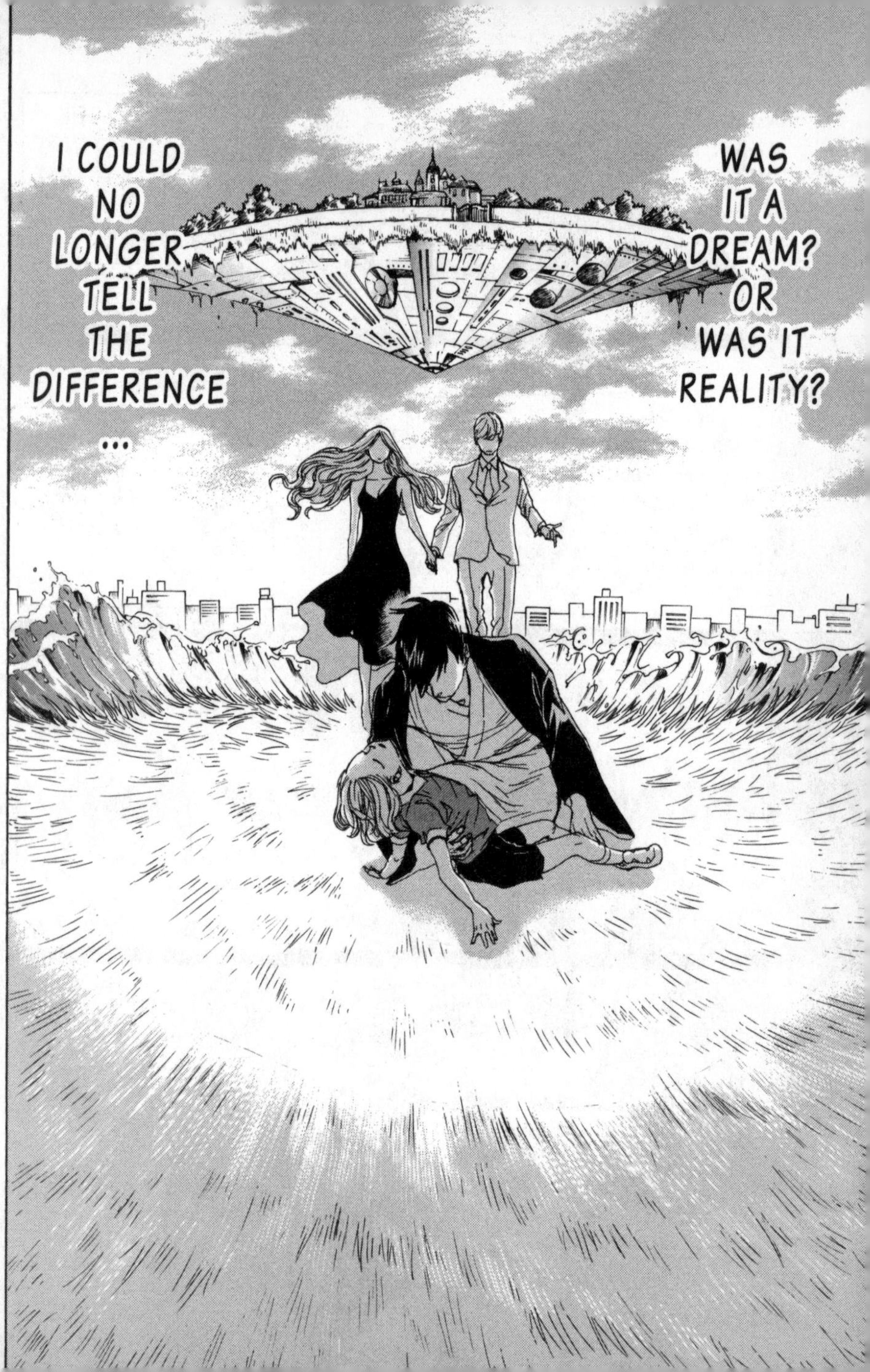
WAS IT A DREAM? OR WAS IT REALITY?
I COULD NO LONGER TELL THE DIFFERENCE...

Chapter 396: The Mole's Dream

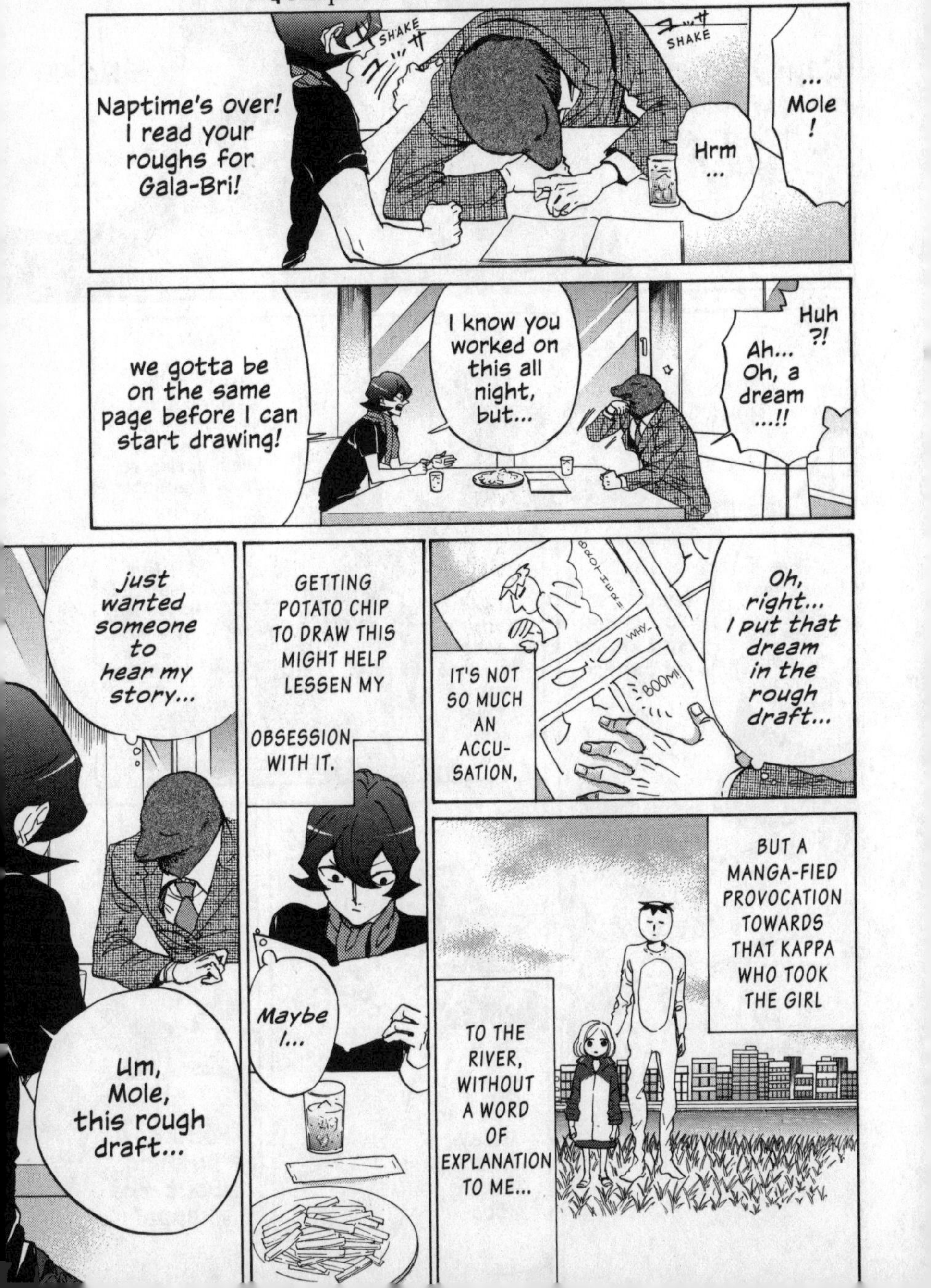
...Mole!
Hrm...
SHAKE
SHAKE
Naptime's over! I read your roughs for Gala-Bri!
Huh?!
Ah... Oh, a dream ...!!
I know you worked on this all night, but...
we gotta be on the same page before I can start drawing!
Oh, right... I put that dream in the rough draft...
IT'S NOT SO MUCH AN ACCUSATION,
BUT A MANGA-FIED PROVOCATION TOWARDS THAT KAPPA WHO TOOK THE GIRL
TO THE RIVER, WITHOUT A WORD OF EXPLANATION TO ME...
GETTING POTATO CHIP TO DRAW THIS MIGHT HELP LESSEN MY
OBSESSION WITH IT.
Maybe I...
just wanted someone to hear my story...
Um, Mole, this rough draft...

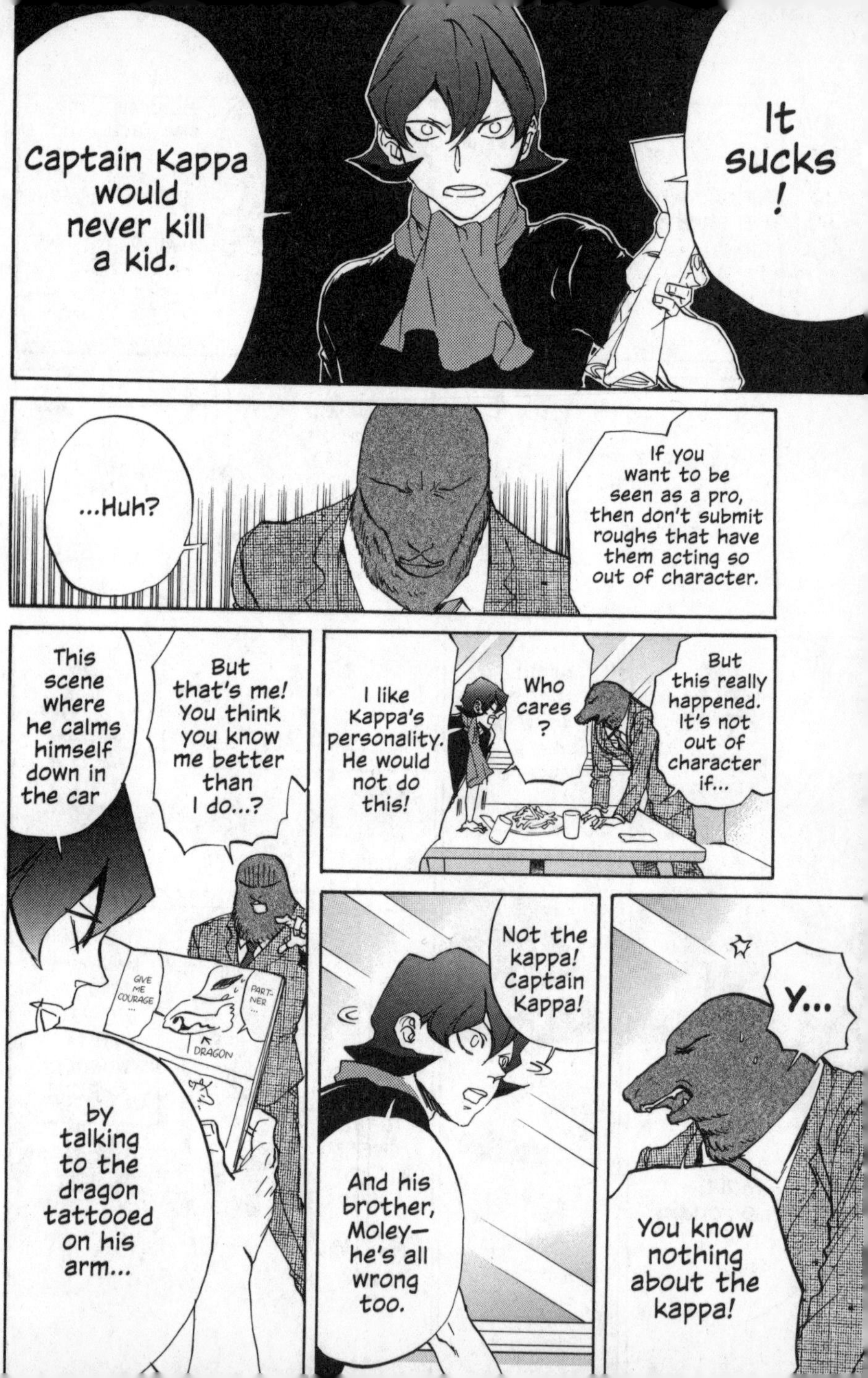
It sucks!
Captain Kappa would never kill a kid.
If you want to be seen as a pro, then don't submit roughs that have them acting so out of character.
...Huh?
But this really happened. It's not out of character if...
Who cares?
I like Kappa's personality. He would not do this!
Y...
You know nothing about the kappa!
Not the kappa! Captain Kappa!
And his brother, Moley—he's all wrong too.
But that's me! You think you know me better than I do...?
This scene where he calms himself down in the car
PART-NER...
GIVE ME COURAGE...
DRAGON
by talking to the dragon tattooed on his arm...

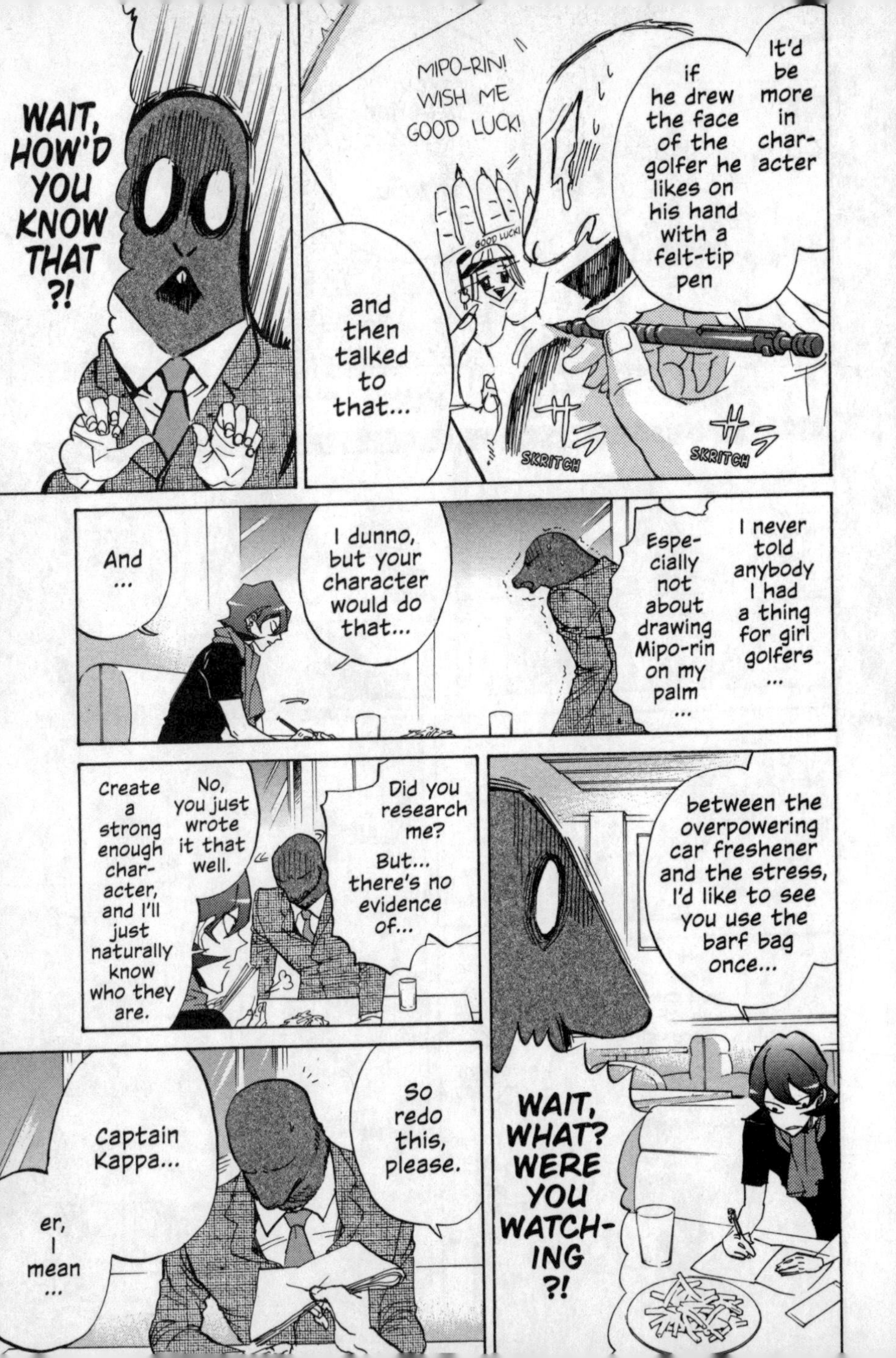
It'd be more in character if he drew the face of the golfer he likes on his hand with a felt-tip pen
MIPO-RIN! WISH ME GOOD LUCK!
GOOD LUCK!
and then talked to that...
SKRITCH
SKRITCH
WAIT, HOW'D YOU KNOW THAT?!
I never told anybody I had a thing for girl golfers ...
Especially not about drawing Mipo-rin on my palm ...
I dunno, but your character would do that...
And ...
between the overpowering car freshener and the stress, I'd like to see you use the barf bag once...
WAIT, WHAT? WERE YOU WATCHING?!
Did you research me?
But... there's no evidence of...
No, you just wrote it that well.
Create a strong enough character, and I'll just naturally know who they are.
So redo this, please.
Captain Kappa...
er, I mean ...

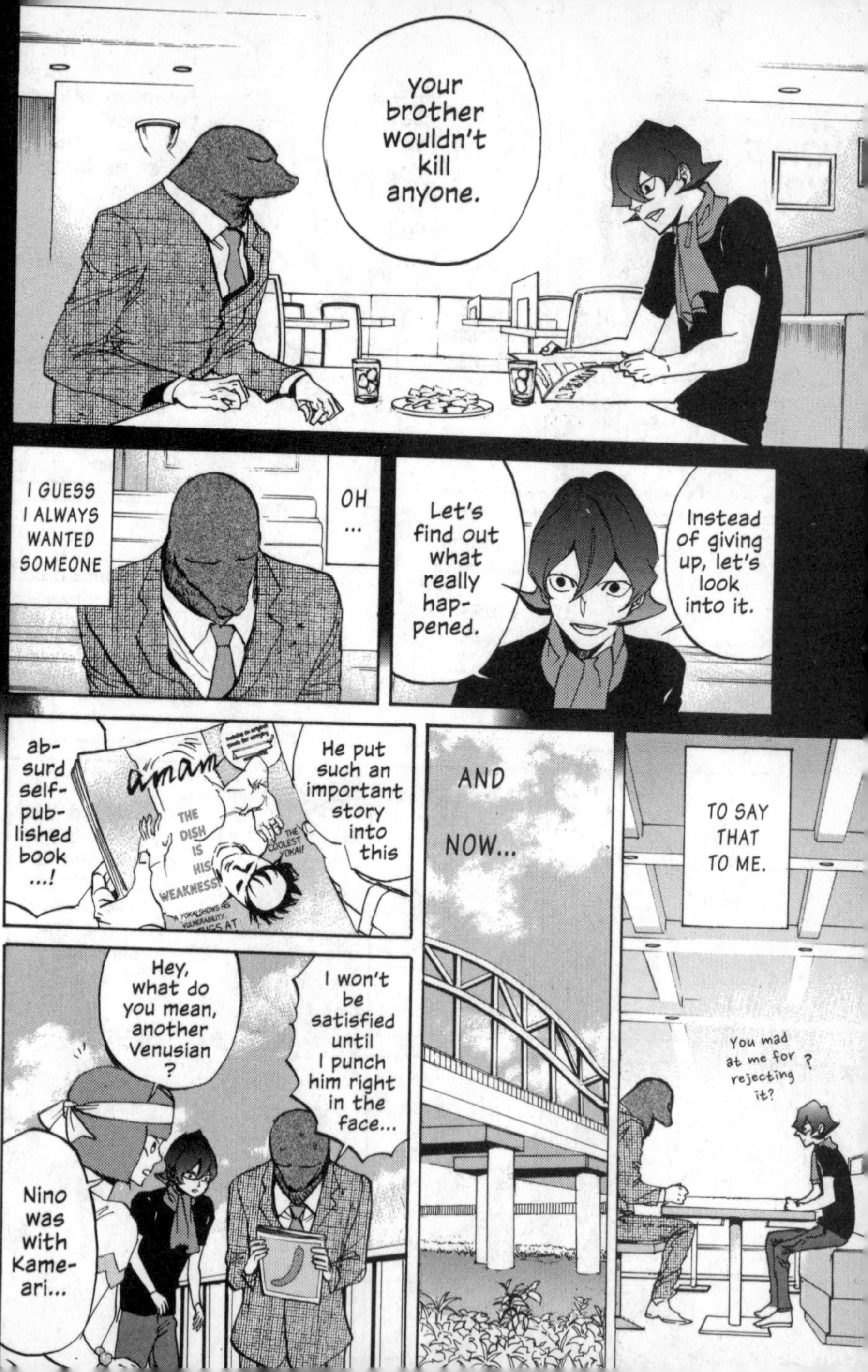
your brother wouldn't kill anyone.
Instead of giving up, let's look into it.
Let's find out what really hap-pened.
OH ...
I GUESS I ALWAYS WANTED SOMEONE
TO SAY THAT TO ME.
You mad at me for rejecting it?
AND NOW...
He put such an important story into this
amam
THE DISH IS HIS WEAKNESS!
THE COOLEST YOKAI!
ab-surd self-pub-lished book ...!
I won't be satisfied until I punch him right in the face...
Hey, what do you mean, another Venusian ?
Nino was with Kame-ari...

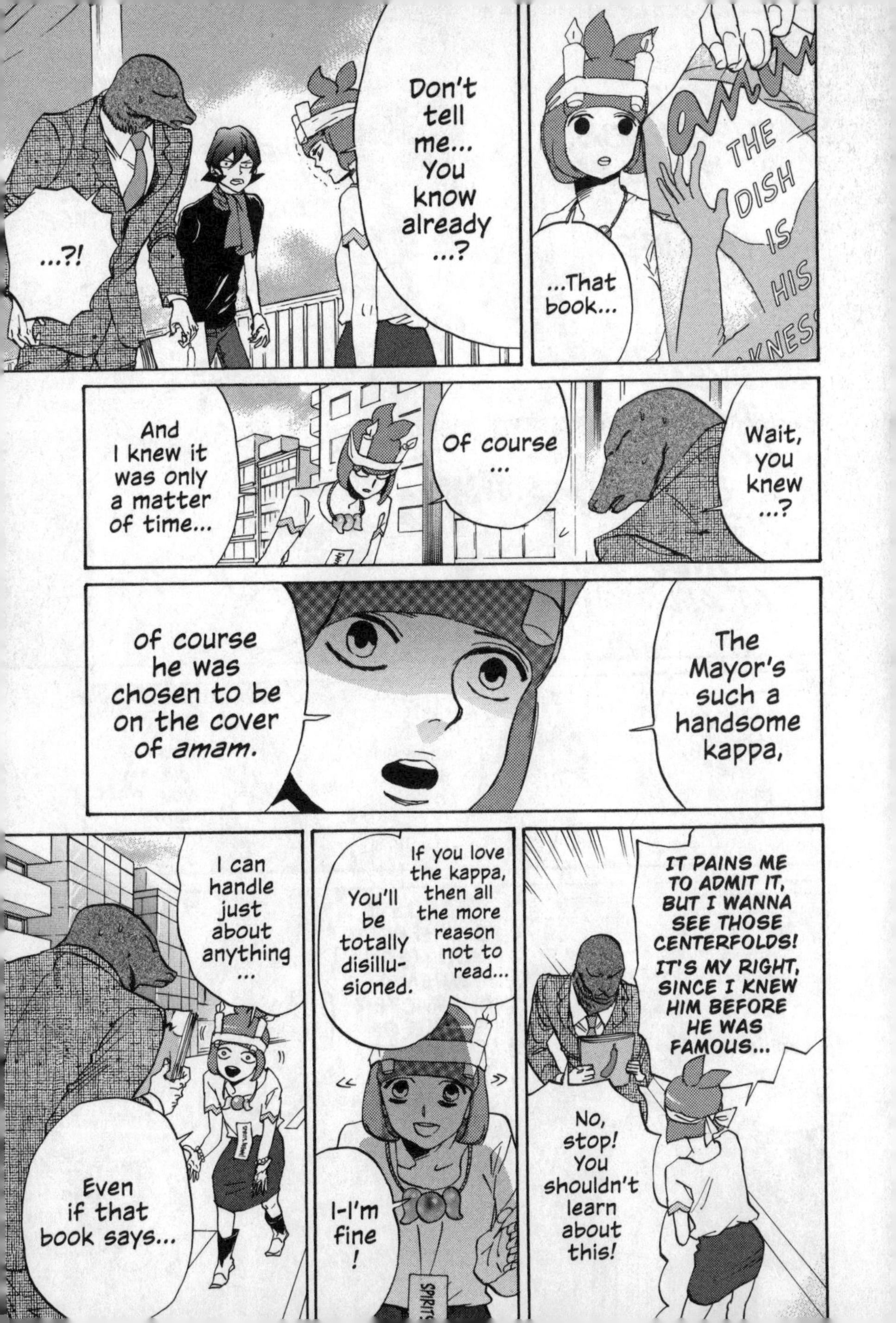
THE DISH IS HIS WEAKNESS
...That book...
Don't tell me... You know already ...?
...?!
Wait, you knew ...?
Of course ...
And I knew it was only a matter of time...
The Mayor's such a handsome kappa,
of course he was chosen to be on the cover of *amam*.
IT PAINS ME TO ADMIT IT, BUT I WANNA SEE THOSE CENTERFOLDS! IT'S MY RIGHT, SINCE I KNEW HIM BEFORE HE WAS FAMOUS...
No, stop! You shouldn't learn about this!
If you love the kappa, then all the more reason not to read...
You'll be totally disillu-sioned.
I-I'm fine!
I can handle just about anything ...
Even if that book says...

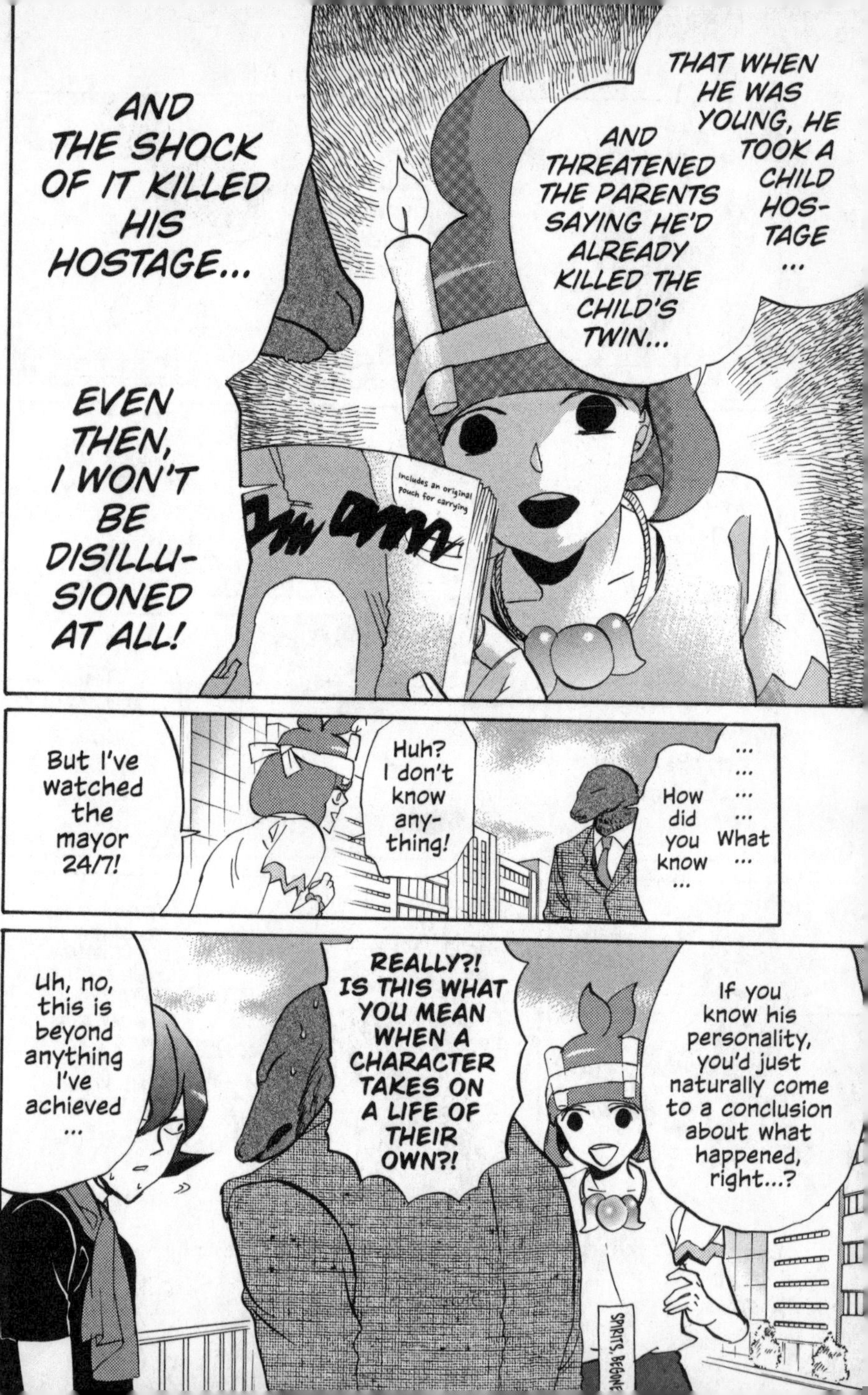
THAT WHEN HE WAS YOUNG, HE TOOK A CHILD HOSTAGE ...
AND THREATENED THE PARENTS SAYING HE'D ALREADY KILLED THE CHILD'S TWIN...
AND THE SHOCK OF IT KILLED HIS HOSTAGE...
Includes an original pouch for carrying
EVEN THEN, I WON'T BE DISILLUSIONED AT ALL!
... ... What ...
How did you know ...
Huh? I don't know anything!
But I've watched the mayor 24/7!
If you know his personality, you'd just naturally come to a conclusion about what happened, right...?
SPIRITS, BEGONE
REALLY?! IS THIS WHAT YOU MEAN WHEN A CHARACTER TAKES ON A LIFE OF THEIR OWN?!
Uh, no, this is beyond anything I've achieved ...

Chapter 397: A Venusian Alone

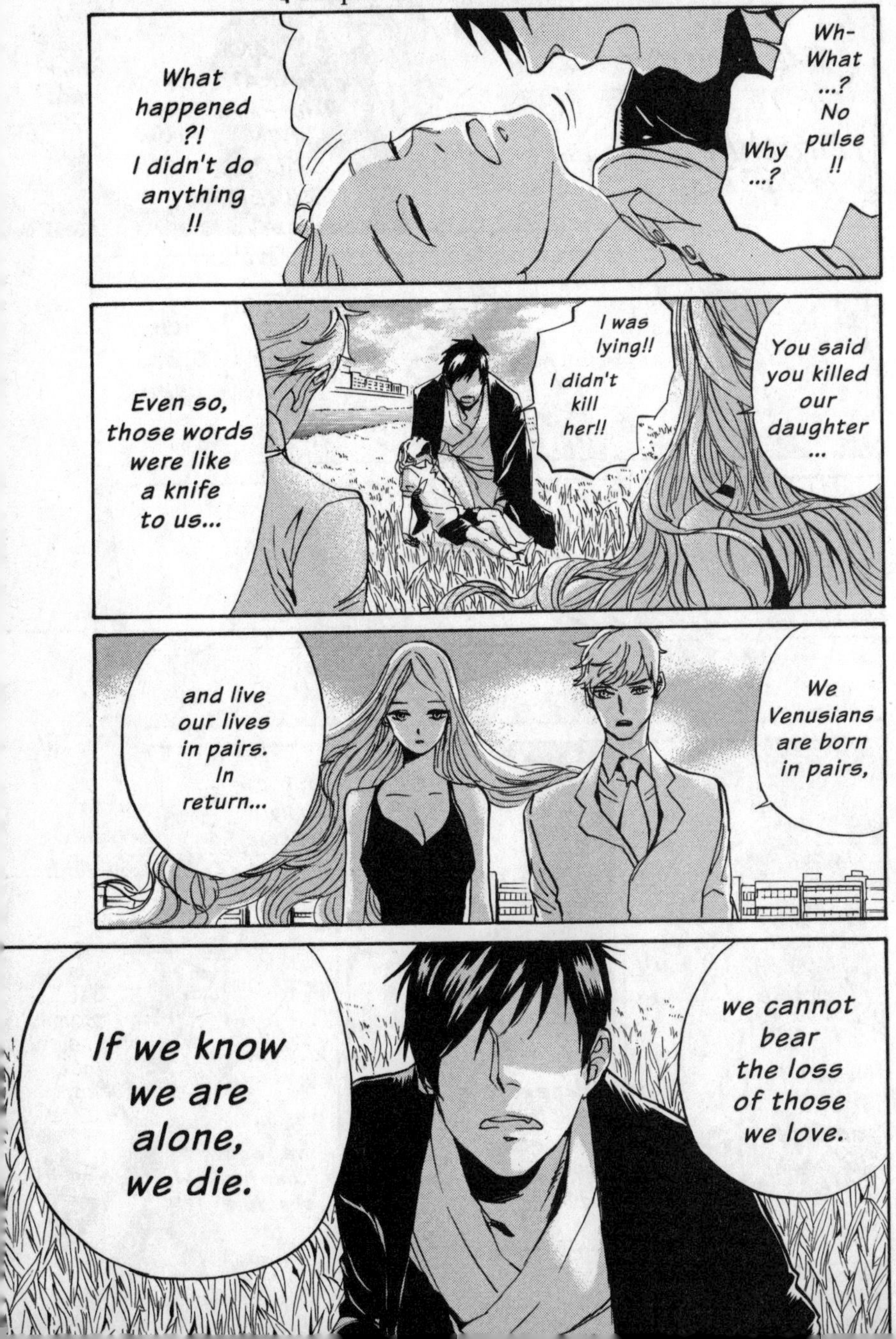
Wh- What ...? No pulse !!
Why ...?
What happened ?! I didn't do anything !!
You said you killed our daughter ...
I was lying!! I didn't kill her!!
Even so, those words were like a knife to us...
We Venusians are born in pairs,
and live our lives in pairs. In return...
we cannot bear the loss of those we love.
If we know we are alone, we die.

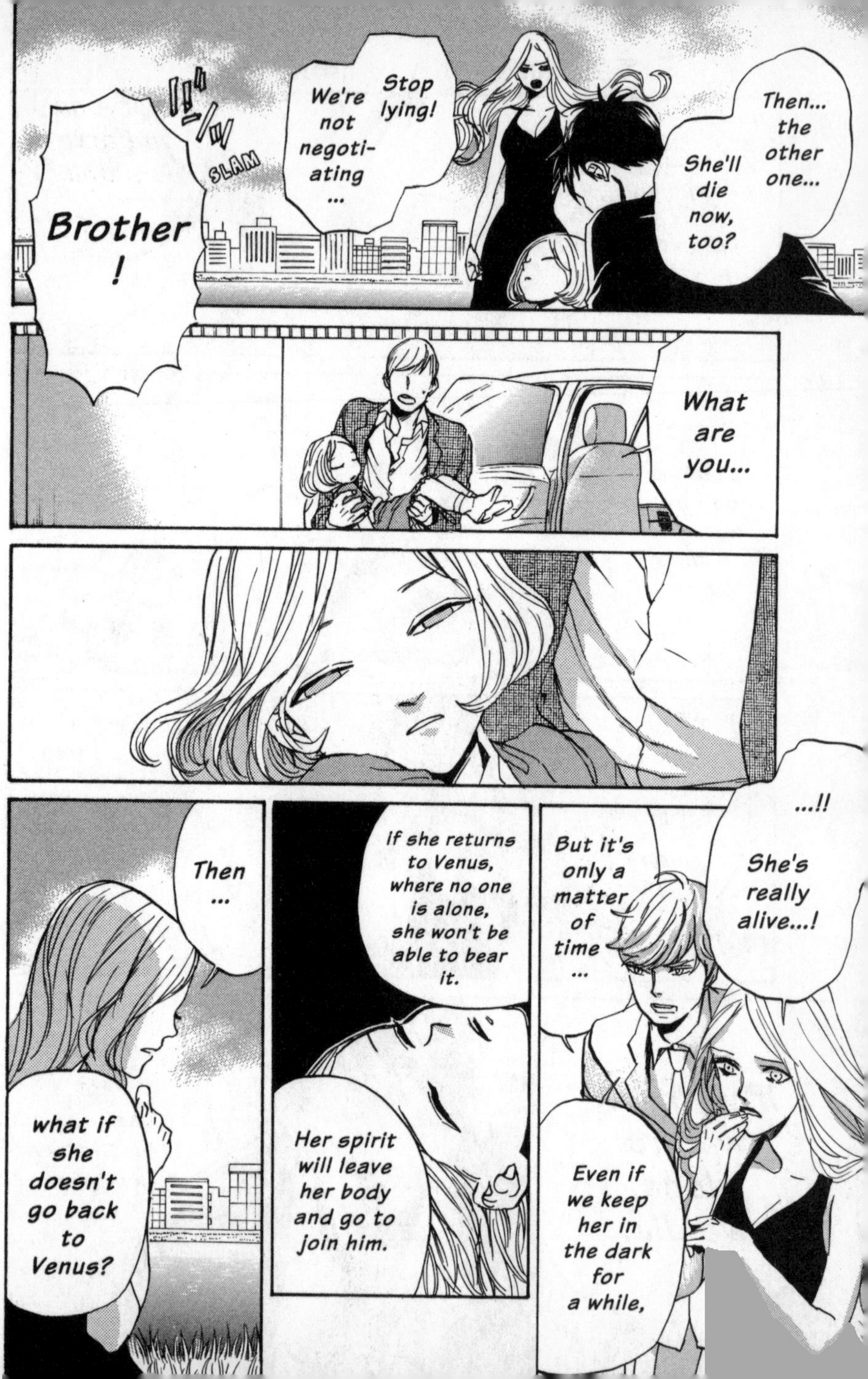
Then... the other one...
She'll die now, too?
Stop lying!
We're not negoti-ating ...
SLAM
Brother!
What are you...
...!!
She's really alive...!
But it's only a matter of time ...
Even if we keep her in the dark for a while,
If she returns to Venus, where no one is alone, she won't be able to bear it.
Her spirit will leave her body and go to join him.
Then ...
what if she doesn't go back to Venus?

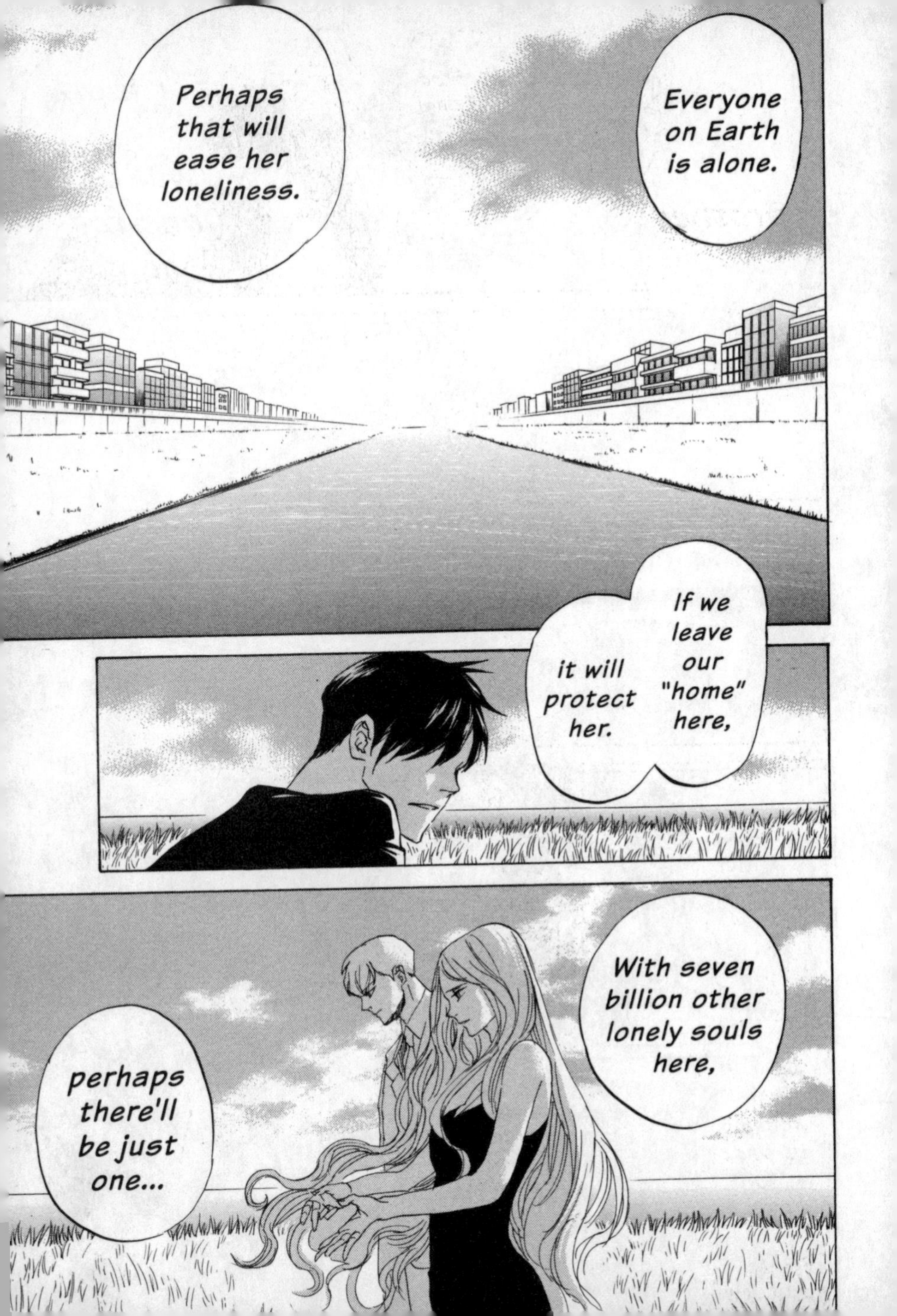
Everyone on Earth is alone.
Perhaps that will ease her loneliness.
If we leave our "home" here,
it will protect her.
With seven billion other lonely souls here,
perhaps there'll be just one...

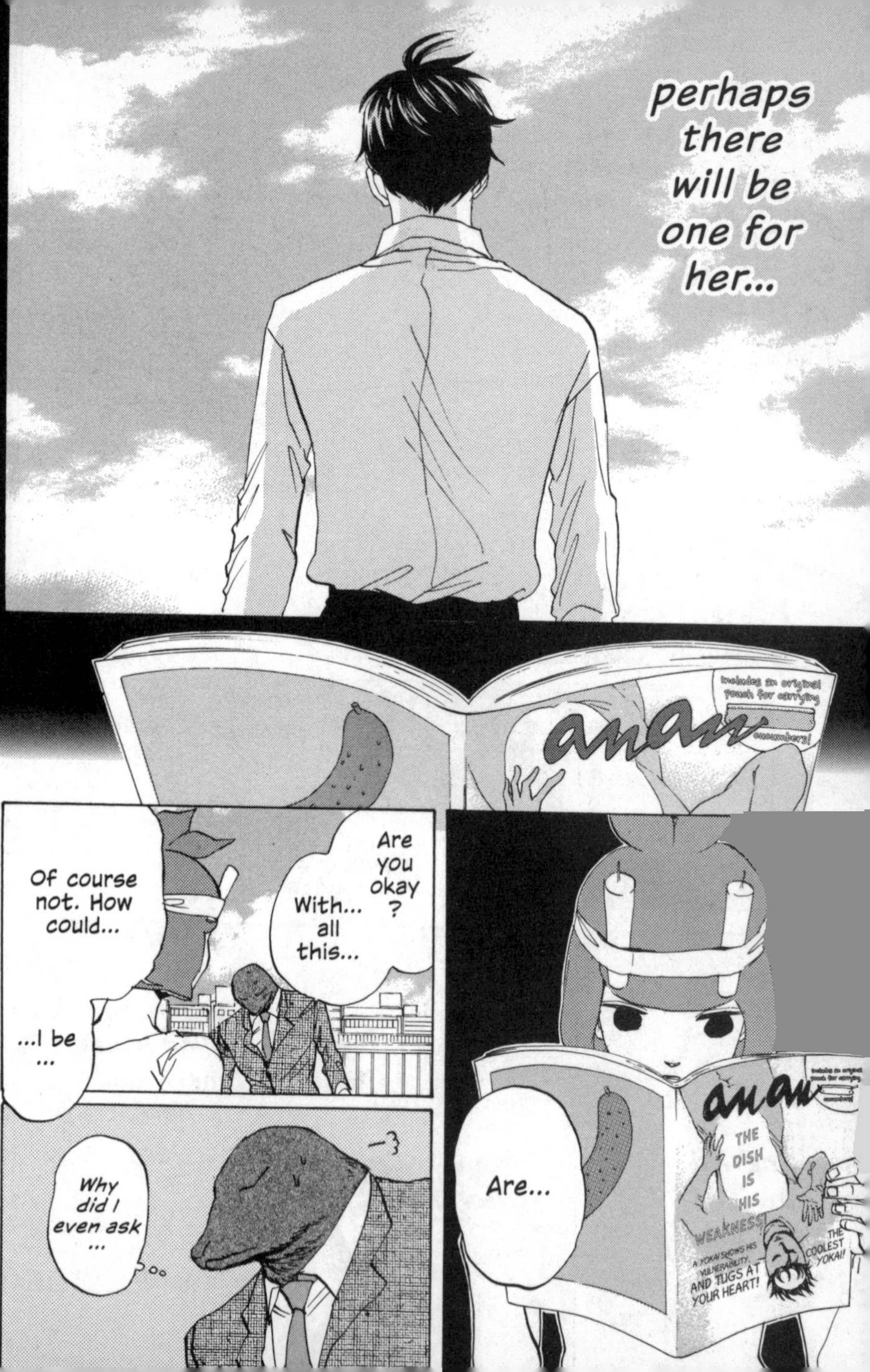
perhaps there will be one for her...
Includes an original pouch for carrying cucumbers!
anan
anan
THE DISH IS HIS WEAKNESS!
A YOKAI SHOWS HIS VULNERABILITY AND TUGS AT YOUR HEART!
THE COOLEST YOKAI!
Are...
Are you okay?
With... all this...
Of course not. How could...
...I be ...
Why did I even ask ...

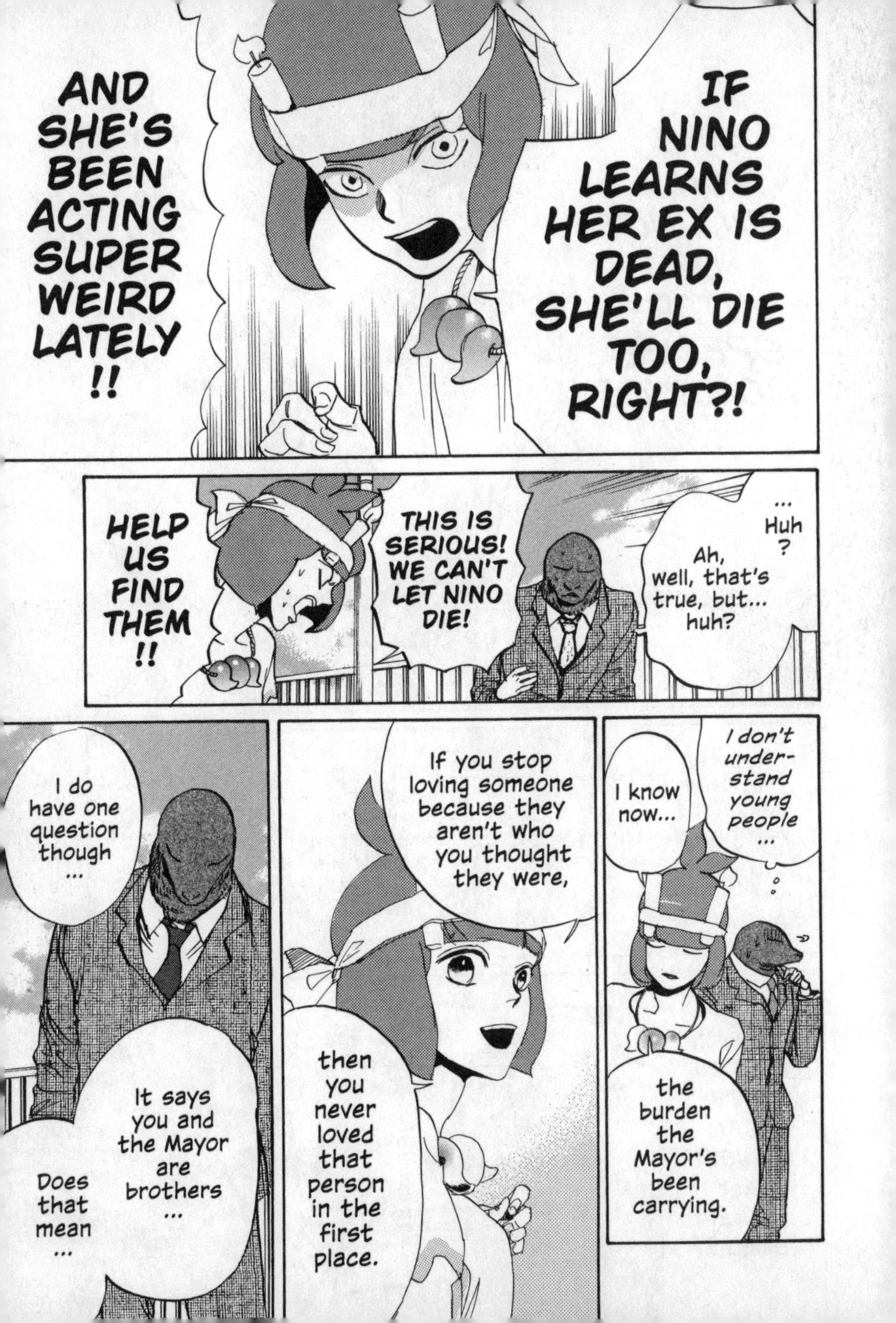
IF NINO LEARNS HER EX IS DEAD, SHE'LL DIE TOO, RIGHT?!
AND SHE'S BEEN ACTING SUPER WEIRD LATELY!!
... Huh?
Ah, well, that's true, but... huh?
THIS IS SERIOUS! WE CAN'T LET NINO DIE!
HELP US FIND THEM!!
I don't understand young people...
I know now...
the burden the Mayor's been carrying.
If you stop loving someone because they aren't who you thought they were,
then you never loved that person in the first place.
I do have one question though...
It says you and the Mayor are brothers...
Does that mean...

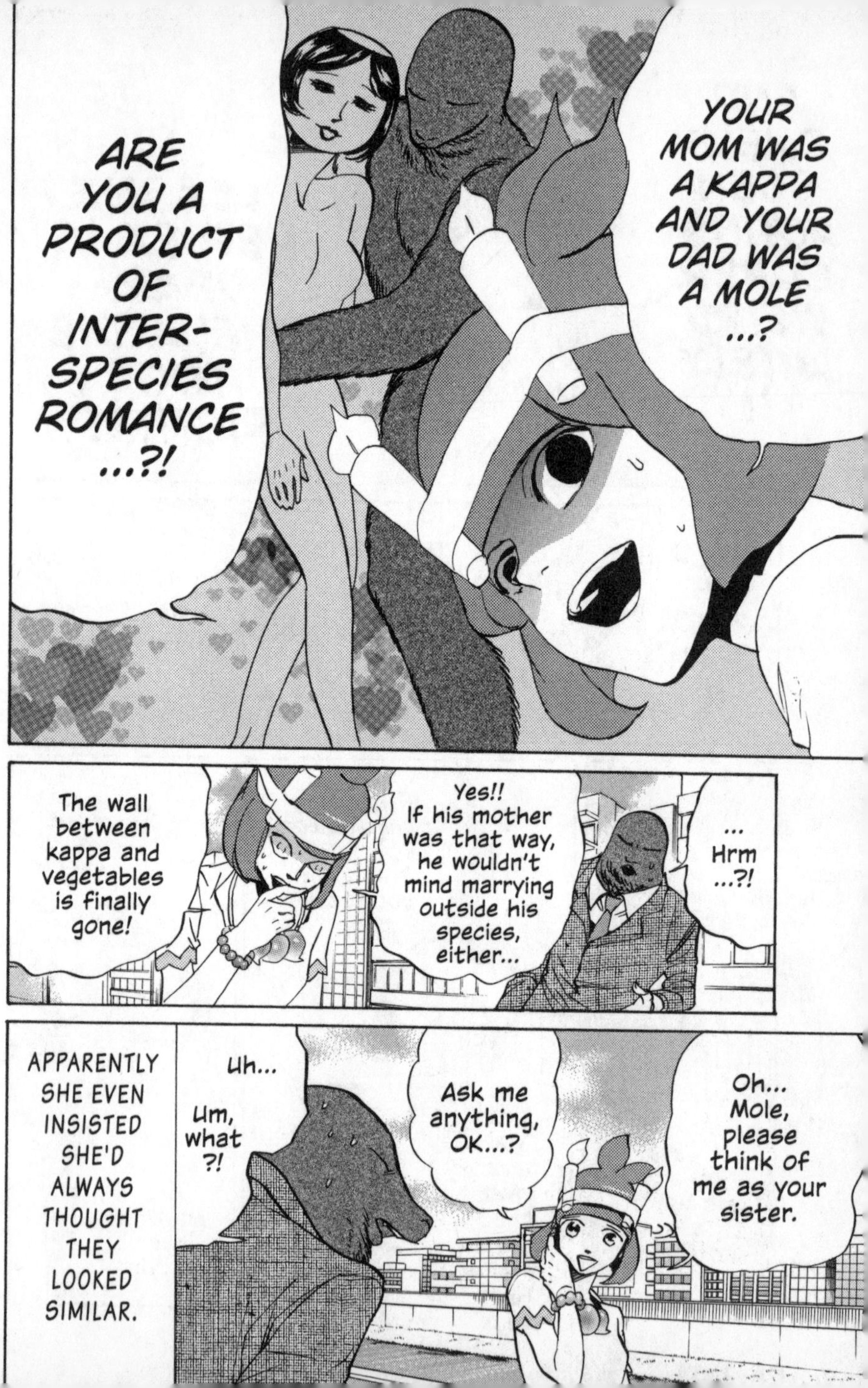
YOUR MOM WAS A KAPPA AND YOUR DAD WAS A MOLE ...?
ARE YOU A PRODUCT OF INTER-SPECIES ROMANCE ...?!
... Hrm ...?!
Yes!! If his mother was that way, he wouldn't mind marrying outside his species, either...
The wall between kappa and vegetables is finally gone!
Oh... Mole, please think of me as your sister.
Ask me anything, OK...?
Uh...
Um, what ?!
APPARENTLY SHE EVEN INSISTED SHE'D ALWAYS THOUGHT THEY LOOKED SIMILAR.

ARAKAWA
UNDER
THE BRIDGE

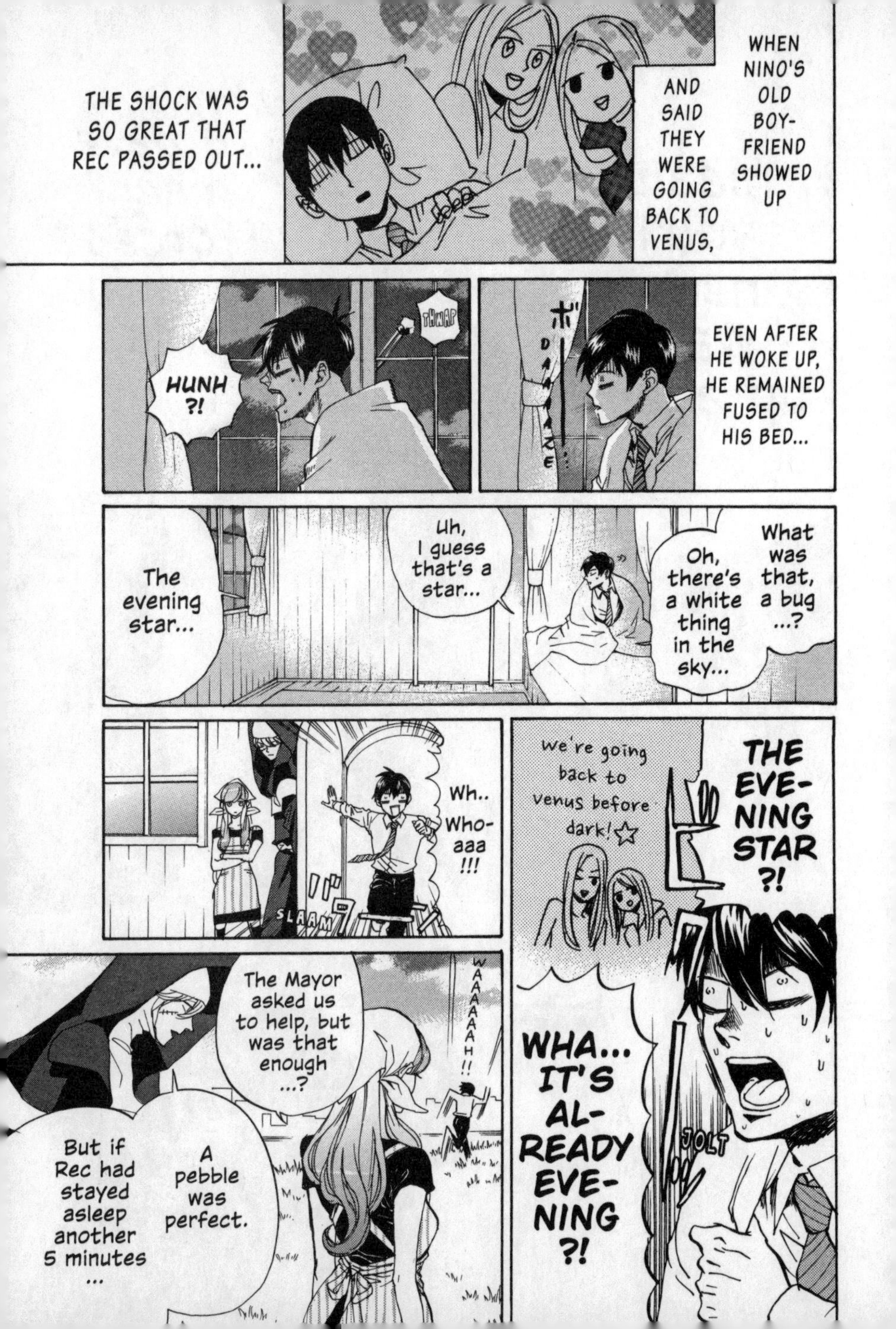
WHEN NINO'S OLD BOY-FRIEND SHOWED UP
AND SAID THEY WERE GOING BACK TO VENUS,
THE SHOCK WAS SO GREAT THAT REC PASSED OUT...
EVEN AFTER HE WOKE UP, HE REMAINED FUSED TO HIS BED...
DAAAAAZE
THWAP
HUNH ?!
What was that, a bug ...?
Oh, there's a white thing in the sky...
Uh, I guess that's a star...
The evening star...
THE EVENING STAR ?!
We're going back to Venus before dark!☆
WHA... IT'S ALREADY EVENING ?!
JOLT
Wh.. Who-aaa !!!
SLAAM
WAAAAAAAH!!
The Mayor asked us to help, but was that enough ...?
A pebble was perfect.
But if Rec had stayed asleep another 5 minutes ...

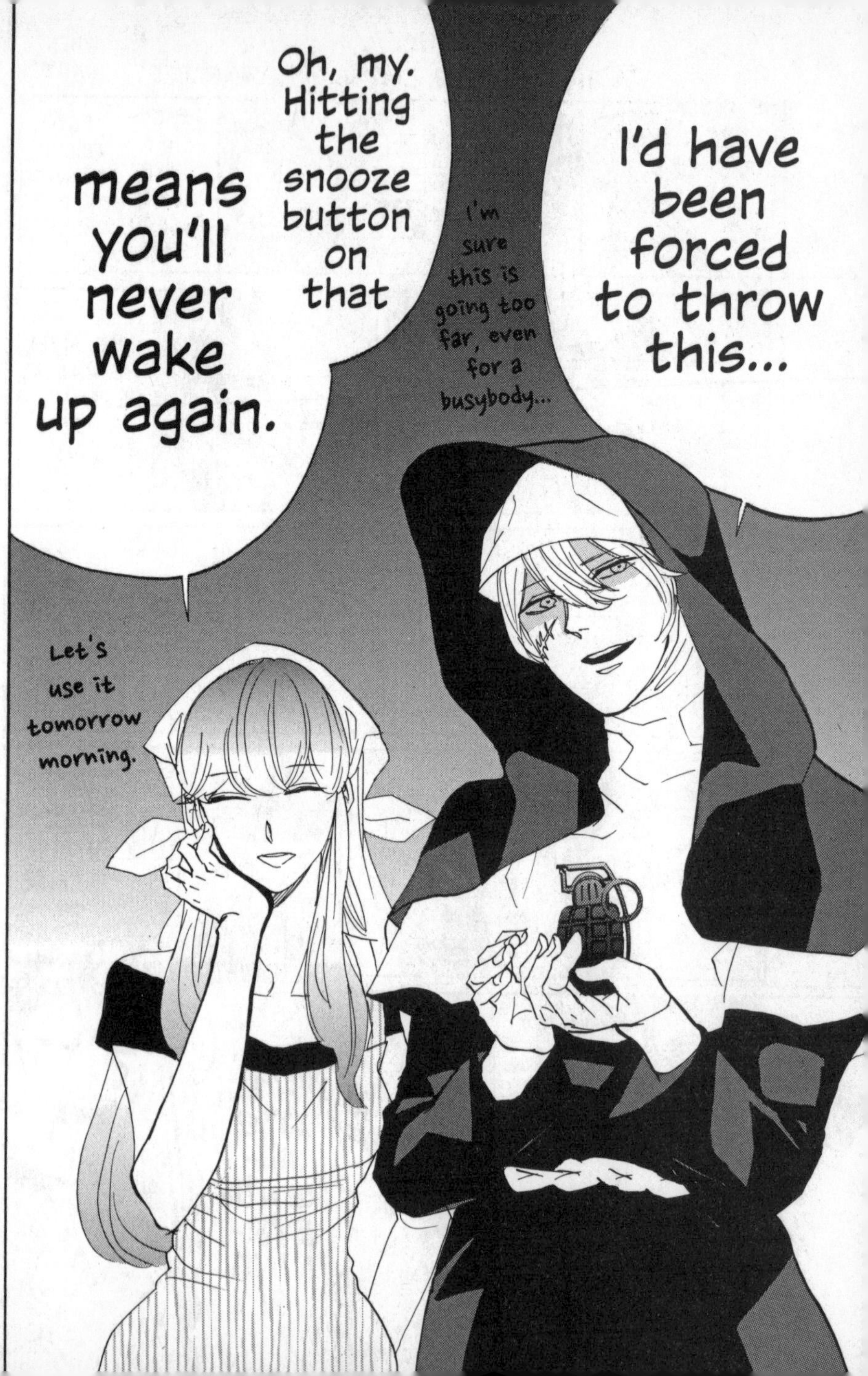
I'd have been forced to throw this...
I'm sure this is going too far, even for a busybody...
Oh, my. Hitting the snooze button on that means you'll never wake up again.
Let's use it tomorrow morning.

Chapter 398: Let Me Call You Papa!

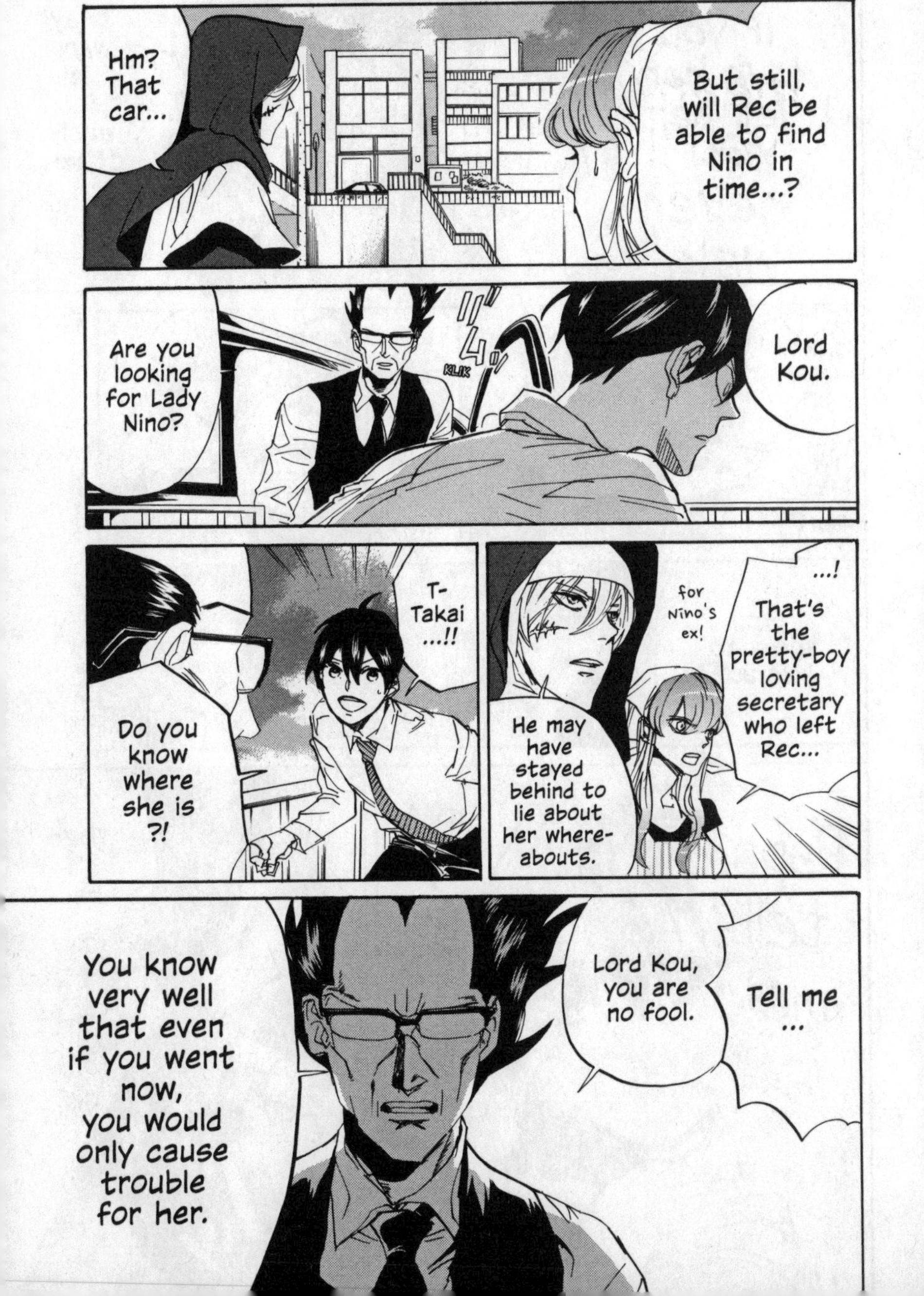
But still, will Rec be able to find Nino in time...?
Hm? That car...
Lord Kou.
KLIK
Are you looking for Lady Nino?
...!
That's the pretty-boy loving secretary who left Rec...
for Nino's ex!
He may have stayed behind to lie about her whereabouts.
T-Takai ...!!
Do you know where she is ?!
Tell me ...
Lord Kou, you are no fool.
You know very well that even if you went now, you would only cause trouble for her.

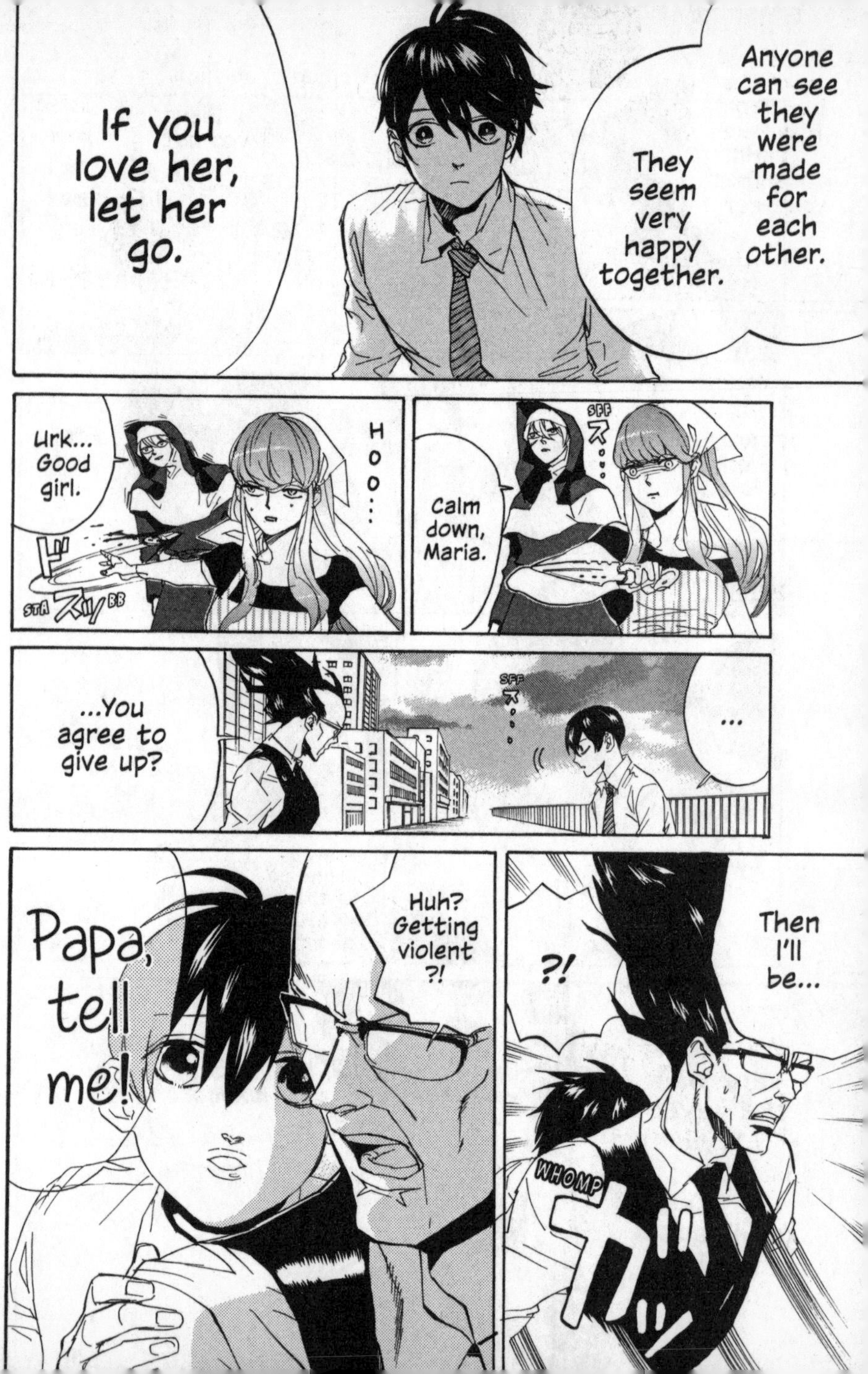
Anyone can see they were made for each other.
They seem very happy together.
If you love her, let her go.
SFF
ス...
Calm down, Maria.
HOO...
Urk... Good girl.
ド
STA
ス!!
BB
...
SFF
ス...
...You agree to give up?
Then I'll be...
?!
WHOMP
ガッ
Huh? Getting violent ?!
Papa, tell me!

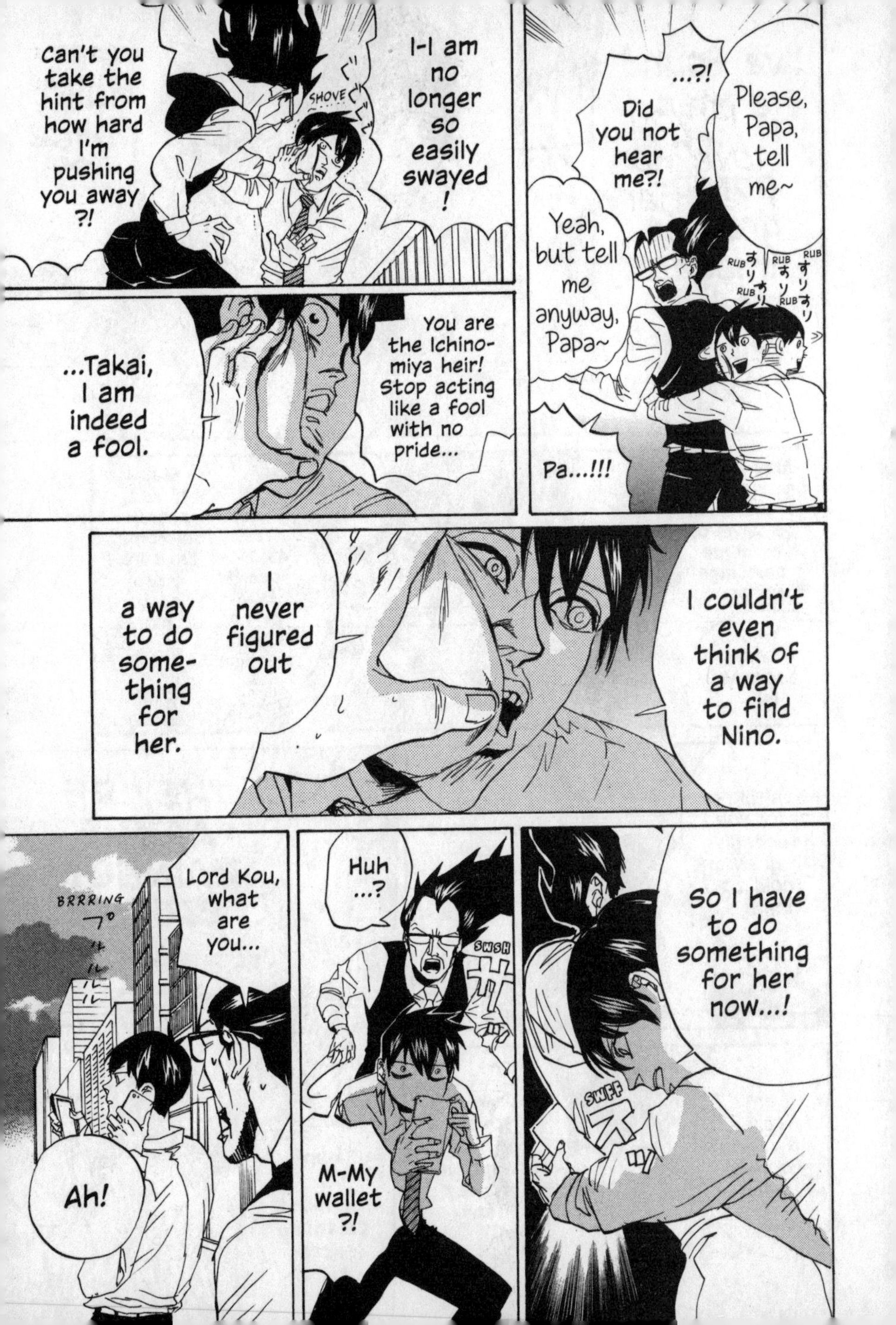
Please, Papa, tell me~
...?!
Did you not hear me?!
Yeah, but tell me anyway, Papa~
RUB すり RUB すり RUB すり RUB すり
Pa...!!!
I-I am no longer so easily swayed!
SHOVE
Can't you take the hint from how hard I'm pushing you away?!
You are the Ichino-miya heir! Stop acting like a fool with no pride...
...Takai, I am indeed a fool.
I couldn't even think of a way to find Nino.
I never figured out
a way to do some-thing for her.
So I have to do something for her now...!
SWFF
Huh...?
SWSH
M-My wallet?!
Lord Kou, what are you...
BRRRING
Ah!

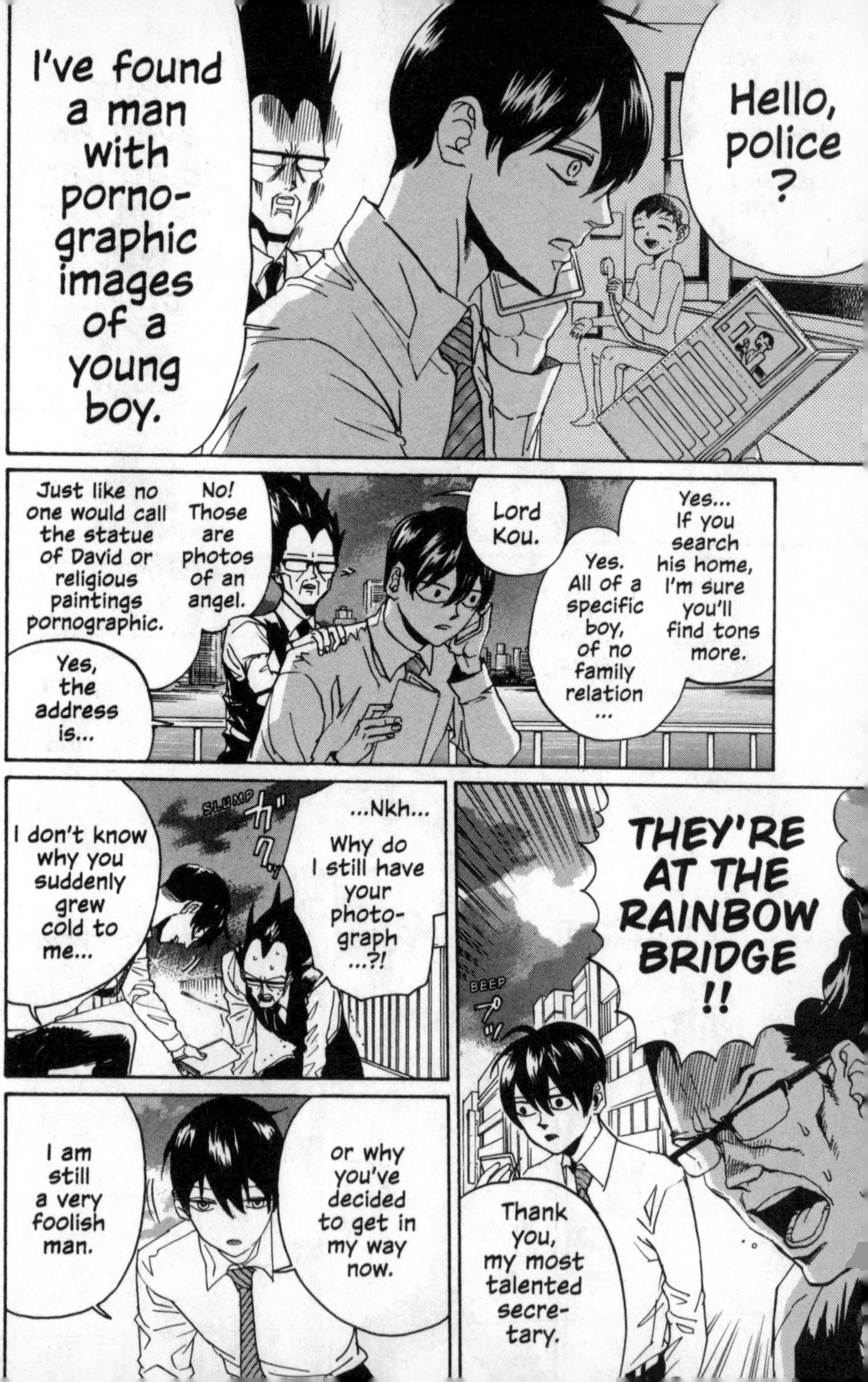
Hello, police?
I've found a man with pornographic images of a young boy.
Yes... If you search his home, I'm sure you'll find tons more.
Lord Kou.
Yes. All of a specific boy, of no family relation...
No! Those are photos of an angel.
Just like no one would call the statue of David or religious paintings pornographic.
Yes, the address is...
THEY'RE AT THE RAINBOW BRIDGE!!
BEEP
Thank you, my most talented secretary.
SLUMP
...Nkh...
Why do I still have your photograph...?!
I don't know why you suddenly grew cold to me...
or why you've decided to get in my way now.
I am still a very foolish man.

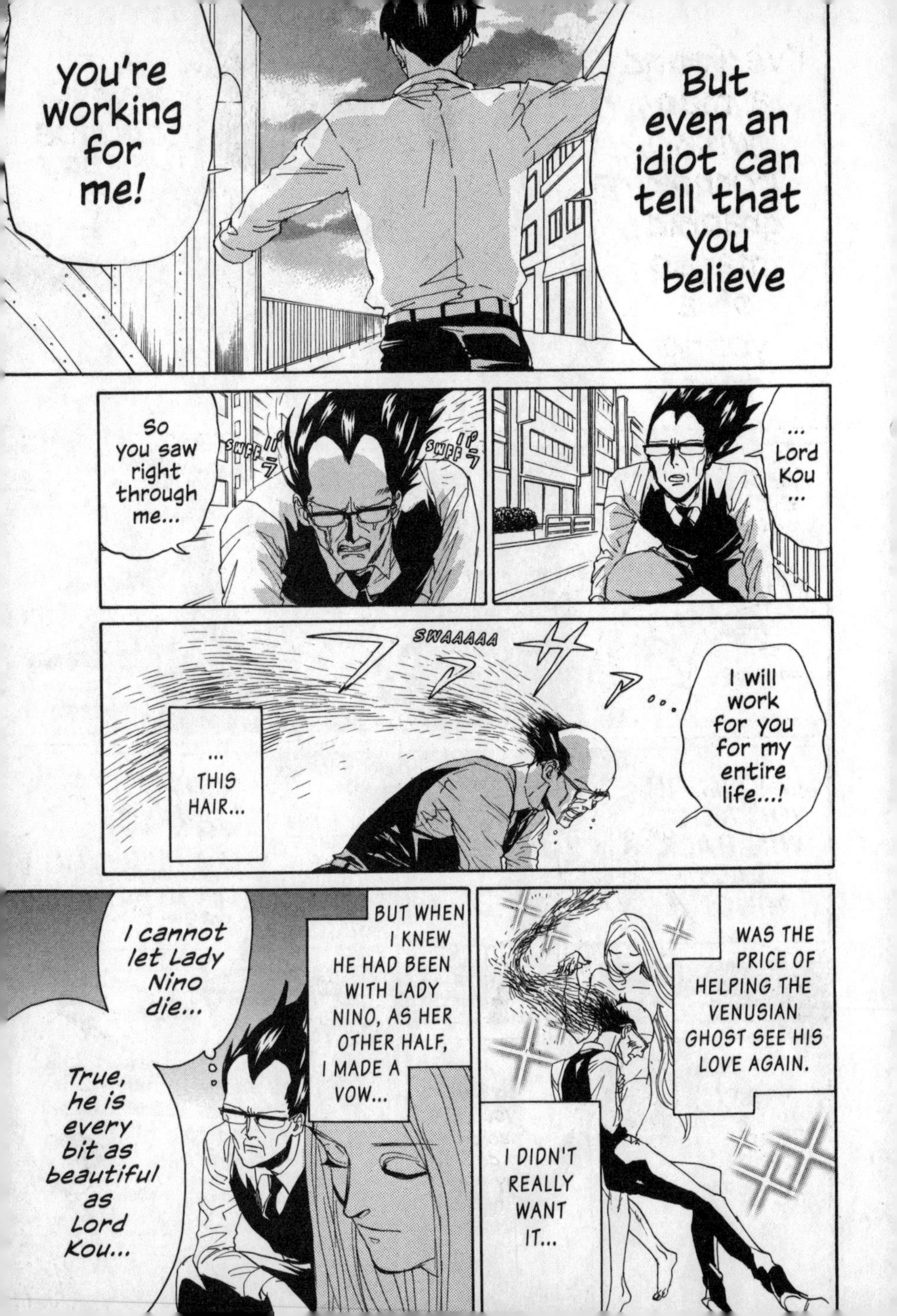
But even an idiot can tell that you believe
you're working for me!
... Lord Kou ...
SWFF
SWFF
So you saw right through me...
SWAAAAA
I will work for you for my entire life...!
... THIS HAIR...
WAS THE PRICE OF HELPING THE VENUSIAN GHOST SEE HIS LOVE AGAIN.
I DIDN'T REALLY WANT IT...
BUT WHEN I KNEW HE HAD BEEN WITH LADY NINO, AS HER OTHER HALF, I MADE A VOW...
I cannot let Lady Nino die...
True, he is every bit as beautiful as Lord Kou...

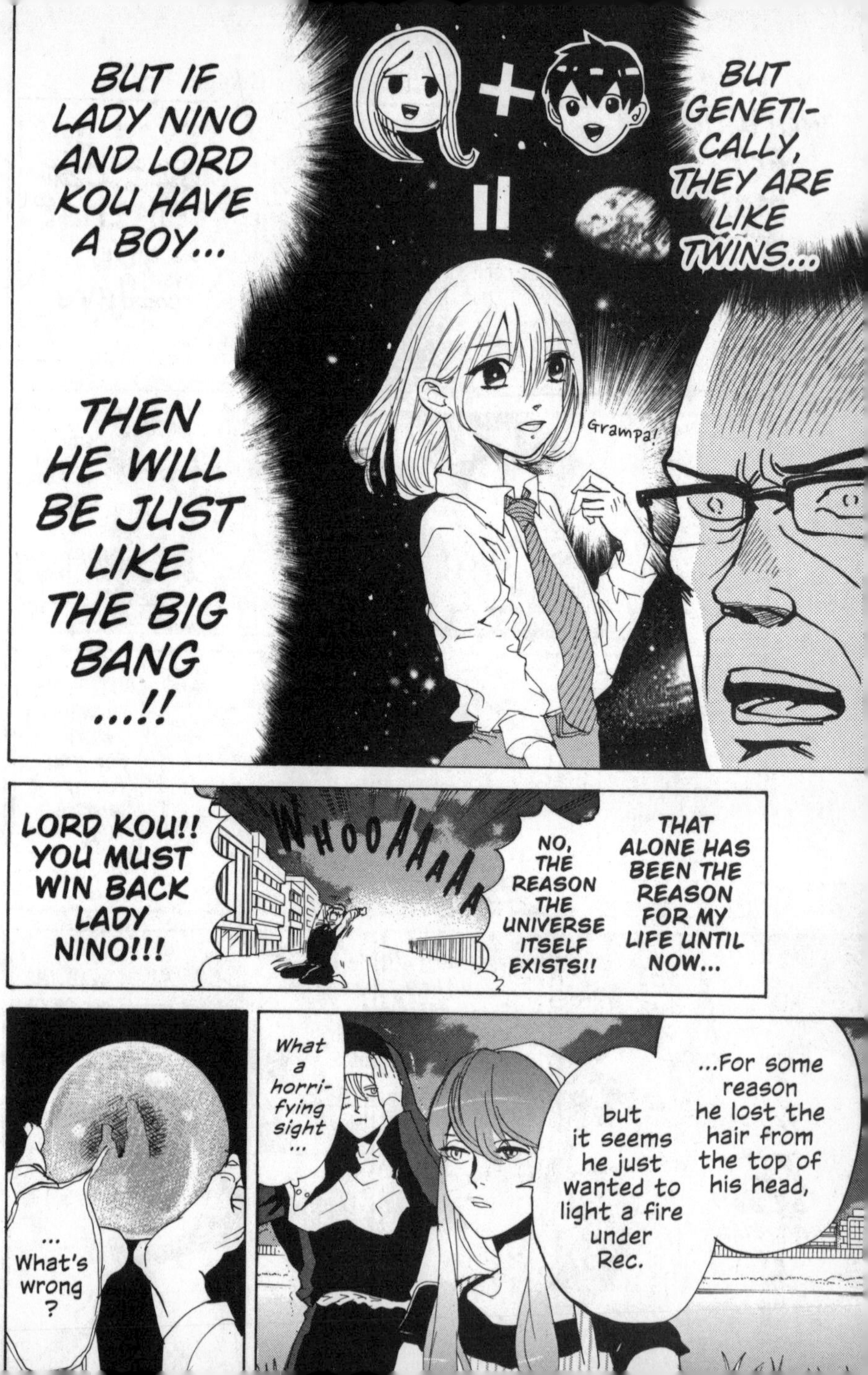
BUT GENETI-CALLY, THEY ARE LIKE TWINS...
BUT IF LADY NINO AND LORD KOU HAVE A BOY...
Grampa!
THEN HE WILL BE JUST LIKE THE BIG BANG ...!!
THAT ALONE HAS BEEN THE REASON FOR MY LIFE UNTIL NOW...
NO, THE REASON THE UNIVERSE ITSELF EXISTS!!
WHOOAAAAAA
LORD KOU!! YOU MUST WIN BACK LADY NINO!!!
...For some reason he lost the hair from the top of his head,
but it seems he just wanted to light a fire under Rec.
What a horri-fying sight...
...What's wrong?

Chapter 399: On the Rainbow Bridge

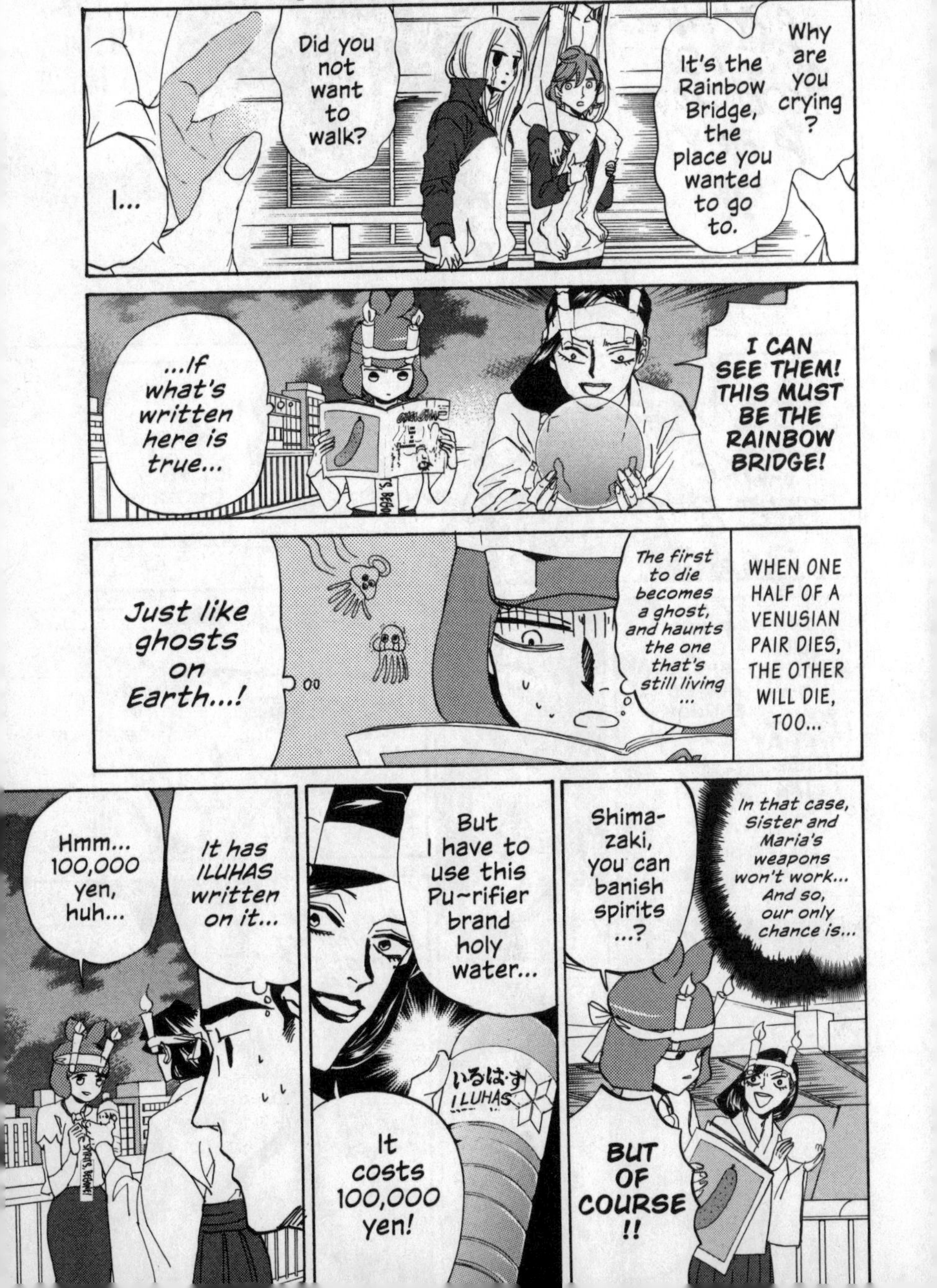
Why are you crying?
It's the Rainbow Bridge, the place you wanted to go to.
Did you not want to walk?
I...
I CAN SEE THEM! THIS MUST BE THE RAINBOW BRIDGE!
...If what's written here is true...
WHEN ONE HALF OF A VENUSIAN PAIR DIES, THE OTHER WILL DIE, TOO...
The first to die becomes a ghost, and haunts the one that's still living...
Just like ghosts on Earth...!
In that case, Sister and Maria's weapons won't work... And so, our only chance is...
Shima-zaki, you can banish spirits...?
BUT OF COURSE!!
But I have to use this Pu~rifier brand holy water...
いるはす
ILUHAS
It costs 100,000 yen!
It has ILUHAS written on it...
Hmm... 100,000 yen, huh...

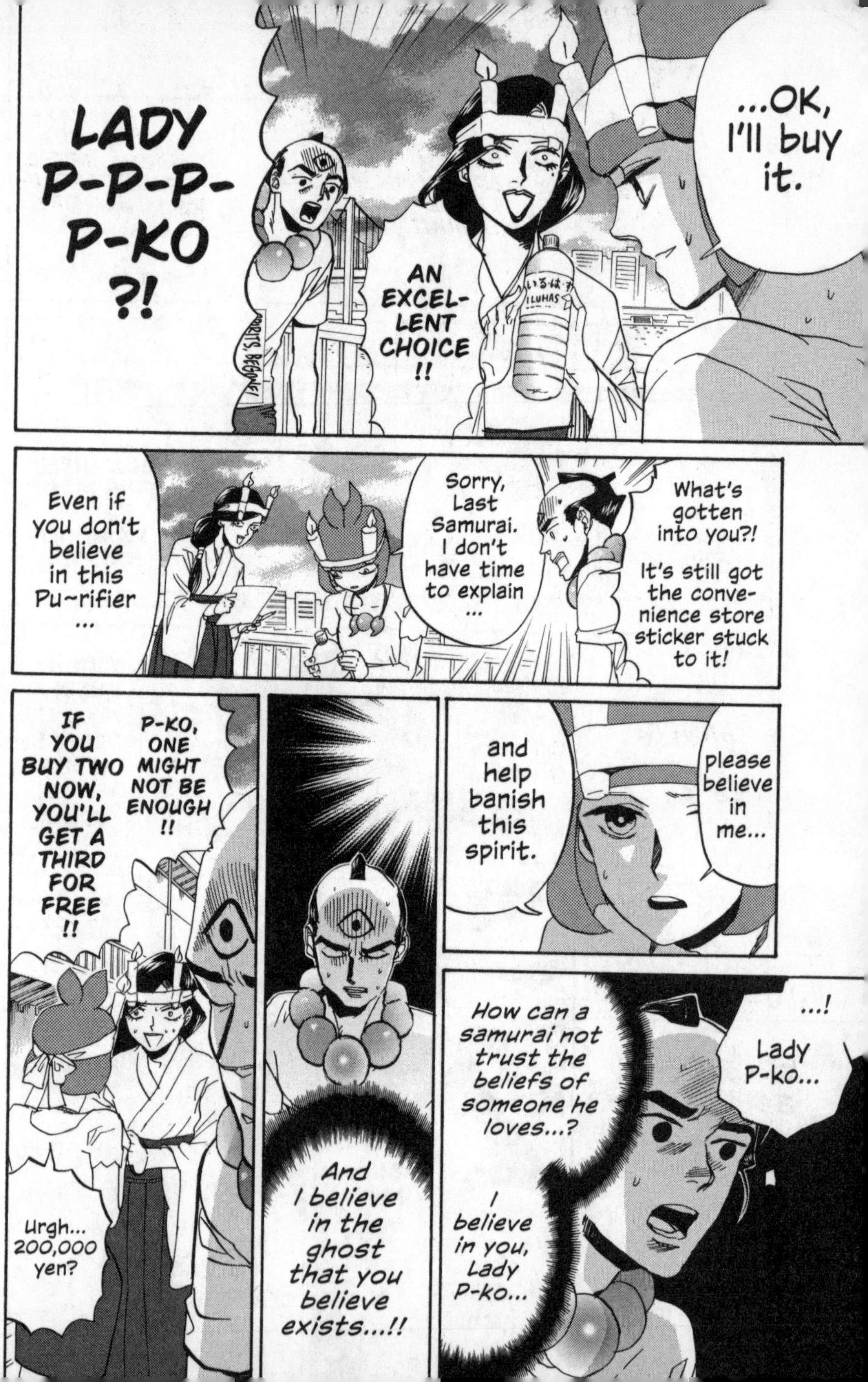
...OK, I'll buy it.
AN EXCEL-LENT CHOICE !!
LADY P-P-P-P-KO ?!
PIRITS, BEGONE!
What's gotten into you?!
It's still got the conve-nience store sticker stuck to it!
Sorry, Last Samurai. I don't have time to explain ...
Even if you don't believe in this Pu~rifier ...
please believe in me...
and help banish this spirit.
...!
Lady P-ko...
How can a samurai not trust the beliefs of someone he loves...?
I believe in you, Lady P-ko...
And I believe in the ghost that you believe exists...!!
P-KO, ONE MIGHT NOT BE ENOUGH !!
IF YOU BUY TWO NOW, YOU'LL GET A THIRD FOR FREE !!
Urgh... 200,000 yen?

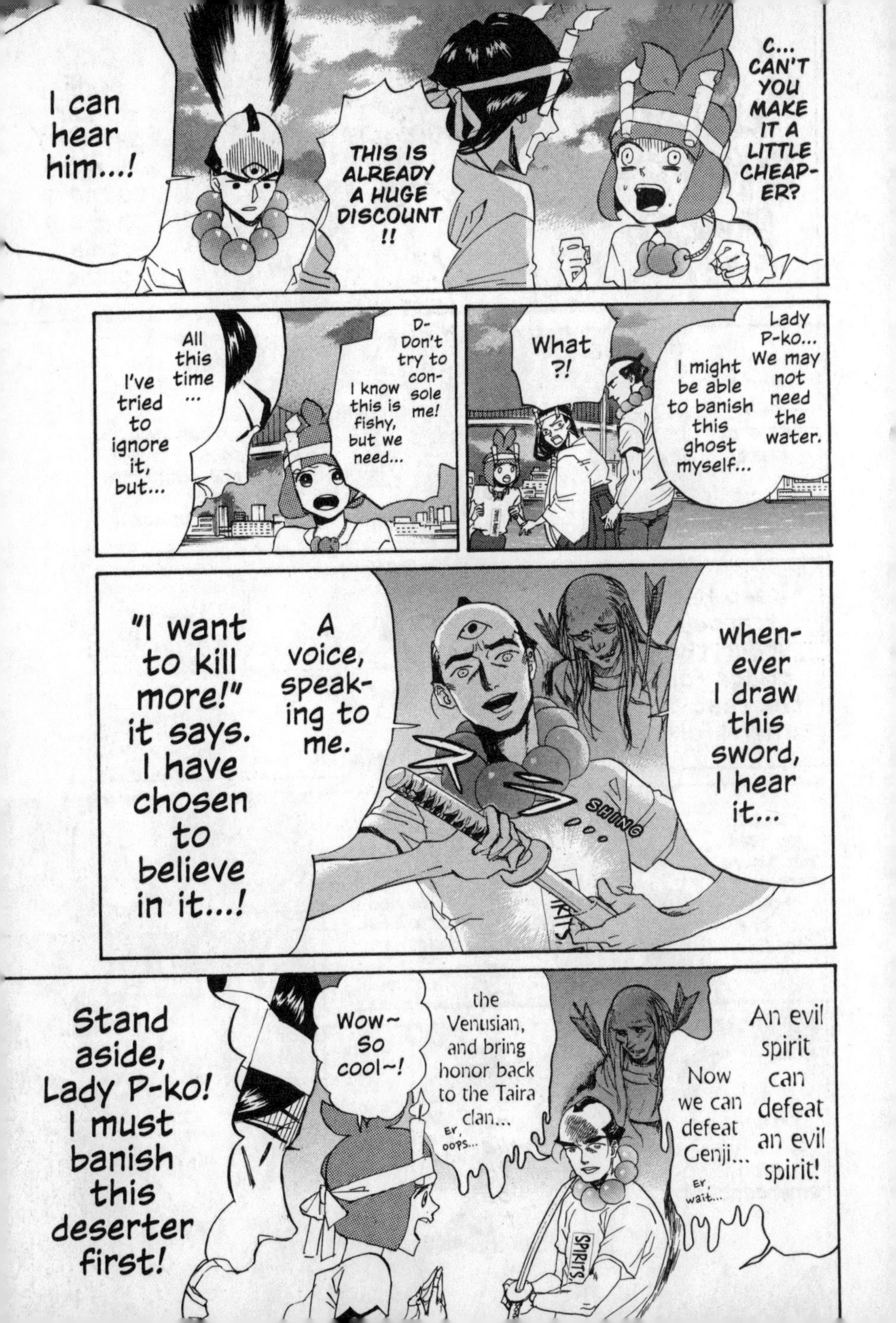
C... CAN'T YOU MAKE IT A LITTLE CHEAPER?
THIS IS ALREADY A HUGE DISCOUNT !!
I can hear him...!
Lady P-ko... We may not need the water.
I might be able to banish this ghost myself...
What ?!
D- Don't try to console me!
I know this is fishy, but we need...
All this time...
I've tried to ignore it, but...
when-ever I draw this sword, I hear it...
A voice, speaking to me.
SHING
"I want to kill more!" it says. I have chosen to believe in it...!
An evil spirit can defeat an evil spirit!
Now we can defeat Genji...
Er, wait...
the Venusian, and bring honor back to the Taira clan...
Er, oops...
Wow~ So cool~!
Stand aside, Lady P-ko! I must banish this deserter first!
SPIRITS

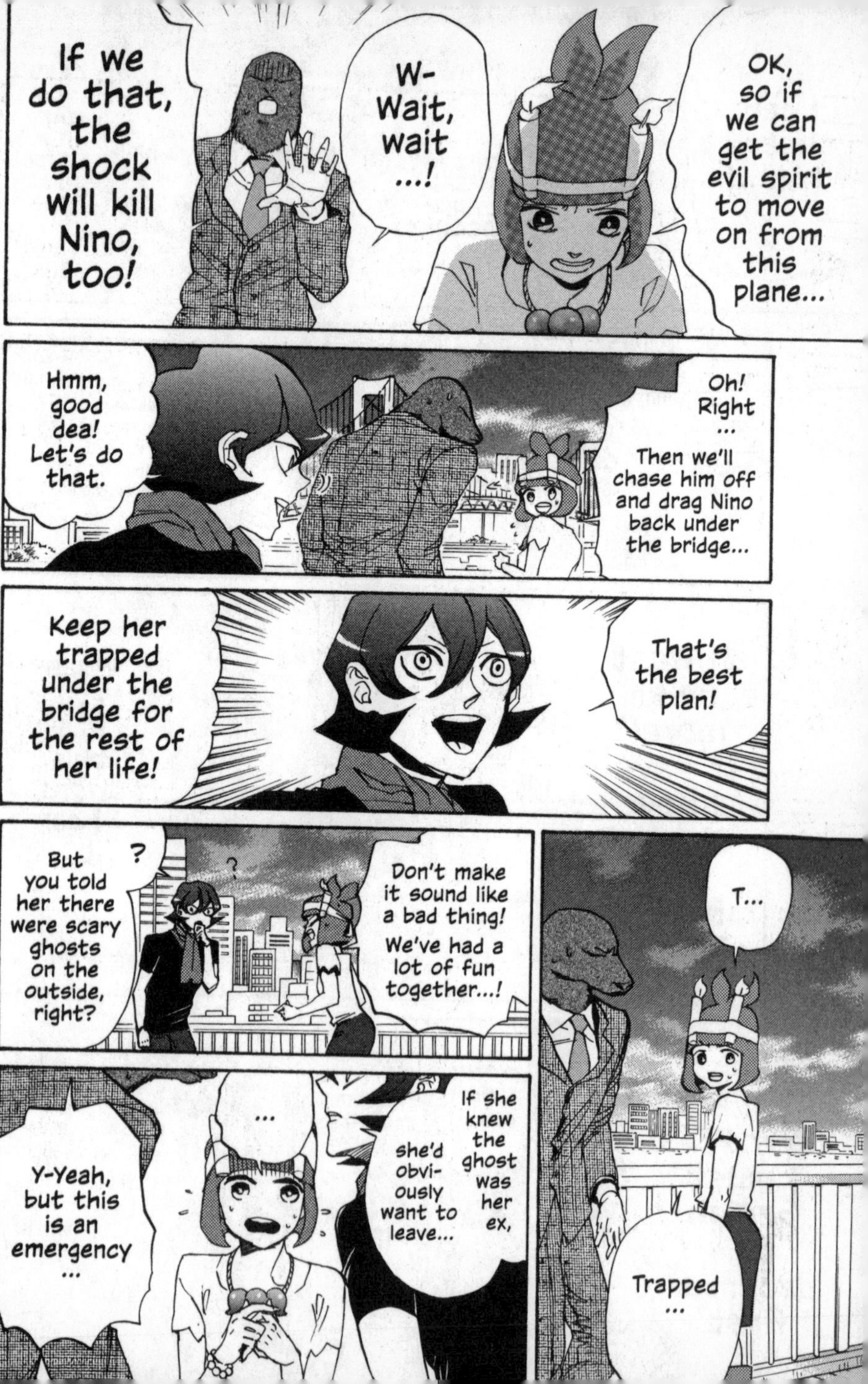
OK, so if we can get the evil spirit to move on from this plane...
W-Wait, wait...!
If we do that, the shock will kill Nino, too!
Oh! Right... Then we'll chase him off and drag Nino back under the bridge...
Hmm, good dea! Let's do that.
That's the best plan!
Keep her trapped under the bridge for the rest of her life!
T...
Trapped...
Don't make it sound like a bad thing! We've had a lot of fun together...!
?
But you told her there were scary ghosts on the outside, right?
If she knew the ghost was her ex,
she'd obviously want to leave...
...
Y-Yeah, but this is an emergency...

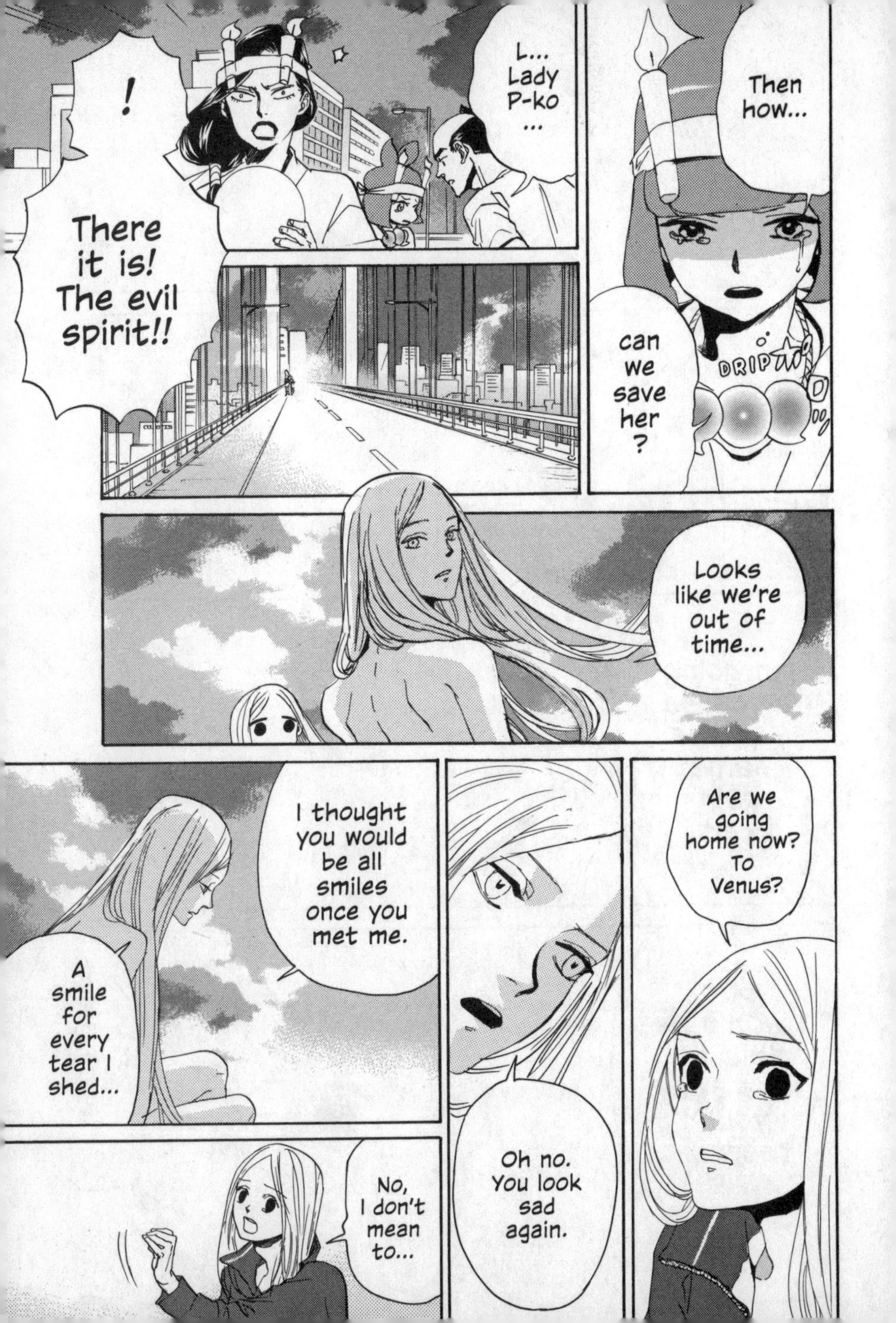
Then how...
can we save her?
DRIP
L... Lady P-ko...
!
There it is! The evil spirit!!
Looks like we're out of time...
Are we going home now? To Venus?
Oh no. You look sad again.
I thought you would be all smiles once you met me.
A smile for every tear I shed...
No, I don't mean to...

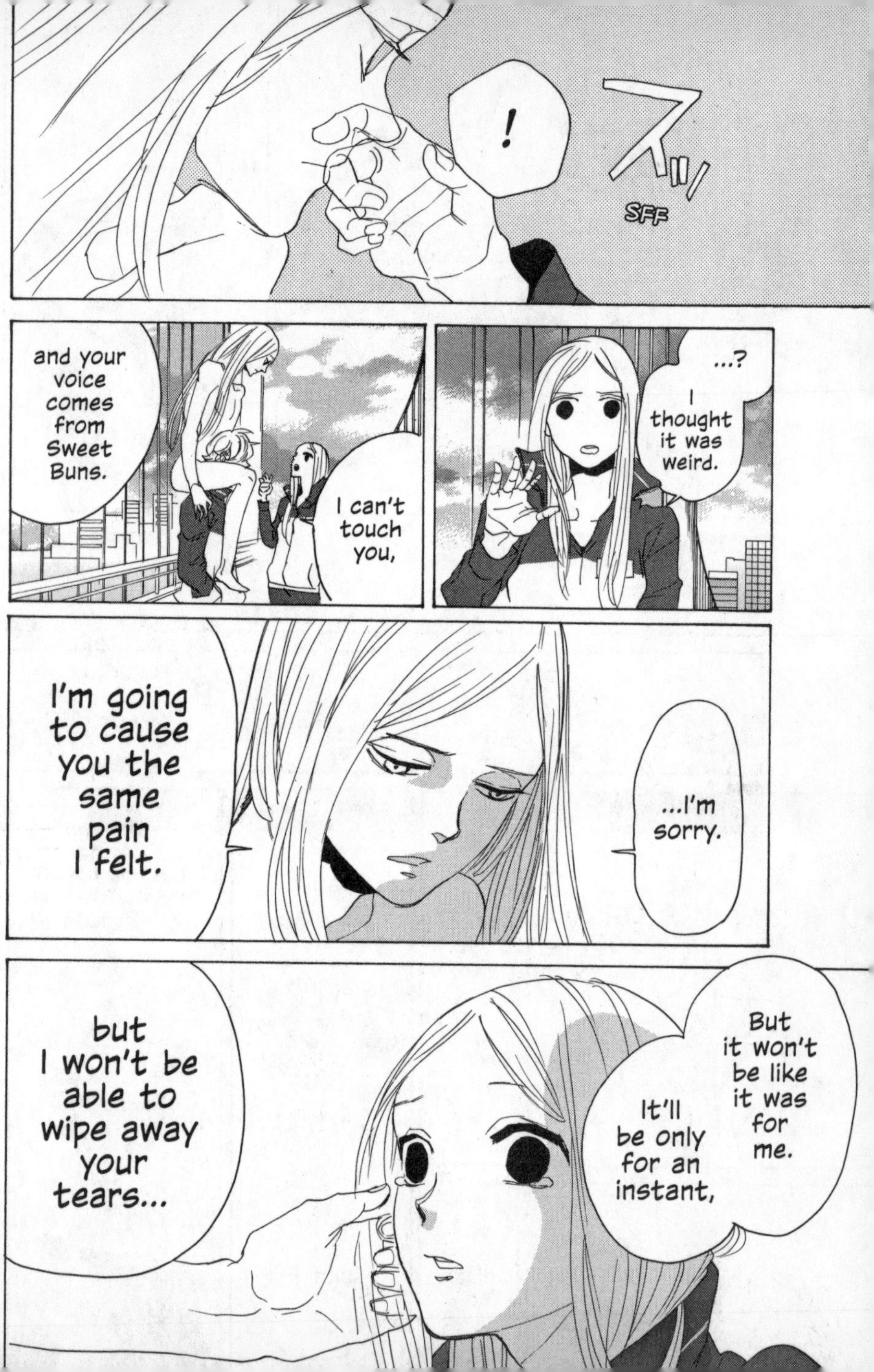
!
SFF
...? I thought it was weird.
I can't touch you,
and your voice comes from Sweet Buns.
...I'm sorry.
I'm going to cause you the same pain I felt.
But it won't be like it was for me.
It'll be only for an instant,
but I won't be able to wipe away your tears...

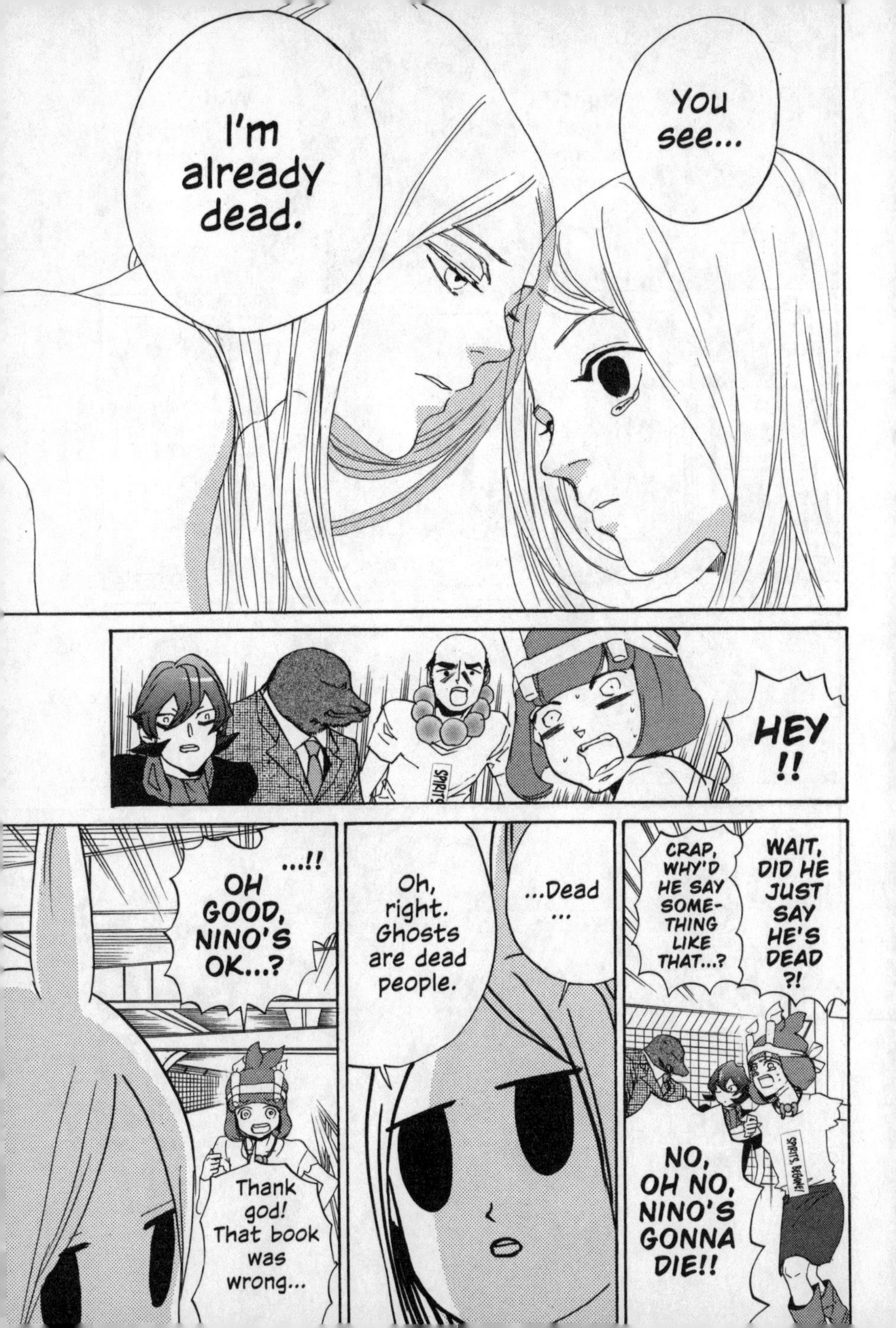
You see...
I'm already dead.
HEY !!
WAIT, DID HE JUST SAY HE'S DEAD ?!
CRAP, WHY'D HE SAY SOME- THING LIKE THAT...?
NO, OH NO, NINO'S GONNA DIE!!
...Dead ...
Oh, right. Ghosts are dead people.
...!!
OH GOOD, NINO'S OK...?
Thank god! That book was wrong...

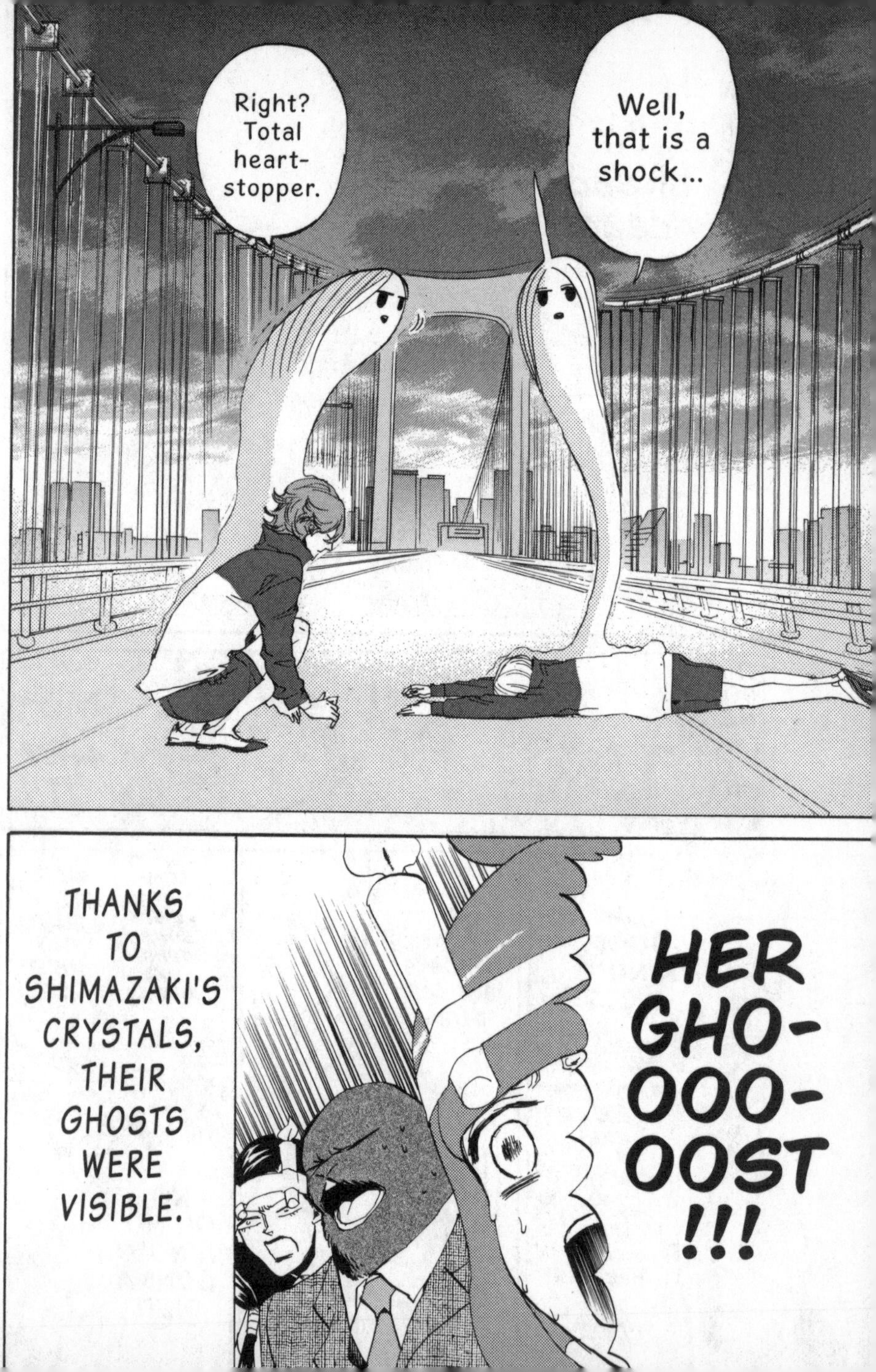
Well, that is a shock...
Right? Total heart-stopper.
HER GHO-OOO-OOST!!!
THANKS TO SHIMAZAKI'S CRYSTALS, THEIR GHOSTS WERE VISIBLE.

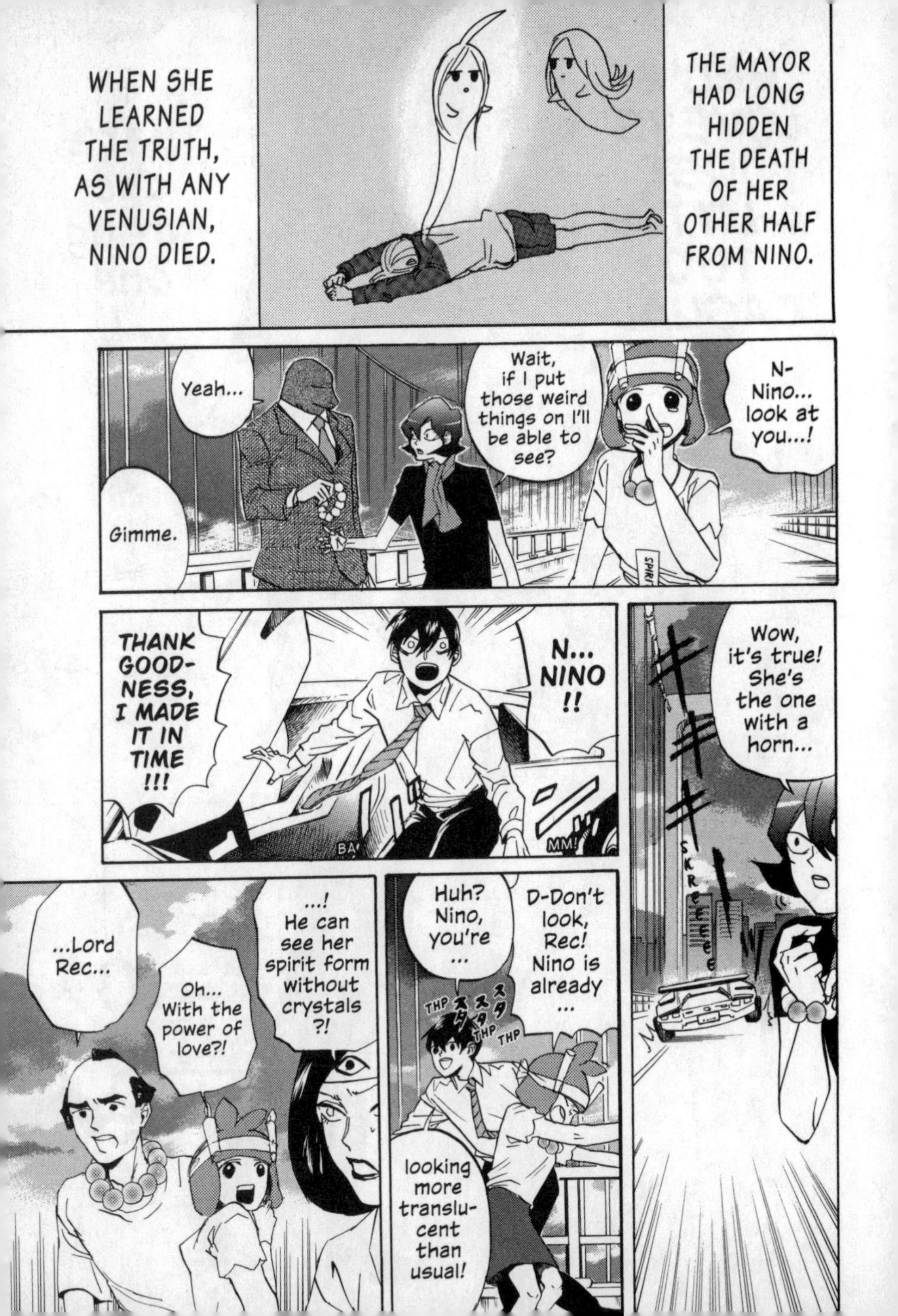
THE MAYOR HAD LONG HIDDEN THE DEATH OF HER OTHER HALF FROM NINO.
WHEN SHE LEARNED THE TRUTH, AS WITH ANY VENUSIAN, NINO DIED.
N-Nino... look at you...!
Wait, if I put those weird things on I'll be able to see?
Yeah...
Gimme.
SPIRIT
Wow, it's true! She's the one with a horn...
SKREEEEEE
N... NINO!!
THANK GOODNESS, I MADE IT IN TIME!!!
BA
MM!
D-Don't look, Rec! Nino is already...
Huh? Nino, you're...
THP スタ THP スタ THP
looking more translucent than usual!
...! He can see her spirit form without crystals?!
...Lord Rec...
Oh... With the power of love?!

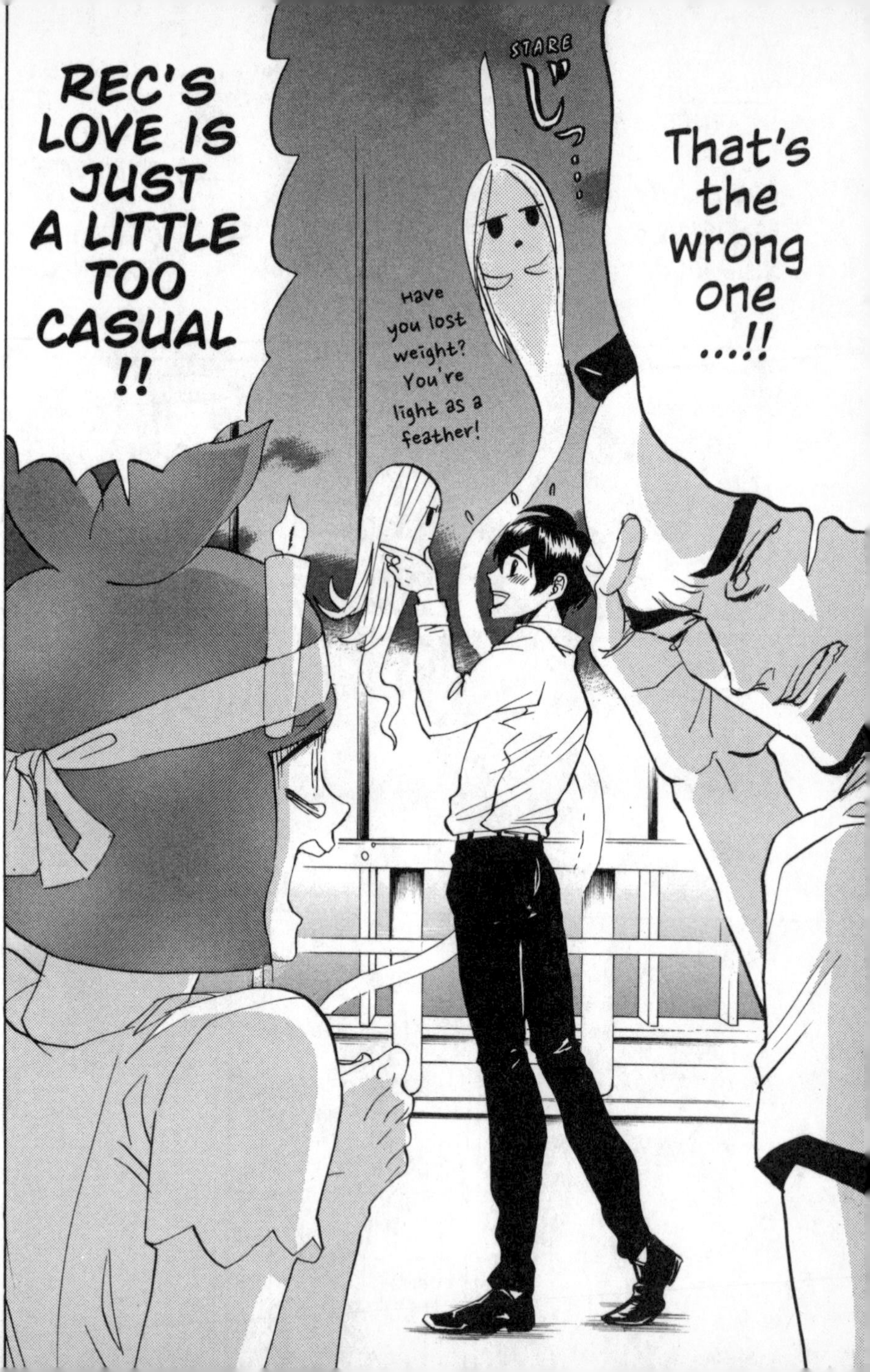
That's the wrong one ...!!
STARE
じっ…
Have you lost weight? You're light as a feather!
REC'S LOVE IS JUST A LITTLE TOO CASUAL !!

Chapter 400: My Girlfriend is a Venusian

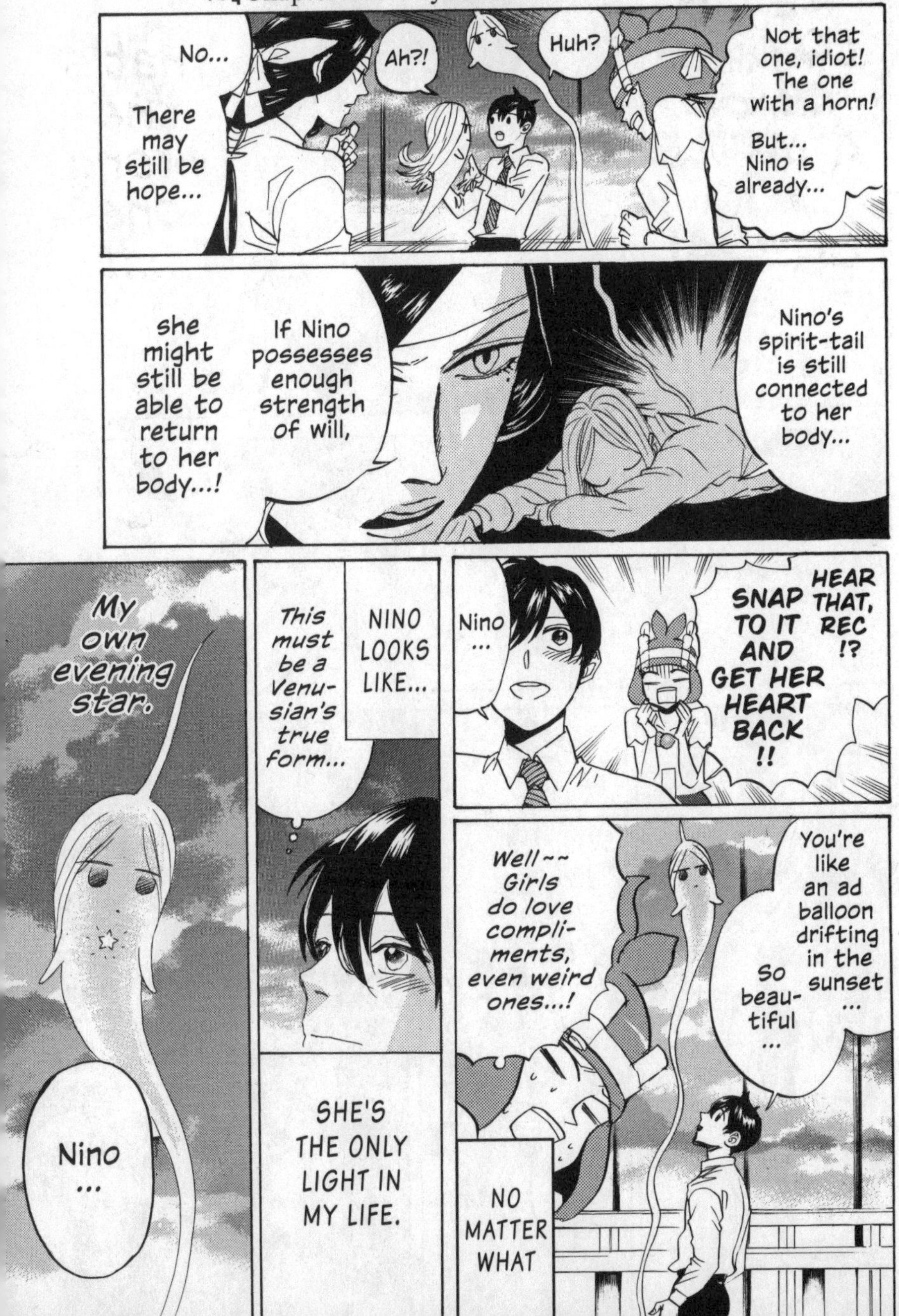

Not that one, idiot! The one with a horn!
But... Nino is already...
Huh?
Ah?!
No... There may still be hope...
Nino's spirit-tail is still connected to her body...
If Nino possesses enough strength of will,
she might still be able to return to her body...!
HEAR THAT, REC!?
SNAP TO IT AND GET HER HEART BACK!!
Nino...
You're like an ad balloon drifting in the sunset...
So beautiful...
Well~~ Girls do love compliments, even weird ones...!
NO MATTER WHAT
NINO LOOKS LIKE...
This must be a Venusian's true form...
SHE'S THE ONLY LIGHT IN MY LIFE.
My own evening star.
Nino...

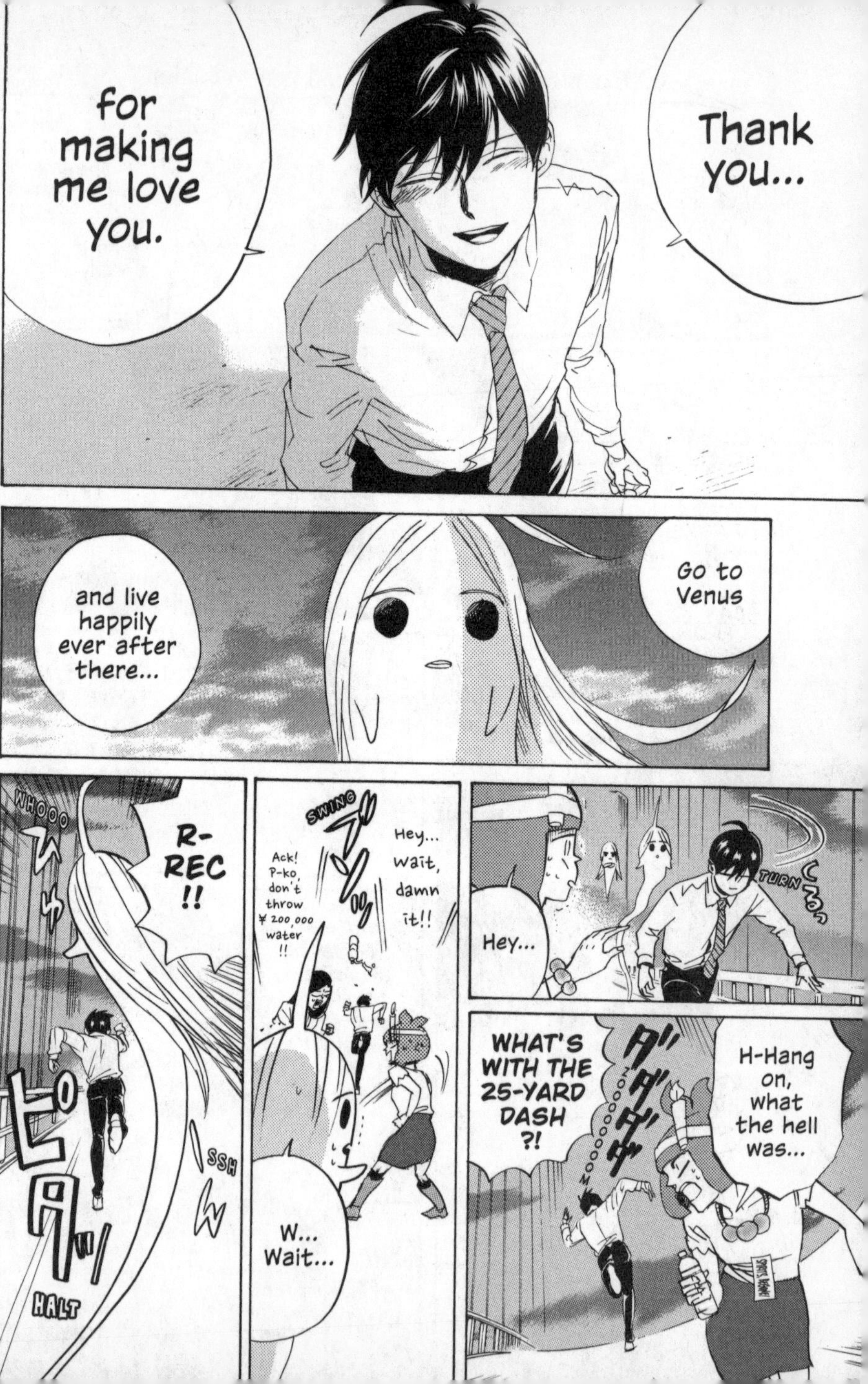

Thank you...
for making me love you.
Go to Venus
and live happily ever after there...
TURN
Hey...
H-Hang on, what the hell was...
WHAT'S WITH THE 25-YARD DASH ?!
SWING
Hey... wait, damn it!!
Ack! P-ko, don't throw ¥200,000 water !!
W... Wait...
WHOOO
R-REC !!
SSH
HALT

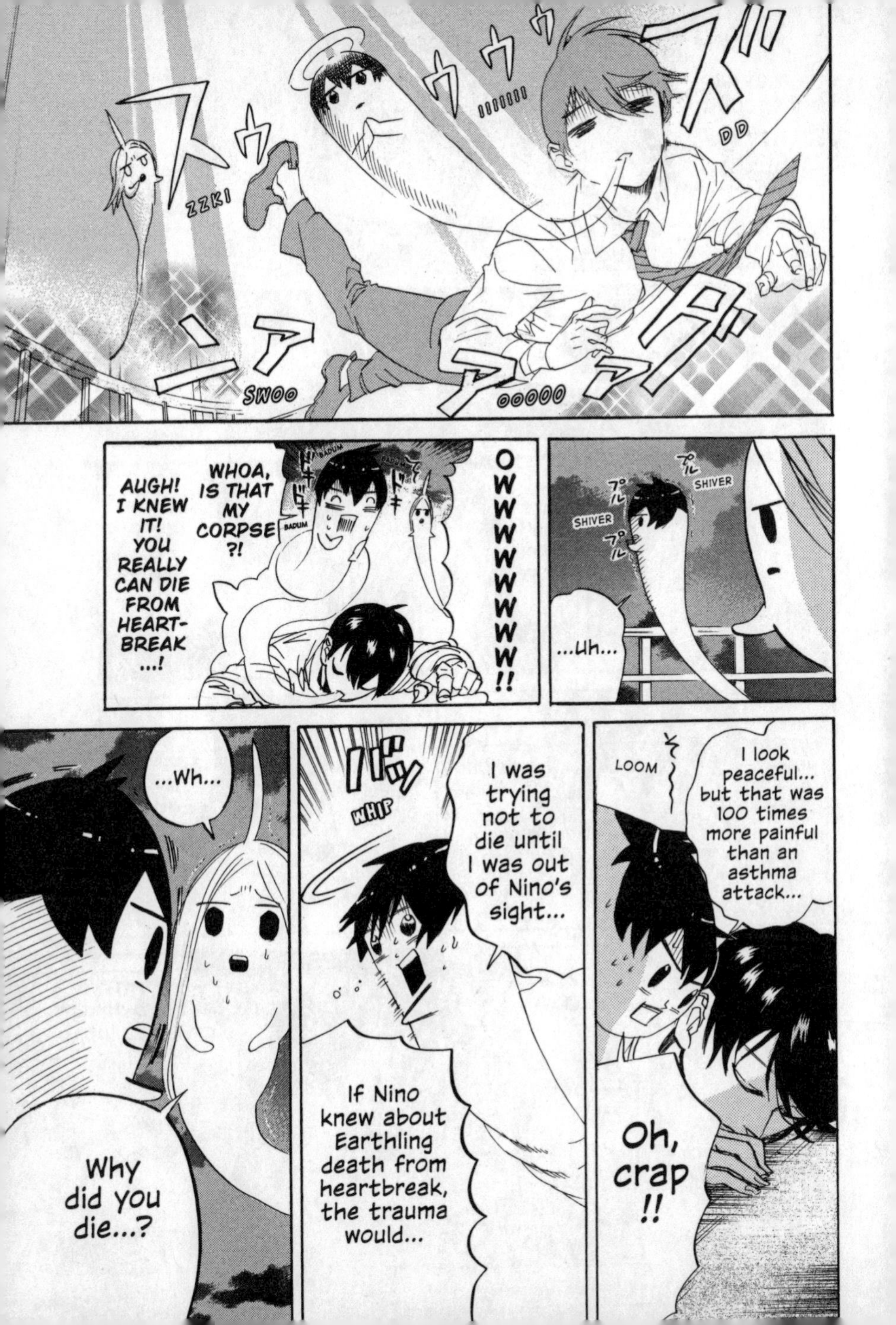
DD
ooooooo
ZZKI
ooooo
SWOO
SHIVER
SHIVER
...uh...
OWWWWWWWWWW!!
BADUM
BADUM
BADUM
WHOA, IS THAT MY CORPSE?!
AUGH! I KNEW IT! YOU REALLY CAN DIE FROM HEARTBREAK...!
LOOM
I look peaceful... but that was 100 times more painful than an asthma attack...
Oh, crap!!
WHIP
I was trying not to die until I was out of Nino's sight...
If Nino knew about Earthling death from heartbreak, the trauma would...
...Wh...
Why did you die...?

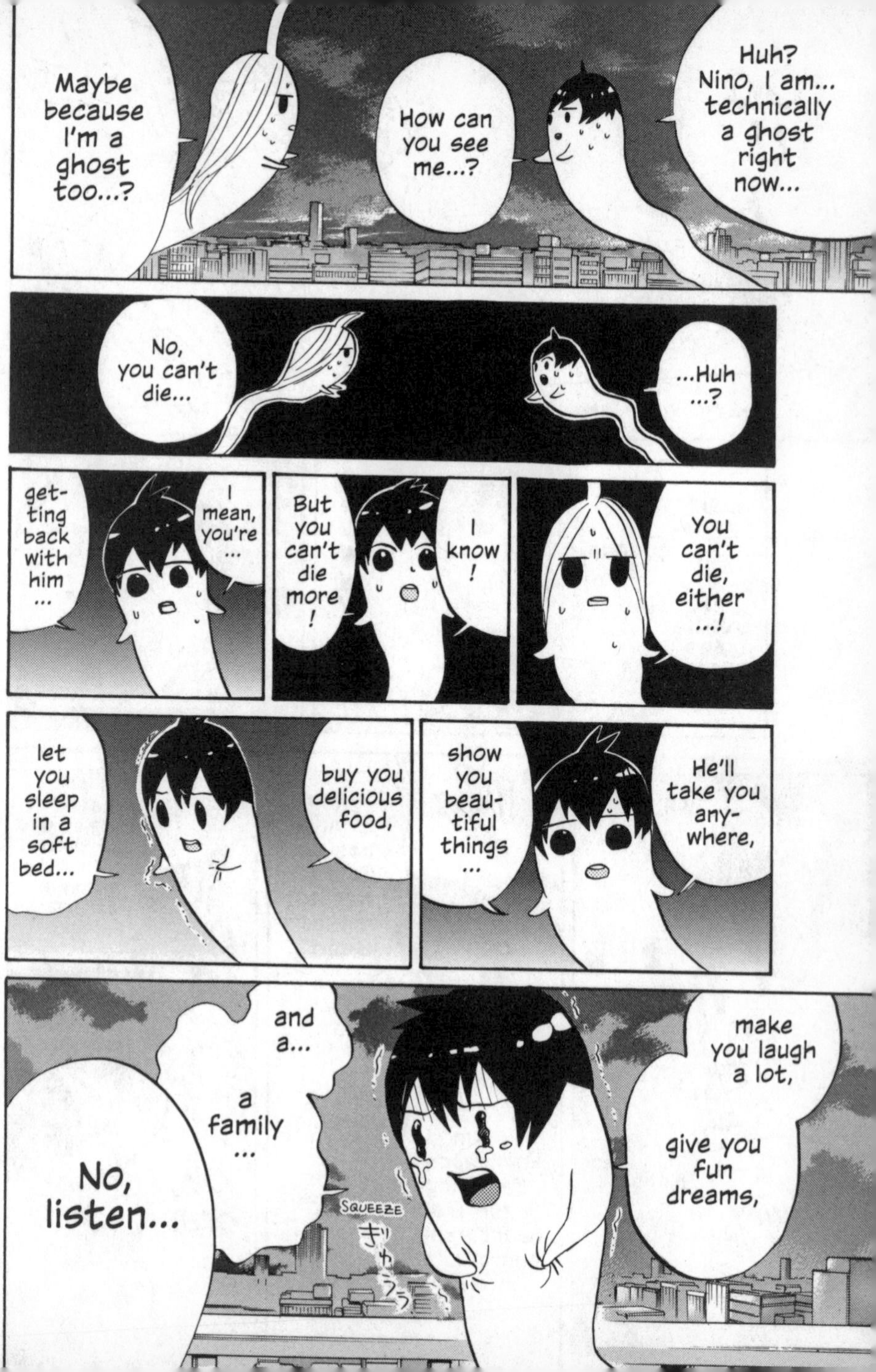
Huh? Nino, I am... technically a ghost right now...
How can you see me...?
Maybe because I'm a ghost too...?
...Huh ...?
No, you can't die...
You can't die, either ...!
I know!
But you can't die more!
I mean, you're ...
getting back with him ...
He'll take you anywhere,
show you beautiful things ...
buy you delicious food,
let you sleep in a soft bed...
make you laugh a lot,
give you fun dreams,
and a...
a family ...
SQUEEZE
ぎゅうう
No, listen...

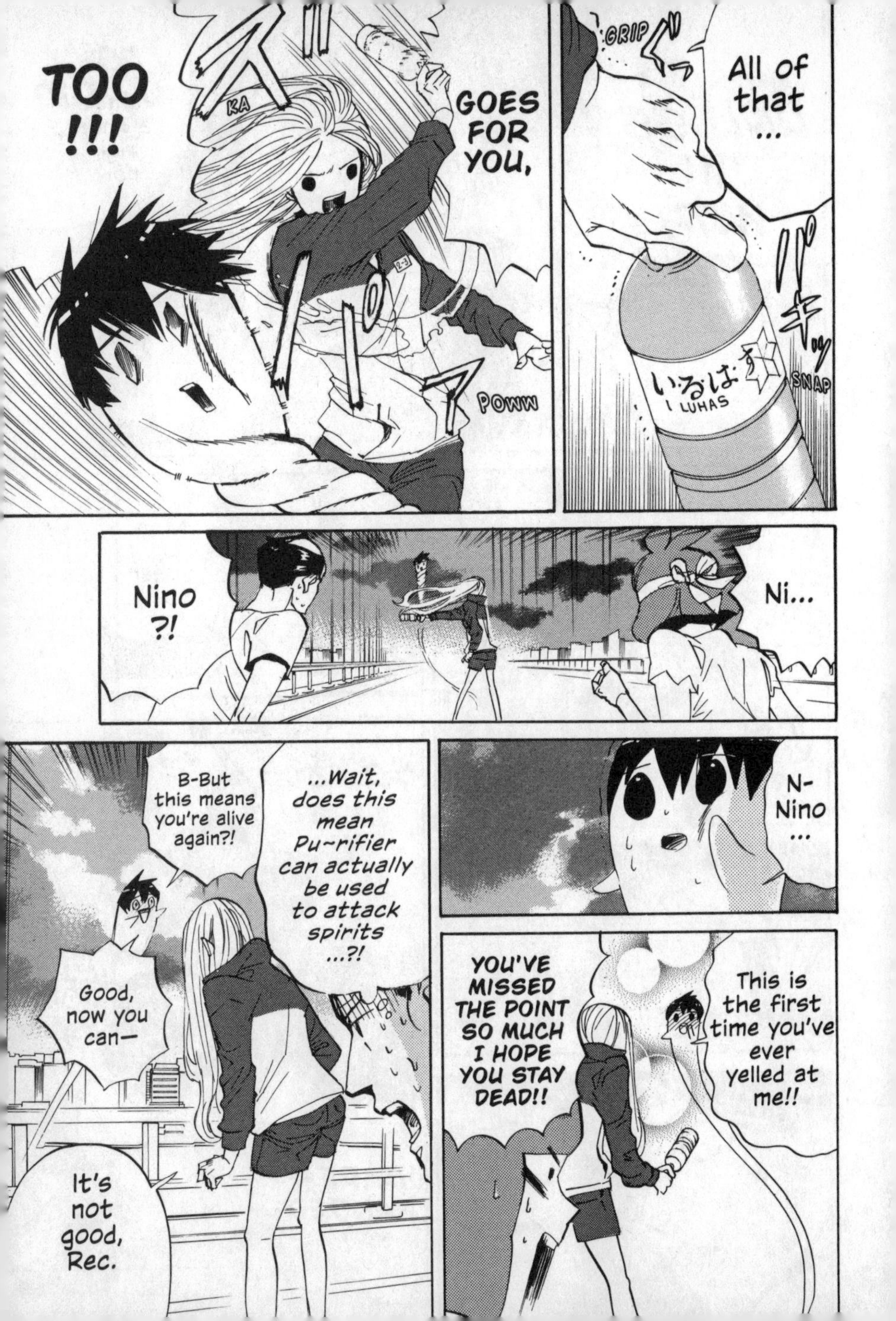
GRIP
All of that ...
いるはす
I LUHAS
SNAP
GOES FOR YOU,
TOO !!!
KA
POWW
Ni...
Nino ?!
N-Nino ...
This is the first time you've ever yelled at me!!
YOU'VE MISSED THE POINT SO MUCH I HOPE YOU STAY DEAD!!
...Wait, does this mean Pu~rifier can actually be used to attack spirits ...?!
B-But this means you're alive again?!
Good, now you can—
It's not good, Rec.

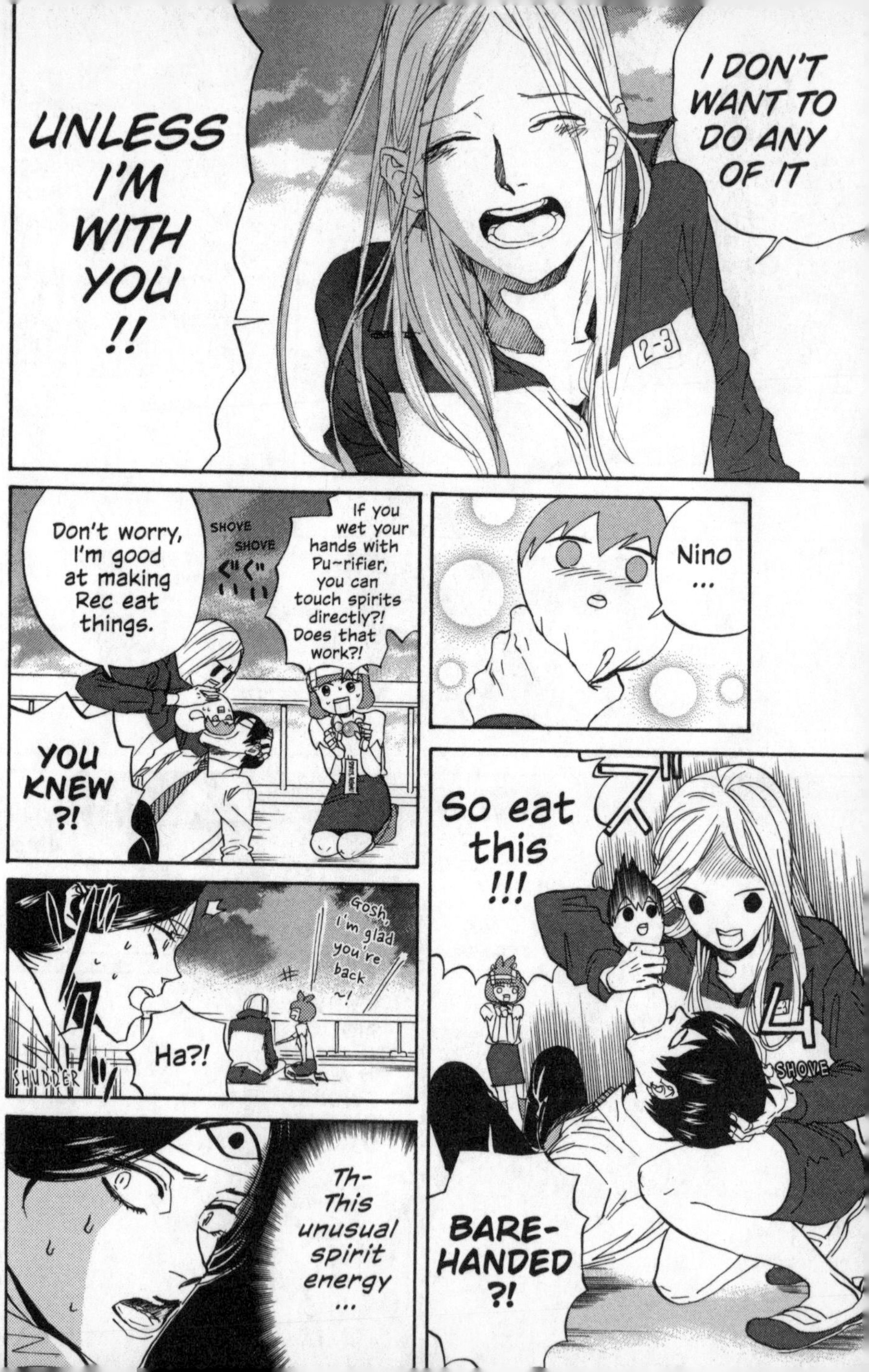
I DON'T WANT TO DO ANY OF IT
UNLESS I'M WITH YOU!!
Nino...
If you wet your hands with Pu~rifier, you can touch spirits directly?! Does that work?!
Don't worry, I'm good at making Rec eat things.
SHOVE SHOVE
YOU KNEW?!
So eat this!!!
SHOVE
BARE-HANDED?!
Gosh, I'm glad you're back~!
Ha?!
SHUDDER
Th- This unusual spirit energy...

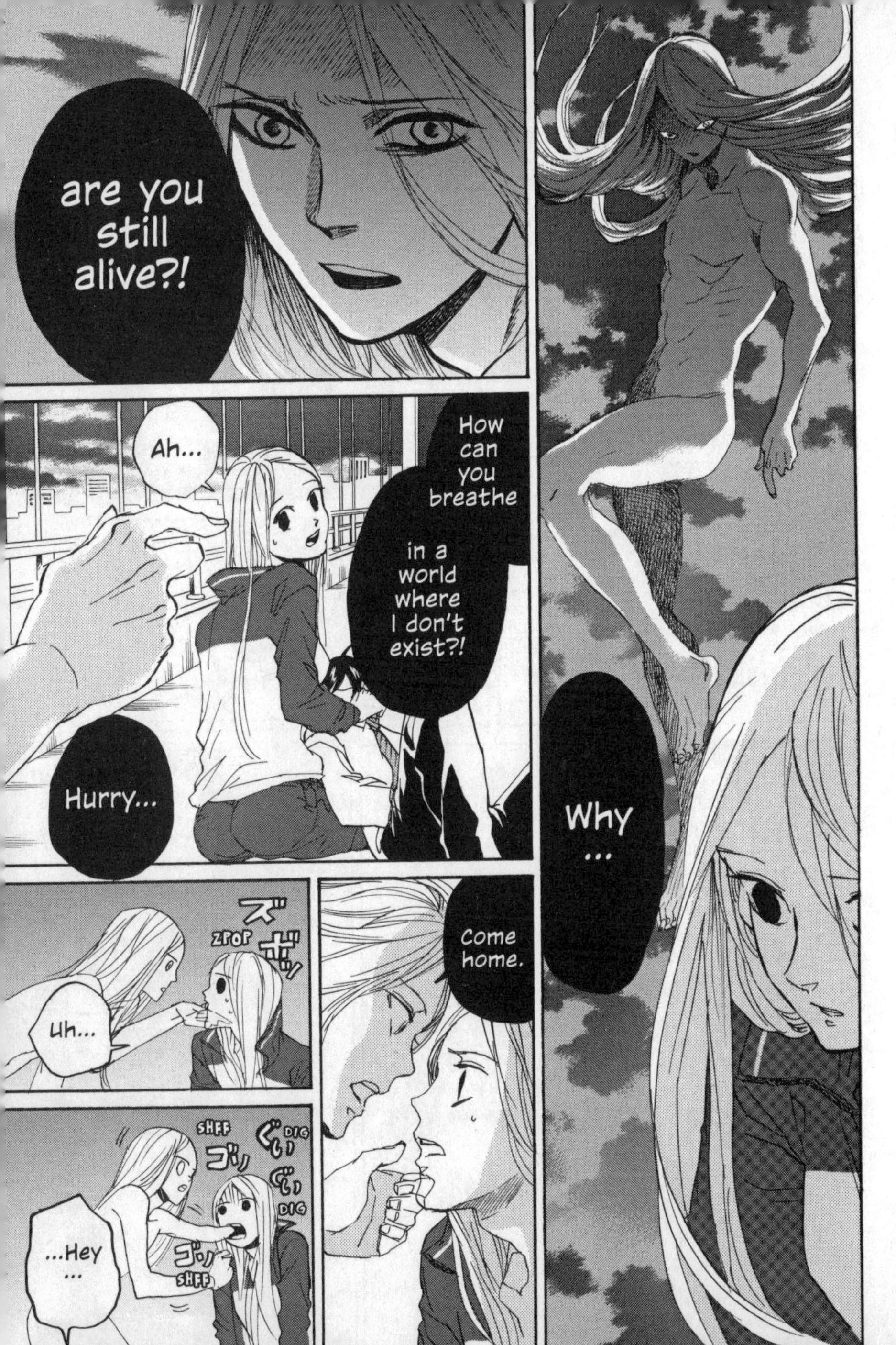
Why ...
are you still alive?!
How can you breathe
in a world where I don't exist?!
Ah...
Hurry...
Come home.
ZPOP
Uh...
SHFF
DIG
DIG
SHFF
...Hey ...

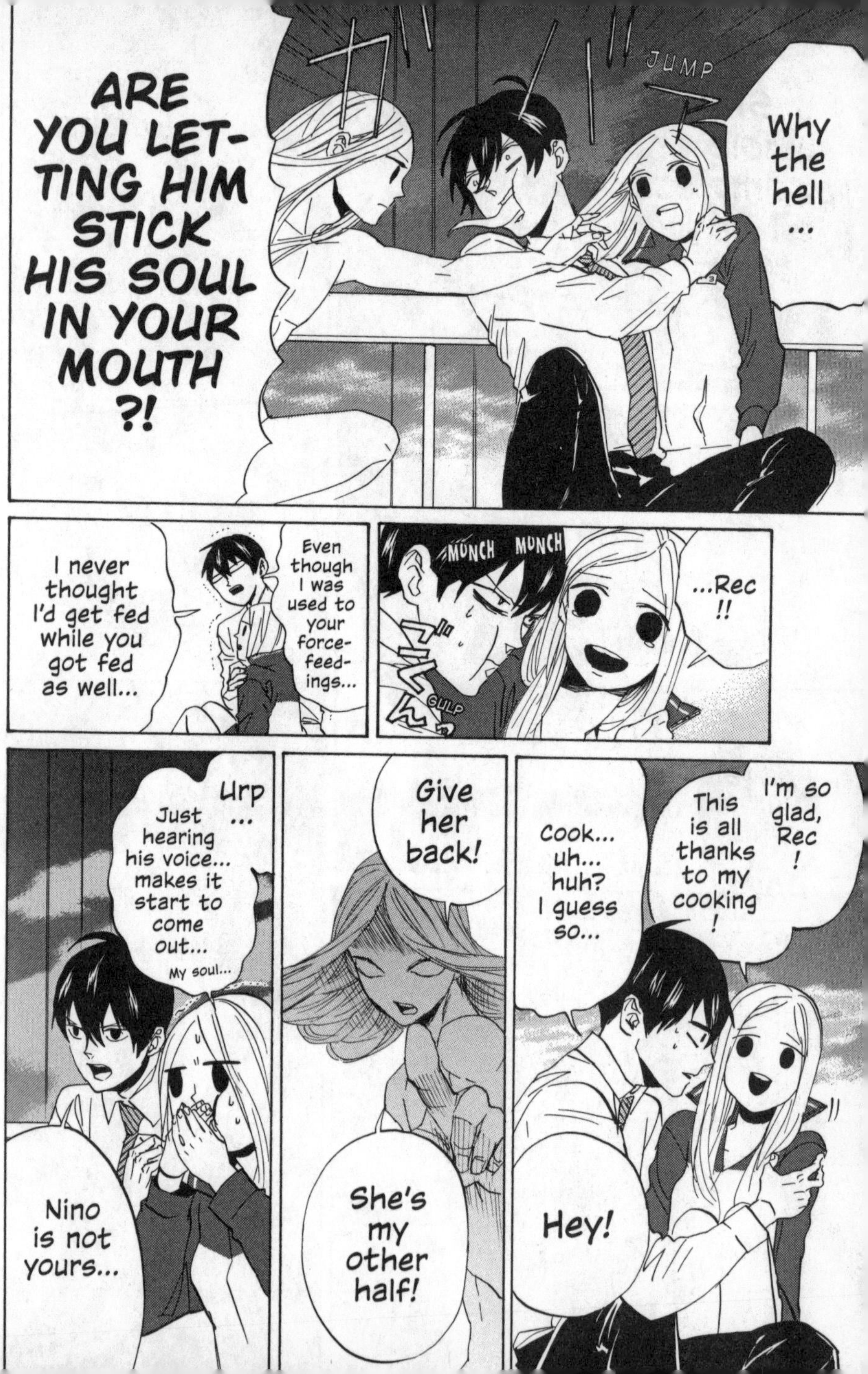
JUMP
Why the hell ...
ARE YOU LET-TING HIM STICK HIS SOUL IN YOUR MOUTH ?!
MUNCH MUNCH
...Rec !!
GULP
Even though I was used to your force-feed-ings...
I never thought I'd get fed while you got fed as well...
I'm so glad, Rec !
This is all thanks to my cooking !
Cook... uh... huh? I guess so...
Hey!
Give her back!
She's my other half!
Urp ...
Just hearing his voice... makes it start to come out...
My soul...
Nino is not yours...

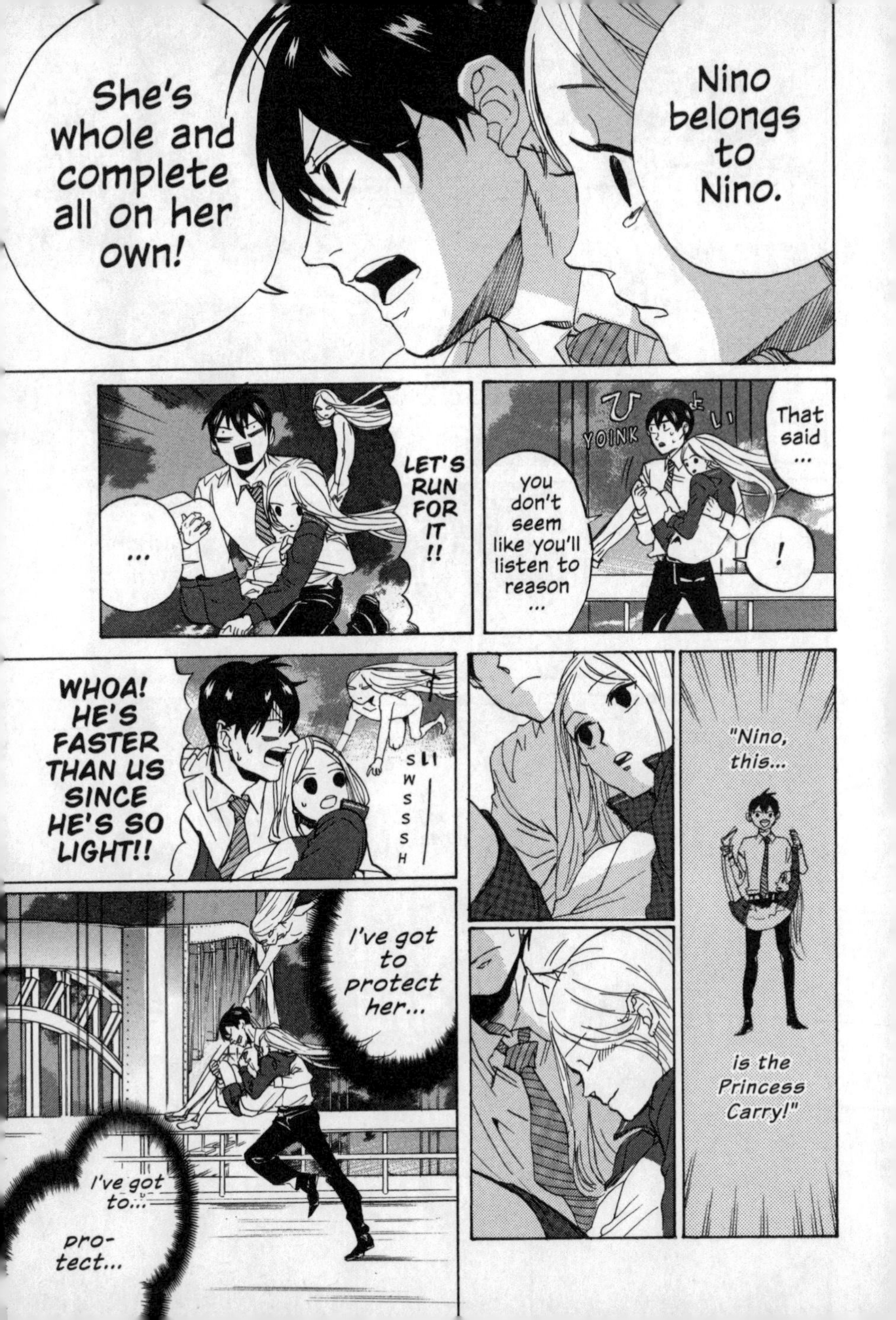
Nino belongs to Nino.
She's whole and complete all on her own!
That said...
ひょい
YOINK
you don't seem like you'll listen to reason...
!
LET'S RUN FOR IT!!
...
"Nino, this...
is the Princess Carry!"
WHOA! HE'S FASTER THAN US SINCE HE'S SO LIGHT!!
I've got to protect her...
I've got to...
pro-tect...

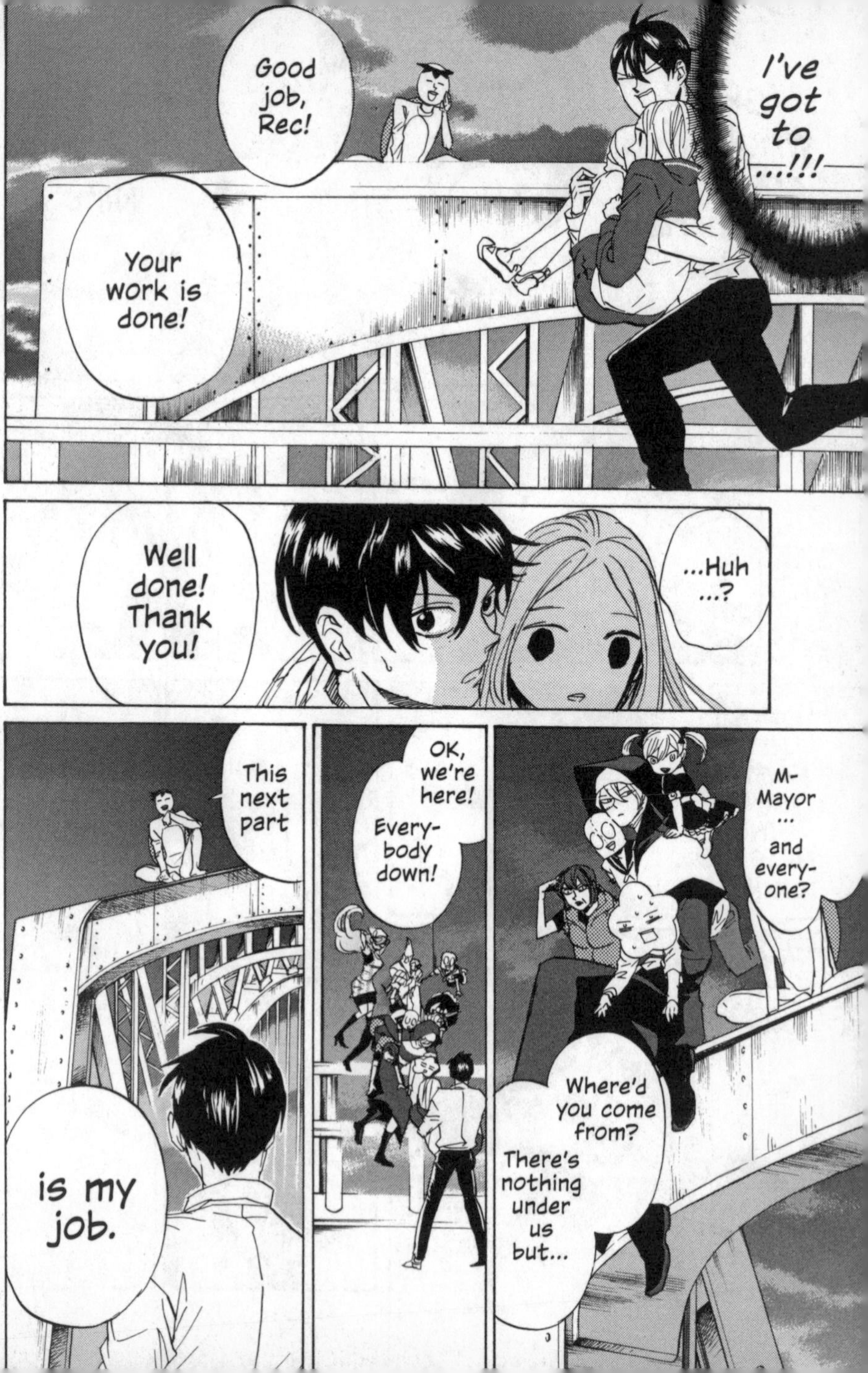
I've got to ...!!!
Good job, Rec!
Your work is done!
...Huh ...?
Well done! Thank you!
M-Mayor ... and every-one?
Where'd you come from?
There's nothing under us but...
OK, we're here!
Every-body down!
This next part
is my job.

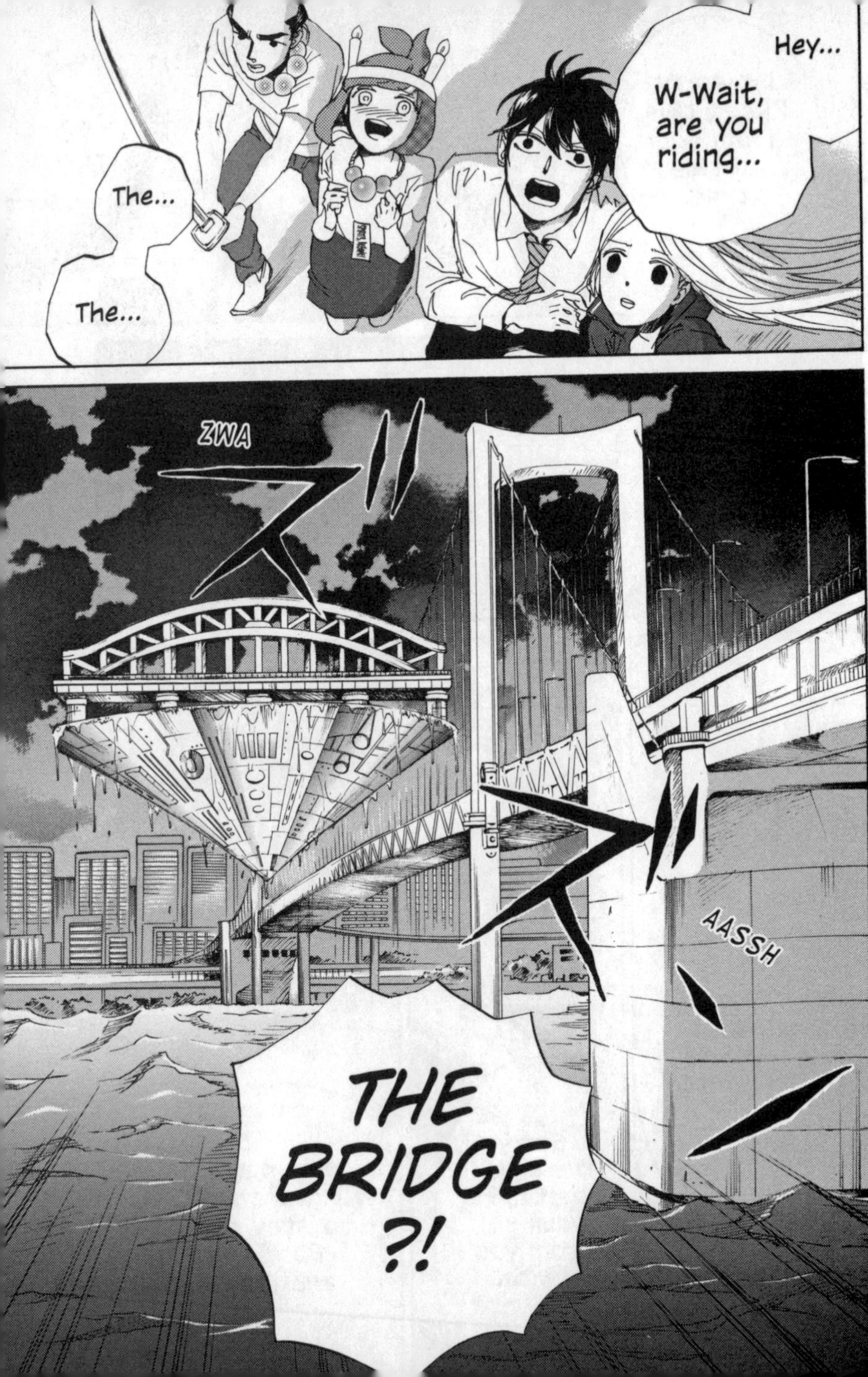
Hey...
W-Wait, are you riding...
The...
The...
ZWA
AASSH
THE BRIDGE ?!

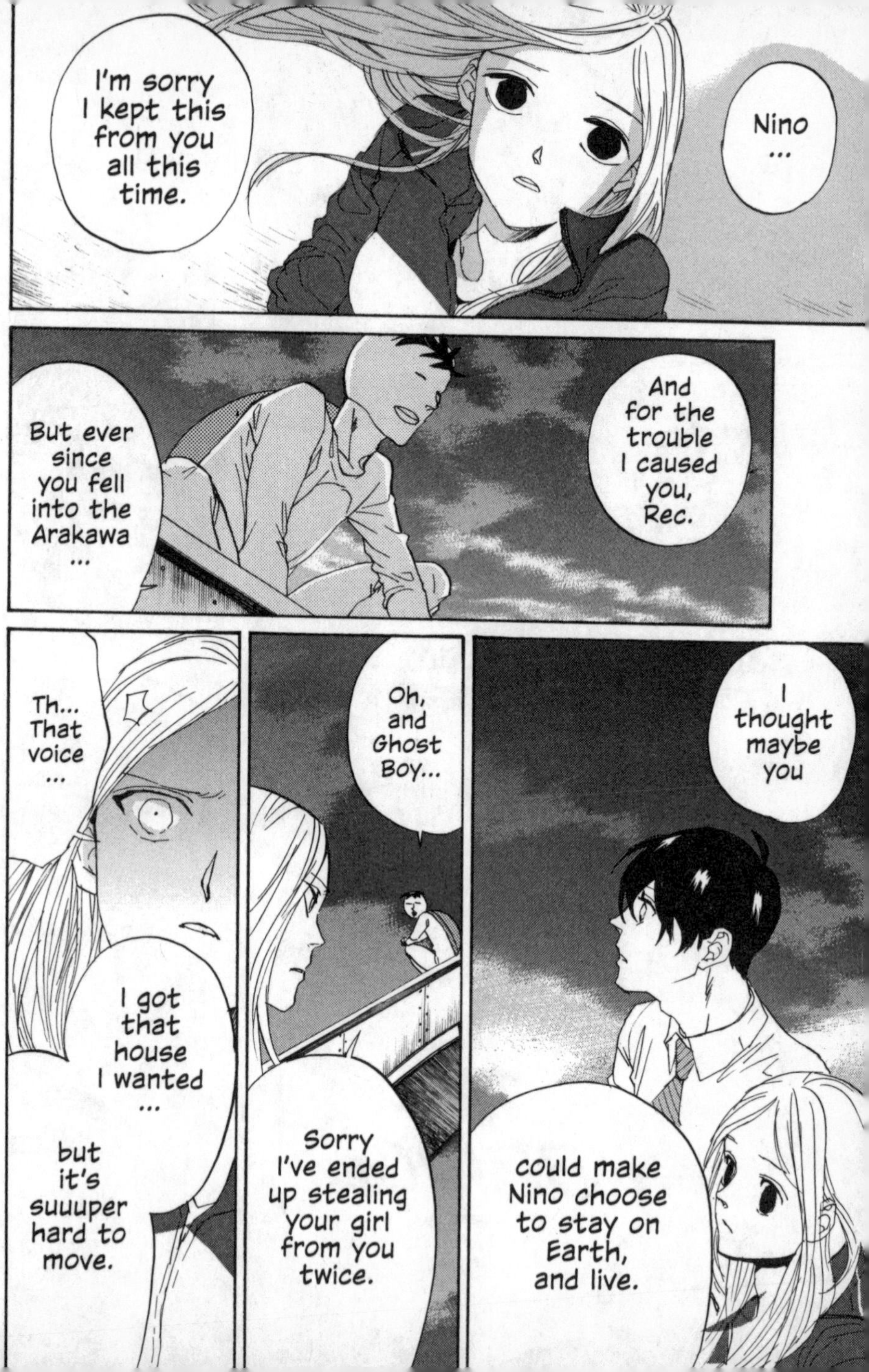
Nino...
I'm sorry I kept this from you all this time.
And for the trouble I caused you, Rec.
But ever since you fell into the Arakawa...
I thought maybe you
could make Nino choose to stay on Earth, and live.
Oh, and Ghost Boy...
Sorry I've ended up stealing your girl from you twice.
Th... That voice...
I got that house I wanted...
but it's suuuper hard to move.

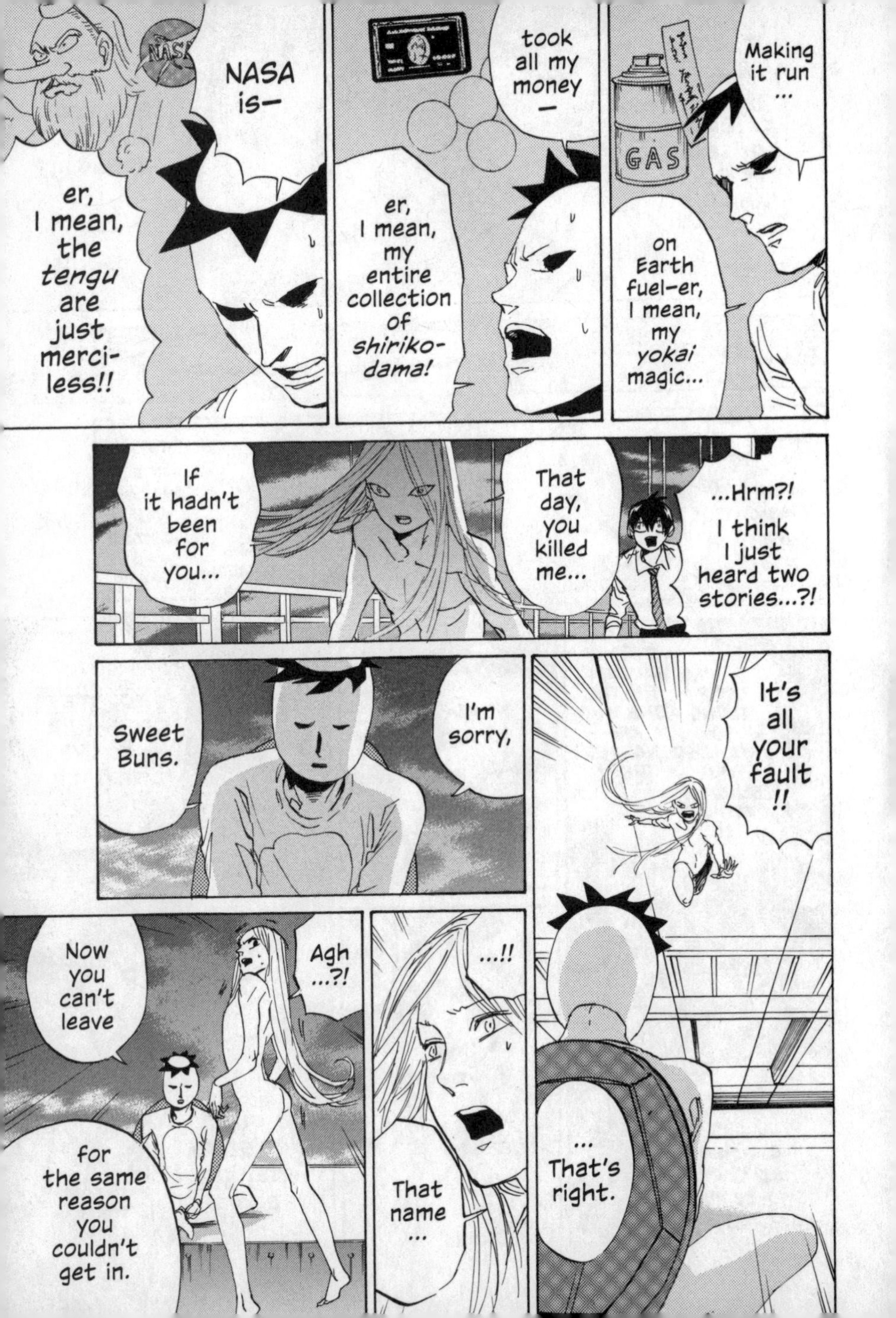

GAS
Making it run ...
on Earth fuel–er, I mean, my *yokai* magic...
took all my money —
er, I mean, my entire collection of *shiriko-dama!*
NASA
NASA is—
er, I mean, the *tengu* are just merciless!!
...Hrm?! I think I just heard two stories...?!
That day, you killed me...
If it hadn't been for you...
It's all your fault !!
I'm sorry,
Sweet Buns.
... That's right.
...!!
That name ...
Agh ...?!
Now you can't leave
for the same reason you couldn't get in.

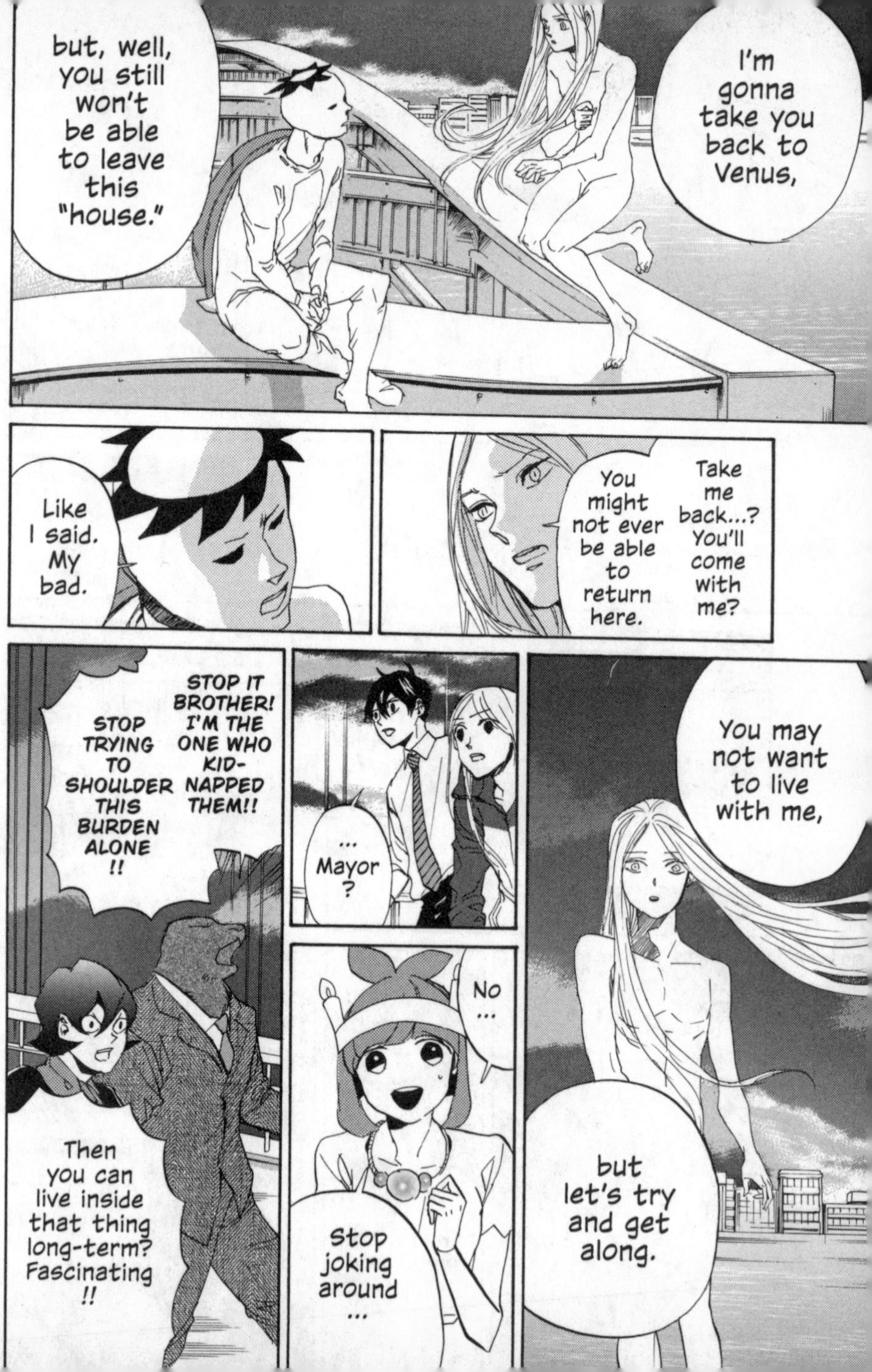
I'm gonna take you back to Venus,
but, well, you still won't be able to leave this "house."
Take me back...? You'll come with me?
You might not ever be able to return here.
Like I said. My bad.
You may not want to live with me,
but let's try and get along.
... Mayor?
No ...
Stop joking around ...
STOP IT BROTHER! I'M THE ONE WHO KID-NAPPED THEM!!
STOP TRYING TO SHOULDER THIS BURDEN ALONE !!
Then you can live inside that thing long-term? Fascinating !!

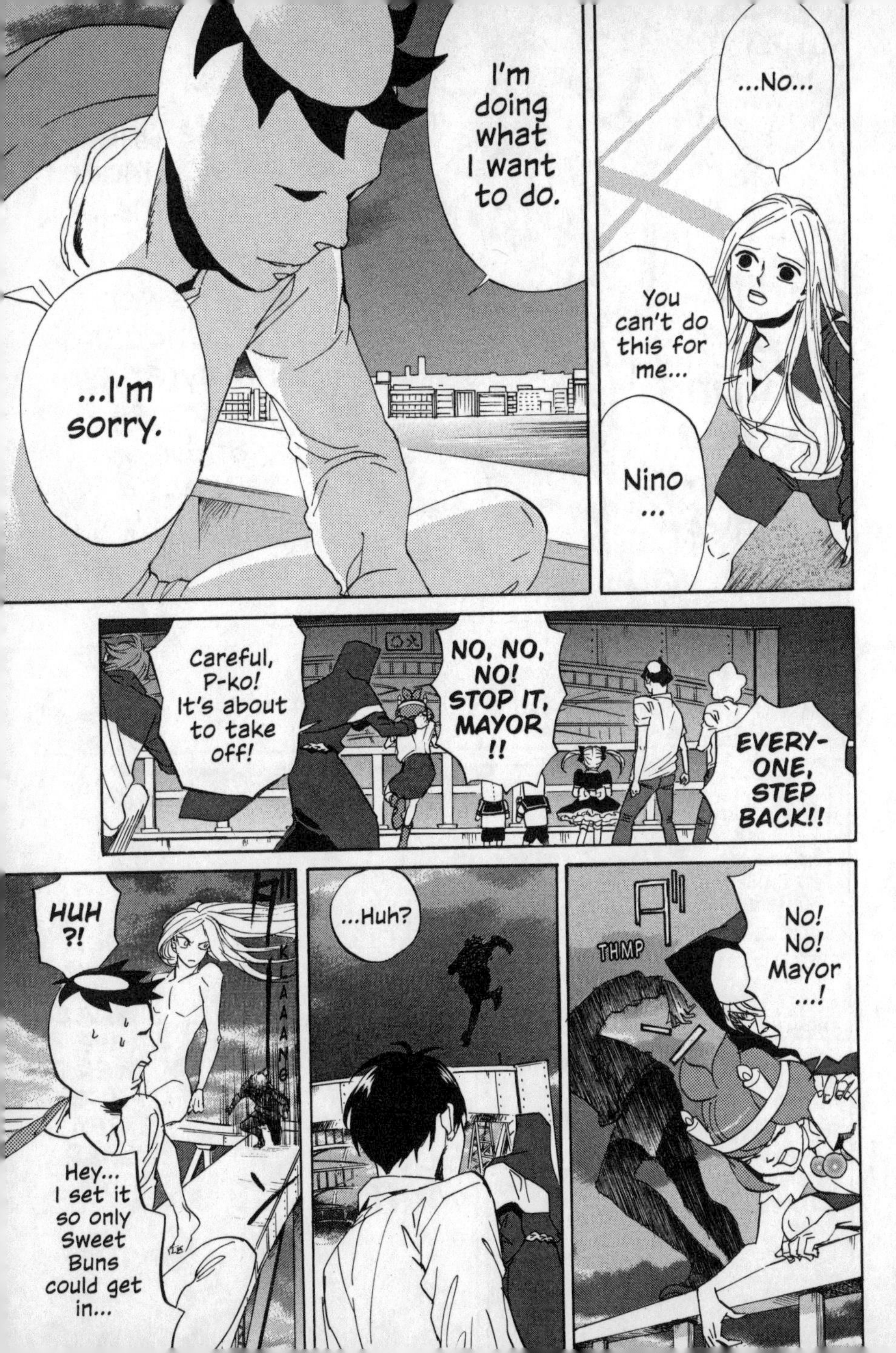
...No...
You can't do this for me...
Nino ...
I'm doing what I want to do.
...I'm sorry.
EVERY-ONE, STEP BACK!!
NO, NO, NO! STOP IT, MAYOR !!
Careful, P-ko! It's about to take off!
THMP
No! No! Mayor ...!
...Huh?
HUH ?!
KLAAAANG
Hey... I set it so only Sweet Buns could get in...

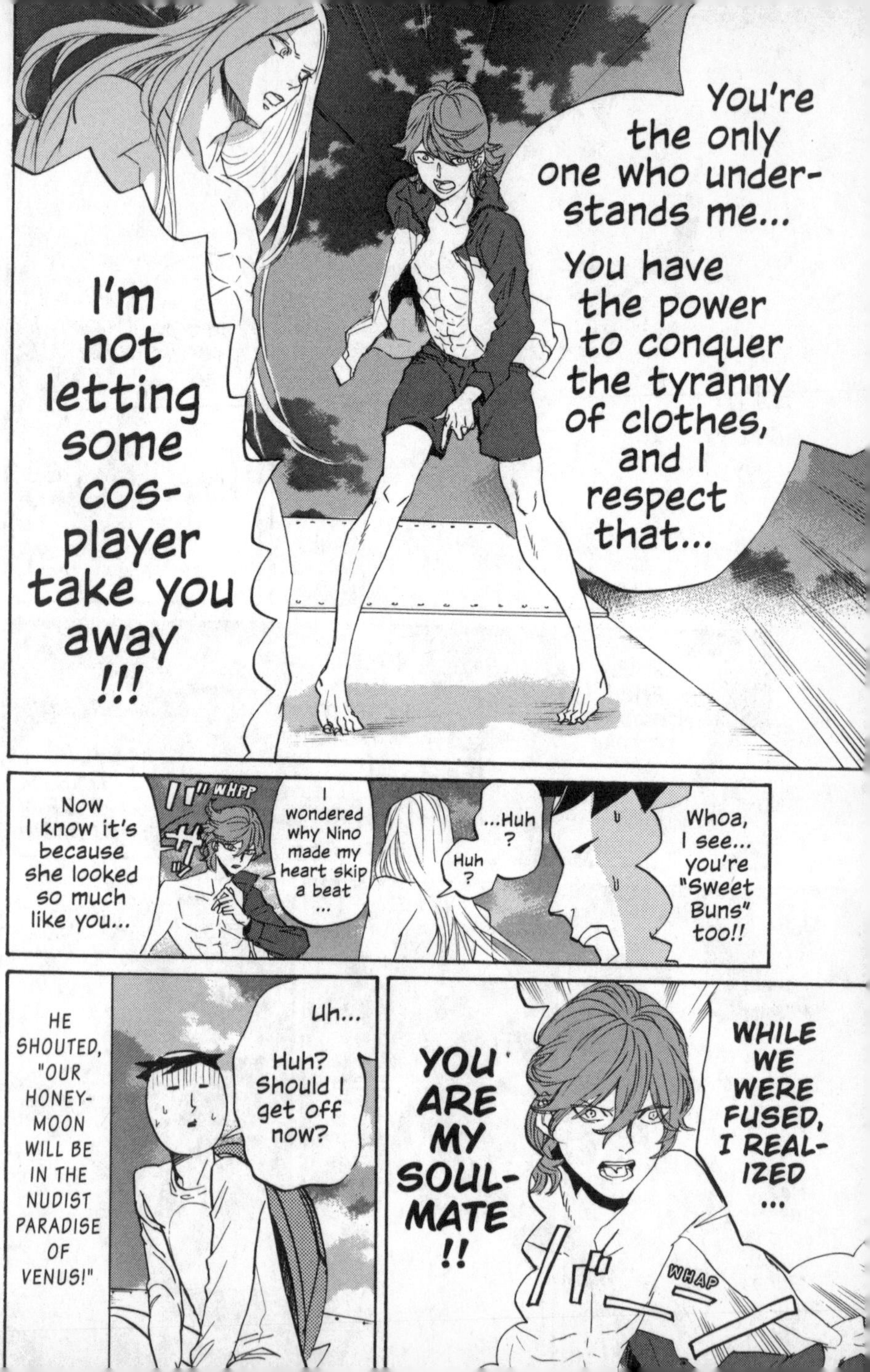
You're the only one who under-stands me... You have the power to conquer the tyranny of clothes, and I respect that...
I'm not letting some cos-player take you away !!!
Whoa, I see... you're "Sweet Buns" too!!
...Huh ?
Huh ?
I wondered why Nino made my heart skip a beat ...
WHPP
Now I know it's because she looked so much like you...
WHILE WE WERE FUSED, I REALIZED ...
YOU ARE MY SOUL-MATE !!
WHAP
Uh...
Huh? Should I get off now?
HE SHOUTED, "OUR HONEY-MOON WILL BE IN THE NUDIST PARADISE OF VENUS!"

ARAKAWA
UNDER
THE BRIDGE

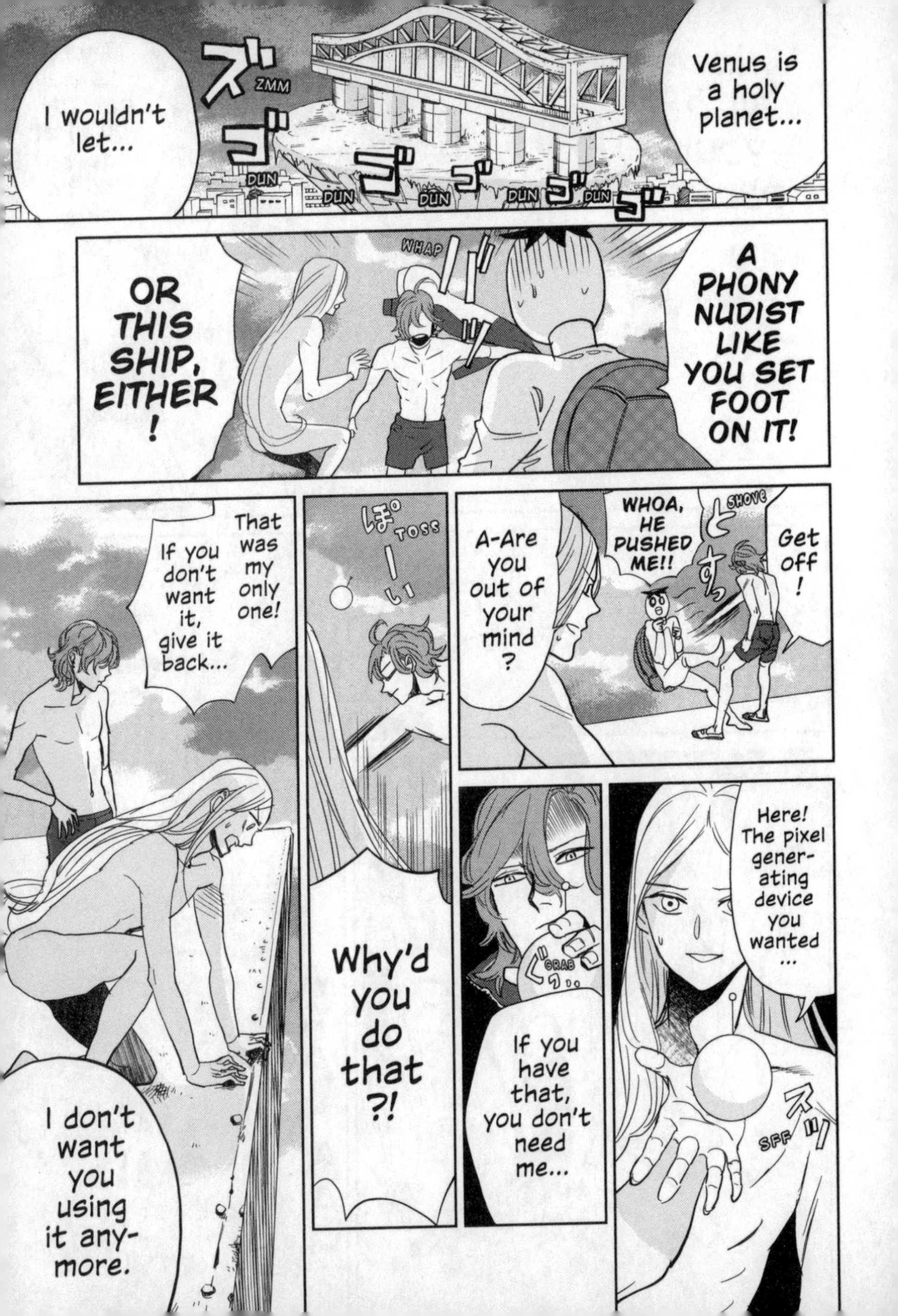
Venus is a holy planet...
ZMM
DUN
DUN
DUN
DUN
DUN
I wouldn't let...
A PHONY NUDIST LIKE YOU SET FOOT ON IT!
WHAP
OR THIS SHIP, EITHER!
Get off!
SHOVE
WHOA, HE PUSHED ME!!
A-Are you out of your mind?
Here! The pixel gener-ating device you wanted...
SFF
GRAB
If you have that, you don't need me...
TOSS
Why'd you do that?!
That was my only one!
If you don't want it, give it back...
I don't want you using it anymore.

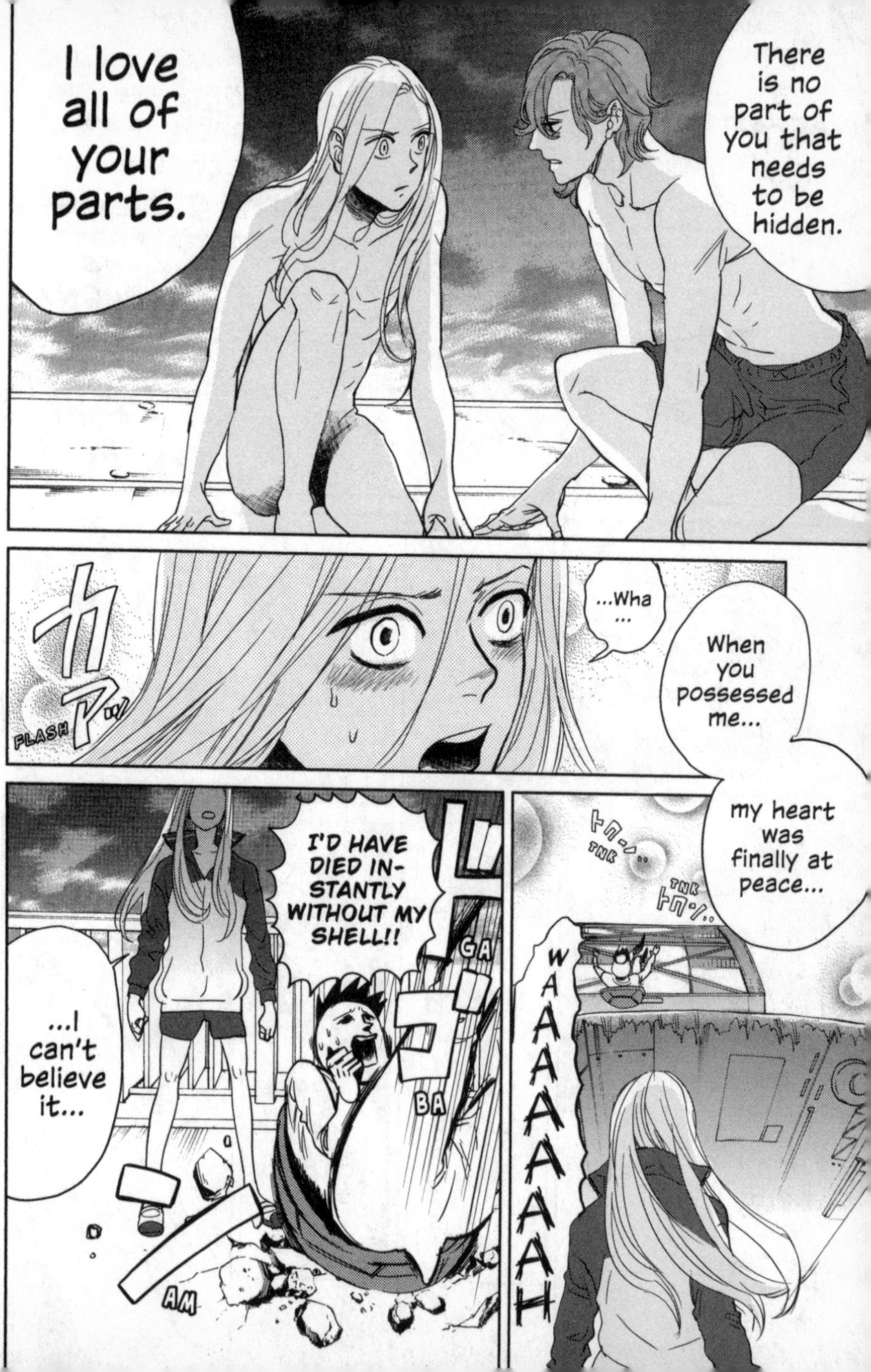
There is no part of you that needs to be hidden.
I love all of your parts.
...Wha...
When you possessed me...
カァッ
FLASH
my heart was finally at peace...
TNK
TNK
WAAAAAAAAAAH
I'D HAVE DIED INSTANTLY WITHOUT MY SHELL!!
GA
BA
AM
...I can't believe it...

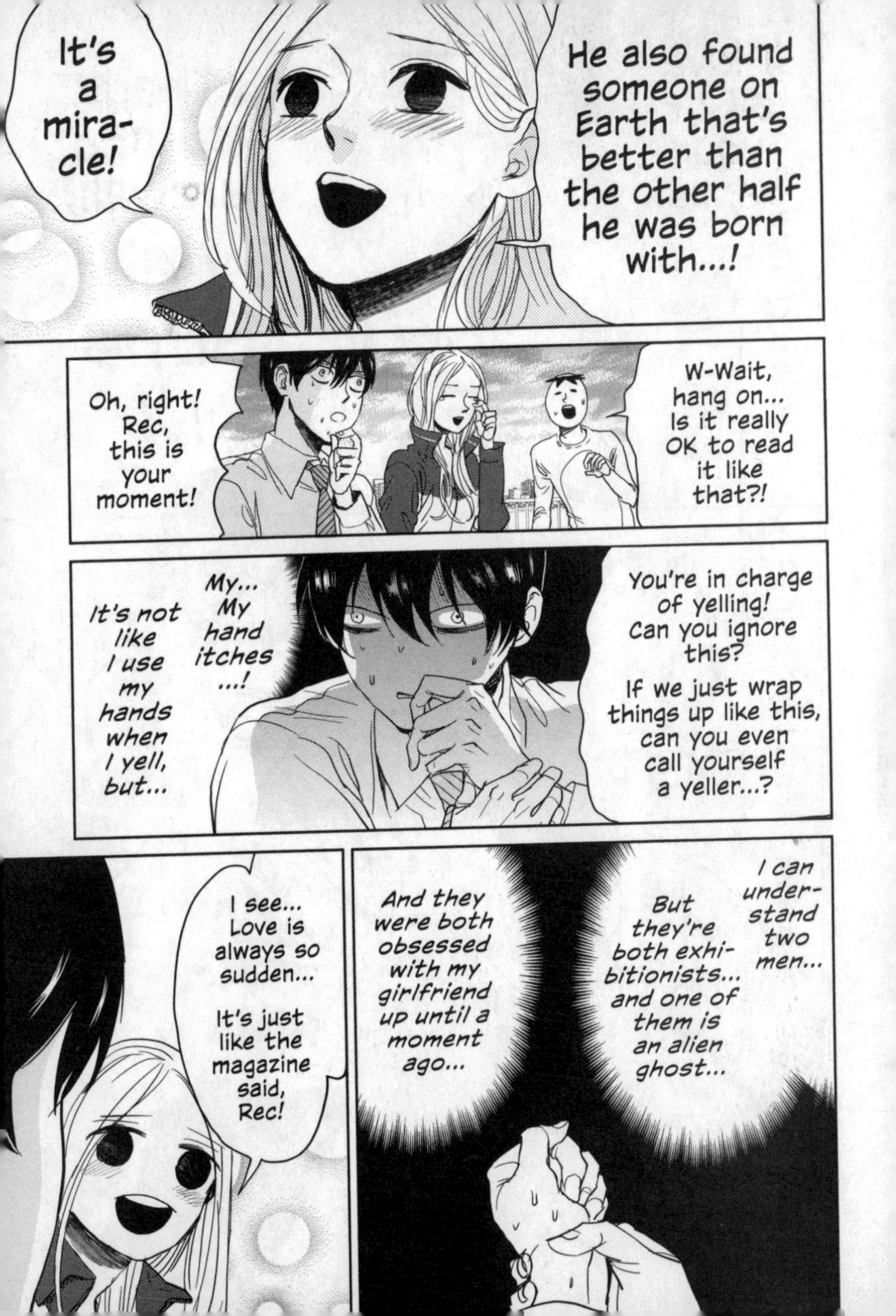
He also found someone on Earth that's better than the other half he was born with...!
It's a mira-cle!
W-Wait, hang on... Is it really OK to read it like that?!
Oh, right! Rec, this is your moment!
You're in charge of yelling! Can you ignore this?
If we just wrap things up like this, can you even call yourself a yeller...?
My... My hand itches ...!
It's not like I use my hands when I yell, but...
I can under-stand two men...
But they're both exhi-bitionists... and one of them is an alien ghost...
And they were both obsessed with my girlfriend up until a moment ago...
I see... Love is always so sudden...
It's just like the magazine said, Rec!

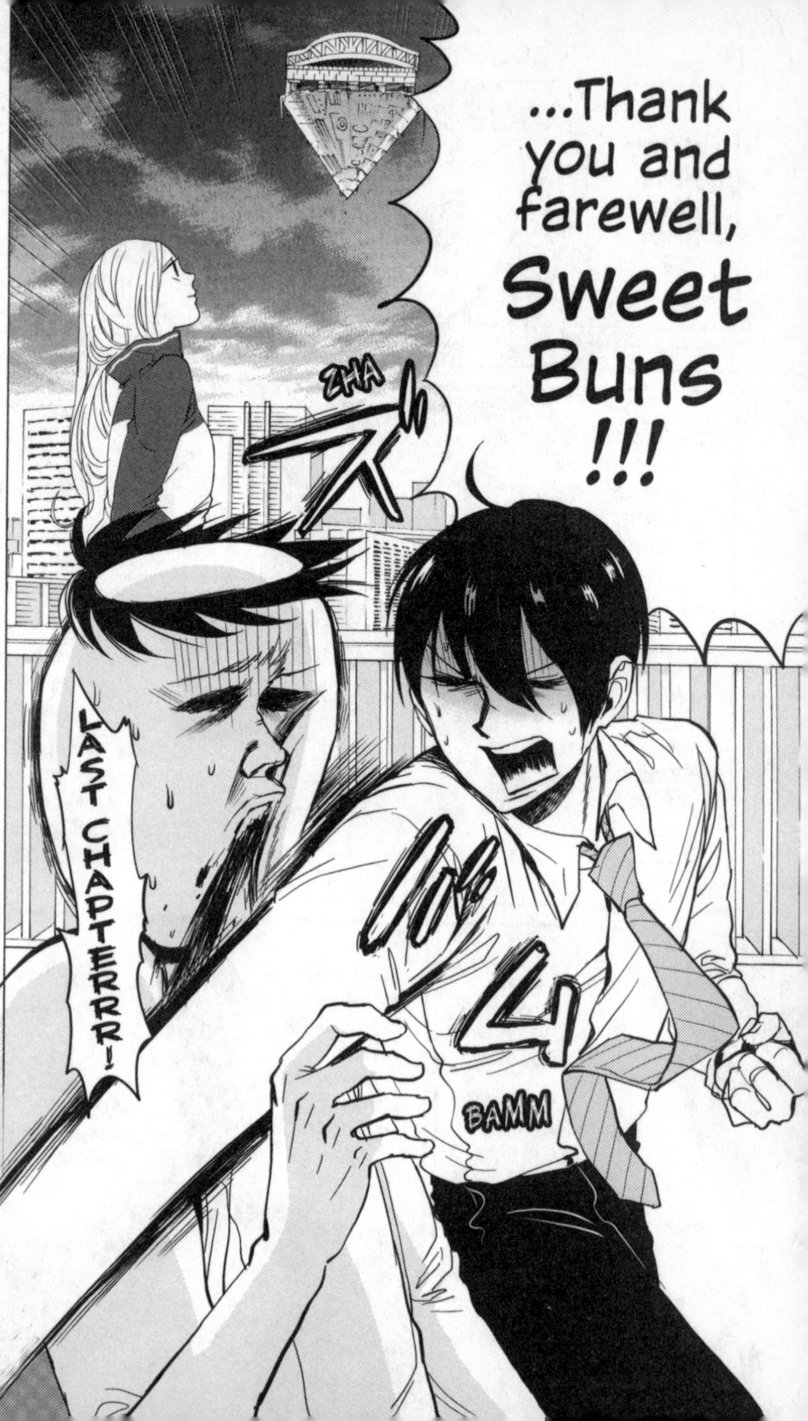
...Thank you and farewell, Sweet Buns!!!
ZHA
LAST CHAPTERRR!
BAMM

THERE WAS SO MUCH TO YELL ABOUT THAT HE JUST PUNCHED THE MAYOR SINCE HE WAS CLOSEST.

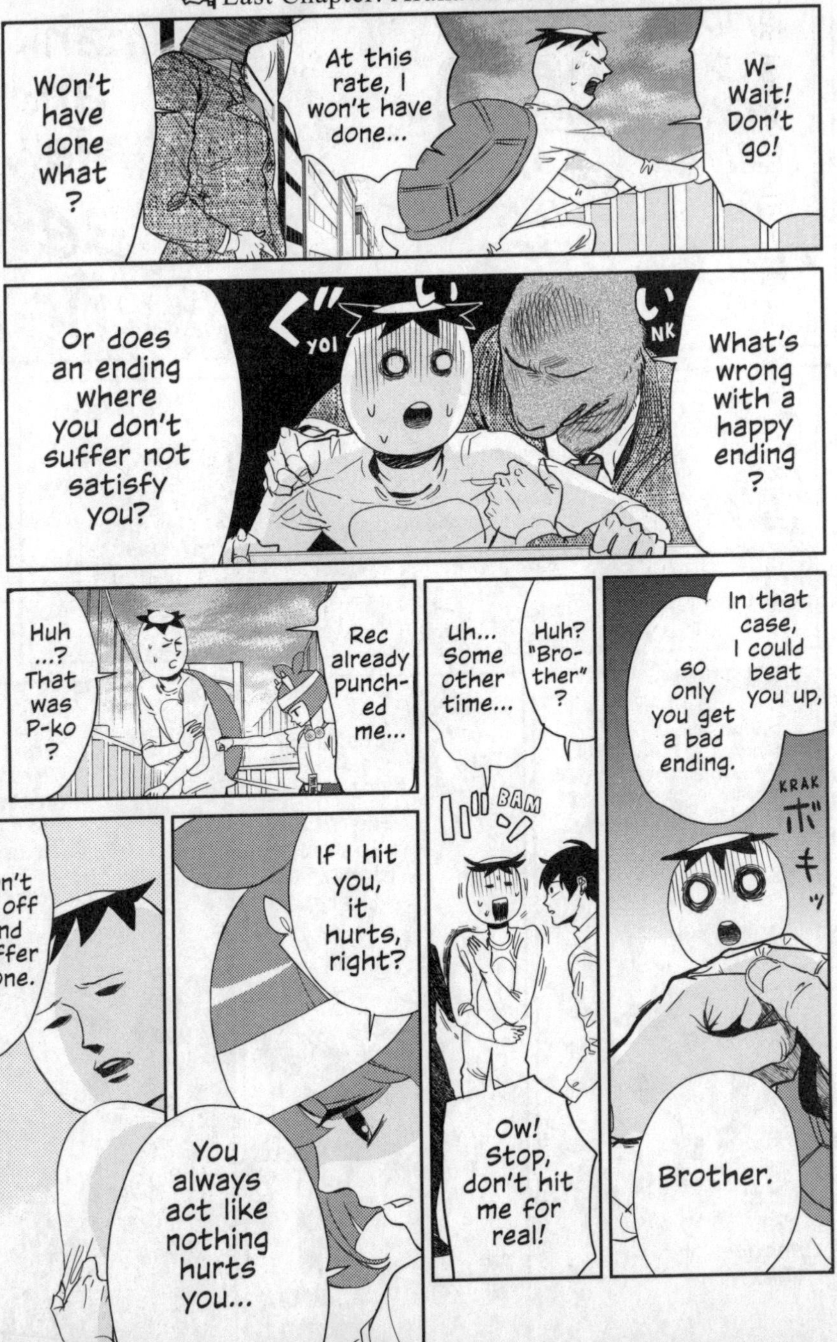
W- Wait! Don't go!
At this rate, I won't have done...
Won't have done what?
What's wrong with a happy ending?
NK
YOI
Or does an ending where you don't suffer not satisfy you?
In that case, I could beat you up,
so only you get a bad ending.
KRAK
Brother.
Huh? "Bro-ther"?
Uh... Some other time...
BAM
Ow! Stop, don't hit me for real!
Rec already punch-ed me...
Huh...? That was P-ko?
If I hit you, it hurts, right?
You always act like nothing hurts you...
Don't go off and suffer alone.

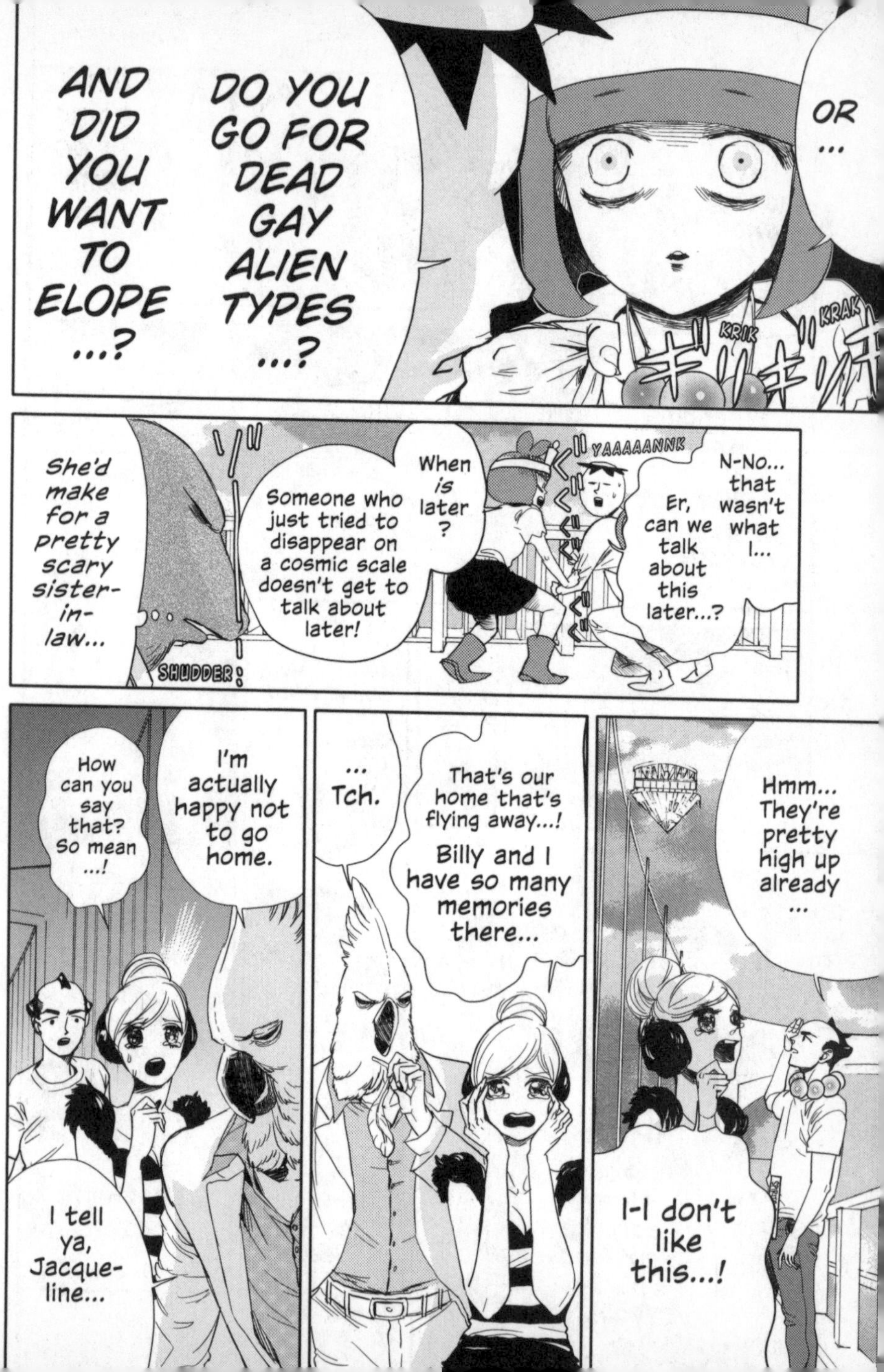
OR ...
DO YOU GO FOR DEAD GAY ALIEN TYPES ...?
AND DID YOU WANT TO ELOPE ...?
KRAK
KRIK
N-No... that wasn't what I...
Er, can we talk about this later...?
YAAAAANNK
When is later?
Someone who just tried to disappear on a cosmic scale doesn't get to talk about later!
She'd make for a pretty scary sister-in-law...
SHUDDER
Hmm... They're pretty high up already ...
I-I don't like this...!
That's our home that's flying away...!
Billy and I have so many memories there...
... Tch.
I'm actually happy not to go home.
How can you say that? So mean ...!
I tell ya, Jacqueline...

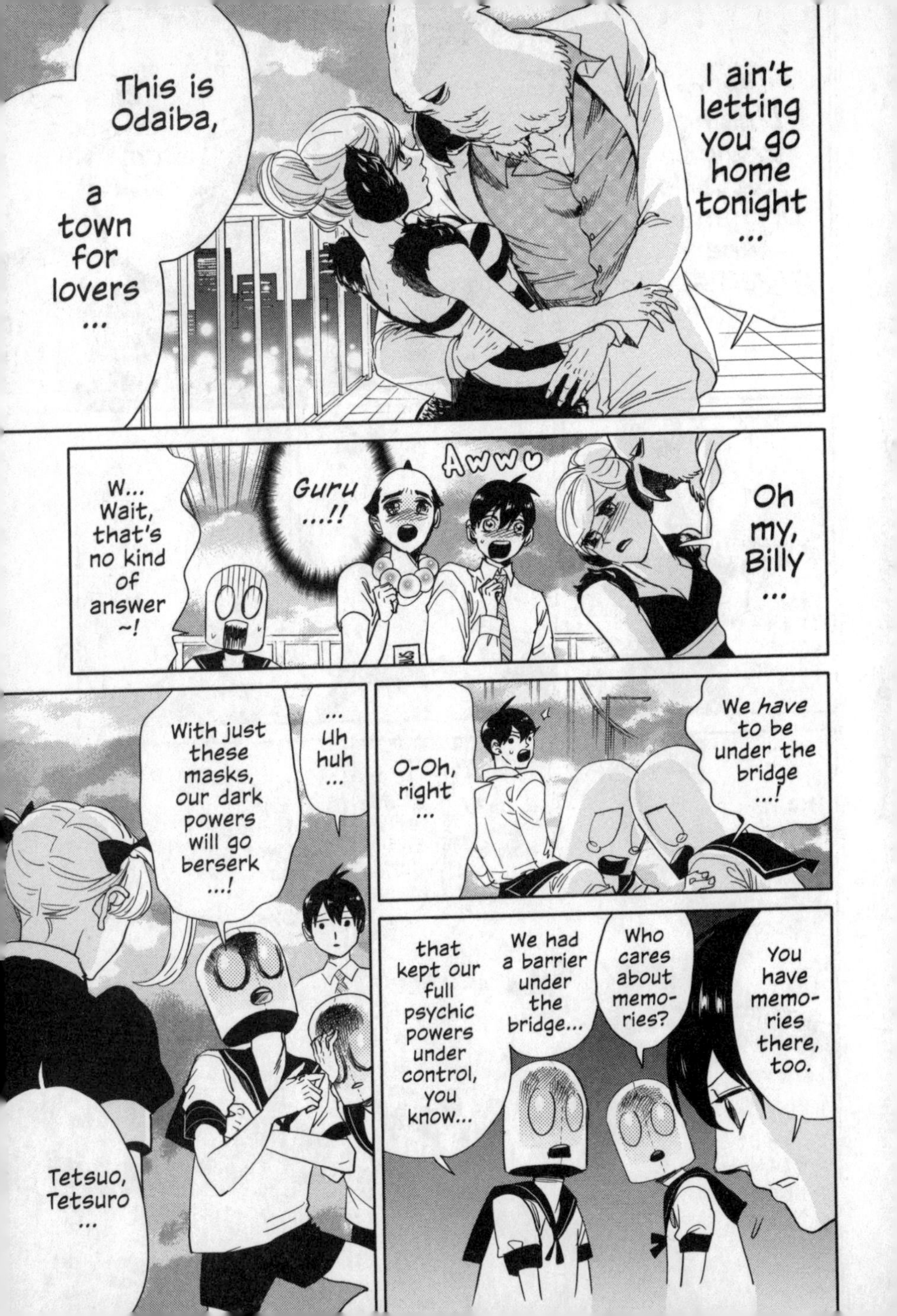
I ain't letting you go home tonight...
This is Odaiba, a town for lovers...
Oh my, Billy...
Awww♡
Guru...!!
W... Wait, that's no kind of answer ~!
We *have* to be under the bridge...!
O-Oh, right...
You have memo-ries there, too.
Who cares about memo-ries?
We had a barrier under the bridge...
that kept our full psychic powers under control, you know...
...Uh huh...
With just these masks, our dark powers will go berserk...!
Tetsuo, Tetsuro...

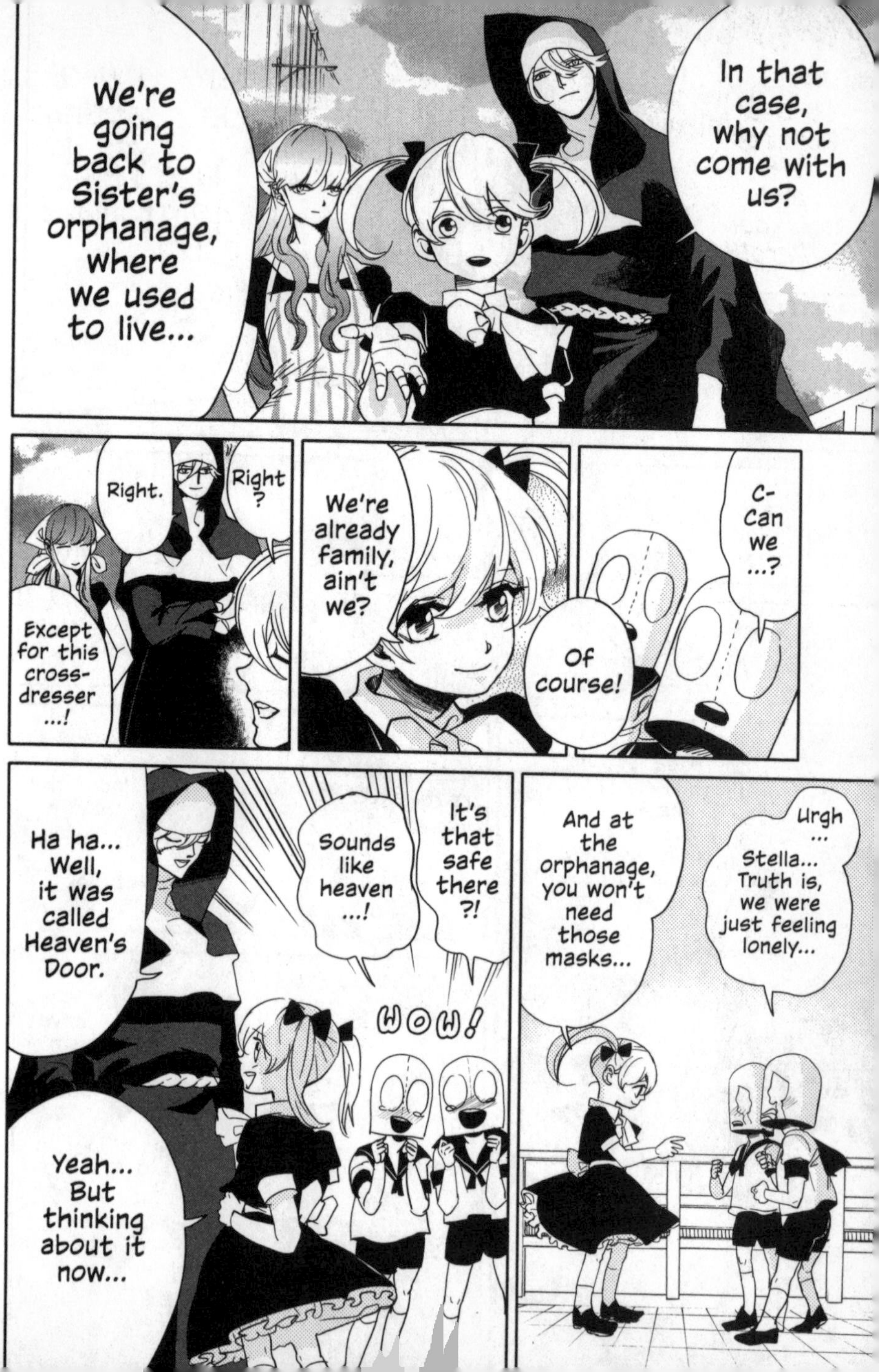
In that case, why not come with us?
We're going back to Sister's orphanage, where we used to live...
C- Can we ...?
Of course!
We're already family, ain't we?
Right?
Right.
Except for this cross-dresser ...!
Urgh ... Stella... Truth is, we were just feeling lonely...
And at the orphanage, you won't need those masks...
It's that safe there?!
Sounds like heaven ...!
Ha ha... Well, it was called Heaven's Door.
WOW!
Yeah... But thinking about it now...

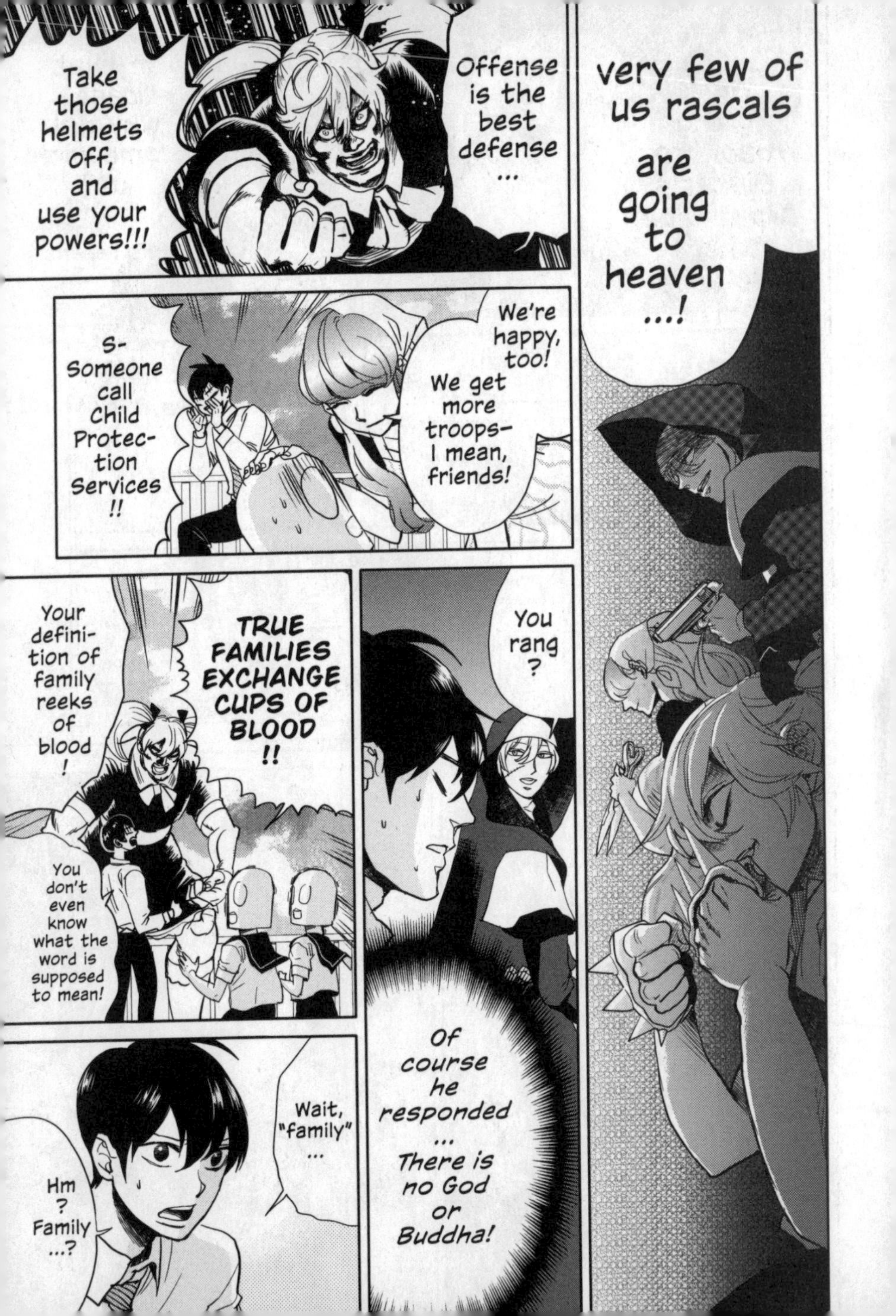
very few of us rascals
are going to heaven ...!
Offense is the best defense ...
Take those helmets off, and use your powers!!!
We're happy, too!
We get more troops- I mean, friends!
S-Someone call Child Protection Services !!
You rang ?
Of course he responded ... There is no God or Buddha!
TRUE FAMILIES EXCHANGE CUPS OF BLOOD !!
Your definition of family reeks of blood !
You don't even know what the word is supposed to mean!
Wait, "family" ...
Hm ? Family ...?

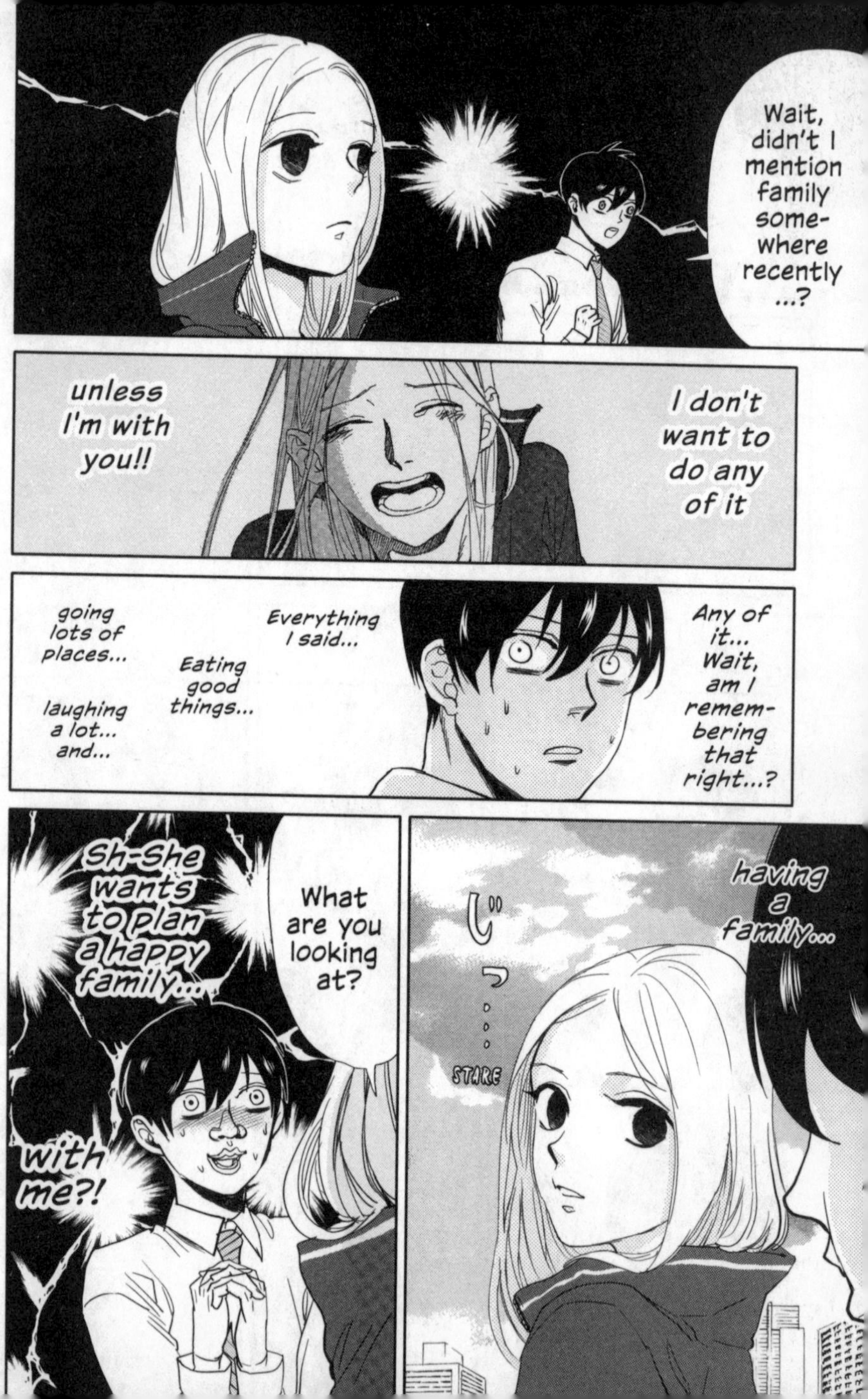
Wait, didn't I mention family somewhere recently...?
I don't want to do any of it
unless I'm with you!!
Any of it... Wait, am I remembering that right...?
Everything I said...
Eating good things...
going lots of places...
laughing a lot... and...
having a family...
じ
STARE
What are you looking at?
Sh-She wants to plan a happy family...
with me?!

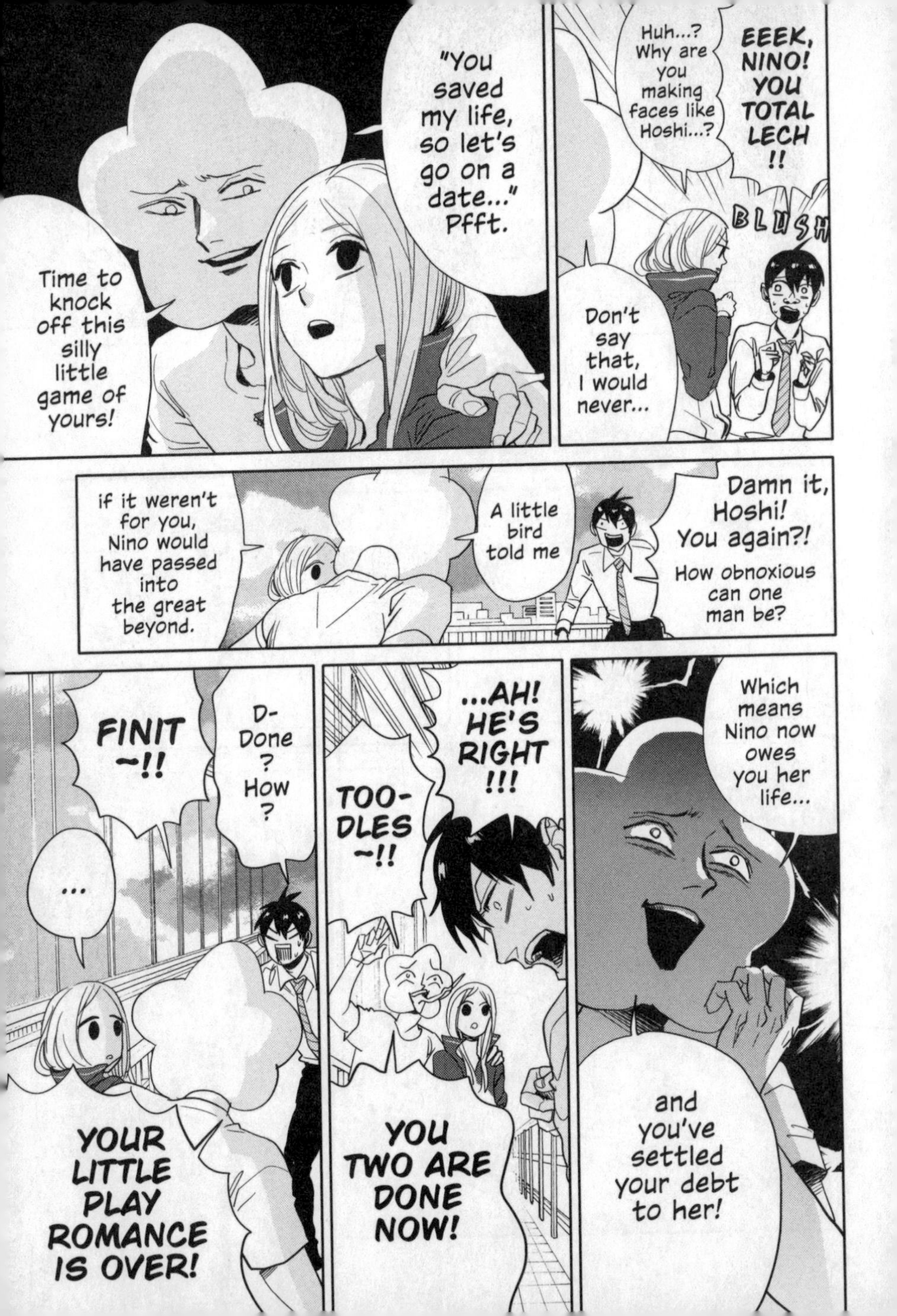
EEEK, NINO! YOU TOTAL LECH!!
Huh...? Why are you making faces like Hoshi...?
BLUSH
Don't say that, I would never...
"You saved my life, so let's go on a date..." Pfft.
Time to knock off this silly little game of yours!
Damn it, Hoshi! You again?!
How obnoxious can one man be?
A little bird told me
if it weren't for you, Nino would have passed into the great beyond.
Which means Nino now owes you her life...
and you've settled your debt to her!
...AH! HE'S RIGHT!!!
TOO-DLES~!!
YOU TWO ARE DONE NOW!
D-Done? How?
FINIT~!!
...
YOUR LITTLE PLAY ROMANCE IS OVER!

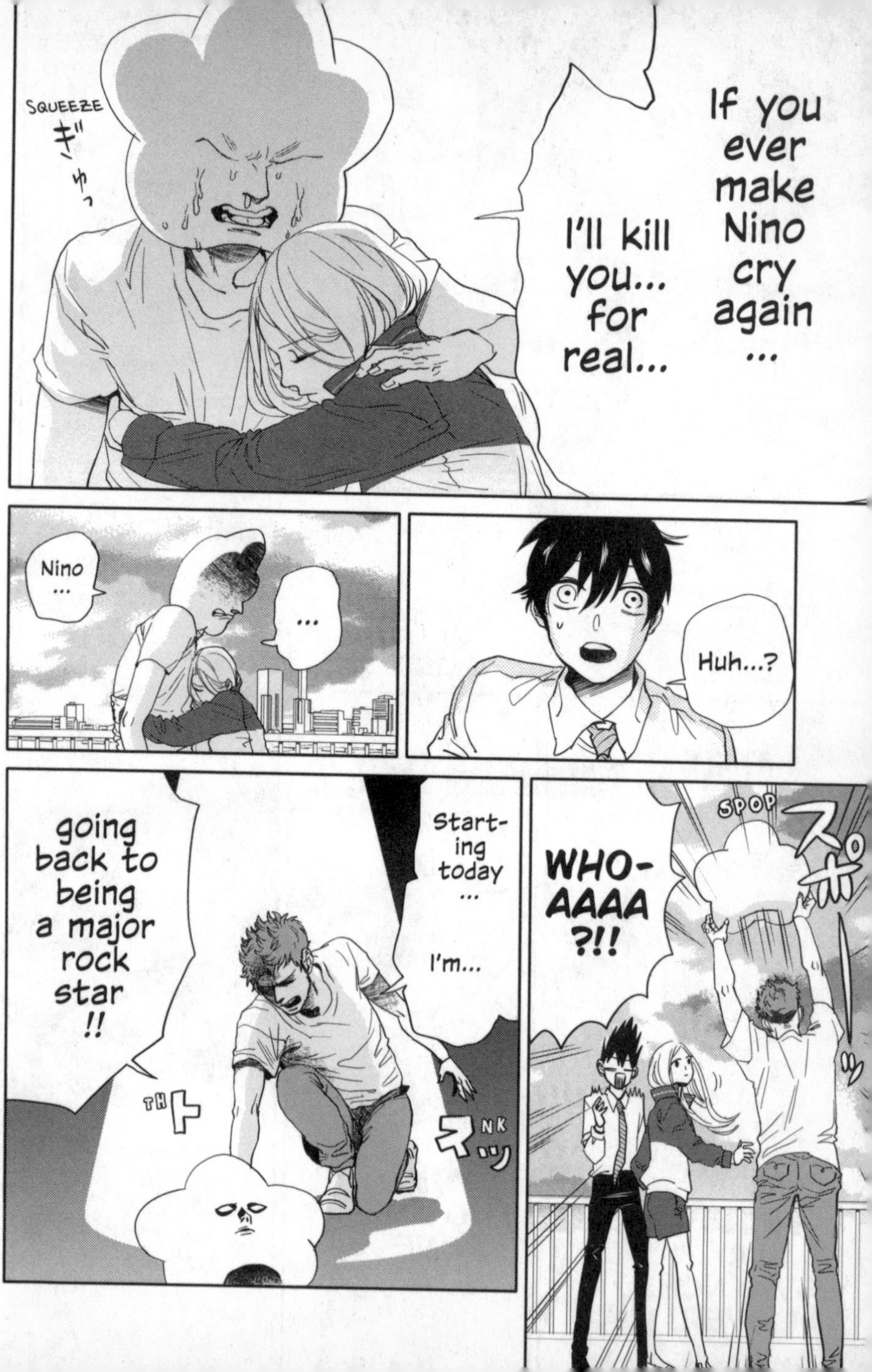
If you ever make Nino cry again ...
I'll kill you... for real...
SQUEEZE
ぎゅっ
Huh...?
...
Nino ...
SPOP
スポッ
WHO-AAAA ?!!
Start-ing today ...
I'm...
going back to being a major rock star !!
TH
ト
NK
ヌッ

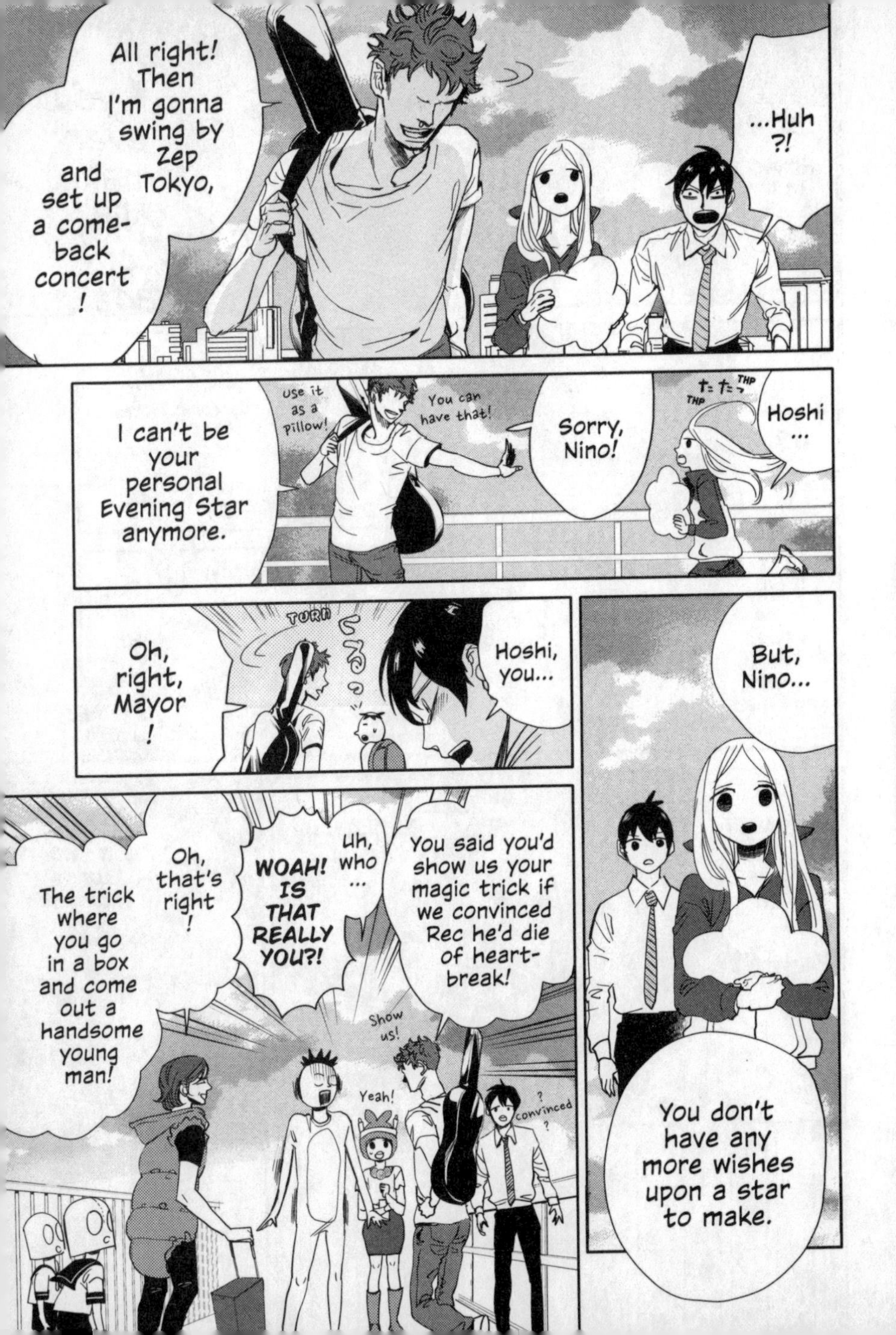
All right! Then I'm gonna swing by Zep Tokyo, and set up a come-back concert!
...Huh ?!
Hoshi ...
たたっ THP THP
Sorry, Nino!
You can have that!
Use it as a pillow!
I can't be your personal Evening Star anymore.
But, Nino...
You don't have any more wishes upon a star to make.
Hoshi, you...
くるっ TURN
Oh, right, Mayor!
You said you'd show us your magic trick if we convinced Rec he'd die of heart-break!
Uh, who ...
WOAH! IS THAT REALLY YOU?!
Oh, that's right!
The trick where you go in a box and come out a handsome young man!
Show us!
Yeah!
? convinced ?

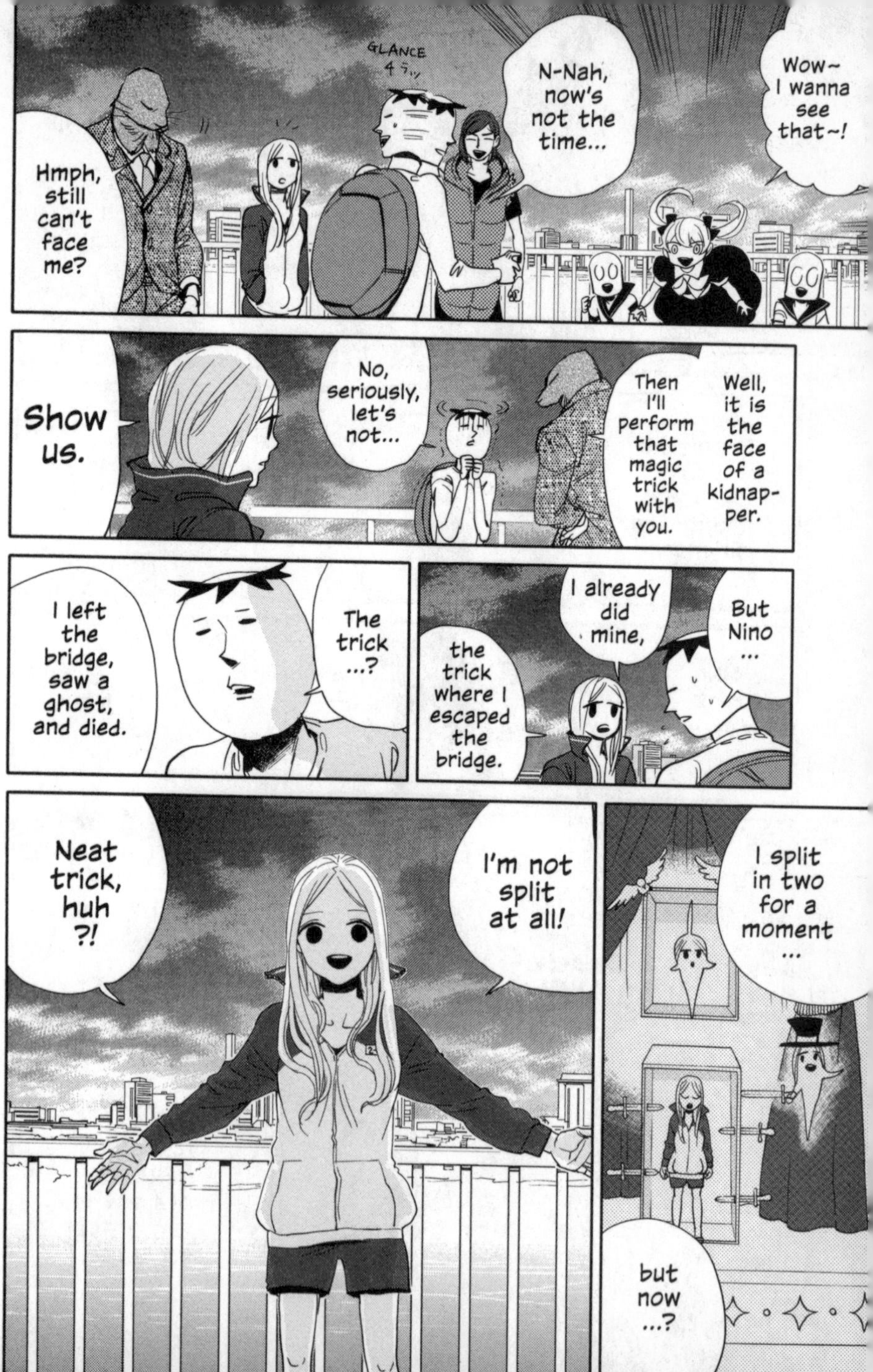
Wow~ I wanna see that~!
N-Nah, now's not the time...
GLANCE
チラッ
Hmph, still can't face me?
Well, it is the face of a kidnapper.
Then I'll perform that magic trick with you.
No, seriously, let's not...
Show us.
But Nino ...
I already did mine,
the trick where I escaped the bridge.
The trick ...?
I left the bridge, saw a ghost, and died.
I split in two for a moment ...
but now ...?
I'm not split at all!
Neat trick, huh ?!

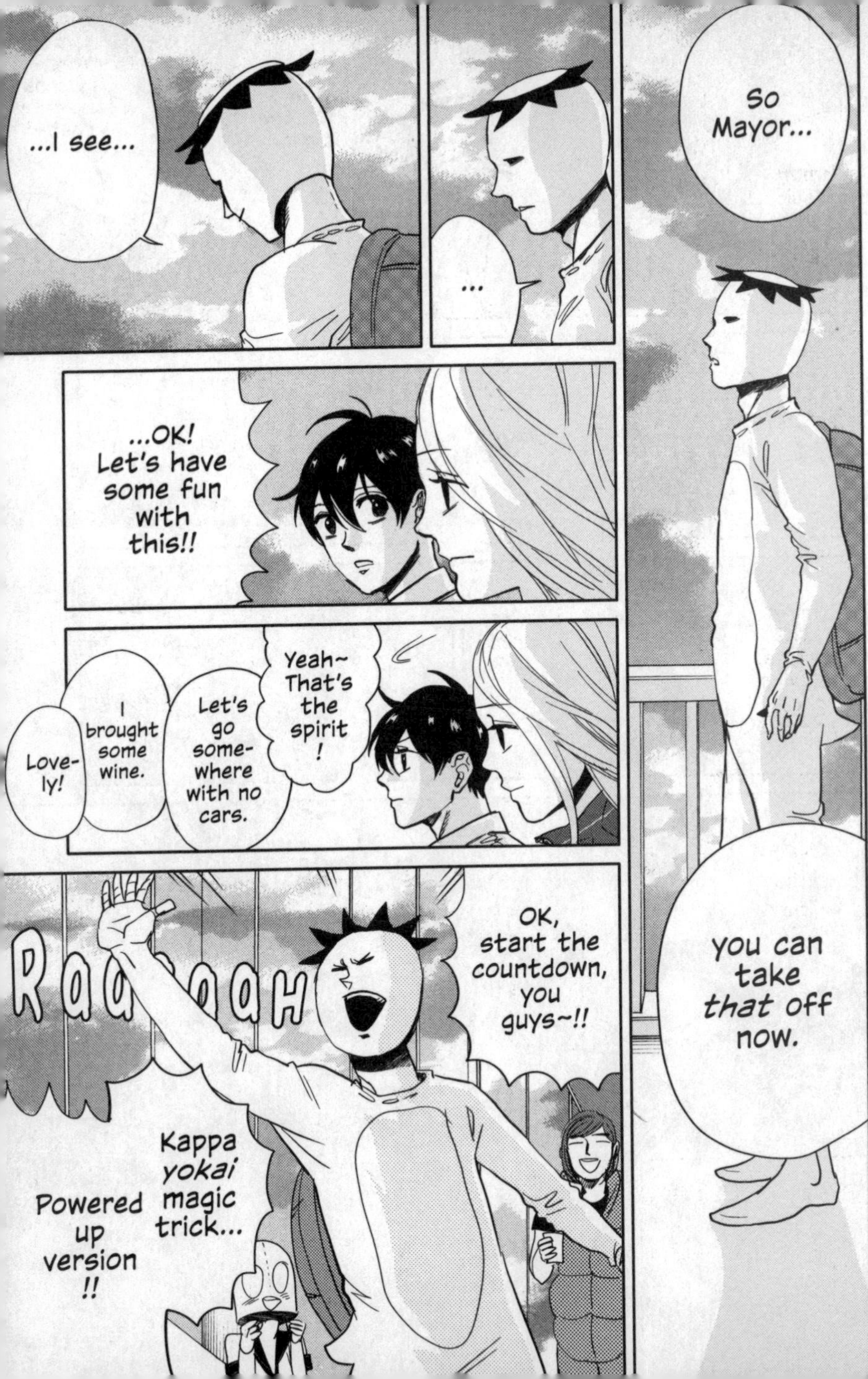
So Mayor...
you can take *that* off now.
...
...I see...
...OK! Let's have some fun with this!!
Yeah~ That's the spirit!
Let's go some-where with no cars.
I brought some wine.
Love-ly!
OK, start the countdown, you guys~!!
Raaaah
Kappa *yokai* magic trick...
Powered up version!!

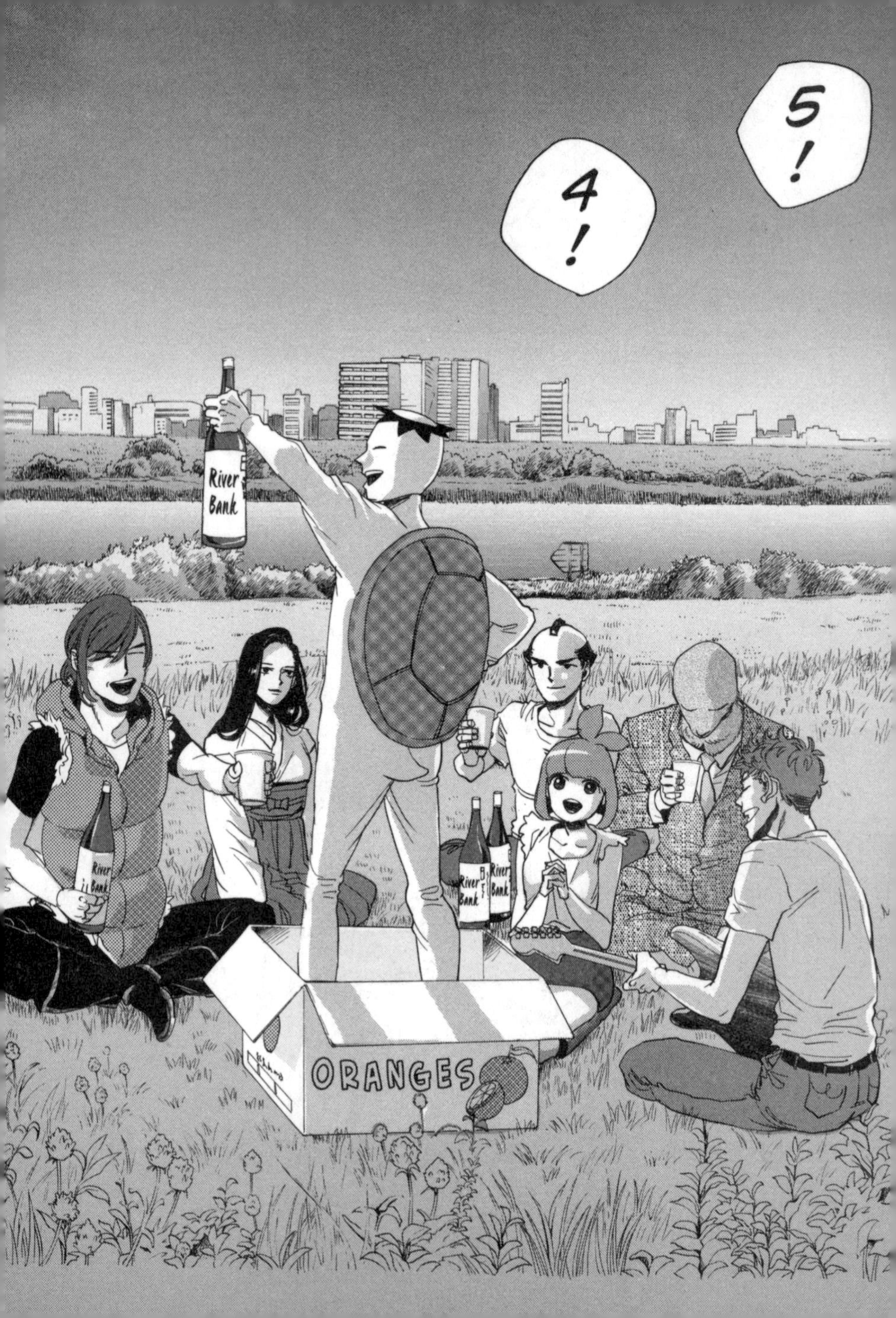
5!
4!
River Bank
River Bank
River Bank
River Bank
ORANGES

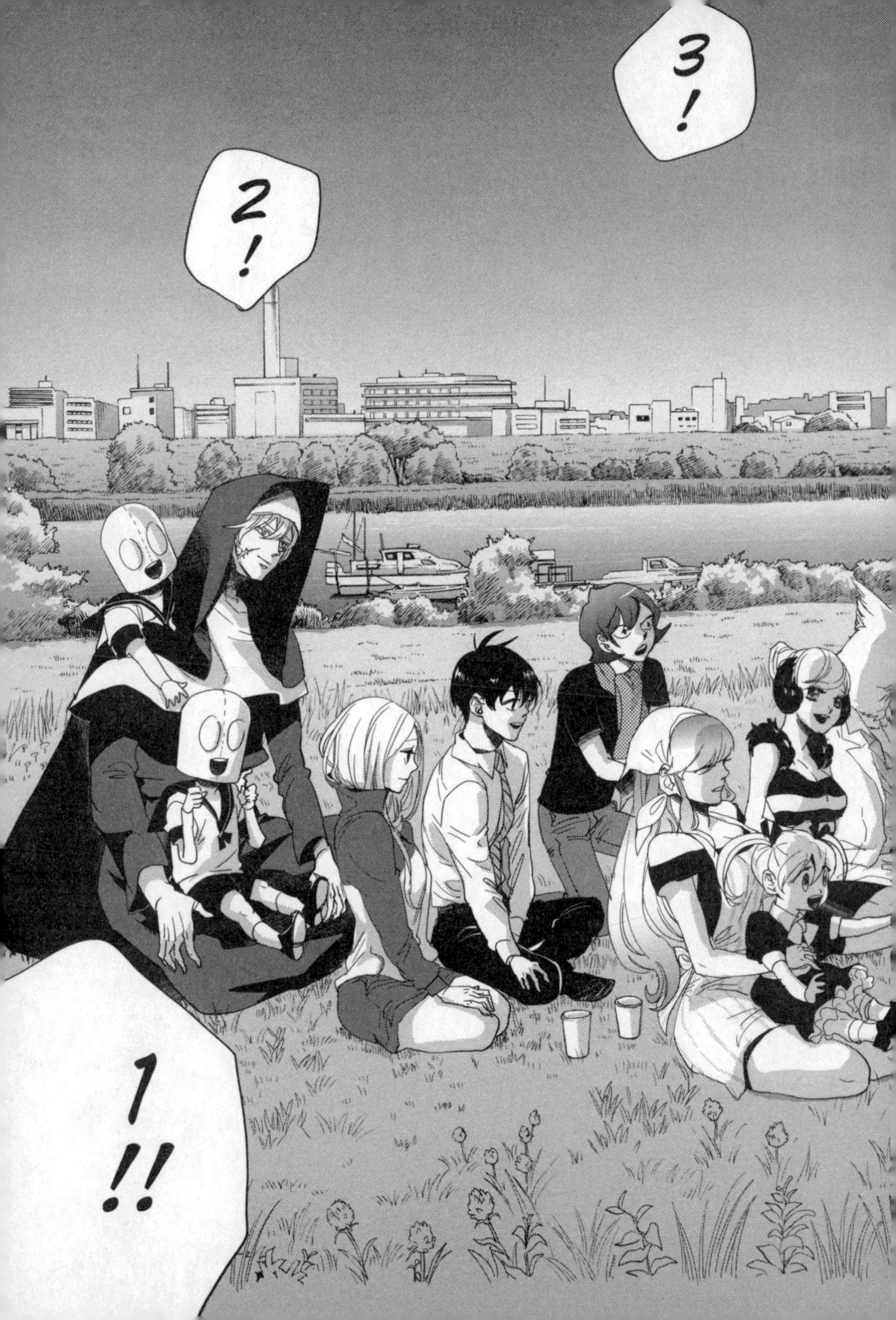
3!
2!
1!!

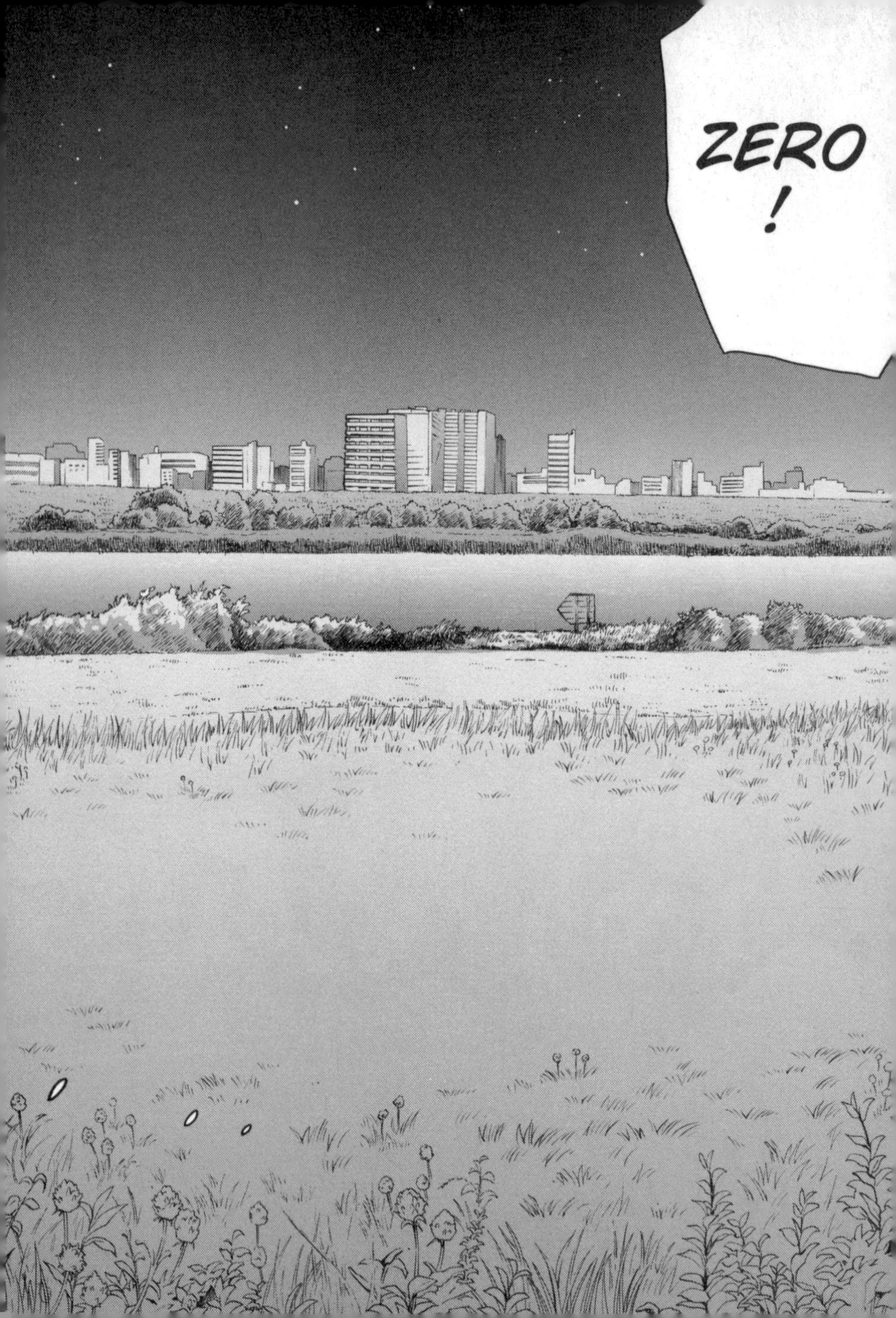
ZERO
!

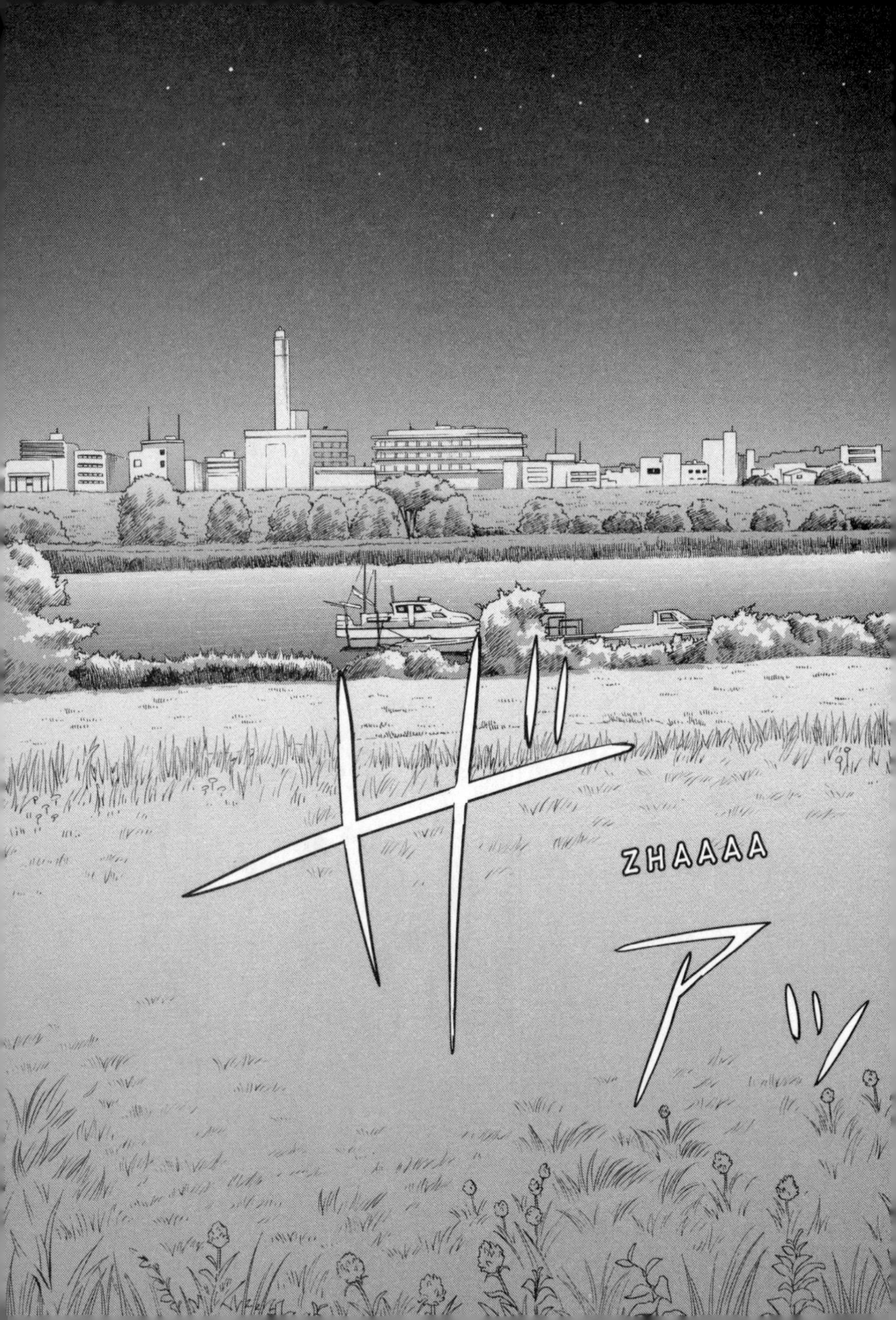
ザアッ
ZHAAAA

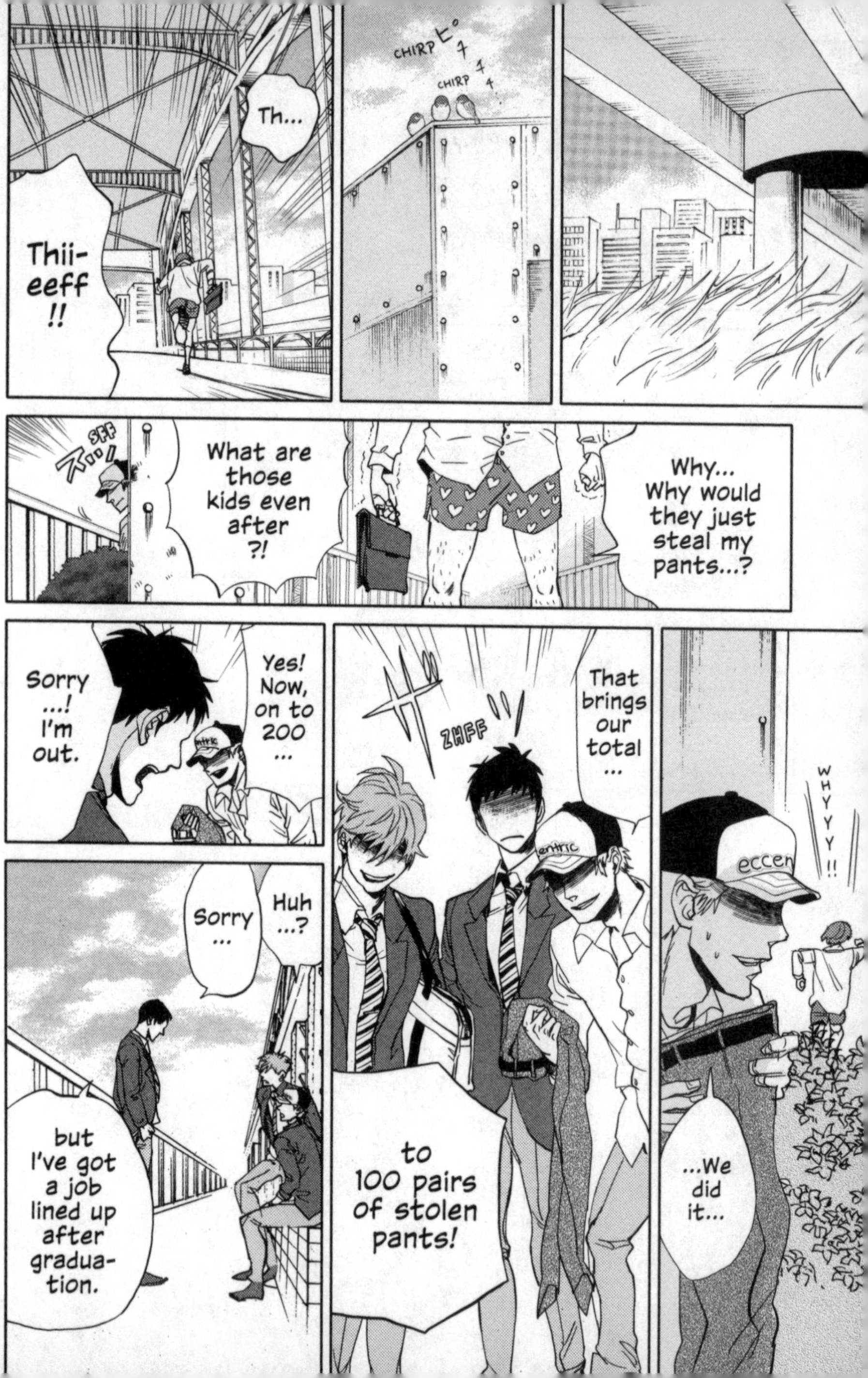

CHIRP ピ チ
CHIRP チ ィ
Th...
Thiieeff !!
Why... Why would they just steal my pants...?
What are those kids even after?!
SFF スッ
WHYYYY!!
...We did it...
That brings our total...
ZHFF
to 100 pairs of stolen pants!
Yes! Now, on to 200...
Sorry...! I'm out.
Huh...?
Sorry...
but I've got a job lined up after graduation.

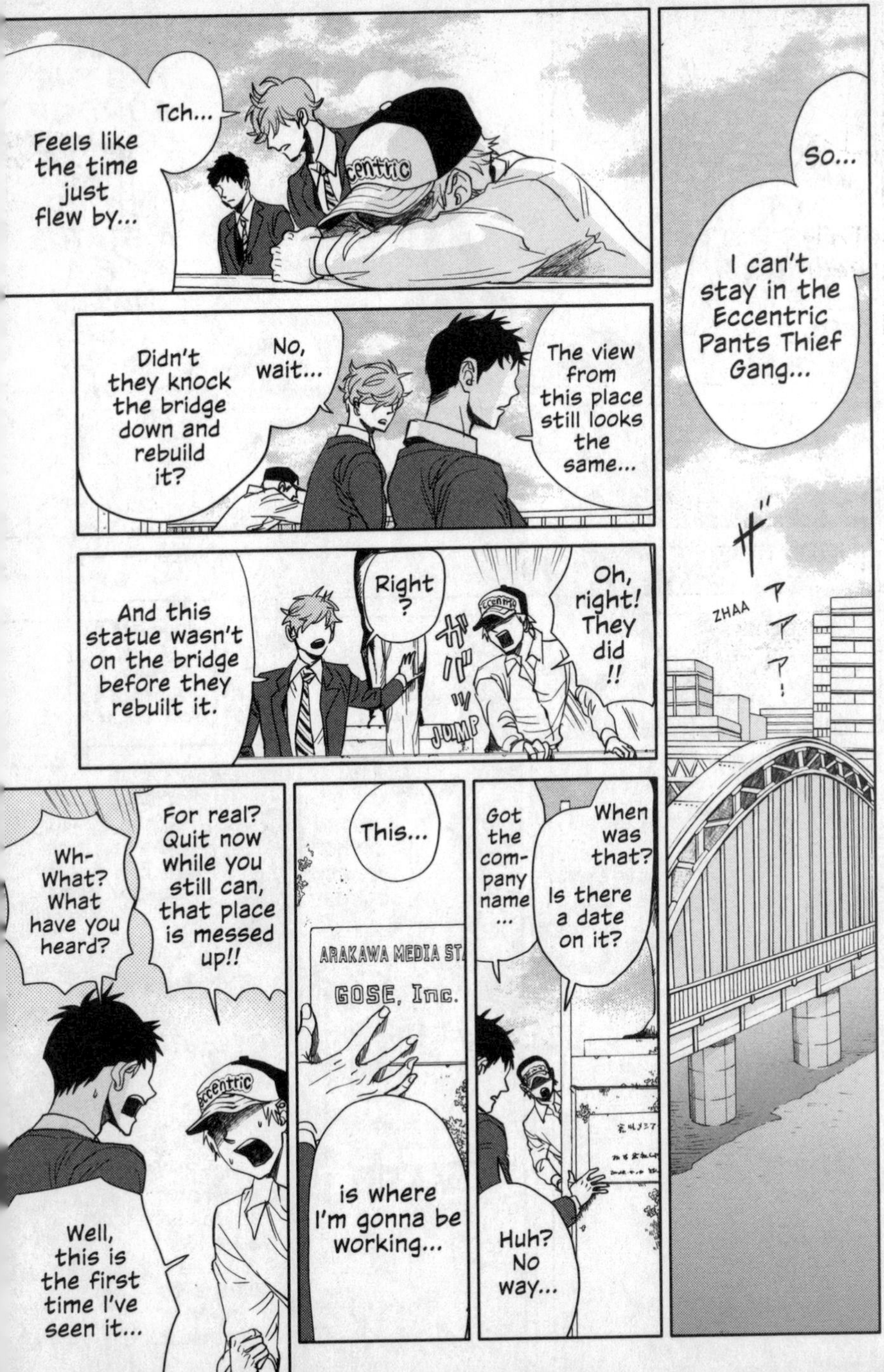
So...
I can't stay in the Eccentric Pants Thief Gang...
ZHAA
Tch...
Feels like the time just flew by...
The view from this place still looks the same...
No, wait...
Didn't they knock the bridge down and rebuild it?
Oh, right! They did!!
JUMP
Right?
And this statue wasn't on the bridge before they rebuilt it.
When was that?
Is there a date on it?
Got the company name...
Huh? No way...
This...
ARAKAWA MEDIA STA
GOSE, Inc.
is where I'm gonna be working...
For real? Quit now while you still can, that place is messed up!!
Wh- What? What have you heard?
Well, this is the first time I've seen it...

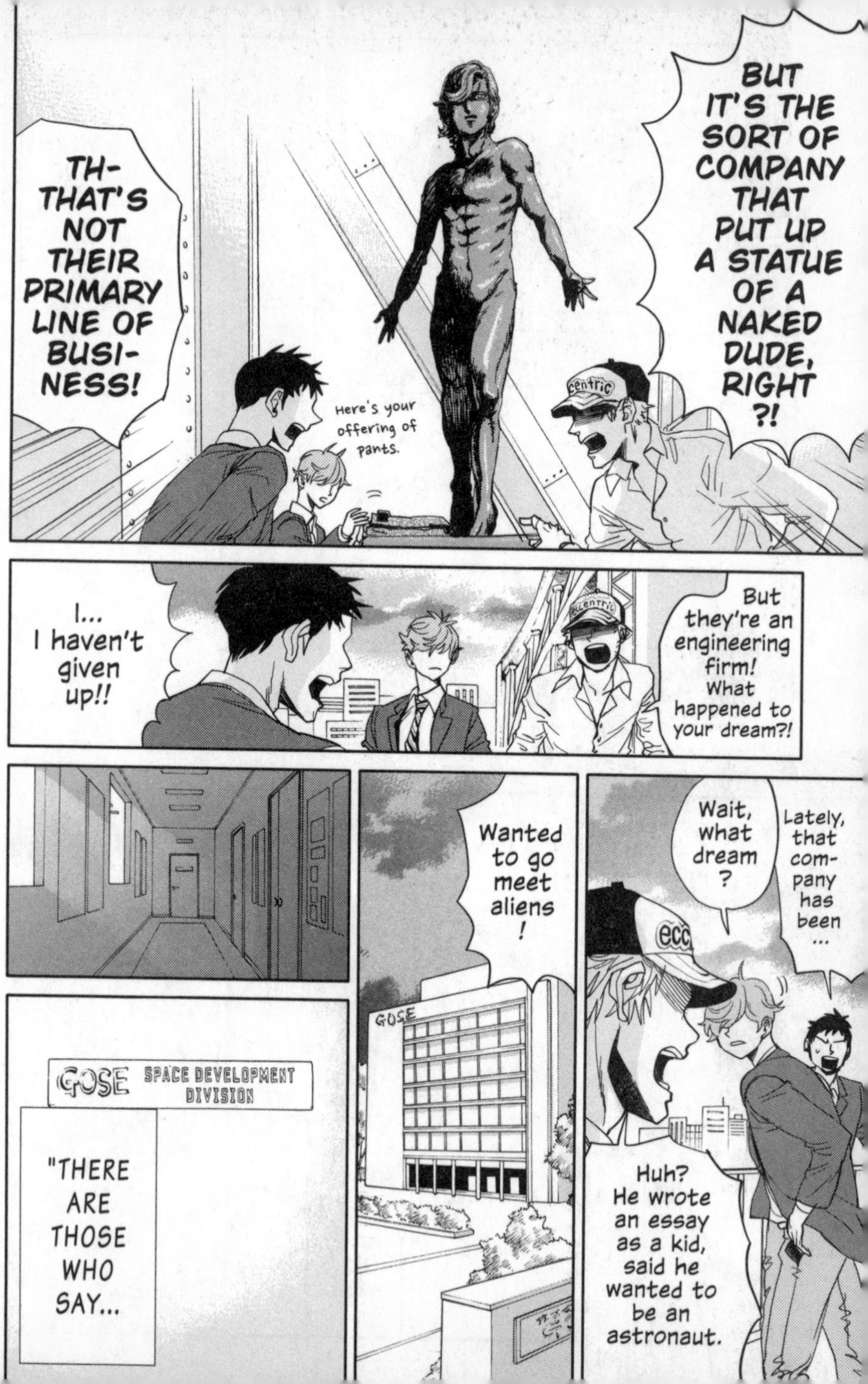
BUT IT'S THE SORT OF COMPANY THAT PUT UP A STATUE OF A NAKED DUDE, RIGHT?!
TH-THAT'S NOT THEIR PRIMARY LINE OF BUSI-NESS!
Here's your offering of pants.
But they're an engineering firm! What happened to your dream?!
I... I haven't given up!!
Lately, that company has been ...
Wait, what dream?
Huh? He wrote an essay as a kid, said he wanted to be an astronaut.
Wanted to go meet aliens!
GOSE
GOSE SPACE DEVELOPMENT DIVISION
"THERE ARE THOSE WHO SAY...

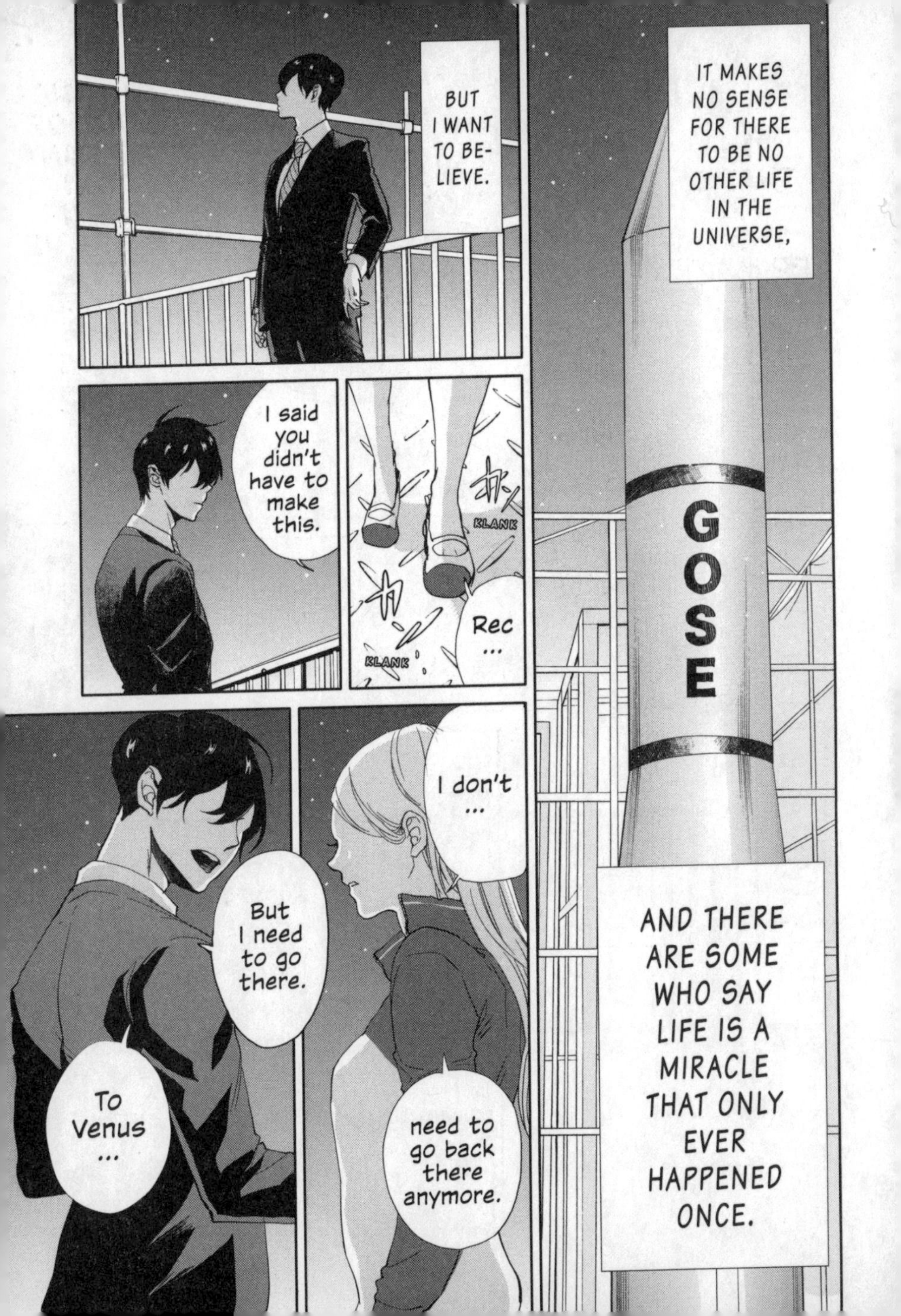
IT MAKES NO SENSE FOR THERE TO BE NO OTHER LIFE IN THE UNIVERSE,
GOSE
AND THERE ARE SOME WHO SAY LIFE IS A MIRACLE THAT ONLY EVER HAPPENED ONCE.
BUT I WANT TO BE-LIEVE.
KLANK
KLANK
Rec ...
I said you didn't have to make this.
I don't ...
need to go back there anymore.
But I need to go there.
To Venus ...

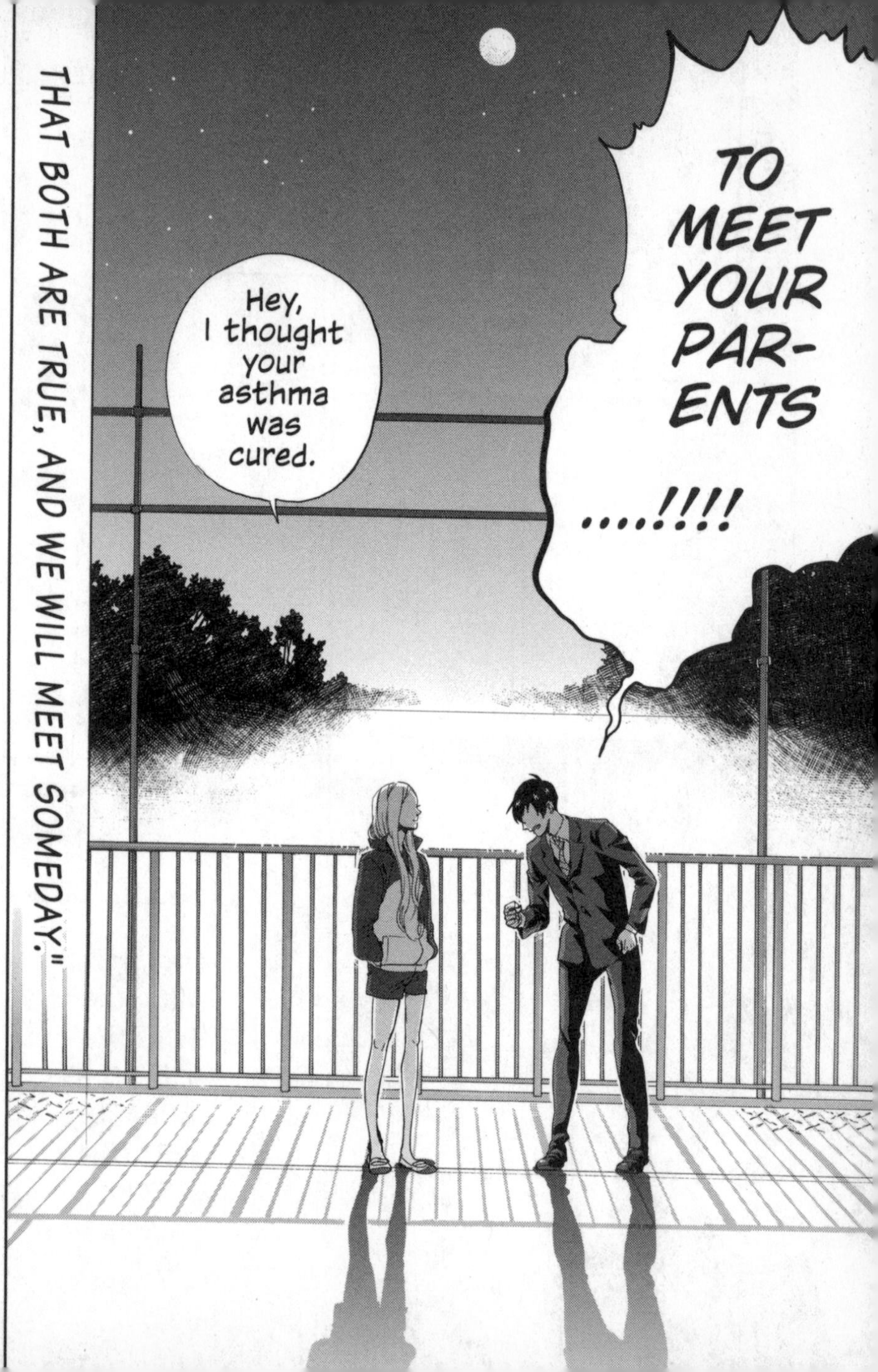
TO MEET YOUR PAR- ENTS ....!!!!
Hey, I thought your asthma was cured.

THAT BOTH ARE TRUE, AND WE WILL MEET SOMEDAY."

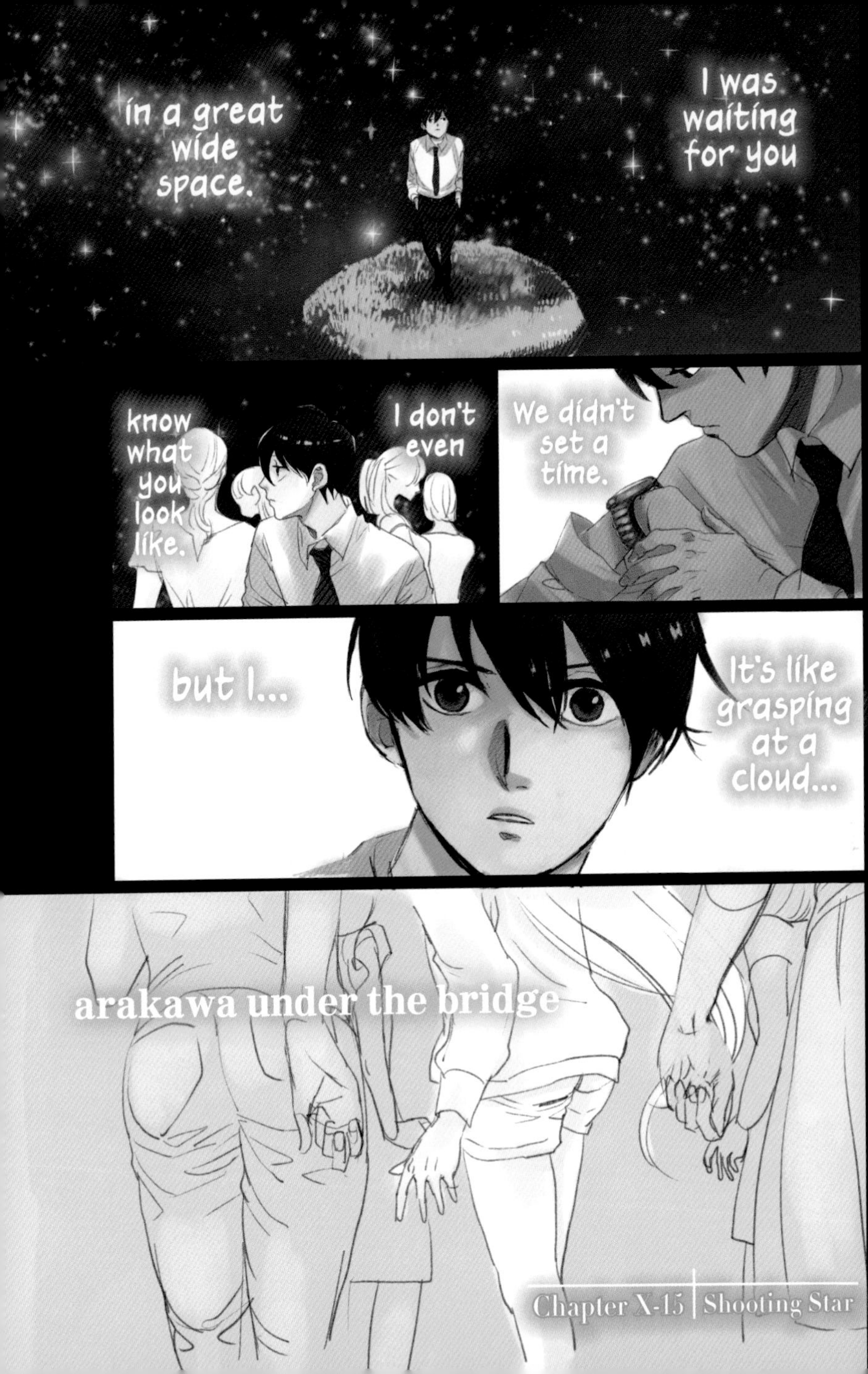
I was waiting for you
in a great wide space.
We didn't set a time.
I don't even
know what you look like.
It's like grasping at a cloud...
but I...
arakawa under the bridge
Chapter X-15 | Shooting Star

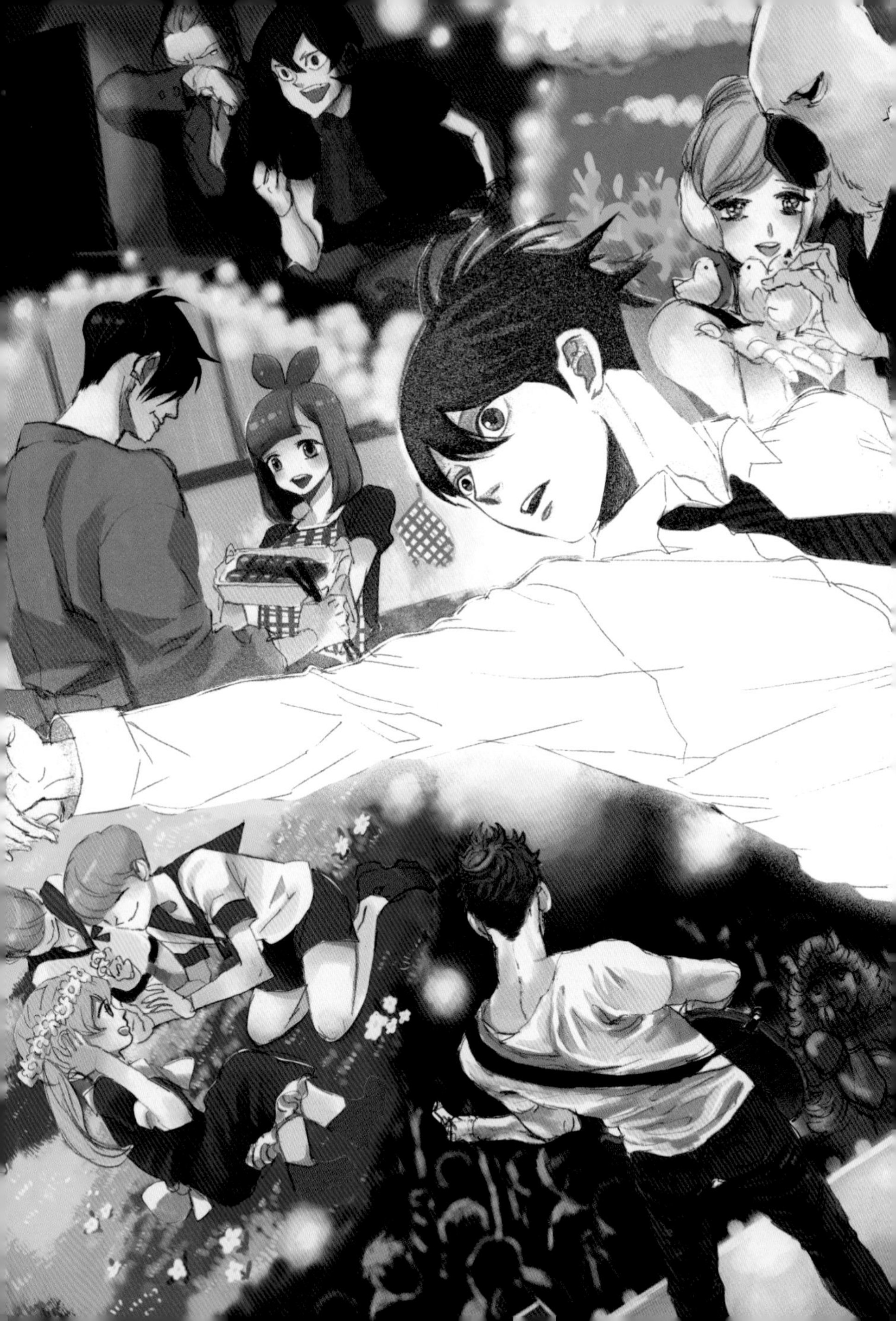

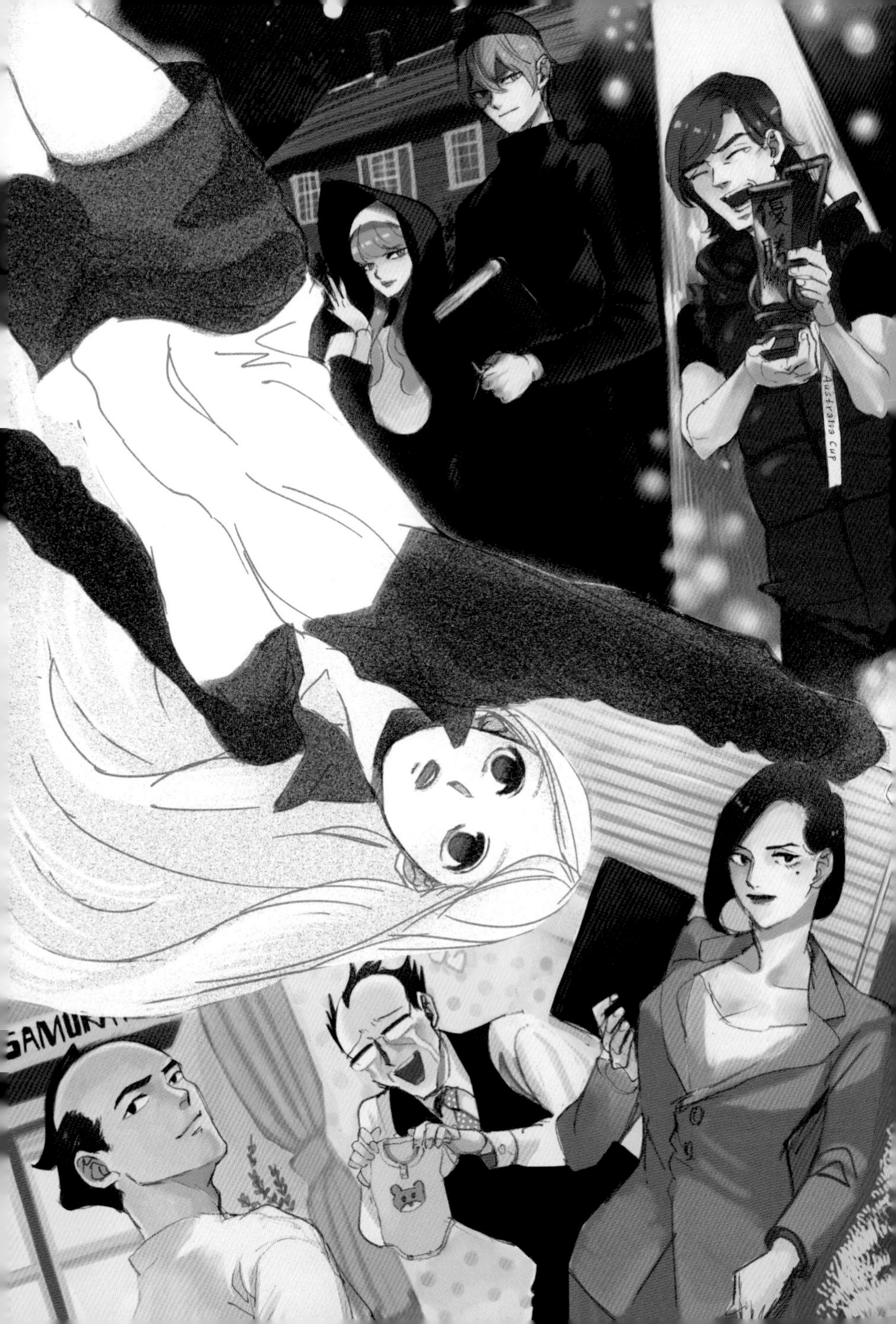
Australia Cup

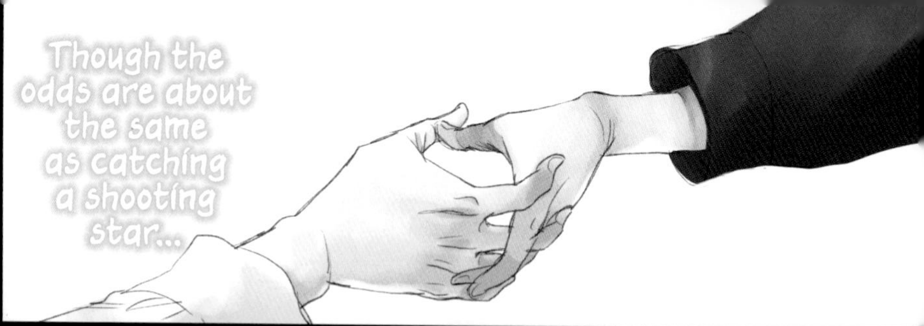
Though the odds are about the same as catching a shooting star...

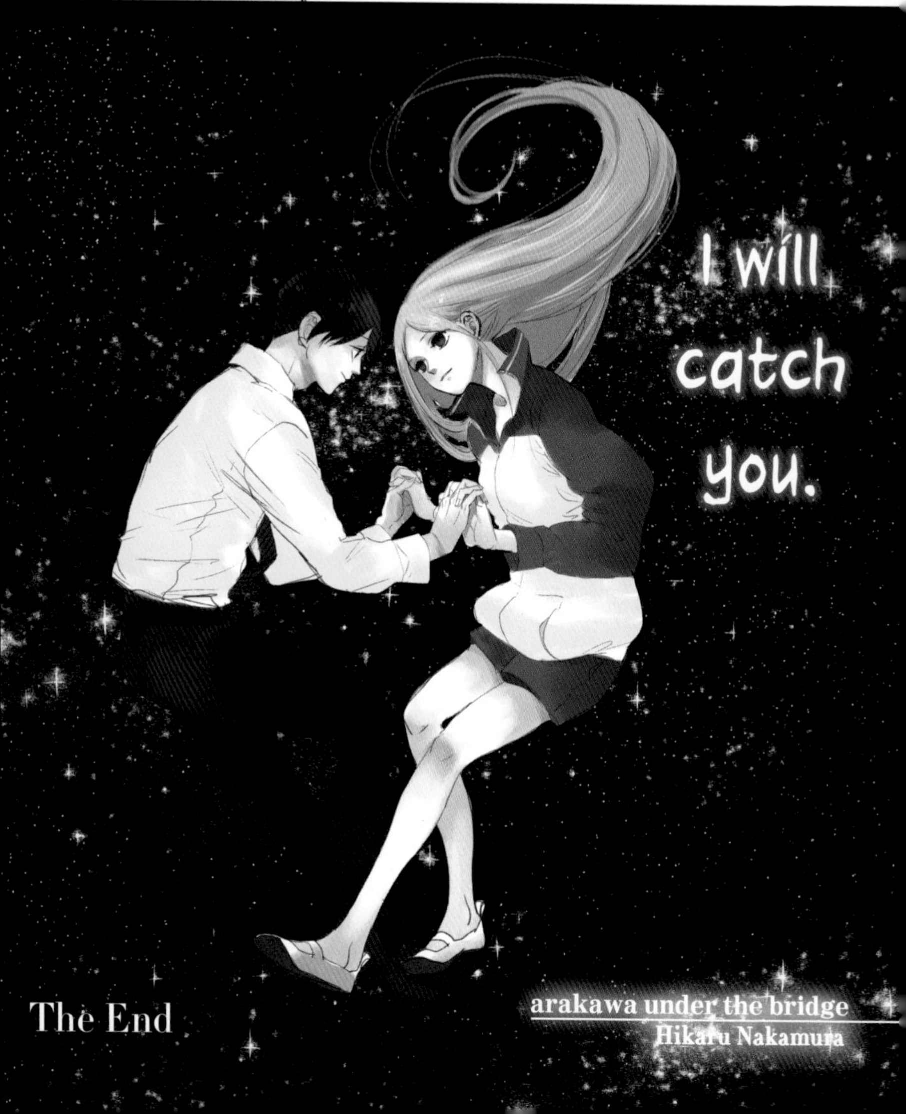
I will catch you.
The End
arakawa under the bridge
Hikaru Nakamura

AFTERWORD MANGA

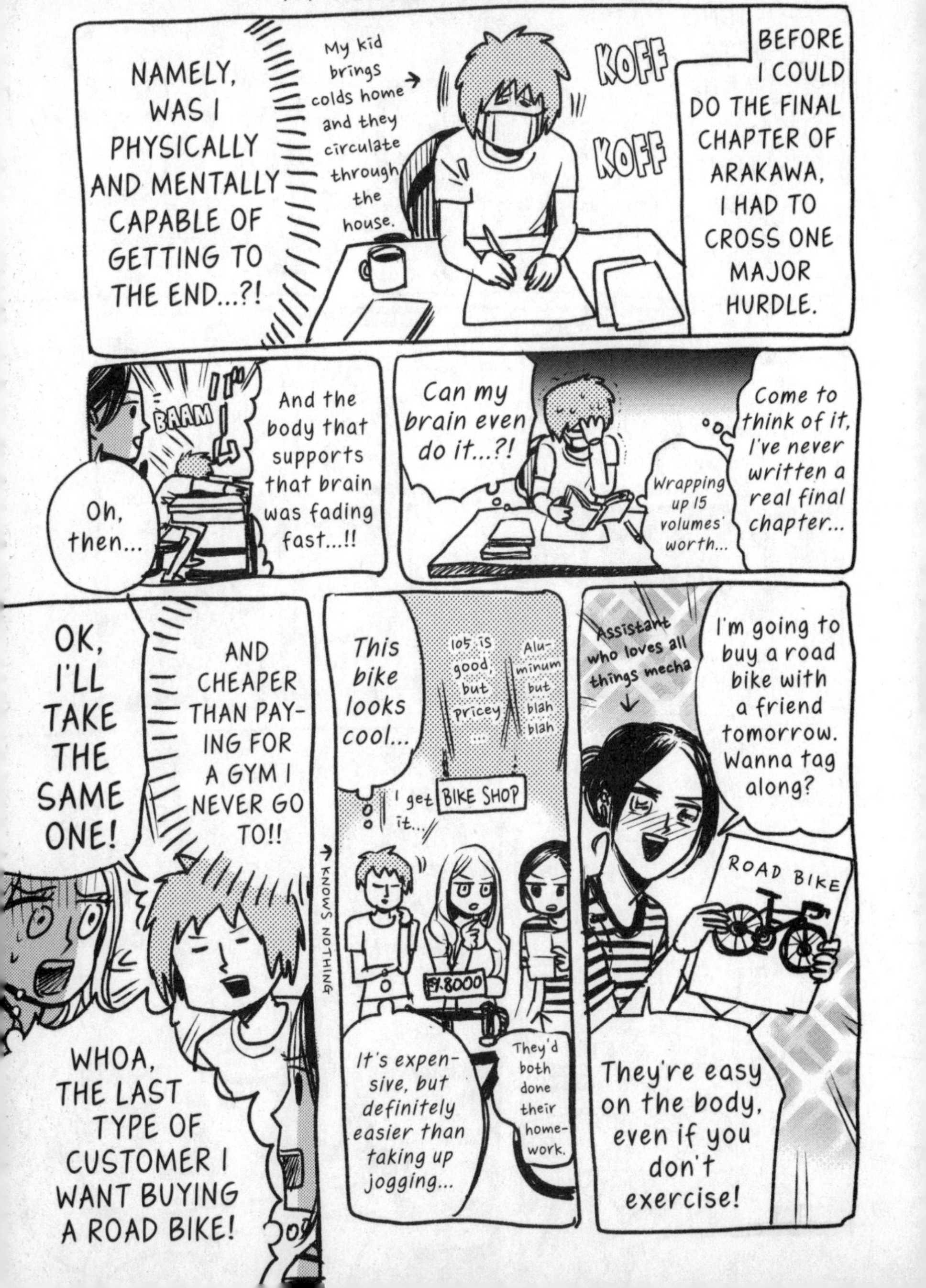
BEFORE I COULD DO THE FINAL CHAPTER OF ARAKAWA, I HAD TO CROSS ONE MAJOR HURDLE.
KOFF
KOFF
My kid brings colds home and they circulate through the house.
NAMELY, WAS I PHYSICALLY AND MENTALLY CAPABLE OF GETTING TO THE END...?!
Come to think of it, I've never written a real final chapter...
Wrapping up 15 volumes' worth...
Can my brain even do it...?!
And the body that supports that brain was fading fast...!!
BAAM
Oh, then...
I'm going to buy a road bike with a friend tomorrow. Wanna tag along?
Assistant who loves all things mecha
ROAD BIKE
They're easy on the body, even if you don't exercise!
BIKE SHOP
This bike looks cool...
105 is good, but pricey...
Aluminum but blah blah
I get it...
KNOWS NOTHING
It's expensive, but definitely easier than taking up jogging...
They'd both done their homework.
AND CHEAPER THAN PAYING FOR A GYM I NEVER GO TO!!
OK, I'LL TAKE THE SAME ONE!
WHOA, THE LAST TYPE OF CUSTOMER I WANT BUYING A ROAD BIKE!

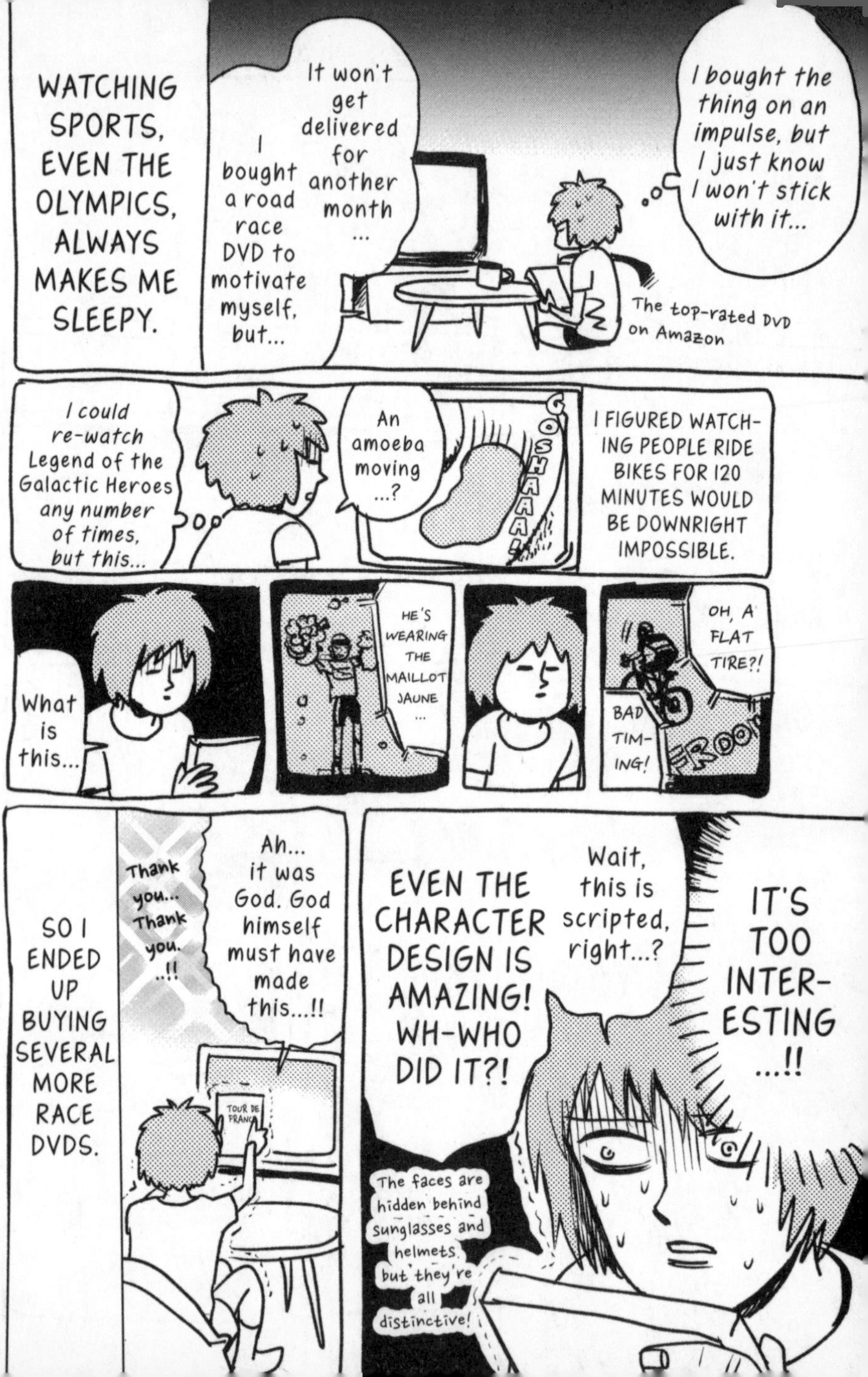
I bought the thing on an impulse, but I just know I won't stick with it...
The top-rated DVD on Amazon
It won't get delivered for another month ...
I bought a road race DVD to motivate myself, but...
WATCHING SPORTS, EVEN THE OLYMPICS, ALWAYS MAKES ME SLEEPY.
I FIGURED WATCHING PEOPLE RIDE BIKES FOR 120 MINUTES WOULD BE DOWNRIGHT IMPOSSIBLE.
GOSHAAAA!
An amoeba moving ...?
I could re-watch Legend of the Galactic Heroes any number of times, but this...
OH, A FLAT TIRE?!
BAD TIMING!
FROO
HE'S WEARING THE MAILLOT JAUNE ...
What is this...
IT'S TOO INTERESTING ...!!
Wait, this is scripted, right...?
EVEN THE CHARACTER DESIGN IS AMAZING! WH-WHO DID IT?!
The faces are hidden behind sunglasses and helmets, but they're all distinctive!
Ah... it was God. God himself must have made this...!!
Thank you... Thank you. ...!!
TOUR DE FRANC
SO I ENDED UP BUYING SEVERAL MORE RACE DVDS.

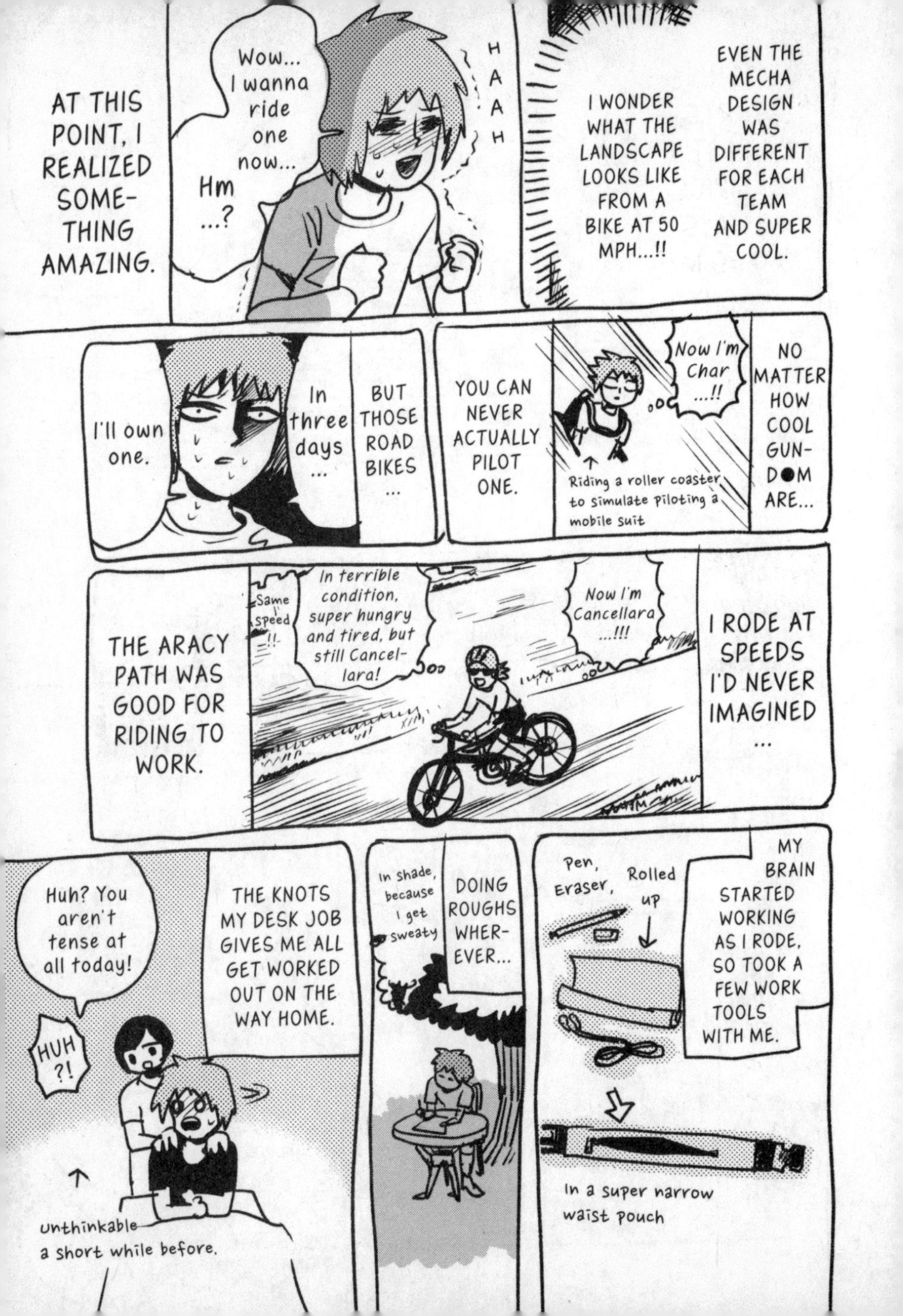
EVEN THE MECHA DESIGN WAS DIFFERENT FOR EACH TEAM AND SUPER COOL.
I WONDER WHAT THE LANDSCAPE LOOKS LIKE FROM A BIKE AT 50 MPH...!!
HAAH
Wow... I wanna ride one now...
Hm ...?
AT THIS POINT, I REALIZED SOME-THING AMAZING.
NO MATTER HOW COOL GUN-D●M ARE...
Now I'm Char ...!!
Riding a roller coaster to simulate piloting a mobile suit
YOU CAN NEVER ACTUALLY PILOT ONE.
BUT THOSE ROAD BIKES ...
In three days ...
I'll own one.
I RODE AT SPEEDS I'D NEVER IMAGINED ...
Now I'm Cancellara ...!!!
In terrible condition, super hungry and tired, but still Cancel-lara!
Same speed !!
THE ARACY PATH WAS GOOD FOR RIDING TO WORK.
MY BRAIN STARTED WORKING AS I RODE, SO TOOK A FEW WORK TOOLS WITH ME.
Rolled up
Pen, Eraser,
In a super narrow waist pouch
DOING ROUGHS WHER-EVER...
In shade, because I get sweaty
THE KNOTS MY DESK JOB GIVES ME ALL GET WORKED OUT ON THE WAY HOME.
Huh? You aren't tense at all today!
HUH ?!
unthinkable a short while before.

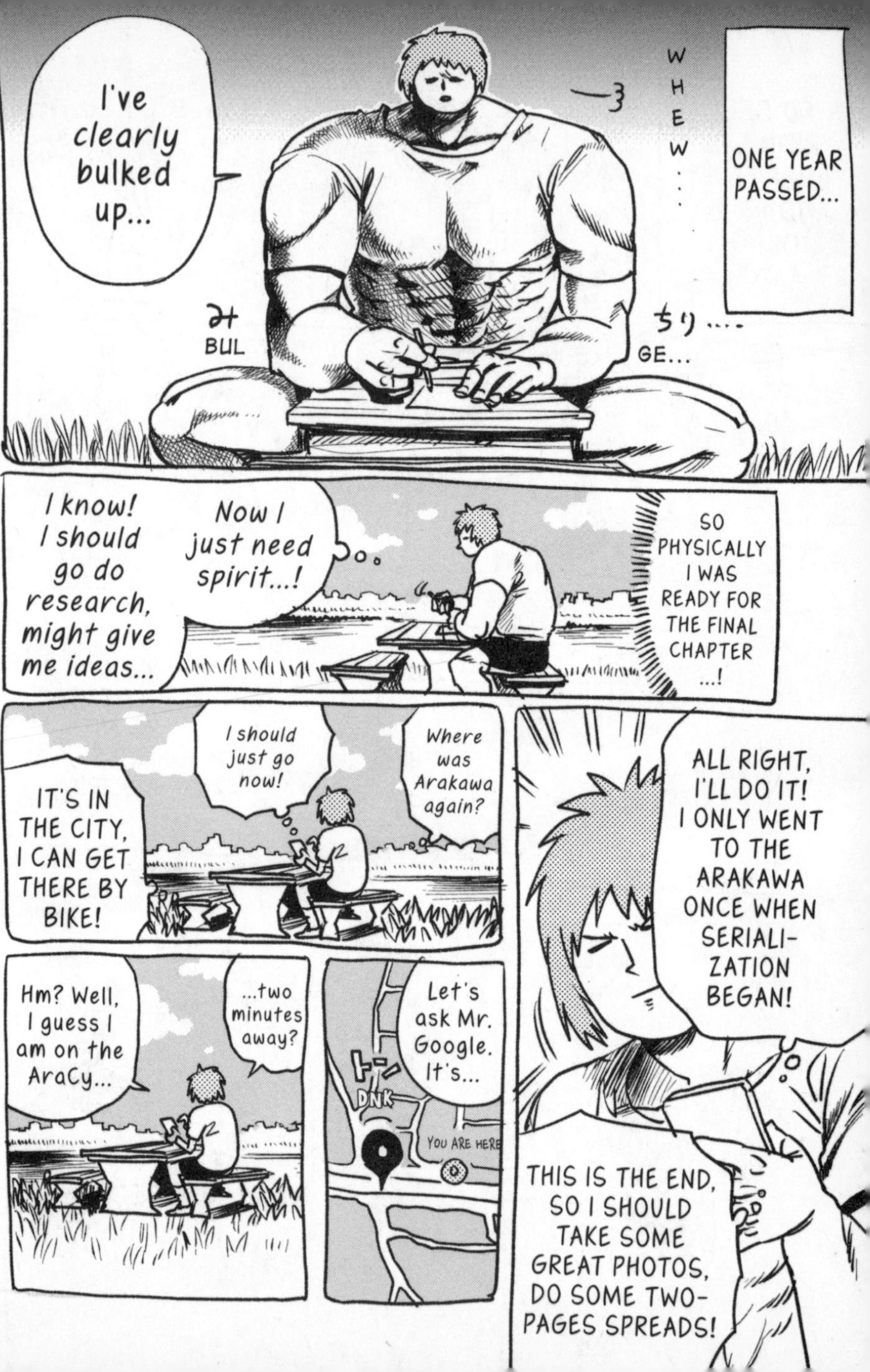
ONE YEAR PASSED...
WHEW...
I've clearly bulked up...
ちり GE...
み BUL
SO PHYSICALLY I WAS READY FOR THE FINAL CHAPTER ...!
Now I just need spirit...!
I know! I should go do research, might give me ideas...
ALL RIGHT, I'LL DO IT! I ONLY WENT TO THE ARAKAWA ONCE WHEN SERIALI-ZATION BEGAN!
THIS IS THE END, SO I SHOULD TAKE SOME GREAT PHOTOS, DO SOME TWO-PAGES SPREADS!
Where was Arakawa again?
I should just go now!
IT'S IN THE CITY, I CAN GET THERE BY BIKE!
Let's ask Mr. Google. It's...
DNK
YOU ARE HERE
...two minutes away?
Hm? Well, I guess I am on the AraCy...

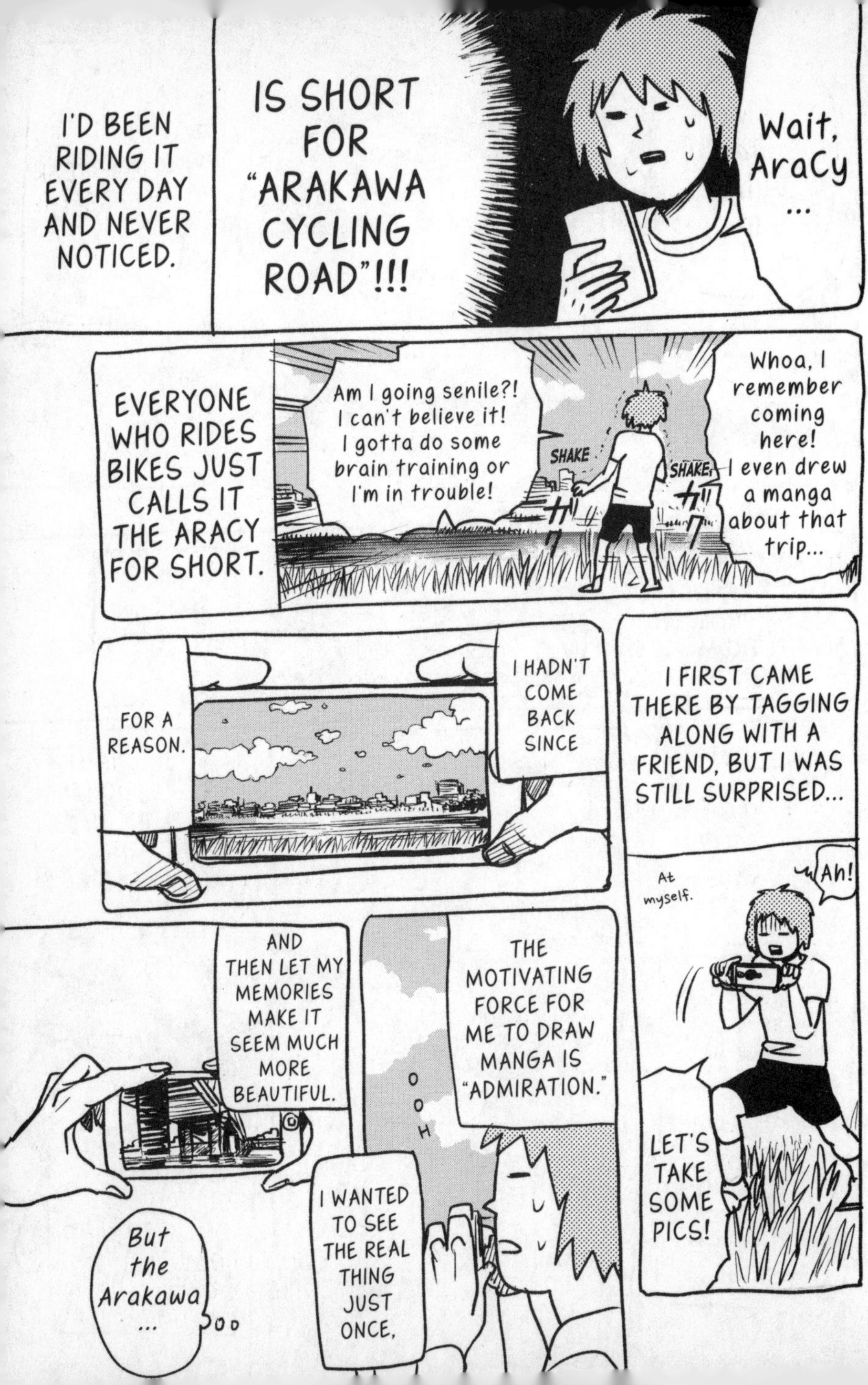

Wait, AraCy ...
IS SHORT FOR "ARAKAWA CYCLING ROAD"!!!
I'D BEEN RIDING IT EVERY DAY AND NEVER NOTICED.
Whoa, I remember coming here! I even drew a manga about that trip...
SHAKE
SHAKE
Am I going senile?! I can't believe it! I gotta do some brain training or I'm in trouble!
EVERYONE WHO RIDES BIKES JUST CALLS IT THE ARACY FOR SHORT.
I FIRST CAME THERE BY TAGGING ALONG WITH A FRIEND, BUT I WAS STILL SURPRISED...
Ah!
At myself.
LET'S TAKE SOME PICS!
I HADN'T COME BACK SINCE
FOR A REASON.
THE MOTIVATING FORCE FOR ME TO DRAW MANGA IS "ADMIRATION."
OOH
I WANTED TO SEE THE REAL THING JUST ONCE,
AND THEN LET MY MEMORIES MAKE IT SEEM MUCH MORE BEAUTIFUL.
But the Arakawa ...
oo

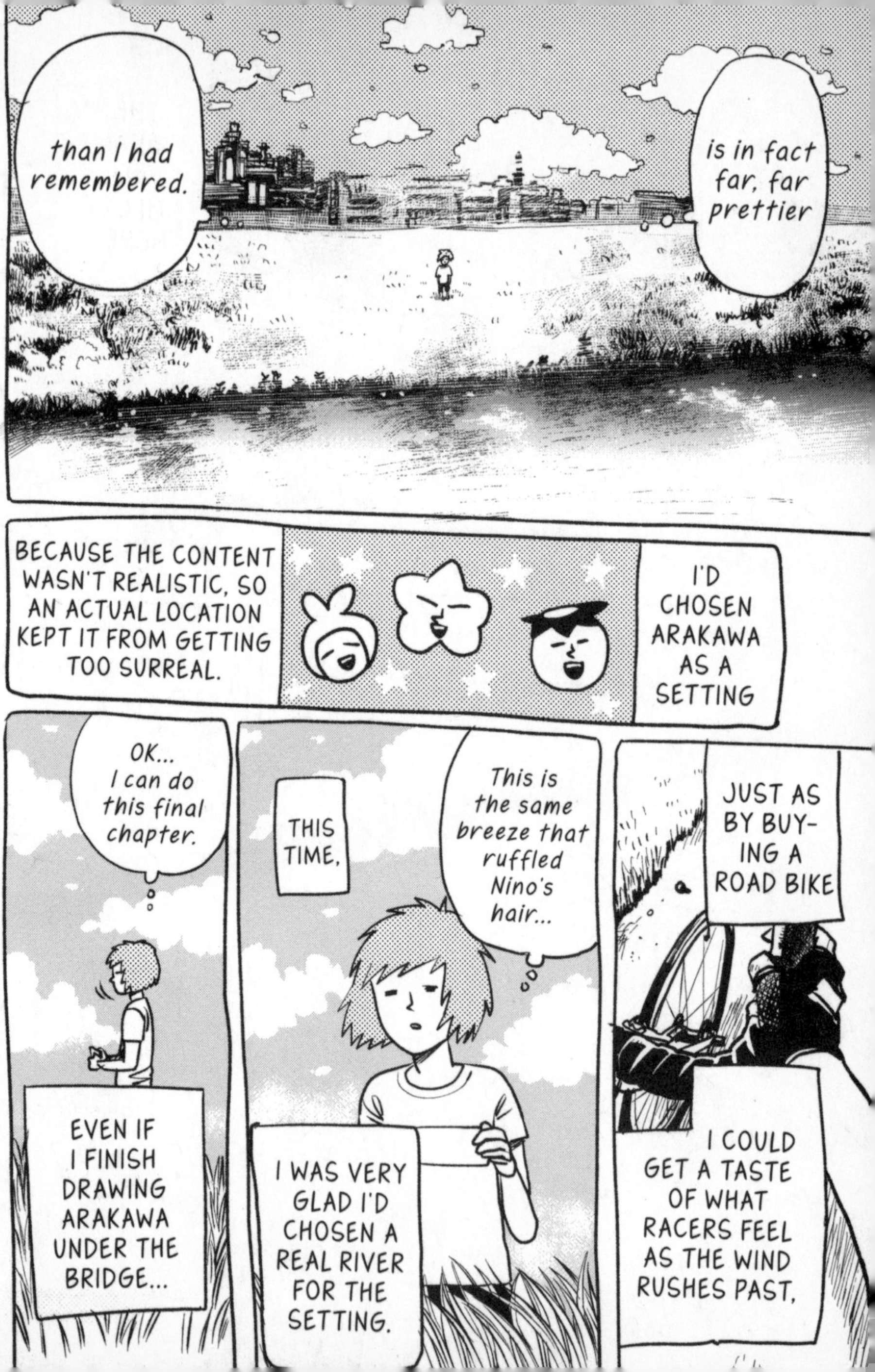
is in fact far, far prettier
than I had remembered.
I'D CHOSEN ARAKAWA AS A SETTING
BECAUSE THE CONTENT WASN'T REALISTIC, SO AN ACTUAL LOCATION KEPT IT FROM GETTING TOO SURREAL.
JUST AS BY BUY-ING A ROAD BIKE
I COULD GET A TASTE OF WHAT RACERS FEEL AS THE WIND RUSHES PAST,
This is the same breeze that ruffled Nino's hair...
THIS TIME,
I WAS VERY GLAD I'D CHOSEN A REAL RIVER FOR THE SETTING.
OK... I can do this final chapter.
EVEN IF I FINISH DRAWING ARAKAWA UNDER THE BRIDGE...

THE ARAKAWA WILL STILL BE HERE.

· THE END ·

While drawing the last volume, I re-read the whole series, and remembered a lot of things from early on in the serialization.

In those early issues, I really wasn't used to the act of drawing manga, and thought about *Arakawa Under the Bridge* from morning 'til night. Just like waking up in the morning and finding your family in the living room, it was a part of my daily life.

I spent my entire 20s with this series.

If nobody reads it, manga is just scrap paper—it never becomes a book. If it hadn't caught anyone's interest, I'd never have reached this page in the final volume.

I am grateful to everyone who kept turning the page all the way to this point.

Thank you for letting me draw the last chapter of *Arakawa*.

I'll keep on drawing in the hope of meeting you again somewhere.

Hikaru Nakamura   Oct. 10, 2015

To those who supported me directly—
my assistants, my editors, salespeople, bookstore owners, designers, everyone at the printers, my family, babysitters... I can't possible express how grateful I am!

ARAKAWA
UNDER
THE BRIDGE

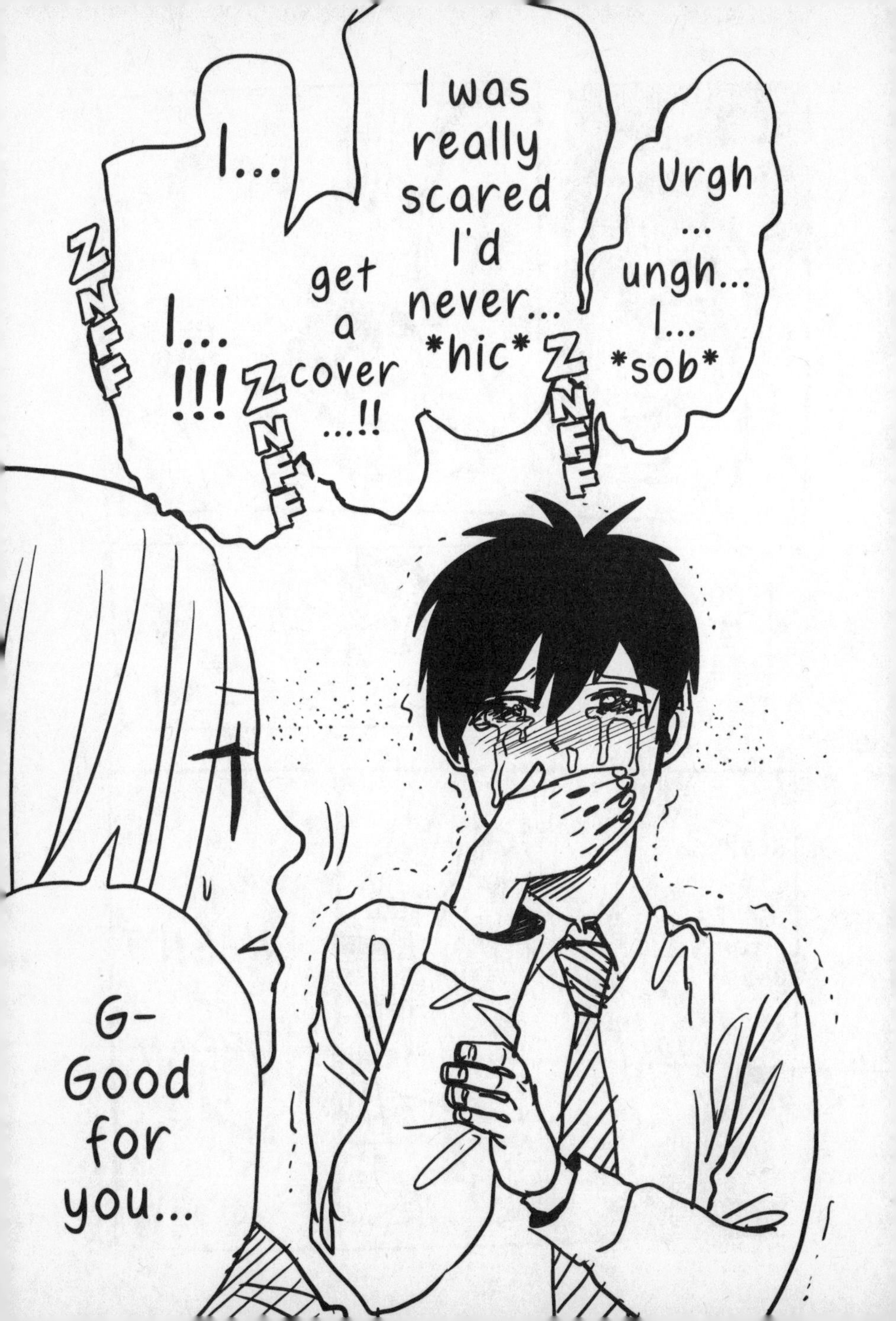
Urgh ... ungh... I... *sob*
ZNFF
I... I was really scared I'd never... *hic*
ZNFF
get a cover ...!!
ZNFF
I... !!!
G- Good for you...

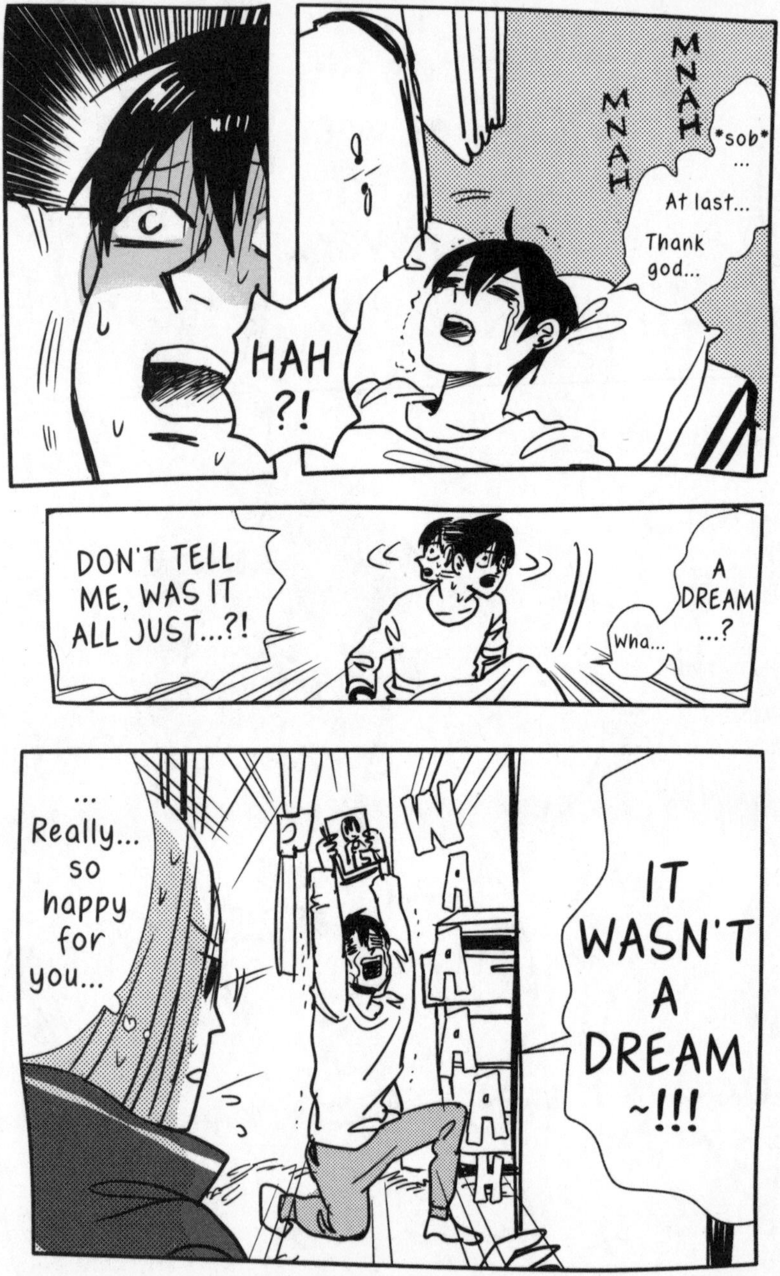
MNAH
MNAH
sob ...
At last...
Thank god...
HAH ?!
A DREAM ...?
Wha...
DON'T TELL ME, WAS IT ALL JUST...?!
IT WASN'T A DREAM ~!!!
WAAAAAH
... Really... so happy for you...

I've been allowed to draw 15 whole volumes of *Arakawa Under the Bridge*, but this is the last one. For 11 years, my pen and paper have let me play in the world under the Arakawa bridge, and that time is precious to me.

This is because of you, dear reader, who read it.

Thank you very much.

I look forward to meeting you again somewhere.

—Hikaru Nakamura

ARAKAWA
UNDER
THE BRIDGE

SAINT ☆ YOUNG MEN

A LONG AWAITED ARRIVAL IN PREMIUM 2-IN-1 HARDCOVER

After centuries of hard work, Jesus and Buddha take a break from their heavenly duties to relax among the people of Japan, and their adventures in this lighthearted buddy comedy are sure to bring mirth and merriment to all!

"Brilliant…the physical comedy and facial expressions will make you literally LOL."
—Sam Humphries
(Host of *DC Daily*; writer, *Green Lanterns, Legendary Star-Lord*)

the daily lives of high school boys

yasunobu yamauchi

Gut-busting antics!

In this slice-of-life comedy, high schoolers Tadakuni, Yoshitake, and Hidenori tackle the wacky and awkward situations they're thrown into in their everyday lives! The trio do everything a normal group of high school boys would do. They play games, they tell ghost stories, and they even...wear skirts?! There's no shortage of witty one-liners in this knee-slapping series!

volumes 1-2
available now!

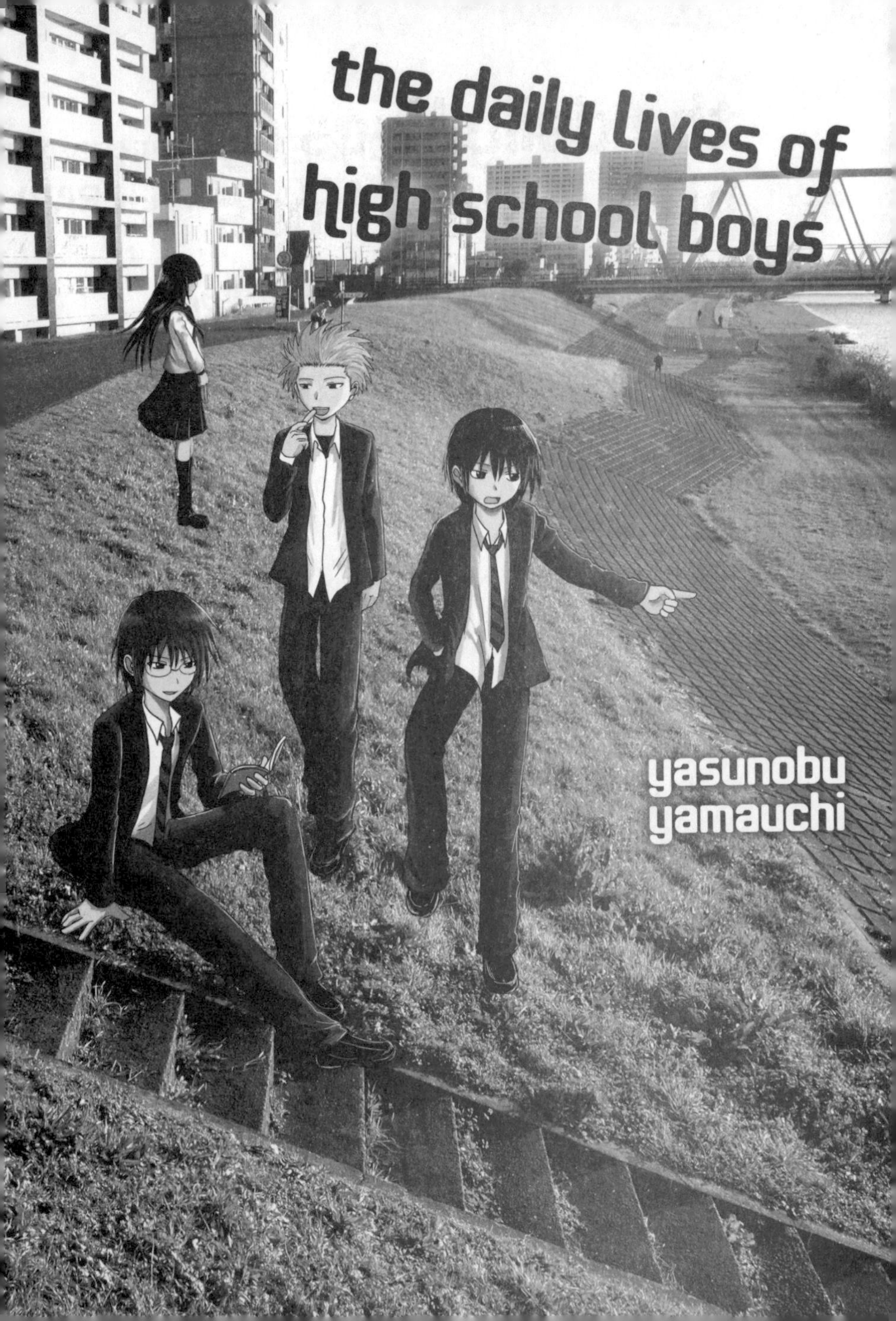
the daily lives of high school boys
yasunobu yamauchi

ARAKAWA UNDER THE BRIDGE 8
Hikaru Nakamura

Translation: Andrew Cunningham
Production: Risa Cho
          Tomoe Tsutsumi

ARAKAWA UNDER THE BRIDGE Vol. 15
© 2015 Hikaru Nakamura / SQUARE ENIX CO., LTD.
First Published in Japan in 2015 by SQUARE ENIX CO., LTD.
Translation rights arranged with SQUARE ENIX CO., LTD. and Vertical,
through Tuttle-Mori Agency, Inc. Translation © 2020 by SQUARE ENIX CO., LTD.

Translation provided by Vertical Comics, 2020
Published by Vertical Comics, an imprint of Kodansha USA Publishing, LLC,
New York

Originally published in Japanese as *Arakawa Andaa Za Burijji 15*
by SQUARE ENIX Co., Ltd., 2015
Arakawa Andaa Za Burijji first serialized in *Young Gangan*, SQUARE ENIX Co.,
Ltd., 2004-2015

This is a work of fiction.

ISBN: 978-1-947194-84-7

Manufactured in Canada

First Edition

Kodansha USA Publishing, LLC
451 Park Avenue South
7th Floor
New York, NY 10016
www.readvertical.com

Vertical books are distributed through Penguin-Random House Publisher Services.